THE DISOBEDIENT GENERATION

THE UNIVERSITY OF CHICAGO PRESS | CHICAGO AND LONDON

The Disobedient Generation

SOCIAL THEORISTS IN THE SIXTIES

Edited by Alan Sica and Stephen Turner

Alan Sica is professor of sociology at Pennsylvania State University. He is the author or editor of several volumes, including, most recently, Social Thought: From Enlightenment to the Present. *Stephen Turner is graduate research professor of philosophy at the University of South Florida. His most recent book is* Liberal Democracy 3.0: Civil Society in an Age of Experts.

The University of Chicago Press, Chicago 60637
The University of Chicago Press, Ltd., London
© 2005 by The University of Chicago
All rights reserved. Published 2005
Printed in the United States of America

14 13 12 11 10 09 08 07 06 05   1 2 3 4 5

ISBN: 0-226-75624-6 (cloth)

ISBN: 0-226-75625-4 (paper)

Library of Congress Cataloging-in-Publication Data

    The disobedient generation : social theorists in the sixties / edited by
    Alan Sica and Stephen Turner — 1st ed.
      p. cm.
    Includes bibliographical references and index.
    ISBN 0-226-75624-6 (cloth : alk. paper) — ISBN 0-226-75625-4 (pbk. :
    alk. paper)
      1. Sociologists—Biography. 2. Sociology—History—20th century.
    I. Sica, Alan, 1949– II. Turner, Stephen P., 1951–
    HM478 .D58 2005
    301′.092′2—dc22

                                      2005008511

For the parents of the Disobedient Generation

Contents

Preface

Alan Sica and Stephen Turner

One might fairly argue that our intellectual period has been colonized by biography and autobiography — that where once stood disembodied ideas we now find personalized reflections. Though decried by some as a degenerate development, for many readers within the academy and beyond, learning about the private mechanisms that give rise to creative endeavors has become at least as intriguing as "the ideas themselves." At minimum, such information often serves as a prolegomenon to more serious analysis of arguments formally stated. The case of philosophy well illustrates this point. Consider the fact that within the past several years two full-length biographies each of René Descartes (Gaukroger 1995; Rodis-Lewis 1998) and of Benedict de Spinoza finally appeared in English (Gullan-Whur 1998; Nadler 1999), the first ever to be offered in this language. These were followed swiftly by equally thorough biographies of Hegel (Pinkard 2000), also unique in the Anglophone circuit, and Kant, the first in English since 1925 and by far the most thorough (Kuehn 2001). Adam Smith also lately received a full-dress treatment (Ross 1995) and a number of other "intellectual biographies" dedicated to thinkers rather than "doers" are forthcoming from major presses. Even more to the point, those self-revelations widely broadcast through published interviews with serious thinkers — several books pertaining to Michel Foucault and Jürgen Habermas most quickly come to mind — seem now, judged by citations, to have attained the status of canonical texts. Perhaps Bryan Magee's best-seller, *Talking Philosophy: Dialogues with Fifteen Leading Philosophers* ([1978] 2001), set the pace for this subgenre of intellectual self-examination some years ago, proving through its success that readers want to know about thinkers' ideas by way of their lives. Autobiographical reflections are a comforting entry-point into published work that is itself often unseemly abstract. This is hardly surprising given the nature of human curiosity, and consider: Could we "know" Johann Goethe without Johann Eckermann, Samuel Johnson without James Boswell?

That said, it remains a fact that most academic lives today do not truly lend themselves to large-scale biography or autobiography. Yet the genre has long been a part of academic life, especially in view of the German tradition of *Erinnerungen* (memoirs) first begun at the turn of the twentieth century. Better-known American psychologists have also institutionalized the practice of writing chapter-length reflections about their life and work. Not only do these become, over time, priceless resources for historians of disciplines, but they also seem to deliver guilty reading pleasures for reflective students of abstract thought, an increasingly useful anchor in an era given more to confession than analysis, even for the most astute audience. For readers who have shared in the historical processes and experiences of autobiographers, or who have been touched by their writings, these works take on more than casual meaning. Is there, for instance, any reader of Richard Rorty's work who was not cheered by his self-revelations in "Trotsky and the Wild Orchids" (in Edmundson 1993)? And a new entry into this general field has been well-reviewed: William Leuchtenburg's edited volume *American Places: Encounters with History* (2001), which collects autobiographical reflections by twenty-eight historians, treating as many different locales.

Sociology has already produced several worthy collections of chapter-length autobiographies (most notably Berger's *Authors of Their Own Lives* [1990]). Although they have not thus far matched the literary charm and commercial success of, say, Gillian Rose's *Love's Work* (1995) or Rorty's brief tale, they nevertheless provided necessary insight into the changing conditions of academic life during the turbulent century just passed, and on occasion have offered surprisingly memorable materials of sheer human interest. The volume we have compiled comprises autobiographical statements with a particular historical purpose and common theme. Everyone invited to write for our book was born between about 1944 and 1951 and, therefore, entered sociology near the time of the great cultural explosion since known as "the events of '68," perhaps the most tumultuous and intellectually exciting year for social science in the post–World War II period. The "generation of '68" has long been identified as such in France and has also been so analyzed for the British case as those students who "went up" to Oxford to study social science in 1968. We believe there is a strong parallel between the intellectual, political, and cultural experiences of these student cohorts abroad and their peers in the United States, though thus far no one to our knowledge has either identified them as such or explained what commonalities and differences connect them with people who would become in due course their European colleagues. We believe this generation of students lived a pedagogical and cultural experience that distinctly separated them from those who came just before and those who followed a few years later. It is this unique perspective that we believe this book illuminates via the solicited autobiographies, for it has since become clear that the student experiences of these now mature and esteemed scholars shaped their outlook and their published work in special ways.

Sociology in 1968 was rapidly approaching its peak in popularity among undergraduate students (which in fact crested in 1972 at U.S. colleges), and this remarkable burst of enthusiasm for the discipline coincided, as most people now know, with student activism and ideological fervor. Students who preceded the "sixty-eighters" were also caught up in similar currents of energetic intellectual and political change. Yet for the most part they found academic outlets within the field, which had carried over from the early sixties: a commitment to disciplinary professionalization, scientism, and a belief that sociology could serve as a politically marketable palliative for the welfare state epitomized by Lyndon B. Johnson's War on Poverty. Randall Collins, for example — for all his differences, theoretically speaking, with the pre-1968 generation — could be taken as one of its representative members, owing to his continuing confidence that sociology and science, uncorrupted by political forces, somehow fit together. The pre-1968 generation also had the huge advantage over their younger siblings of an exploding job market, where boundless opportunity for academics had become standard from the mid- to late sixties. Stories of having a dozen job offers in hand before completing one's dissertation had become common before the contraction of the early 1970s. Thus, the '68 cohort began, as sociology undergraduates, on a very high note, but by the early seventies retrenchment had set in with a vengeance. Without warning, they faced a fratricidal environment in which the already entrenched generation that preceded them — in many cases only a few years older than these suddenly dispossessed young sociologists — had swallowed up most of the available jobs. The course of events in different academic settings in subsequent years differed internationally, but everywhere, and especially in the United States through the effect of affirmative action and the women's movement, powerful changes were felt in sociology and, in an attenuated form, within social theory circles as well.

Despite this handicapped beginning to their careers (when it was not uncommon to hear of five hundred applicants for one assistant professorship in sociology), some members of the generation survived. Within a few years, their initial enthusiasms, often politically anchored, were converted into energy for the long climb up the academic ladder. How the members of this "radical" generation struggled to make peace with the powers that were says a great deal about the future of sociology as a locus for social theory, as well as illuminating the evolution of social thought in the post-1968 period. This generation, it could reasonably be argued, has already made its mark and is of sufficient historical interest even now to justify a volume of the sort we have assembled. Moreover, these scholars are by virtue of their distinctive background and experiences also interesting as an academic generation. Many of the great figures of academic sociology and particularly sociological theory are now in their seventies and departing the scene. By contrast, the generation that received its doctorates in the early sixties, the pre-sixty-eighters, is peculiarly thin. Yet they are now inheriting the institution of scholarship which was shaped by the GI Bill generation of former soldiers. This inheritance, like so many, has turned out to be deeply problematic. Just how the sixty-eighters deal with it will determine the future prospects of sociology and of social thought. For this reason our book, so we believe, holds far more than merely historical interest.

The contributors to this book are each scholars of substantial publishing achievements and, in each case, have also had significant institutional responsibilities in universities and/or as editors. The group is multinational, but with the greatest concentration from the United States and the United Kingdom. We, as editors, have been fortunate in being able to secure writers whose names most immediately come to mind when considering theoretical achievements, both from the United States and Europe. All are well-known to social theorists and, more broadly, to social scientists at large.

One reason for the lack of true "celebrity status" (compared with, say, Rorty or Derrida) is that this particular group retained close ties to the classical tradition of social theory and sociology, avoiding the passing enthusiasms of the past fifteen years, from rational choice theory at one end to transgender theories at the other. What one might make of this committed fidelity to scholarly tradition is obviously itself open to inquiry, for it has perhaps not served them very well as a mechanism for climbing into intellectual eminence—which often calls for the invention of a "new thing," real or imagined. Nevertheless, there is a sense in which it became their generational mission to return to and reengage classi-

cal social theory at its most basic level, while preserving it from the simplification and interpretive crudities they saw about them among competing scholarly
circles. Perhaps this was their response to the problem they faced as a generation: how to salvage something intellectually legitimate from the delegitimation
of Talcott Parsons's edifice on one side, and the political collapse of Marxism on
the other.

A project of this sort might be viewed as yet another instance of boomer self-
indulgence and self-regard, since academic autobiographies often suffer from
precisely these failings. The editors applied firm editorial control in order to ex-
punge preciosity and the accompanying temptations to restate a curriculum vita
in essay form. The reward is a book filled with interesting and informative components to these recounted lives, where life experiences at critical moments
helped define and determine ultimate scholarly aspirations and achievements.
We have managed, we hope, to capture these events in a "class portrait" of those
who lived through a cultural and political period of history which was fraught
with anxiety, even danger, and that virtually pushed these scholars into sociology
and social theory, sometimes even against their will.

One of our inspirations in this task came from reconsidering the history of theory as captured in key texts. We are reminded that Don Martindale's classic work,
The Nature and Types of Sociological Theory ([1960] 1981), was first published
when some of the theorists he scrutinized were relatively young. Parsons, Robert K. Merton, and Marion Levy, for example, were scarcely fifty when the first
edition of this bestselling textbook appeared. That volume marked a dramatic
generational transition in American sociology, a change evident by comparing
Harry Elmer Barnes's two influential collections, *Contemporary Social Theory*
(1940) and *An Introduction to the History of Sociology* (1948), the latter of which
(in its eighth printing in 1970) included chapters on the founders of sociology
and the first generation of American sociologists, who were then dying off. That
situation was not unlike the generation of Parsons's and Merton's students who
are rapidly disappearing from active professional work vis-à-vis the sixty-eighters.
Though the circumstances differ, to be sure, as does the literary form, this book
might nevertheless function as did Martindale's vis-à-vis Barnes's, by returning
the corpus of social theory to its homeland in the larger sociological tradition.
And because teaching social theory is notoriously difficult, owing to the nature
of the primary texts, we hope that our book might well serve as a textbook for the
study of contemporary theory, providing students with a user friendly framework
with which to comprehend today's theoretical landscape.

It should also be noted that the book was Turner's idea, and the editors' names are listed alphabetically on the title page since they split the work once they had agreed on the book's scope and the most desirable autobiographers.

Finally, we would like to thank for their expert help in creating this book Douglas Mitchell, Tim McGovern, and Yvonne Zipter at the University of Chicago Press and Eileen Kahl for creating the index. Anne Sica helped with a French translation and also gave stylistic advice throughout.

References

Barnes, Harry Elmer, ed. 1948. *An Introduction to the History of Sociology*. Chicago: University of Chicago Press.

Barnes, Harry Elmer, Howard P. Becker, and Frances Bennett Becker, eds. 1940. *Contemporary Social Theory*. New York: D. Appleton-Century Co.

Berger, Bennett M., ed. 1990. *Authors of Their Own Lives: Intellectual Autobiographies by Twenty American Sociologists*. Berkeley: University of California Press.

Edmundson, Edmund. 1993. *Wild Orchids and Trotsky: Messages from American Universities*. New York: Penguin Books.

Gaukroger, Stephen. 1995. *Descartes: An Intellectual Biography*. Oxford: Clarendon Press.

Gullan-Whur, Margaret. 1998. *Within Reason: A Life of Spinoza*. London: Jonathan Cape. U.S. ed., New York: St. Martin's Press, 2000.

Kuehn, Manfred. 2001. *Kant: A Biography*. Cambridge: Cambridge University Press.

Leuchtenburg, William, ed. 2001. *American Places: Encounters with History*. Oxford: Oxford University Press.

Magee, Bryan. [1978] 2001. *Talking Philosophy: Dialogues with Fifteen Leading Philosophers*. Oxford: Oxford University Press.

Martindale, Don. [1960] 1981. *The Nature and Types of Sociological Theory*. 2d ed. New York: Houghton Mifflin.

Nadler, Steven. 1999. *Spinoza: A Life*. Cambridge: Cambridge University Press.

Pinkard, Terry 2000. *Hegel: A Biography*. Cambridge: Cambridge University Press.

Rodis-Lewis, Genevieve. 1998. *Descartes: A Biography*. Ithaca, NY: Cornell University Press.

Rorty, Richard. 1993. "Trotsky and the Wild Orchids" Pp. 29–50 in *Wild Orchids and Trotsky: Messages from American Universities*, ed. Edmund Edmnunson. New York: Penguin Books.

Rose, Gillian. 1995. *Love's Work: A Reckoning with Life*. New York: Schocken Books.

Ross, Ian Simpson. 1995. *The Life of Adam Smith*. Oxford: Clarendon.

Jeffrey C. Alexander

Craig Calhoun

Patricia Hill Collins

Hans Joas

Karin Knorr Cetina

Laurent Thévenot

Stephen Turner

Steve Woolgar

Erik Olin Wright

Introduction

What Has 1968 Come to Mean?

During the sixties, Alan Sica worked full-time in a paper mill, as a luggage handler at a Greyhound Bus station, in a Philip Morris factory on the Marlboro assembly line, in a bank reconcilement unit, and in several libraries. He also played guitar and harmonica, rode motorcycles, and tried not to be arrested for incorrect political attitudes. After that, he taught at Amherst College, University of Chicago, University of Kansas, University of California, Riverside, Pennsylvania State University, and University of Pennsylvania. He was associate editor of the American Journal of Sociology *and* Contemporary Sociology, *editor and then publisher of* History of Sociology, *and editor-in-chief of the American Sociological Association (ASA) journal,* Sociological Theory. *He was chair of the Theory Section of the ASA in 1997. Between 1989 and 1998 he served as associate editor (for social sciences) and contributor to the* American National Biography. *In 1997–98, he was deputy editor of the* American Sociological Review. *Since 1991 he has been professor of sociology at Penn State, where he is founder and director of the interdisciplinary Social Thought Program. His books include* Hermeneutics: Questions and Prospects; Weber, Irrationality and Social Order; Ideologies and the Corruption of Thought: Essays of Joseph Gabel; What Is Social Theory? The Philosophical Debates; The Unknown Max Weber: Selected Essays of Paul Honigsheim; Max Weber and the New Century; Max Weber: A Comprehensive Bibliography; *and* Social Thought: From the Enlightenment to the Present. *He has also worked as a professional violinist. He has been married for thirty-four years and helped raise three sons.*

This book comprises autobiographical chapters written by noted scholars and activists, most of whom were born between 1947 and 1950, with a few outliers as far back as 1944 and up to 1952. They therefore came of age during the cultural revolution of the late 1960s and early 1970s that swept over Europe and the United States and even penetrated Mao's China (though in a different form, of course). This unforgettably raucous period has ever since been recognized as a distinct cultural/political epoch that in reductionistic shorthand is called "the Sixties," unique as much for its popular music and films as for its more durable political and social changes. This disparate group of authors (who agreed in this rare instance, uncharacteristically and not without genuine initial hesitation, to evaluate themselves rather than society at large) are unified principally by their substantial scholarly reputations and not by any standard "party line" that might reflect their experiences as students or apprentice intellectuals. They now work in Britain (3), Canada (1), France (2), Germany (2), Italy (1), and the United States (10), but despite the obvious differences the specific conditions of work lend to their stories, there are common threads that clearly bind them to a special generational experience, the influence of which has not left their imaginations these thirty-five years later. Each was invited to consider the impact this vast sea change — symbolically capsulized as "the events of '68" — had on their development as individuals, scholars, and politically astute participants during the more pacific decades that followed. What did it mean to be formed, intellectually, politically, and personally, between about 1966 and 1972? Is there a definably "Sixties" way of seeing the social world and of reacting to it as a scholar and social theorist?

Our autobiographers have answered this invitation with brilliant diversity of tone and substance, and all speak eloquently for themselves, thus relieving me of the standard duty, as the volume's introducer, of recapitulating their analyses and stories. What these memoirs do presuppose, however, is some general knowledge of what the French have ever since called "the events of May" — the global political conflagration that actually began in late April 1968 and continued for most of that year. What historians have termed "the hard year" (O'Neill 1971), "the pivotal year" (Morgan 1991, 154), or even "America's *annus horribilis*" (Marwick 1998, 642–75) is perhaps best revived in memory by these words of the time: "The May Revolution of 1968 was a disturbance in French society on a scale to break the seismograph. It was the sort of event that sets your mind reeling for months afterwards as you try to make sense of it" (Seale and McConville 1968a, 9). The "ruckus" or "troubles" (as the Right tagged this period) began among a small group of students in New York City at Columbia University and quickly spread to Paris, Oxford, London, Rome, Madrid, Berlin, Prague, Belgrade, and Peking (now Beijing), not to mention Berkeley, Madison, Ann Arbor, and dozens of other American college campuses. Many thousands of students took part, sometimes aided by the working classes (especially in France and Italy), and no one who read a newspaper or watched television news doubted that indeed (forgive the cliché), "the times they were a 'changin.'"

Epochal 1968 has become more or less unimaginable when set beside any single subsequent year in Western history. It is not easy to conjure up that time, both for those who were not there and for those participants whose memories can no longer contain the fearsome thrill of societal chaos that seemed to engulf the most "civilized" parts of the modern world. The uniquely re-creative societal setting that gave rise to the chapters that fill this book can most efficiently be recalled by listening to the semiofficial voice of the era, *Time* magazine's feature writers. The "shocking" cover for June 7, 1968, displayed a headshot of an unsmiling college graduate (University of California, Los Angeles, student-newspaper editor, Brian Weiss) wearing a peace symbol on a chain, in full beard and mortarboard, over the caption, "The Graduate 1968" (an obvious reuse of the 1967 Dustin Hoffman film that made him a star and helped define a generation: "Plastics, son, plastics"). A diagonal banner across *Time's* cover coyly read "Can You Trust Anyone under 30?" an ironic play on a famous contemporary expression about "elders" over thirty and their inherent duplicity. The six-page article that followed, entitled "The Cynical Idealists of '68" (1968, 78), began this way:

> The troubled and troublesome college Class of 1968 tends to have a sober, even tragic view of life. They were high school seniors in [the] year that John Kennedy . . . was shot. . . . They were college seniors in the year that Martin Luther King, the Negro leader who tapped their idealism and drew them into social protest, was murdered in Memphis. Throughout all of their college careers, the war in Viet Nam has tormented their conscience, forced them to come to personal decisions relating self and society, country and humanity, life and death. With the lifting of most of the graduate school deferments, the men of '68 face the war and those existential issues as an immediate, wrenching reality.
>
> Such pressures, direct and indirect, have had a profound impact on the 630,000 seniors who will pick up diplomas this spring. . . . Those who are in the really new

mold sometimes show it by a defiance in dress: beards beneath the mortarboards, microskirts or faded Levis under the academic gowns. More often, and far more significantly, it emerges in a growing skepticism and concern about the accepted values and traditions of American society. Some of these graduates will become draft dodgers. Many smoke pot. Fewer than ever remain virginal. Yet it is also true that the cutting edge of this class includes the most conscience-stricken, moralistic, and, perhaps, the most promising graduates in U.S. academic history.

The authors then point out that students (and, surprisingly, allied factory workers) brought the French economy to a standstill and humiliated the previously untouchable de Gaulle, forced Czechoslovakia into an anti-Soviet openness, pressured the authoritarian government of Spain, demonstrated angrily in Germany, and did the same thing in Italy. In the United States, the most unlikely candidate, Eugene McCarthy, a peacemonger, became the first "young people's" representative in the race for the presidency. Observers all over the world, most of them "over thirty" and therefore by definition "the enemy of youth," agreed that the world had been turned upside down almost entirely without warning and that the bases of social order and control were under attack globally. It must have seemed to those familiar with German folklore that the Pied Piper of Hamelin (perhaps in the person of Bob Dylan or Mick Jagger) had gaily crossed the world that spring of 1968, and young people heard the tune and began a frenzied dance, even while the seductive sounds escaped their parents' ears entirely: "Something is happening here, but you don't know what it is—do you, Mr. Jones?" (Dylan 1965).

As a way of reentering that enchanted, but dangerous period, consider some voices of the time at their most unvarnished:

"We are tired of seeing the same old fogies running everything, making promises and not fulfilling them. We have realized that students and young people in this country must take things into their own hands." These sentiments, tumbling angrily out of the mouth of an intense student, were, as it happens, uttered in Serbian. But they could equally well have been delivered in French, Italian, or English [or German, Polish, or Spanish]. For in widely separated corners of Europe last week, thousands of youngsters were battling for what their intellectual mentor, German-born sociologist Herbert Marcuse, has taught them to think of as "the liberation of individuals from politics over which they have no effective control." ("Into Their Own Hands," 1968)

An intelligent but dyspeptic account of Marcuse soon appeared in the *haute bourgeois* hardbound "magazine," *Horizon*, along with a long companion piece denouncing the new face of "anarchism" (Burrow 1969; Stillman 1969). In simpler syntax and without the Marcusean pedigree, note this heartfelt observation published on May 3, 1968, from Mrs. M. H. Medearis of Brentwood, Missouri, in a letter to *Life* magazine (the most popular outlet of middle-brow sentiment at the time), where she confessed that, "since the death of Martin Luther King, I've wished that I were a Negro. I want to fully understand and hurt even more than I do. My sympathetic, complacent, Midwestern attitude hasn't done me or anyone else any good." One week later, in the May 14 issue of *Life's* main competitor, *Look*, the letters page revealed an entirely different mindset, though one could easily imagine Mrs. Medearis sharing the sentiments of her countrymen when they wrote as follows about the Ohio "draft dodgers" who had been featured in the April 2 issue of that magazine: "I must say, I was appalled by your article. I mean, after reading it several times, I got the idea that you were in favor of that kid. He deserved to be put in 1-A [for immediate draft into the army for Viet Nam duty]. After all, he didn't belong to a church, and he believed in a lot of crazy foreign writers like Socrates. The trouble with kids nowadays is that they get all involved with opposition to war, and they worry so much about morality and kindness to others that they forget the basic teachings of Christianity that have made America great. . . . Frederick George Farley, Prospect Park, Pennsylvania." One must assume (in a pre-*Monty Python*, pre-*Saturday Night Live* public sphere) that this was written sincerely, especially considering the rest of the letter, which becomes ever more earnest and self-righteous. None other than Senator Edward M. Kennedy added that "the [entire] issue was interesting and informative, and I was particularly pleased at the intelligent discussion of problems in the current selective service system." Brent Parsons of Central Michigan University seconded Kennedy's opinion: "Congratulations to Anthony Wolff on his candid article on local draft boards ["Draft Board No. 13, Springfield, Ohio"]. Certainly exposure of this archaic and reprehensible system is long overdue. The author's comments reflect the thoughts of many young people today who find themselves in a desperate quandary. Because of an 'implied' threat by many draft boards, the freedom of speech and assembly has been blatantly denied. To travel 10,000 miles to fight despotism is hardly necessary when we can find it at any one of 4,084 local draft boards." Yet once again from the other side, Dianne Cohen of Westfield, Massachusetts, had this to say: "I was thoroughly disgusted by the attitude taken in your article. Why is the draft dodger made a celebrity? Their little speeches are quoted, pictures are taken of them and their wives with various anti-American captions such as 'No political idea is worth another man's life.' If we used that as our doctrine, we'd still be paying tea taxes to England!" Were I asked to produce a short document that summarized the zeitgeist prevalent in spring 1968, these four letters from page 16 of *Look* would serve well enough.

Returning to the letters section of *Life*'s May 3 issue, a range of topics are brought up, including the presidential run of "Clean Gene" McCarthy, "who has sensed the unprecedented potential of American youth, who has dared to challenge the strategy of political and union 'bossism,'" wrote John D. McCarthy of Brooklyn. Robert Kennedy's candidacy, Lyndon Johnson's decision not to run again, military supply lines in Viet Nam, and "the piousness of joggers" all occasioned letters, but by far the most numerous (eight letters), irate, and argumentative pertain to the rock group, The Doors: the "article 'Wicked Go the Doors' (April 12) is the first intelligent and serious coverage of the progressive sounds that I have seen in a non-underground publication" (Richard B. Davidon, Broomall, PA). T. P. Lynch from Troy, NY, wrote "It seems obvious the author is suffering from the first stages of the ever-spreading middle-age syndrome. This phase is marked by the sufferer's pawky ability to perceive great beauty in something he does not understand" (which may be the last time any writer to a news-magazine used the word "pawky," meaning shrewd, witty, crafty, or sly). Mrs. A. M. Ingalls (Pasadena) could not contain herself: .

> One is revolted not just by the behavior of The Doors' "leader," Jim Morrison. After all, when one imagines diapers in place of leather jeans and a pacifier in place of the microphone, everything else — the baby curls, sullen pout, spitting, yelling, and the use of the universal 2-year-old vocabulary, 'I want' and 'now' — seems quite in keeping. What repels one more is the misplaced sentiments of those who not only give attention to such behavior but marvel at it, pay for it, take their children to witness it, write about it, *stand* for it! Infantilism is the major affliction of our society today.

— and not, presumably, warmongering, racism, poverty, sexism, environmental ruin, and the other dozen "causes" with which the Sixties have since been permanently linked.

Extremely typical of the time, at least as I recall it at eighteen, was this commentary from Salt Lake City, Utah, by Theron D. Gregg: "Certain authors seem to glorify the acid-tripping, pot-smoking, speed-shooting type of movement that rock groups, like The Doors, seem to be associated with. On the other hand, police, people over 25 and authority in general get a bum-rapping. If someone had given the jerks like Morrison a good shot in the can when they were 9 years old, they might have become social-climate changers like John Kennedy or Abe Lincoln, instead of the youth-exploiting fops that they are." Sociologists of the media, of knowledge, of politics, and of culture will point out that a "self-selection bias" is at work in the words of letter writers, since such a tiny percentage of people with strong sentiments ever bother(ed) to send their remarks to a magazine or newspaper for public dispersal (particularly in the days before e-mail). Nevertheless, as I remember, and judging from the commentaries by my colleagues in this book, the accumulated bile that sprang from older people as they evaluated "The Youth Movement," "The Generation Gap," "The Counterculture," "The Antiwar Movement," "The Psychedelic Scene," "Haight-Ashbury/ Hashbury," "The Woodstock Generation"—however one chooses to label this congeries of semirelated events and persons—could have filled a small lake in Orange County. Mr. Gregg's letter could have been read in virtually any newspaper or magazine of the time—and probably was.

But perhaps, due to my age at the time, I overstate the case. Talking about the past is less trying when one was not a participant in the events under discussion, which is why it is existentially easier to write medieval than contemporary history, for there is nobody around to contradict one's conclusions based on their uncooperative memories, nor does one burn with the personal memory of shame or injustice. That said, the most difficult task, it seems to me, facing someone who was born between 1944 and 1952 when speaking about "the Sixties" is to recall truthfully the bitter, even murderous dislikes of the era: between Veterans of Foreign Wars and "long-hairs" or "peaceniks"; between radicalized blacks and conservative whites; draft dodgers versus gung-ho militarists, with John Wayne as their totem (who himself craftily sidestepped service in World War II); Yankee, liberal integrationists versus Southern, conservative segregationists; the Depression elders versus their affluent young; the Federal Bureau of Investigation under Hoover versus everybody he did not like—a very long list indeed; northern, often Jewish radicals versus southern, often Baptist reactionaries; the Black Panthers versus "collaborationist" blacks in the National Association for the Advancement of Colored People; blue-collar workers versus the leisure class, particularly their collegiate children; Sinatra admirers versus Rolling Stones fans—a comprehensive list could cover several pages. Long after the fact, *Time* magazine coyly dubbed June through August 1967 as "The Summer of Love," principally because *Sgt. Pepper's Lonely Hearts Club Band* was released then, and if nothing else, popular music had hit a high point not equaled since.

Yet for most young people and their ambivalent elders, enduring the very quotidian lives that popular music was designed to ameliorate, it was anything but. In fact, there seemed to be almost nothing but depressing "hard" news on the national level between the defining moment of Kennedy's assassination in November 1963 and the calamitous global events that filled 1968 with so many "bad vibes," from Berkeley to Paris to Saigon. A mere recitation of what occurred in 1968 alone—when *Time* magazine cost twelve cents a copy through subscription, and a new MGB British two-seater sports car was $2,670—is quite difficult to grasp when posed beside today's relatively calm winds: the vicious Tet Offensive in Viet Nam, oil wars in Nigeria (still familiar to us today), the violent general strike in France involving 8–10 million workers, the King and (second) Kennedy assassinations, the Soviet invasion of Czechoslovakia and the crushing of "Prague Spring," police criminality at Columbia University against its own students, more police criminality at the Democratic Convention in Chicago and the resultant trials of the "Chicago Seven," Muhammad Ali's conviction for draft evasion based on his Muslim principles, the shocking American athletes at the Olympics displaying Black Power salutes while receiving their medals, the moon orbited by *Apollo 8*, and lastly, international student protests against the war in Viet Nam and any number of other "Establishment" evils, many of them ending in death and imprisonment (see Kurlansky [2004] for the most recent and thorough analysis; for a solid chronology, see Fišera [1978], 35–40, passim).

In the context of the early Sixties—burning cities, the first Kennedy assassination (which ever fewer people believed had been solely the work of Oswald), the increasing hopelessness of the war effort and Lyndon Johnson's own political defeat because of it, and escalating racial tensions, not to mention the earliest outbursts of angry, braless feminism—*Time* magazine's inept description, "The Summer of Love," seems not only tasteless but almost perversely irresponsible, a breach of journalistic ethics. "Bliss was it in that dawn to be alive, But to be young was very Heaven!" said Wordsworth in *The Prelude*, though "Everybody's youth is a dream, a form of chemical madness" was Fitzgerald's response in "The Diamond as Big as the Ritz." But for most young people of the mid- to late 1960s in the United States, especially young males who were subject to the draft, youth was neither bliss nor a dream—and chemicals were used to escape it all.

As I demonstrated above, to transcend the sepia-toned mental footage that has enveloped that period, inspired by the dreadful films that have thus far been made about it — nostalgia's comforting fog that crowds out disturbing aspects of the past — some perusal of contemporary periodicals is a handy corrective, even allowing for their inherent limitations as reliable historical sources. At that time, news magazines existed in greater numbers and were read more widely than today, and the detailed reports they offered their readers far outstrips our own most common sources of social and political news, both quantitatively as well as in matters of "balance." With corporate media unblushingly pushing Rightist agendas nowadays, it is hard to recall that heterodox views and actions were at one time accorded some measure of "objective reporting," and stables of print reporters who have since been transmogrified into TV personnel wrote at length when portraying new developments on the national and international scenes. The "Edward R. Murrow ethic" was still in place.

More important, a sympathy for the downtrodden and powerless was at that time not yet considered "unmanly" or the sure sign of the newly despised "bleeding-heart liberal." For instance, in May 1968 *Time* ran a thirteen-page cover story that contained thousands of words reported from all over the nation, plus photographs of the named, working poor in their "natural settings," culminating in a detailed, two-page guide for the conscience-stricken reader: "What Can I Do?" From the charmingly ingenuous side of Los Angeles: "Dr. Curtis Stevens, a white psychologist, opened his backyard swimming pool to Negro children, and was soon playing host to two shifts a day, five days a week. By the end of summer, as Stevens' example spread, 2,000 Negro youngsters were regularly and happily splashing in 22 private pools" (36). As was the custom in those days, no advertisements appeared in this section of the magazine. It is very hard to remember when an equivalent outpouring of journalistic concern for the underprivileged appeared in a national news magazine in the United States that was not saturated in a strongly revisionist, "welfare-reform" rhetoric.

Marx's claim that the "real foundations" of social life always lie in its political-economic transactions is surely correct and, as such, leads one to inquire precisely what said foundations were like in 1968, and what role they played in precipitating the vast "superstructural" changes which enveloped the world shortly thereafter. From a May 1968 *Time* article, we find the macrofeatures. Since peace talks had just begun in Paris (oddly in tandem with student riots), Arthur Smith, National Bank of Dallas, said "No single event would do more good for the nation's economy than ending the war." Hope for yet another "peace dividend" was in the air, and the Dow rocketed up .87 for the week to a "record high of 54.26" [*sic*]. The conventional economic arguments were made, just as they have always been during wartime, that "resolving the Vietnamese conflict would free the United States to attack domestic problems deferred too long — and will create great demands." The army would shrink from 2.6 to 1.5 million men [*sic*], and the country could begin spending the "$30 billion 'fiscal dividend'" that would come with war's end (which in fact occurred ingloriously, of course, eight years later). The military-industrial complex about which Mills wrote and Eisenhower warned publicly pretended that Viet Nam was not especially important to its business — Lockheed claimed "only 5% of our business results directly from Viet Nam" — but that is a standard line for such industries. In fact, they did extremely well: Witness Howard Hughes (Hughes Aircraft; Hughes Tool), who at sixty-two was the nation's richest man, along with J. Paul Getty (Getty Oil Co.), each with $1–1.5 billion. It is interesting that William Benton, also one of the richest with between $150 and $200 million, was owner of the *Encyclopaedia Britannica*, to-day the merest shadow of its former self ("The Economy: If Peace Comes," 1968).[1]

A political-economic snapshot of the United States at the time might include some basic figures. The war was costing $29 billion per year, or 3 percent of gross national product, about half what the Korean war cost, with total defense at 9 percent of gross national product, compared with 41 percent during World War II and 13 percent during Korea (peak figures). Clearly, then, it was not so much the relative cost of the war that disturbed the average citizen but the intent and meaning of it. It was argued that a "moderate recession" would follow the war, whereas in fact a minidepression gripped the economy from the mid-seventies to mid-eighties, precipitated by the 1973 Organization of Petroleum Exporting Countries oil embargo and the stupendous inflation, then "stagflation," that followed. The balance of trade deficit had "ballooned" in 1967 to $4 billion, 41 percent of it blamed on the war (which seems comical now, when hundreds of billions in deficits have become the norm): "Last week the Commerce Department reported that shrinking exports gave the United States a trade deficit of $157M during March, the first since January 1963. As a result, the nation's normally robust trade surplus shriveled in the first quarter to a meager annual rate of $731M, about a sixth of the surplus the U.S. achieved last year."

To say we live in a different political-economic world is not to say nearly enough: consider that as of December 1967, American consumers owed no money in "revolving credit debt" because credit cards did not become nationally

1. Based on *Fortune* data.

available until January 1968. At last tally, the current figure was rapidly approaching the trillion-dollar mark, having leapt exponentially since 1985 into an almost vertical ascent (*Federal Reserve Statistical Release: Consumer Credit*). Meanwhile, the minimum wage in 1968 had just grown to $1.60 per hour in February (up from $1.40, which remained the national norm) and paid only 50 percent of the average manufacturing job. But a black, male cotton chopper in Mississippi was paid $3 for a twelve-hour day in the fields and only did such work one month a year ("Poverty in America," 1968, 30). Median family annual income was nearly $8,000, $2,000 more than the next richest country, Sweden: "In aggregate wealth and individual opportunity, no nation in history can match the U.S." (24), with 170 million people living in relative comfort. That said, 30 million Americans lived below the newly created "poverty line," which even then, of course, was a politically derived figure that understated human needs, and 10 million people were, technically speaking, malnourished.

The principal reason that *Time* ran its enormous cover story on poverty was in response to what we might now call "citizen action": "In the Los Angeles district of Watts, California's most notorious Slough of Despond [from *Pilgrim's Progress*], the orderly rows of one-story stucco houses reflect the sun in gay pastels, and only the weed-grown gaps between stores along the wide main streets — 'instant parking lots' — hint at the volcanic mob fury that three years ago erupted out of poverty to take 34 lives and destroy $40 million worth of property" — $216 million in adjusted dollars (ibid.). What is most interesting about these ordinary socioeconomic data is the fact that conditions then for the bottom two economic quintiles of the population were not much worse than now, in relative terms, and in some ways even better, particularly if one considers such things as incarceration rates for young black males. The difference is one of social conscience. At that time, ordinary people read Michael Harrington's exposé, *The Other America* (1962), in vast numbers, and under the Kennedy/Johnson view of the world, poverty and its attendant ills should be eradicated from the country. Today, no such voices exist with any political clout, and that has made all the difference ever since Reagan took office in 1980 and began the astringent Rightist counterrevolution through which we are still living. What took official, governmentally sponsored liberalism only a few years to enact, and the youthful counterculture perhaps a half-dozen years to act out, the Right has spent a quarter-century dismantling, piece by piece. It is in realizing precisely what this about-face means for the polity at large that seems to mark the "Sixties generation" more than anything else, whether such people ended up as "bleeding-heart liberal sociologists" or as a Republican president whose principal allegiance is to corporate wealth and religious conservatism.

The question of what to do about the less fortunate, both at home and abroad (when the Peace Corps was considered an entirely noble "calling"), occupied the country's collective conscience ever since Kennedy's inauguration speech in 1961. But between April and the fall of 1968, the focus shifted to "The Generation Gap," not least because many of the general magazine subscribers were upper middle-class professional men and their homemaker wives, whose very children had become the avant-garde of "The Movement." *Life* magazine went so far as to run a cover story called "The Generation Gap," which featured a heartfelt, almost unbearably earnest dialogue between a forty-two-year-old uncle (Ernest Fladell) and his twenty-year-old nephew (Richard Lorber), by whose kindness the latter was able to attend Columbia University while living in the elder's home in Manhattan. Their dialogue runs for many pages and is a worthwhile document of the time (published simultaneously as a book by McGraw-Hill called *The Gap*). They smoke dope together, talk, attempt to work at the uncle's ad agency together (not very successfully), and "hang out" with nubile young women who seem troubled but attracted — to both of them. At one point, Lorber is intensely worried about losing his draft deferment and his uncle avows that "for one irrational moment I couldn't help taking some satisfaction in seeing Richie's smugness shattered and knowing that my nephew would now face some of the experiences, indignities, fears, frustrations, and the loss of momentum that I had suffered when I was 18 [in 1944, as a soldier]. But this was also my nephew, my sister's boy, my friend. All at once I wanted to cry" (82). In a nutshell, that says as much about "the generation gap" as any other document I have read: the Depression-era World War II generation of heroic GIs deeply resented the free sex, dope, antiwar sentiment, and loud, obscene, overt confrontation with authority that their children were promulgating on them, even as they paid for tuition and otherwise behaved as "the good parent."

Newsweek ran a detailed "Special Report" on Columbia University students: "rather than change themselves, they propose to change society" ("Columbia at Bay," 1968, 53). In some ways the most thorough treatment of the recent tumult, it began by noting that a Viet Cong flag was flying from the Eiffel Tower, German students had attacked a reactionary publisher's offices (Axel Springer), Czech students risked imprisonment and confrontations with Soviet tanks to take to the streets in solidarity with a peace march in New York, plus students at Boston University, Colgate College, Trinity College in Connecticut, Duke University, and elsewhere had carried out rude and enterprising experiments in social fomentation. And in a move that by today's standards is almost a fairy tale, the Duke divinity school faculty "unanimously voted to divert their annual raises into the pay envelopes of campus maids and policeman. Under such moral pressure, the trustees agreed to raise salaries to $1.45 an hour starting May 6 [still 15 cents below minimum wage, by the way]. But at Columbia, students' protests were not started so innocently, nor settled so amicably" (40).

Ever since James Kunen's *The Strawberry Statement* (the book and the film), the Columbia "riots" have been the best documented of all the student commotions during 1968 in the United States. Though minuscule in scale, cost, injury, or ultimate consequences when compared with the events of May in Paris, they carried enormous symbolic weight, since Columbia was at the time an extraordinarily staid institution, was full of its own self-importance, and for decades had been in the hands of an autocratic administration which had frozen out any notion of student or faculty voices in their decision making. For many faculty, it was just as well, since they seemed to prefer writing books, but for the students who had taken up the cause of the poor in Harlem, freedom of speech, antiwar activity, and so on, their takeover of five campus buildings and the subsequent 2 a.m. "attack" by a thousand New York City police became a defining moment for many who lived through it. (The fact that Columbia and its famed journalism school was the hometown college of the *New York Times* also helped bring it front and center to world attention.) One participant whom I interviewed recently claimed that much of the *Times* reporting was wrong — that, for instance, the students did not trash the dean's office, but in fact the police did to provide a photoop for the press and to justify their absurd overreaction. Whereas, in Paris, thirty thousand students built fifty large barricades throughout the city, using the time-honored method of unearthing paving stones for use in high walls, and then fought police tooth and nail, at Columbia the students seemed to do very little other than sit nervously in campus buildings, let Mark Rudd talk to the press, and quickly ask for forgiveness for their obstreperous behavior. Their radical action was mostly limited to lots of talk and wearing different colored armbands: white for supportive faculty, blue for students who opposed the protest, which were quickly assumed then by jocks who threatened the protestors with physical expulsion, orange for leaders of this so-called majority coalition, green for those who wanted amnesty for the protestors, yellow for those in fear, black for anarchists, and so on. Perhaps the fact that black students and some famous confederates from Harlem had taken over other buildings and had evicted all the white students sent a particular chill up the spines of those who ran the university. Oddly, though, the blacks knew enough to leave quietly when pressed, whereas the affluent white students did not and were therefore arrested en masse. The local and national response to these events now seems quite overdone, reaching even the House of Representatives, where a bill was passed that denied grants or loans to any student who participated in such "unpatriotic" activities ("The Two Columbias," 1968, 63).

The follow-up story, "It's Happening All Over" (1968), gave a quick recounting of student rebellions in Germany, Italy ("We must preserve confusion!"), France, Belgium, Great Britain, Spain, Czechoslovakia, Japan (where 5,500 police handled 2,200 demonstrators), and Poland (where students who protested were immediately drafted into the army!). The political graffiti that was born during these few weeks is perhaps its most lasting cultural contribution to similar future events: "Power to the imagination" is almost universally known but is not so creative as "Don't look back now, God, but the world is collapsing behind you! The more I make revolution the more I want to make love!" ("Battle for Survival," 1968, 21; "Columbia at Bay," 1968, 46). Even more creative, "Humanity will not be happy until the last capitalist is hanged with the entrails of the last bureaucrat," while nearby the bust of Auguste Comte (inventor of the term "sociology") "was draped with a red bandanna," thus recruiting him for the Left ("Anarchy Revisited," 1968, 33). But far more seriously, and with truly long-term consequences, *Newsweek* named, pictured, and summarized the ideas of five "revolutionary gurus" to the young: Guevara, Marcuse, Debray, Fanon, and Mao ("Ideas in Action," 1968, 47). It is significant that nowadays, during this notably unrevolutionary era of international student life, these very authors (excepting possibly Mao) have become standards in the "postmodern, postcolonial" canon and, in many quarters, are held virtually above reproach as social theorists and visionaries.

Keenly aware of the relatively mild goings-on at Columbia University, students in the land that spawned Gabriel Tarde's famous theory of behavior-as-imitation became restive in May 1968, mostly for sheerly practical reasons: bad teaching, huge classes, leaking dorms, cramped study space, outmoded curricula, and inadequate libraries. They also realized that the French social structure had ossified into a form that permitted only 10 percent of college students to stem from the working or lower middle classes. Despite its revolutionary tradition, France had remained notoriously caste-bound, and as students began studying sociological and political works that investigated this phenomenon (culminating many years later in Bourdieu's *Distinction*), they learned that "of 2530 prominent French, ranging from pop singer Sylvie Vartan to Charles de Gaulle . . . 68% came from families that belong to the top 5% of French society" and "only 5% of prominent French men and women came from what could be classified as the working class" ("The Workers of France," 1968, 33). Women were joining the workforce in larger numbers, not due to feminism but because consumer goods were extremely expensive and usually bought on credit (an innovation) that required two incomes to service. Even skilled workers earned only $195 per month, savings disappeared and life insurance was "virtually unknown." The astonishing and unanticipated convergence of students' complaints about the quality of their education, and the factory workers' sense that their standard of living was rapidly declining, tossed aside the traditional animosities of modern France. Together these unlikely groups produced what *Newsweek* called "French Revolution 1968" on its May 27 cover. The former group—who led 250,000 in Paris protests— came from privileged sectors of the economy and lived a life wholly removed from the materially straitened conditions of the workers, whose only real ally on the political front was the French Communist Party (the leadership of which, truth be told, was also the bailiwick of intellectuals). Nobody, least of all de Gaulle, imagined that the students' uproar in the vast Parisian university system would spill over into factories all over the nation and that in short order police, air traffic controllers, tugboat captains, subway operators, garbage men — in short, the entire blue-collar workforce of the country—would execute a work stoppage that began costing the nation enormous financial losses.

And amid this revolutionary moment, the man most often quoted in the media was Daniel "Red Danny" Cohn-Bendit, a twenty-three-year-old, third-year sociology student at Nanterre (though a native German), previously unknown, with a gift for political theater and rhetoric that equaled the American "Yippies" who upended the Democratic Convention later that summer in Chicago. Cohn-Bendit became a national figure when he orally confronted a government authority–figure inspecting a swimming pool on the Nanterre campus, who had insulted and patronized him, to which Danny responded in characteristic style by refusing to be the least intimidated, then launching a counterattack which put the government entirely on the defensive. Historians of the day argue that without Cohn-Bendit, the student agitations would never have begun. He was expelled from the university on May 21, and French police then formed a cordon trying to refuse him reentrance into France after he had visited Germany. When news of this infraction became public, riots of "extreme violence" occurred in

Paris on May 23 and 24 (Marwick 1998, 615). But he dyed his hair black, snuck back into Paris, and carried on his political speechifying, eventually writing political philosophy and becoming as much an international icon among student protesters as Abbie Hoffman or Mark Rudd were on the U.S. scene. Although he never published a book after his international best-seller, *Obsolete Communism: The Left-Wing Alternative* in 1968, today he has his own spiffy Web site, accessible in three languages, heads the European Union's Green Party, and seems to have settled very comfortably into the role of professional politician. When one compares his public persona in the summer of 1968—when his photo and speeches filled the airwaves in France and elsewhere, and he became officially persona non grata in his adopted country—with the matured politician today, he might serve as the "poster man" for a successful transformation between impudent youth and polished politico. He probably had more fun back then.

Select Bibliography

Absalom, Roger Neil Lewis. 1971. *France: The May Events, 1968.* London: Longman.
Aldgate, Anthony, James Chapman, and Arthur Marwick, eds. 2000. *Windows on the Sixties: Exploring Key Texts of Media and Culture.* London: I. B. Tauris.
"Anarchy Revisited." 1968. *Time,* May 24.
Anderson, Terry. 1995. *The Movement and the Sixties.* New York: Oxford University Press.
Aron, Raymond. 1969. *The Elusive Revolution: Anatomy of a Student Revolt.* Translated by Gordon Clough. New York: Praeger Publishers.
Art Gallery of Greater Victoria. 1968. *Younger Vancouver: Cross Section '68—May 22–June 9, 1968.* Organized by Will Hoare. Vancouver: Art Gallery of Greater Victoria.
Atack, Margaret. 1999. *May 1968 in French Fiction and Film: Rethinking Society, Rethinking Representation.* Oxford: Oxford University Press.
"Battle for Survival." 1968. *Time,* May 31.
Blackburn, Robin. 2004. "You Had to Be There." Review essay on *1968: The Year That Rocked the World,* by Mark Kurlansky. *Nation,* February 9, 30–35.
Bloom, Alexander, and Wini Breines, eds. 1995. *"Takin' It to the Streets": A Sixties Reader.* New York: Oxford University Press.
Bourges, Hervé. 1968. *The French Student Revolt: The Leaders Speak.* Translated by B. R. Brewster. New York: Hill & Wang.
Brown, Bernard E. 1974. *Protest in Paris: Anatomy of a Revolt.* Morristown, NJ: General Learning Press.
Burner, David. 1996. *Making Peace with the 60s.* Princeton, NJ: Princeton University Press.
Burrow, J. W. 1969. "The Anarchists (Who Are with Us Again)." *Horizon: A Magazine of the Arts* 11, no. 3 (Summer): 32–43.
Caldwell, Christopher. 1998. "1968: A Revolting Generation Looks Back." *Weekly Standard,* September 7, 19–23.

Cavallo, Dominick. 1999. *A Fiction of the Past: The Sixties in American History.* New York: St. Martin's Press.

Chalmers, David. 1996. *And the Crooked Places Made Straight: The Struggle for Social Change in the 1960s.* Baltimore: Johns Hopkins University Press.

Cohen, Patricia. 1998. "New Slant on the 60s." *New York Times,* June 13.

Cohn-Bendit, Daniel. 1968. *Obsolete Communism: The Left-Wing Alternative.* New York: McGraw-Hill.

Cohn-Bendit, Daniel, et al. 1968. *The French Student Revolt: The Leaders Speak.* Presented by Hérve Bourges. Translated by B. R. Brewster. New York: Hill & Wang.

"Columbia at Bay: When Students Revolt, the Target Can Be Cafeteria Food—or Society Itself." 1968. *Newsweek,* May 6, 40–53.

"The Cynical Idealists of '68." 1968. *Time,* June 7.

Dickstein, Morris. 1977. *The Gates of Eden: American Culture in the Sixties.* New York: Basic Books.

Dylan, Bob. 1965. "Ballad of a Thin Man." From *Highway 61 Revisited.* New York: Columbia Records.

Echols, Alice. 2002. *Shaky Ground: The '60s and Its Aftermath.* New York: Columbia University Press.

"The Economy: If Peace Comes." 1968. *Time,* May 3.

Editors of Time/Life Books. 1998. *Turbulent Years: The 60s.* Alexandria, VA: Time/Life Books.

Ehrenreich, Barbara. 1992. "Legacies of the 1960s: New Right and New Lefts." Pp. 227–234 in *Sights on the Sixties,* edited by Barbara Tischler.

Erikson, Erik H. 1970. "Reflections on the Dissent of Contemporary Youth." *Daedalus* 99, no. 1 (Winter): 154–76.

Farber, David. 1994. *The Age of Great Dreams: America in the 1960s.* New York: Hill & Wang.

Farrell, James J. 1997. *The Spirit of the Sixties.* New York: Routledge.

Federal Reserve. *Federal Reserve Statistical Release: Consumer Credit.* G.19. http://www.federalreserve.gov/releases/g19/hist/cc_hist_mt.html.

Feenberg, Andrew, and Jim Freedman. 2001. *When Poetry Ruled the Streets: The French May Events of 1968.* Albany, NY: SUNY Press.

Fišera, Vladimir, ed. 1978. *Writing on the Wall/May 1968: A Documentary Anthology.* New York: St. Martin's Press.

Gitlin, Todd. 1993. *The Sixties: Years of Hope, Days of Rage.* Rev. ed. New York: Bantam Books.

Goodman, Mitchell, comp. 1970. *The Movement Toward a New America: The Beginning of a Long Revolution (A Collage) A What?* Philadelphia: Pilgrim Press; New York: Alfred A. Knopf.

Hayes, Harold, ed. 1971. *Smiling through the Apocalypse: Esquire's History of the Sixties.* New York: Dell.

Hobsbawm, Eric, and Marc Weitzmann. 1998. *1968, Magnum throughout the World.* Sorbonne Exhibition Catalog. Paris: Hazan.

"Ideas in Action: Revolutionary Gurus." 1968. *Newsweek,* May 6.

"Into Their Own Hands." 1968. *Newsweek,* June 17, 64E.

Isserman, Maurice, and Michael Kazin. 2004. *America Divided: The Civil War of the 1960s.* 2d ed. New York: Oxford University Press.

"It's Happening All Over." 1968. *Newsweek,* May 6, 45–48.

Johnson, Richard. 1972. *The French Communist Party versus the Students: Revolutionary Politics in May–June, 1968.* New Haven, CT: Yale University Press.

Judis, John B. 1998. "The Spirit of '68: What Really Caused 'The Sixties.'" *New Republic,* August 31, 20–27.

Kurlansky, Mark. 2004. *1968: The Year That Rocked the World*. New York: Ballantine Books.

Lefebvre, Henri. 1969. *The Explosion: Marxism and the French Revolution*. Translated by Alfred Ehrenfeld. New York: Monthly Review Press.

Lorber, Richard, and Ernest Fladell. 1968. "The Generation Gap." *Life*, May 17, 81–92.

Macedo, Stephen, ed. 1997. *Reassessing the Sixties: Debating the Political and Cultural Legacy*. New York: W. W. Norton.

Manchester, William. 1974. "The Year Everything Went Wrong." Pp. 1122–54 in *The Glory and the Dream: A Narrative History of America, 1932–1972*. New York: Bantam Books.

Marwick, Arthur. 1998. *The Sixties: Cultural Revolution in Britain, France, Italy, and the United States, c. 1958–1974*. New York: Oxford University Press.

McWilliams, John C. 2000. *The 1960s Cultural Revolution*. Greenwood Press Guides to Historic Events of the Twentieth Century. Westport, CT: Greenwood Press.

Morgan, Edward P. 1991. *The 60s Experience: Hard Lessons about Modern America*. Philadelphia: Temple University Press.

O'Neill, William L. 1971. *Coming Apart: An Informal History of America in the 1960's*. New York: Times Books.

Pagès, Yves. 1998. *No ©opyright: Sorbonne '68, Graffiti/documents réunis et présentés par Yves Pagès*. Paris: Ed. verticales.

"Poverty in America: Its Cause and Extent." 1968. *Time*, May 17, 24–37.

Priaulx, Allan, and Sanford Ungar. 1969. *The Almost Revolution: France—1968*. New York: Dell.

Quinn, Edward, and Paul J. Dolan, eds. 1968. *The Sense of the Sixties*. New York: Free Press.

Reader, Keith. 1987. *Intellectuals and the Left in France since 1968*. New York: St. Martin's Press.

Reader, Keith, with Khursheed Wadia. 1993. *The May 1968 Events in France: Reproductions and Interpretations*. New York: St. Martin's Press.

Rohan, Marc, comp. 1988. *Paris '68: Graffiti, Posters, Newspapers, and Poems of the Events of May 1968*. London: Impact Books.

Ross, Kristin. 2002. *May '68 and Its Afterlives*. Chicago: University of Chicago Press.

Sayre, Nora. 1973. *Sixties Going on Seventies*. New York: Arbor House.

———. 1996. *Sixties Going on Seventies*. Rev. ed. New Brunswick, NJ: Rutgers University Press.

Sayres, Sohnya, et al., eds. 1984. *The 60s without Apology*. Minneapolis: University of Minnesota Press.

Seale, Patrick, and Maureen McConville. 1968a. *French Revolution 1968*. Harmondsworth: Penguin Books.

Seale, Patrick, and Maureen McConville. 1968b. *Red Flag Black Flag: French Revolution 1968*. New York: G. P. Putnam's Sons.

Servan-Schreiber, Jean Jacques. 1969. *The Spirit of May*. Translated by Ronald Steel. New York: McGraw-Hill.

Singer, Daniel. 2002. *Prelude to Revolution: France in May 1968*. 2d ed. Cambridge, MA: South End Press.

Starr, Peter. 1995. *Logics of Failed Revolt: French Theory after May '68*. Stanford, CA: Stanford University Press.

Steigerwald, David. 1995. *The Sixties and the End of Modern America*. New York: St. Martin's Press.

Stephens, Julie. 1998. *Anti-Disciplinary Protest: Sixties Radicalism and Post-Modernism*. Cambridge: Cambridge University Press.

Stern, Jane, and Michael. 1990. *Sixties People*. New York: Alfred A. Knopf.

Stillman, Edward. 1969. "Herbert Marcuse." *Horizon: A Magazine of the Arts* 11, no. 3 (Summer): 26–31.

Sur, Jean. 1998. *68 Forever* [in French]. Paris: Arléa.

Tischler, Barbara, ed. 1992. *Sights on the Sixties*. New Brunswick, NJ: Transaction Publishers.

Touraine, Alain. 1971. *The May Movement: Revolt and Reform/May 1968 — the Student Rebellion and Workers' Strikes — the Birth of a Social Movement*. Translated by Leonard Mayhew. New York: Random House.

Townsley, Eleanor. 2001. "'The Sixties' Trope." *Theory, Culture, and Society* 18, no. 6:99–123.

"The Two Columbias." 1968. *Newsweek*, May 20, 63)

Unger, Irwin, and Debi Unger, eds. 1998. *The Times Were a Changin': The Sixties Reader*. New York: Three Rivers Press.

Vinen, Richard. 2000. *A History in Fragments: Europe in the Twentieth Century*. Boston: Little, Brown, 331 ff.

Wallerstein, Immanuel, and Paul Starr, eds. 1971. *The University Crisis Reader: Confrontation and Counter-Attack*. 2 vols. New York: Random House.

Wells, Tom. 1994. *The War Within: America's Battle over Vietnam*. Berkeley: University of California Press.

"What Can I Do?" 1968. *Time*, May 17, 36–37.

Wheen, Francis. 1982. *The Sixties: A Fresh Look at the Decade of Change*. New York: Arrow/Random House.

Winston, Michael R. 1974. "Reflections on Student Unrest, Institutional Response, and Curricular Change." *Daedalus* 103, no. 4 (Fall): 212–16.

"The Workers of France." 1968. *Time*, June 7, 32–33.

Losing Faith

Andrew Abbott is the Gustavus F. and Anne M. Swift Distinguished Service Pro-
fessor at the University of Chicago. After graduate work at Chicago (PhD 1982),
Abbott taught at Rutgers University from 1978 to 1991, when he returned to Chi-
cago. Known for his ecological theories of occupations, Abbott has also pioneered
algorithmic analysis of social sequence data. He has written on social theory, on
social science methodology, and on the history of the social sciences and the aca-
demic system. His books include The System of Professions; Department and Discipline; Time Matters; *and* Methods of Discovery. *He is currently writing a book*
of general social theory as well as studying the microdemography and career struc-
ture of occupational therapy. An active teacher, Abbott has served on or chaired
over fifty dissertation committees. He served from 1993 to 1996 as Master of Chi-
cago's Social Science Collegiate Division and has edited Work and Occupations
(1991–94) as well as the American Journal of Sociology *(2000–).*

In the 1960s I grew up. I was not happy about it. I thought I had lost my direction
and my principles. Long retrospect says that what I lost were illusions. But they
were my illusions, and I loved them.

 I began to recognize the public's 1960s around the time of the March on Washington in 1963. I was fourteen. These public 1960s seem to me to have lasted until 1973, which saw the Watergate scandal, the first oil crisis, the end of the draft,
and the dismantling of the Bretton Woods system: a new world indeed. My personal 1960s had the same dates but for different reasons: 1963 marked puberty
and my first year in high school while 1973 marked the end of my all-too-short

graduate fellowship and the beginning of my first steady job. But while the historical 1960s are thus for me temporally indistinguishable from a personal life-
epoch, their mark on me stands out nonetheless. For they set the terms of my
adolescence; there were no private histories in that stormy decade.

I

The boy who entered this tumultuous time wanted to be a scientist and had
recreational enthusiasms for stargazing, butterfly collecting, and woodland exploring. Bored to the point of psychosomatic illness by my public school classes,
I left in fifth grade for a more challenging private school. From age eight on, I
was effectively an only child, my older brother's health problems having taken
him to Colorado. We lived in a huge old house on a rural lane, surrounded by a
thousand acres of dying farms and town forest. I perforce spent my free time —
and private school meant there were nearly four months of it between Labor Day
and late June — alone at home in the day (my mother worked full-time to make
my school fees) and alone with my parents at night. From the endless day-time
solitude I acquired the lifelong habit of talking to myself. From the nighttime
with my parents I learned to expect adult attention and to prefer it to that of my
age-mates. The precocious contact with adults made me profoundly earnest and
serious, while the lack of age-mate friends left me unskilled in friendship and
even routine interaction. Combined with my scholastic preeminence in the very
competitive Fay School, all these qualities made me seem — in the eyes of my
age-mates — self-absorbed and conceited but also curiously defensive and inse-
cure. They found me desperately in need of deflation and, lucky for them, surprisingly easy to deflate. Predictably, I was unwilling to close ranks with peers
against the adult world. (My peers never wanted me in their closed ranks, in any
case.) I was much more likely to define myself against my age-mates, whom I pri-
vately viewed as a bunch of peer-pressured sheep following the prescribed age-
grade fashion of rejecting adults. This attitude was hardened by the extraordinary
competitiveness of Fay, where each boy's weekly effort grades were read aloud at
a school meeting every Monday afternoon.

   The boy so far described we might call Abbott A, the smart kid who did the
right things, never got into trouble, and so forth. With puberty there arrived an
Abbott B, who was more sociable, did the wrong things, had a nasty temper,
swore volubly, and so on. Abbott B had his day in the sun at summer camp, freed
from the constraints of school culture and parents' rules. I teased younger vic-

tims, taunted counselors, and practiced the voluble cursing my brother brought home on visits. Underneath this rubbish was a positive side to Abbott B, who unlike Abbott A could at least be freely passionate. The best of my camp moments synthesized the achievements of the one character with the passions of the other. This synthesis has proved a longstanding difficulty; even today friends are sometimes bewildered by my running off the rails. I have never become conventionally unconventional.

Politics was nowhere in this world. Like many—probably most—American kids of my time, I thought America the best of countries, the logical culmination of a history that began with Greece and Rome, ripened in Western Europe, and flowered in the American Revolution and the triumphs of the two World Wars. I knew about Little Rock and Governor Faubus and gave thanks that we weren't like that. I thought the problems of the country could be solved by democracy and fair play, by good faith and compromise. I thought individuals decided their values and commitments by unbiased reflection and rational consideration. I had no more idea of irreconcilably opposed interests than I had of flying cattle or babies with webbed feet.

In particular, class and ethnicity had almost no place in my consciousness. This was not entirely because we were upper-middle-class WASPs or because class or ethnic differences were invisible to me—they were not. Rather, my parents came from differing and complicated class and ethnic backgrounds and did not talk about them. My father's father, from an old Philadelphia family, had made himself the owner of three New Hampshire textile mills. But when my father was seven, my grandmother deserted her husband, leaving my father and his two younger brothers to be raised alone by the hard-driving businessman. In practice, my father was raised by my grandfather's cook and maid, unmarried sisters from the Irish working class. By contrast, my mother's father was an Irish-speaking peasant who had somehow won the youngest daughter of declining Catholic smallholders one market day in Kenmare. Their passage paid by my grandmother's spinster elder sister, my grandparents came around 1910 to Manchester, New Hampshire, where my mother was born in 1916 and her mother died two years later of TB and the Spanish flu. The spinster sister raised my mother; she became a housekeeper for a middle-class bachelor and raised my mother as her dependent in that household. My parents were thus one rich, one poor, one WASP, one Irish, one Episcopalian, one Roman Catholic. They met at a party given by their common piano teacher and married six years later.

Like many first generation Americans and like many a woman marrying above her class, my mother assimilated with a vengeance, turning her back on Irish culture, the giant Amoskeag Mill, even the Roman Catholic Church. But her father-in-law detested her and threw my father out of the family. When my parents began life anew outside Boston, their tastes remained upper class — my father's by birth and my mother's by hypergamy — but their income did not match their tastes. By most external measures, they were upper middle class: they worked for master's degrees part-time, subscribed to the *Saturday Review*, and listened to Artur Schnabel playing Beethoven. Ethnically, my parents raised us WASP, in keeping with my mother's assimilation to her husband's heritage. I somewhere learned the language of ethnic slurs — probably from my brother — but such words were never on my parents' lips, nor the sentiments in their hearts, so far as I knew. Indeed, my lack of a language for class and ethnicity was so strong that I never understood that the Fay School was a crucible of class microconflict between the 130 boarders — scions of very old WASP money — and the forty day students — usually upper-middle-class boys (half of us Jewish) escaping weak public schools.

My parents were quietly conservative, taking Boston's Republican paper and consistently voting Republican. This is hardly surprising given my father's background and my mother's assimilation. There was only one real edge to their politics, a dislike of unions on the part of my father that I later learned was traceable to his father having (characteristically) made him the fall guy when the National Labor Relations Board investigated the mills in the mid-1930s. Although he has never mentioned the experience, my father clearly felt deeply betrayed on both sides.

By tenth grade I started to have my first real arguments about politics, mainly about civil rights and unions. By this time, I was a boarder at Phillips Academy in Andover, Massachusetts, then at a kind of intellectual zenith as a flood of talented outsiders to the old Protestant elite — upper-middle-class kids, Jews, Catholics, and others — swarmed in to take advantage of the school's pipelines to the Ivies,. Civil rights seemed a simple matter to us at Andover — the laws would be passed and everything would be fine. Many of us had become folk singers and were caught up in that optimistic world, whose conflict-ridden heritage we did not know. Thus it was not about civil rights, but about unions that I had my first political arguments. Woody Weiss — a doctor's son from New York and another of the class's more earnest souls — began to wake me up to the fundamentally opposed interests of capital and labor. Of course we both thought labor issues were ultimately resolvable through negotiation and compromise, but we raised more questions than we could answer: Why do we believe what we believe? Which values should predominate over others? How can society change? For us as for millions of others all over young America in those days, these were the grist for late-night arguments of a kind that only adolescents can sustain, filled with passion and dogmatism and foolishness and — given our school situation — with the faint eroticism that permeates single-sex environments.

All the same, these arguments were not the foreground of Andover for me. That foreground was intense intellectual effort in the toughest courses of my life, voracious reading outside of classes, and attempts to prove myself as an athlete. Most important, although I retained from earlier years an overwhelming ambition for scholarly preeminence, I was not the top scholar of my class. Some were simply smarter than me and quite a few had more cultural capital. But I gradually developed a secret set of personal criteria according to which I was the best or at least among the best. It was a rationalization of failure, to be sure, but my personal criteria set high standards nonetheless: I would know about many different things; I would care about ideas for their own sake; I would read off the beaten track; I would be second-best in many subjects, if first in none; I would not specialize. By the time I was midway through Harvard, these rules would coalesce into a militant eclecticism and a barely suppressed pretense at omniscience. The whole pattern grafted easily onto the self-preoccupation and set-apartness born of my solitary childhood but was gradually hidden under a surface of gregarious piffle as boarding school (and later, college) taught me a modicum of interactional skills.

Such nonspecialization also characterized my place in Andover's complex social system. I had no single group of close friends, as most of my classmates did. Nor was I clearly located as a grind or a jock. Rather I was on the boundaries of each group — a three-season varsity athlete who was not cool, a veteran of the school's most advanced courses who was not regarded as an intellectual. I became a hyperastute student of the detailed sociometry of the school, a master player of the thrice-daily who-sits-with-whom game in the dining hall. As always, I was in a crowd but not of it.

In the summers I began to nuzzle up to the new social issues. In particular, 1965 found me as a tutor (one of four whites and two blacks) at the Roxbury Boys Club in the Boston ghetto. When I read today the daily logs we were required to keep, they seem unbearably earnest — I am very much the concerned teacher obsessing about his kids and reading Maria Montessori on the side. But on 13 August, while Watts burned a continent away, someone came to speak to us who represented the new wave of black consciousness. Whatever she said — apparently a vehement condemnation of white suburbia — my reaction shows that I had finally gotten the picture that there were some people for whom I and mine were the bad guy a priori. I was very angry about it and said so.

II

I arrived at Harvard in the fall of 1966. There I continued my Andover pattern of multiple locations, playing varsity sports all four years in addition to manufacturing an intellectual personality, working ten hours a week, and spending four or five hours a day schmoozing in the dining hall. My goals were vaguely intellectual. But unlike those who lived their intellectuality publicly as newspaper or literary magazine writers, I remained in the closet, continuing my secret but self-conscious cultivation as a comprehensive intellectual.

My coursework was systematically omnivorous. Five advanced placement credits already guaranteed my college-level mastery of science, math, and language. Prevented by a bureaucratic restriction from majoring in multidisciplinary social studies, I majored in the next broadest thing — history and literature — then took most of my courses in the social sciences, looking for answers to Woody Weiss's questions. By the end, my thirty-two courses comprised six in literature, five in history, five in government, five in "social relations" (Harvard's umbrella for sociology, social psychology and social anthropology), three in philosophy, and two in economics, in addition to four years of individual tutorial in English history and literature and year-long audits of introductions to music and art history. From an adviser's perspective, this record was pathological or wonderful, depending on your attitude toward general education.

Politics was in the background. My political interlocutors — and there were many, from many points of view — were told "I'll study and find out the facts and then tell you what I think about the issues." I cannot now regenerate the development of my views about Viet Nam, but my ultimate view was that the war was stupid politically and unwinnable militarily. I never argued that it was immoral, having given up such concepts in the chill light of Clausewitz, whom I read as a sophomore. I was personally drawn to radical students, who were the most intellectually lively people around, but I found their group identity all too sheeplike.

In the fall of 1968 (my junior year) I stood as a dormitory candidate for Harvard's Student Faculty Advisory Committee, proposing the interrogation of the university's dependence on government funding, then around one-third of its income. But my elaborate printed analysis of this problem left Kirkland House voters cold. I was soundly defeated by Frank Raines, a sophomore running on a platform of ominous platitudes, who after a brief college career as a middle of the road activist went on to Lazard Freres and OMB, ending up as CEO of Fannie Mae. Indeed, many of the people with armbands are now the "capitalist pigs" they once decried. Student radicals were simply a new form of "big men on campus."

As for more open political action, I detested the groupthink it seemed to enforce. My decisive experience came on Moratorium Day in October 1969. Guilt-tripped into going by friends, I found myself walking up Commonwealth Avenue to get to the Boston Common and hearing from two blocks away 100,000 people shouting "Peace Now, Peace Now." And from two blocks away, shorn of its consonants, it sounded like "Eee Ahh, Eee Ahh." Suddenly I had a vision of the great Nuremberg rallies. There, too, the vowels in the distance would have been "Eee Ahh, Eee Ahh." But close up one would have heard "Sieg Heil, Sieg Heil," and the ultimate result would have been not peace but the death of 60 million people. I wanted no such submerging of my judgment and individuality. I turned around and walked the four miles back to Cambridge.

Indeed, my reading and reflection in college had led me to despair of the ability of rational political institutions to deal with short-run irreconcilable differences. By the middle of my college years I had concluded that all real social change — indeed even all real intellectual change — has its roots in irrationality. For a young man committed to rational reflection, this was a profoundly destructive conclusion. What Gandhi and Napoleon and Churchill shared with Freud and Marx was not an open mind but precisely the reverse — a mind completely committed and therefore able to subordinate all details to its master ideas. Eclecticism — my chosen intellectual way — was clearly the way of failure.

But I have ignored so far what was probably the central determinant of my political life. By a fluke I became, in 1967, undergraduate research assistant to Roger Revelle, director of the Harvard Population Center, remaining with him for four years. Roger was a physical giant and a preeminent oceanographer, a university founder (UCSD) and a scientific statesman, the architect of the near-legendary Mohole drilling project and the author of the foundational paper on the greenhouse effect. His enormous vision and charisma powered a multidisciplinary institute for social change. Population Center scholars worked on family planning, hydrology, river control, ethical analysis, and development economics — everything, in fact, but politics, a criticism I threw at Roger when I dared. The center's faculty included many eminent figures, and Roger's personal networks included many of the great names of American academia. I was around such people all day at the center and, since the Revelles often invited me home, could find myself chatting with them (continuously and completely out of my depth) at dinner. This ongoing intimacy with the very established, if very liberal, adult world of the center strongly restrained whatever small inclination I had for the more extravagant varieties of political activity.

Politically, Roger was of the technological modernizing school. Despite my efforts to persuade him to the contrary, he thought that third-world peasants were simple rationalizers who just needed to be presented with the right incentives and the right technologies. As close as I ever got to political activism was arguing with this successful, powerful, and famous man that he was ignoring the crucial forces that were shaping developing countries. Apparently I tried pretty hard. Roger spoke for many people in my life when he turned to me on the center stairs one day and said in a rage, "You're so goddamn arrogant you're never going to learn a goddamn thing from anybody." But a few weeks later he carted me to Washington to say the same things to a National Research Council meeting on population. They probably had the same reaction.

To be political one must know the events of the moment. Yet it was in this time — my later years at Harvard — that I gave up on the media. As a child, I had had little contact with the news. My parents had scanned a newspaper quickly, over the breakfast table, but did not routinely watch a news program or take any news periodical. We watched almost no television. But since I arrived first on summer mornings at the Population Center, I began reading the center's copy of the *New York Times* while making the coffee. I then became a serious *Times* reader until some point in my senior year. But I gradually evolved the view that what matters is the conjunctural news — the long-term trends that require serious theoretical work to recognize. And at some point in this period also, disenchanted with the "who heard about which coup first" competition at Kirkland House, I began to make the argument that "the news is the sports [i.e., entertainment] page of the upper classes." I was willing to be extremely offensive about this antinews attitude. I made Roger toweringly angry when in July 1969 I refused to watch the moon landing (for him one of the great triumphs of the sciences he so loved), characterizing the whole thing as a media event, down to the scripted words. I told him the money would have been better spent on alleviating poverty and solving social problems. Saying that to one of America's most powerful and devoted scientists was political action for me.

But the real reason I disattended to news — and by extension to politics — was

the incapacitating rage that it often produced in me. I have always had an aston-
ished, rage-filled hatred of what I deem blatant untruth and unfairness, whether
it be a camp counselor changing the rules of a game, a colleague misrepresent-
ing a job candidate, or a politician telling a known and obvious lie. This rage is
a negative synthesis of the passions of Abbott B as directed by the rigorous but
sometimes censorious and ungenerous thinking of Abbott A. A peak of this rage
came as I watched the Republican Convention of 1968. Up until then, I believed
that American politics embodied some kind of rationality and concern, that
reflective patriotism was possible and that a spirit of compromise and humanity
could solve the problems of the country. But when David Eisenhower crowed
that history would vindicate Nixon and the Republicans, I became incoherent
with rage at his fatuous, complacent drivel. I turned the TV off. I have never
watched a major political newscast since — not a State of the Union address, a
campaign speech, a presidential debate, or even the Watergate hearings. They're
all well-scripted lies, as far as I'm concerned. I don't own a television.

Thus in the late 1960s I was at Harvard, refraining from active politics, driven
more and more to social science to find answers to embarrassing political questions, confident that answers would be found, paying less and less attention to the
news. My friends were all over the political map. One of my roommates went out
to work for Gene McCarthy and came back with good stories, a new girlfriend,
and a failed candidate. Other friends talked earnestly about the "worker-student
alliance," carried little red books, and grew sententious hairdos. Still others imbibed novel organic concoctions and took extended voyages to parts unknown.
Another group quietly marched around in ROTC uniforms on Thursday afternoons. What is missing in this picture?

III

Behind this frenzy, of course, was the draft. Given the context of Viet Nam, doing something about the draft—finding a deferment, burning a draft card, signing up — was really the elementary male political act. After all, only when a man
had done that something for three years could he vote. For men, the draft was the
1960s.

A few facts are important, since many young people today don't know them.
First, huge numbers of men served in the armed forces: two-thirds of those coming of age between 1945 and 1965 and about one-half of those after 1965. Second,
draft eligibility ran for eight years (from age eighteen to twenty-six), and until De-

cember 1969 the oldest were drafted first. Third, the draft was administered by four thousand local boards, and since a man remained permanently under the jurisdiction of the draft board where he registered, chances of induction varied widely between individuals because of the large differences between the local demographics of their draft boards. Fourth, induction could be postponed or in some cases avoided by various deferments: parental, occupational (e.g., farmer), educational (e.g., college student), moral (conscientious objector), or personal (e.g., medical or mental reject). Extended steadily during the peacetime years, these deferments were steadily withdrawn (except for conscientious objector, which was expanded) in the late 1960s. Once his deferments were lost, a man might still fail the preinduction physical. If he passed that, there were many further choices, such as getting drafted, enlisting, serving as an officer, or joining the reserves, all with varying lengths of (active and reserve) service, varying degrees of choice of military occupation, and varying chances of combat. There were also four possible branches—Army, Navy, Air Force, and Marines—each with its own entry requirements and internal occupational choices.

By the late 1960s this system was thought to be inequitable and irrational. The occupational and educational deferments favored the privileged, while the mental requirements favored the deprived. The graduate school deferment led to thousands of otherwise unwanted PhD's, while the marriage and parenthood deferments fostered equally unwanted marriages and children. So on 1 December 1969 (the fall of my senior year in college), a lottery was held involving all men from eighteen to twenty-six, aiming to order draft eligibility by a random selection of birthdays and to move, for subsequent cohorts, to one year of nondeferable vulnerability at age eighteen. A generation of men watched the televised picking of the numbers. (I did not.) Absurdly—the 1969 draft lottery is now a textbook example of poor design—the results were nonrandom.

From the point of view of the draftable man, the draft was a complex, arbitrary game involving a bewildering variety of choices. Associated with these choices were equally bewildering probabilities, varying widely by draft board, induction center, and service branch, most of them unknown and indeed unknowable. And these bewildering choices and probabilities made up a particular kind of game—a zero-sum game; for every man who got out, another had to go. (Ironically, the experience most widely shared by the supposedly cohesive 1960s generation was this war of all against all.) The stakes were high: a one-in-two chance of serving, with consequent life disruption of varying periods; a one-in-four chance of going to the war theater if you entered service; and once there, a one-in seven-chance of being a casualty and a one-in forty-chance of death. In short, life-course disruption, combat, injury, and death were the fourth, third, second, and grand prizes, respectively, in this macabre parody of the American game of success, complete with "equal opportunity," "free choice," unpredictable risks, resource inequities, and so on. I got a minor fourth prize. (My brother, incidentally, won several third prizes between 1963 and 1971.)

I and my college peers of course enjoyed a number of advantages in this game. But these were not enough to avoid it. They merely put off the play and helped out when we rolled the dice. I worried far more about the draft in my last two years of college than I did about war protest or civil rights or my BA thesis or where to go to graduate school. I certainly didn't think the antiwar movement was going to solve my personal problem with the draft, nor did I think demonstrating was a very effective way to express my rage. Like most of my peers, I more or less hoped the draft would go away as a problem—that the war would wind down or that I would suddenly figure out a new deferment possibility or that I would get a high number in the lottery or whatever.

The horror was that the draft virtually forced you to barter your values. Only three kinds of men really had the option of acting on the basis of coherent principles: men whose conscientious objection stemmed from broader personal ethical systems that antedated the time they were at risk, men who genuinely believed in the war and in the government's right to ask them in particular to fight it, and the tiny handful who openly and personally refused induction and went to jail. All the rest of us were trying to adjudicate between competing principles in a context where our getting out meant that others would go. Obviously, there were intense pressures to ignore the consequences for others, to favor the principles that let us down easy, and to justify lying and misrepresentation (usually by invoking the unfairness of the system). For it was clear that those who favored themselves this way would free ride on those who did not. As a result, virtually all of us lied to ourselves and others, one way or another. Those of us with permanent deferments lied to ourselves about how we would have acted had we lacked them. Those of us who found easy berths lied to ourselves about how fairly those were allocated. Those of us who became conscientious objectors for the moment lied to ourselves about our beliefs. Those of us who went to Canada lied to ourselves about the benefits citizenship had conferred. All of us ignored the ways we free rode on others who fared worse.

The truth was that very few men came through this experience with their principles in one piece. I did not want to think of myself as someone who was frightened and dishonest with himself, who couldn't think straight, wanted others to bear the load, wanted to avoid serving his country, and spent time thinking about how to beat the draft. And I didn't want to think that my peers were what so many of them seemed to be, as they surfaced throughout that spring of 1970 with previously unknown medical problems, sudden transformations into conscientious objectors, and the like. But the result was in fact the destruction of my faith in myself and of much of my respect for my peers.

Even thinking about the draft — making the calculations — mocked the ideals of rationality, rigor, cooperation, patriotism, and compromise that I brought to the late 1960s. And in the event, I retained exactly enough of my principles to be completely ineffectual at saving myself. I could lie, but not at the right time and not enough. More than all my readings about Nazism and the discontents of civilization, the draft persuaded me of the utter irrationality of political life — indeed, of public life. I arrived at Harvard a believer in rational government and a profound, if occasional, patriot. I left it persuaded that government policy was mostly irrational and that national symbolism was cynical propaganda. More personally, I arrived at age eighteen thinking myself a young man of honor and principle. I had done some things in my life that embodied those principles and was proud of them. But the draft taught me that like most other young men, when the stakes were high, I believed in *sauve qui peut* and, moreover, that I wasn't very good even at that.

By whatever path, I stumbled into the Army Reserve on 30 April 1970. Shortly afterward, my undergraduate BA thesis was turned down, and my relationship of three years' standing entered the last stages of its long decomposition. My senior year in college was a glacial horror, flowing slowly but inevitably toward its late summer nadir, my entry to active duty on 26 August 1970.

IV

Active military service was painful but enlightening. Much of basic didn't bother me because boarding school life and athletic competition made me used to close quarters, excessive physical training, and being ordered around. But the lack of foreknowledge and the absolute heteronomy weighed heavily. To my surprise, there was no indoctrination about the war. The Army was just a conveyor belt delivering young men to what my philosophical drill sergeant — whose spine was still full of Viet Cong lead — wryly called "the two-way firing range" in Viet Nam.

As advertised, yet still surprising to me, cultural diversity was the most important, although also the most painful, experience of basic. For the first time I lived
at close quarters with men from other social classes and educational strata in the
deliberately classless regimentation of enlisted life. But I did not at the time
see how valuable this experience was. I was too overwhelmed by a stabbing ache
for the cultured life of my youth—for classical music, real literature, complex
thought. My letters to my parents from basic capture this painful, almost frozen,
attitude. I buried my enormous loss in an invented hyperresponsibility for my
platoon, of which I became leader on the first day.

I spent my entire time at "advanced training" (on-the-job training in typing!)
reflecting on the disaster of my final year in college. In letters that now seem morbid and disturbing, the issue of action versus reflection was my central concern.
On 4 November I wrote to my basic drill sergeant in Kentucky returning to him
the illicit barracks key he had slipped me in order to run things a little more
smoothly. Discussing my general position about 1960s politics, I wrote: "[People]
seem divided but have so much in common. My answer to this problem is to es-
chew action, to study, to try to understand, and through understanding to create
community."

But my old friend Jon Lipman—one of the few real conscientious objectors I
knew—wrote to chide me for seeming to accept the military, for failing to resist.
I wrote back (28 January 1971) summing up my whole experience of the previous
few years: "I am really only a man of thought, even though I feel that inaction is
immoral. Hence *guilt.*"

In a letter of 11 December 1970 to my college roommate, I restated the aims of
what I ruefully called my "project of omniscience," with its attempt to see reality
even from the point of view of those I despised. (I was naively developing the per-
spectivalism I would find when I read Mannheim two years later.) "One must try
to engulf everything and hold it in, retaining its ambiguities, and then postulate
an answer if one dares. I am homesick not for home, but for the old me, the me
who dreamed this could be done."

Even at the moment it was obvious to me that some kind of enormous watershed had been passed. A set of basic illusions about myself were gone. But if in
1970 I could see that I was basically a reflective not an active man, now I can see
that I was a man almost incapable of making decisions, even between largely arbitrary alternatives. We call this quality open-mindedness or eclecticism if we
like it or an inability to make choices and to commit if we don't. Of course it is
both things, the context deciding what meaning it has in each present moment.

For me, the problem of the draft had been that it forced me to make choices when in fact I was constitutionally reluctant to do so.

My draft behavior was by no means the only example of this. My entire academic career had been about avoiding choices. At Andover, I took honors courses in the sciences and the humanities, one of the only kids in my class to do so. At Harvard, my BA thesis was unable to choose between deep historical analysis and the social science theory that so offended the thesis graders. At the Population Center, the background paper I was supposed to write on population studies and psychiatry turned into a comprehensive review of everything I had learned about social and personal life. In graduate school, I went into sociology because it was the least specialized of the social sciences. Even my PhD thesis would be four separable theses combined into a massive document of 200,000 words because I couldn't decide whether the historical or demographic or cultural or functional approach worked best. It is little surprising that my thesis adviser, Morris Janowitz, once said to me with evident disgust, "You have an undergraduate mind."

This unwillingness to make choices also expressed itself in my insistence on having many different kinds of friends — jocks and intellectuals and artsy types at Andover, people across the entire political spectrum at Harvard. Often interested in finding new friends, I was equally unwilling to completely ditch the old. So I ended up with nodding acquaintances with dozens of people representing a large variety of past and present selves. Having many different types of friends meant having to justify myself again and again, to people of wildly differing views, who very often hated each other and despised each other's values. And it meant puzzling again and again about why so many people I liked believed so many different things. From this puzzling, I began to evolve a set of basic questions that had to be answered before I felt I could have a defensible basis for my own positions. The questions involved were, of course, simple and timeless. They seem contentless now, but they arose in burning experience at the time.

1. What is the relation of individual and society? Is the individual utterly free? Utterly determined? Which comes first, individual or society?

2. From where do values come? Decision? Faith? Social origins? Arbitrary sources?

3. How can social change happen? Is irrationality the only mode of change?

4. Why do we see the world as we do? What is the "sociology" of knowledge itself? Is truth completely relative to social position?

5. What are social groups? How do they stay together?

This agenda of questions became the basis of my scholarly career, just as the passion behind it became the passion that drove that career. Coming to a notion of who I was, in the complex array of friends and political positions that my indecisiveness created around me, more or less required that I become a sociologist. Not necessarily in the professional sense—I spent much of graduate school bewildered by peers who seemed to think sociology was a profession or, even worse, a way of making a living. No, for me sociology was about finding out who I was and who I could be. I recognized none of this at the time. I knew I was eclectic. I knew I had friends of vastly different kinds. I was proud of both things. But I did not associate these things with, nor did I see my particular version of trouble with the draft as the result of, the same personality characteristic.

V

When I started graduate school in the fall of 1971, the political environment was quieting down as public battles over policies dwindled into academic debates over Marxism. A small amount of Marx was on the department's famous preliminary reading list, but the devotees read him on their own. Their leader was the noisy, brilliant, and charismatic Michael Burawoy. For various reasons, Michael and I got on like oil and water. Moreover, I had my usual distaste for crowds. So I never moved toward the engaged political scholarship he was creating for himself and his friends, although I admired his huge intelligence and energy and very much wanted him to like me. We got on better once we were both in the field doing ethnography.

The subject of that ethnography—psychiatric knowledge—came from a chance conversation with Professor Janowitz about my research on psychiatry at the Population Center, a conversation that put me into the field only two weeks later. As a result, my agenda of burning personal questions as well as the residue of my political concerns got focused into a decade-long study of psychiatry as a knowledge system, first as an ethnographer (in a clinic for a year and in a mental hospital for five years) and later as a historical sociologist. This research area was already full of openly political fights over things like insanity law, community mental health, biological psychiatry, and "the myth of mental illness." But these and other great debates decomposed, in the field, into incomprehensibilities. In the hospital, one seldom knew who was telling the truth, because everything there was profoundly damaged: the patients crazy, the professionals unlicensed or defrocked, the custodial staff adroit liars, the larger mental health and criminal justice systems (we had insane criminals, too) corrupt as well as bureaucrat-ically irrational. All the grand oppositions — hospital and community, biology and psychology, freedom and constraint, custodial staff and professionals, liber-als and fascists — were turned round and recombined and ironized and undercut till one could have few "politics" other than a kind of personal loyalty to the people one knew at first hand to be humane people.

For me, then, the enormous agenda of issues formed in my college years was focused into this narrower task of understanding mental illness and society's re-action to it. Here alone did I study politics, and the practical lesson I eventually drew was that coherent political positions — general categorizations of the kind Michael Burawoy used without a second thought — didn't make sense. The pa-pers I wrote on madness and mental hospitals in the mid-1970s all took a broadly humanistic and traditionally ethnographic stance: trying to understand, trying to reconcile, seeking a basis for a comprehensive view in a kind of rigorous com-mon sense. They are filled with passion, but the passion of humanism, not of rigorous political analysis. Not until more than two decades later, in the last chapter of Chaos of Disciplines, did I attempt to turn this understanding into something like a general analysis. And it is quite significant that Michael — by then a much-admired old friend — liked the rest of the book but thought I was out of my depth in that chapter.

As the war faded, feminism loomed as the new issue. The public transforma-tion of gender rules was echoed by private renegotiations all over America. And like most men of that era, I fought out an understanding of feminism on the in-timate turf of a long-term relationship. But the evolutions of this private politics would take us far beyond the 1960s. Nonetheless, remembering feminism points to the useful closing insight that my experience of the 1960s was explicitly mas-culine. The draft was a man's problem. Women could commiserate, support, ig-nore, despise. But they couldn't live the draft experience, and they were, in any case, increasingly preoccupied with their own oppressions.

In the 1960s, I grew up. I was not happy about it.

JEFFREY C. ALEXANDER

The Sixties and Me

From Cultural Revolution to Cultural Theory

Jeffrey Alexander is the Lillian Chavenson Saden Professor of Sociology and codirector of the Center for Cultural Sociology at Yale University. He has chaired the sociology departments at Yale (2002–5) and the University of California, Los Angeles (1989–92), the ASA's Theory (1984) and Culture (2005) sections and the International Sociological Association's Research Committee on Social Theory (1990–94). He works in the areas of theory, culture, and civil society. He is the author of The Meanings of Social Life: A Cultural Sociology *and* Cultural Trauma and Collective Identity *(with R. Eyerman, B. Giesen, N. Smelser, and P. Sztompka) and the editor, with Philip Smith, of* The Cambridge Companion to Durkheim.

There are currents that run through the affairs of men and women. They wash over us, cleanse us, and push us head over heels into some unknown place. They knock us over, wear us out, and sometimes almost kill us. They leave us gasping in their wake and grateful for being left alive.

The Sixties[1] marked one of those gigantic rebellions against this-worldly asceticism that can make you think twice about "modernity." Even modernity's greatest champions knew that the rationalization of the world comes at a price.

---

1. See the fascinating discussion by Eleanor Townsely, "The Sixties' Trope," *Theory, Culture, and Society* 18, no. 6 (2001): 99–123.

Max Weber heard the sirens of this-worldly mysticism, eroticism, aestheticism, and fundamentalism but thought they could be resisted. Karl Marx believed that communism would get the answers right and provide an alternative modern world. Émile Durkheim put his faith in the secular sacred. Georg Simmel looked to art. Talcott Parsons saw the other side of the pattern variables, and the strains modernity placed on men, but believed that balance could be preserved by hearth and home. Jürgen Habermas looked nostalgically at the life world but thought it could be insulated from instrumental rationality and segregated in the ethical sphere. Modernity's critics had an easier time. Friedrich Nietzsche condemned abstract morality, yearning for myth and Dionysus. While condemning the rational public as surveillance, Michel Foucault pursued the private cultivation of the self, finding release through ecstatic, transgressive experience.

These awarenesses of the doubleness of modernity have never been organized into a systematic theory of the emotional and moral contradictions that simultaneously fuel modernity and threaten to destroy it. But the contradictions are there, nonetheless, in the real life of modern societies for all to experience and sometimes even to see.

The cost of rationalization is a tumultuous unconscious. Individuals slip into the unconscious during dreams; they are motivated by it when they are unable to maintain logical control, and stick to the reality principle, when they are awake. The social unconscious is revealed in the fantasies and nightmares that propel popular symbolic life, in movies and television dramas about love and sex, death and violence; in painted and sculpted representations of primordial archetypes, transcendental tranquility, and chaotic passion; in novels about adventure beyond control, intimacy beyond conflict, and remorse without end; in music that is apocalyptic beyond imagination, ecstatic beyond reason, and sublime beyond our most luxuriant dreams.

The dreams of popular culture are the messengers of the social unconscious. They reveal the underside of the modern order. This underside is real. It may not take an institutionalized form, but it provides constant temptation, promising transcendence beyond good and evil. It fuels social and religious movements and hopes, not only for civil but personal repair, for social justice and love.

There are times in human history when the social unconscious breaks boldly into the light of day. Such outbreaks mark wars and revolution but, as well, the great public movements of moral compassion and religious awakening that try to set things right in a fundamental way. Inchoate and diffuse, these moments point to alternative social orders even if they do not clearly define them, much less in-

THE SIXTIES AND ME | 39

dicate how they can be achieved. For all their unrealism, these outbreaks provide the fuel that societies need to create and procreate. Rationalization can kill. Social life needs to be fed by the social unconscious to survive.

The Sixties marked a great outbreak of the social unconscious. In the last part of the nineteenth century, there had also been enormous waves of anxiety, utopia, and rebellion in response to the ratcheting up of economic rationalization in the bureaucracy-building age. In some national contexts, these outbreaks helped to humanize capitalism and create social democracy. In others, they unleashed the fanaticisms of communism, fascism, and militarism that threatened to destroy civilization, and almost succeeded. Yet, the frenzy of the Second World War created another surge of social rationalization. The postwar settlement upgraded and enlarged rational control. Should it have been surprising, two decades later, that surplus repression in the most modernized societies was becoming difficult to bear?

The Sixties were sparked by specific events and not by such fateful fits of the collective unconscious alone. The civil rights movement opened up dreams of interracial harmony. The horrendous war in Viet Nam polluted America, the vanguard of modern rationalization, and triggered a vast social movement for peace. There was also the emergence of a new kind of music, rock and roll, which fueled a youth culture and allowed private visions of love and violence to take on new public texture and economic might.

These secular rhythms and historically specific events entered the life cycle of my generation at a formative stage. Our socialization in the quiet 1950s and early 1960s had nurtured an ambition to fit in and to get ahead. We postwar baby boomers, like our parents, were models of this-worldly asceticism and disciplined self-control. Yet, as the popular culture of that time reveals, we also experienced the anxiety and the romantic yearning that marks the doubleness of modern life.

During the Sixties, the social unconscious reached up and grabbed us by our collective throat. It shook us violently and turned our world upside down.[2] Our parents had deceived us, our teachers were oppressors, our political leaders criminals, our criminals saints. The old world was dying, a new one was being born. My generation experienced the Sixties as a liminal state. Teetering at the edge of

---

2. Binary references to the dystopia of apocalypse and the utopia of salvation were continuous themes in contemporary efforts to understand the Sixties — e.g., Harold Hayes, ed., *Smiling through the Apocalypse: Esquire's History of the Sixties* (New York: Esquire, 1969); and Morris Dickstein, *Gates of Eden: American Culture in the Sixties* (New York: Basic Books, 1977).

the old times, we lived in a *communitas* that adumbrated the new age, when the fragmented, isolated, and rationalized world of modernity would be left behind.

I was a Sixties communard, a noncommissioned foot soldier in this new generational army of social and personal salvation, struggling with "my brothers and my sisters" to bring about the new world that was already being made. Fresh from the ascetics and romantics of Los Angeles public high school life, I arrived at Harvard in 1965, just in time to catch the generational tidal wave as it gathered strength. Experiencing drugs, sex, and rock and roll in real time, my modernist dreams of grace through achievement faded away. So did my once powerful sense of the realness of social reality, of the legitimacy of social power, of the reasoned basis for the social and cultural structures of modern American life. The abyss had opened up. Everything holy was profaned; all that was solid was melting into air. I experienced the social construction of reality. I became an intellectual to understand this experience in a more cognitive way.

Liminality ruled my sophomore year. My most rigorous education was provided by fellow editors at the *Harvard Crimson*, and my most coherent writing appeared in its feature pages. The year is frenetic in memory, an often unhappy, sometimes ecstatic blur. When spring came, I threw open my living room windows to blare Beatles and Stones songs into the Lowell House yard.

In my junior year I began to stick my head above the ether and breathe the intellectual air. With the bemused good will of my social studies tutor, Mark Roberts, I structured an individual tutorial around writings on social utopia. Paul Goodman, Herbert Marcuse, David Riesman, and Kenneth Keniston gave me my first sense of what social theory might try to be — utopian theory to match my liminal social and personal life, intellectual imagination stretching to connect with emotional and moral need.

In my senior year, I joined Students for a Democratic Society, or SDS as it is probably more commonly known, and sunk baby teeth into critical social thought. Disrupting a Harvard faculty meeting to protest the Reserve Officers' Training Corps (ROTC), we received a "disciplinary warning." We threatened a "sleep in" against Harvard's restrictive female visiting hours, but they were relaxed before we could try it out. We organized a New Left study group, which met in Michael Kazin's room. We wondered whether there was a social theory that could tie things together, fold them into our angst and hope, and tell us how radical social change would make it all go away. In these intense, occasional meetings, I encountered the concepts of cultural contradiction and postindustrial society. Such ideas seemed to explain our unhappy feelings and rebellious actions. We felt angry because we were fodder for the new class, which was being trained to produce commodities that nobody would need.

I experienced the aesthetic pleasure of an intellectual system. The same theory could explain the liberating qualities of the new world and the oppression of the old. This pleasure was so vivid that I became a lifelong theorist. It made me thirsty for even bigger things. I would eventually give up Marxism, and later Parsonianism, but I would remain nostalgic for a grand theory, the kind that C. Wright Mills, he of the pragmatic school of American radicalism, roundly despised.

That one could tie normative hope and empirical realism neatly together hooked me for life. Sociological theory became Sixties manqué. Intellectual ratiocination would provide an antidote to social rationalization. The commitment to intellectual play remained long after the commitment to a world organized by social play disappeared. Properly disciplined and rationalized, it would eventually provide a pathway from liminality to adulthood. Eventually, it would even pay.

The Sixties made me into a social theorist. It created the space not only to make the world anew but to think it anew as well, and to think about thinking it. I shared this experience with many others, not only in the United States but around the world. But my Sixties was not only representative. Distinctive experiences in my life course separated me from some of the influential themes of my intellectual generation, even as I remained deeply connected to others. This dialectic of separation and connection led me to cultural and democratic theory, which I continue to pursue today.

The cultural and political radicalism of the Sixties focused on emotions and morality, on the structure and restructuring of internal life. Subjectivity was everything, and "changing" or "raising" consciousness were the mantras of the day. When I became a Marxist, it was decidedly of the New Left kind.[3] Materi-

3. For some representative texts of this very particular Marxism, see, e.g., Martin J. Sklar, "On the Proletarian Revolution and the End of Political-Economic Society," *Radical America: An SDS Journal of American Radicalism* 3, no. 3 (1969): 1–41; The New Left Review, eds., *Western Marxism: A Critical Reader* (London: New Left Review Editions, 1977); Mark Poster, *Existential Marxism in Postwar France: From Sartre to Althusser* (Princeton, NJ: Princeton University Press, 1975); Shlomo Avineri, *The Social and Political Thought of Karl Marx* (Cambridge: Cambridge University Press, 1969); Alex-

alism was our enemy not only in society but also in social theory. We associated orthodox, economistic Marxism with Soviet communism, and we considered the latter to be an object lesson in social rationalization, not its alternative. Commodity fetishism was the force against which we fought, not the poverty of scarce commodities. Weber's iron cage and bureaucratic rationality were the main dangers, not a particular kind of distributive regime. This was "Western Marxism" with a vengeance, the very embodiment of the theoretical perspective at which Perry Anderson would later take aim but that he and his friends in the *New Left Review* had done so much to spawn.[4]

We conceived "interest" in qualitative terms. Making revolution meant engaging in intensive dialogue, passionate social drama, and radical reinterpretation. We could not rely on objective contradictions, on necessity produced by economic force. Georg Lukács had discovered reification, moving critical thought from Marx to Marcuse. Antonio Gramsci had discarded *Das Kapital*, replacing its economic laws with ideological hegemony. Jean-Paul Sartre connected Marxism with inner subjectivity. André Gorz linked consciousness to a new strategy for labor.[5]

New Left Marxism taught that the objective only seemed so. The economic and political were infused with subjectivity. If everything in bourgeois life were ideologically constructed, then everything was up for grabs. If it could reinterpreted, then it could be redefined. If these new readings were dramatized, they could penetrate people's inner lives. If conscious changed, there would be a new world of sentiment and feeling, and institutional transformation after that.

These foundational beliefs of the Sixties generation stayed with me. They were crystallized in different ways at different times. While the translation into New Left idioms disappeared, the general sensibility retained its feeling and form.

The political and intellectual axes of my personal life always cross cut. My intellectual life was defined by the tension between socialism and liberalism. My

---

ander Cockburn and Robin Blackburn, eds., *Student Power: Problems, Diagnosis, Action* (London: Penguin, 1969); Herbert Marcuse, *One Dimensional Man* (Boston: Beacon, 1964); Albrecht Wellmer, *Critical Theory of Society* (New York: Herder & Herder, 1971).

4. Perry Anderson, *Considerations on Western Marxism* (London: New Left Review Books, 1976).

5. Georg Lukács, *History and Class Consciousness* (1924; reprint, Cambridge, MIT Press, 1971); Antonio Gramsci, *Selections from "The Prison Notebooks"* (New York: International Publishers, 1971); Jean-Paul Sartre, *Search for a Method* (New York: Alfred A. Knopf, 1963); and André Gorz, *Strategy for Labor* (Boston: Beacon, 1967).

politics revolved around the tension between revolutionary militancy and democratic social reform.

At Harvard, I was initiated into the intellectual culture of critical liberalism. Motivated by intense antagonism to the Viet Nam war and a personal commitment to civil rights, I audited Michael Walzer's lectures on democratic obligation and civil disobedience. Watching this deeply moral thinker use abstraction to grapple with the most pressing problems of my time made a deep impression on me. It introduced me to notions of mutual respect and solidarity that would later inform my work on civil society. I also closely followed H. Stuart Hughes's elegantly crafted lectures on twentieth-century intellectual history, which began with the discovery of intellectual cosmopolitanism in his *Consciousness and Society* (1958) and concluded with the claim that Marcuse embraced a primordialism that threatened to undermine it. At the time, I couldn't entertain the latter point, but I was nonetheless fascinated by the method. Hughes's books and lectures implanted in my mind a model of theoretically informed historical text interpretation that would later sustain my first book, *Theoretical Logic in Sociology*.

My most ardent academic enthusiasms at Harvard were reserved for the humanities, from the ancient Greeks to the Reformation and Renaissance, nineteenth-century novels, and the postwar avant-garde. The one big thing I had learned in public high school was New Criticism. Interpreting novels, plays, and paintings were what I enjoyed most during my college days. The continuity with my later interest in cultural methods is clear.

Under the influence of Walzer's and Hughes's lectures, my tutorial in utopian social theory, and my gradually increasing involvement in radical politics, I did begin to get some sense for social science. My undergraduate honors thesis in social studies, with Barrington Moore, focused on the American labor movement in the late nineteenth century, though I had yet hardly read Marx.

My argument was that labor radicalism had been muted at a critical juncture not by liberal cooptation but by the subjective impact of antilabor violence. This rather blunt, simplistic thesis was informed by an interpretation of inner life. The idea had come to me while reading Samuel Gompers's autobiography, *Seventy Years of Life and Labor* (1920). It struck me that the centerpiece of that bildungsroman was Gompers's vivid account of his narrow escape from horse-mounted militia during a labor strike in 1877, the "year of violence." If he had not leaped into a sewer and pulled a manhole cover over his head, Gompers believed, he would have been beaten, possibly even killed. This psychological trauma, generated by imminent violence, remained with Gompers for the rest of his life. It seemed to provide a subjective explanation for his commitment to nonpolitical, economic unionism. In *Cultural Trauma and Collective Identity*, I formalized this early intellectual gut feeling in a more rigorous way.

During this last year at Harvard, my political experience became defined by the sharpening tension between revolutionary militancy and democratic reform. When I joined SDS, it was already deeply split between New Left and Progressive Labor Party (PLP) factions. Initiates into the New Left caucus, like me, still read the Port Huron statement, the animating and not very Marxist principle of which was that people had the right to participate in the decisions that affect their lives. This political maximum defined the spirit of the Sixties' New Left activists. It was because we were animated by this spirit that we would spend hours talking things through at meetings. Our politics were a passionate commitment to discursive and disruptive engagement with the community outside. By contrast, PLP students viewed themselves as labor militants, and created an organization call the Worker Student Alliance. Rather than following the early Marx, they emulated bolshevism. They were a cadre, following policies decided by a central committee in secret meetings. We idolized Marcuse and Sartre; their gods were Lenin, Stalin, and Mao.

During a tense and chaotic meeting that stretched long into a night in April 1969, members of Harvard SDS struggled over the question of whether taking over a Harvard administration building would help to stop the war. The majority voted against initiating such a militant confrontation. A few hours later, in the darkness of dawn, PLP militants who had lost the vote stormed Harvard's central administration building. They pulled the deans from their offices and threw them violently down the stairs. Fearing the revolution would pass us by, the New Left caucus sucked in their pride and joined the occupation. Administrative missteps, police brutality, and a restive youth culture transformed this political misadventure into an act of liberation. The rest of the academic year became political carnival. Silk-screened poetry festooned the Harvard yard. We experienced our own Prague spring. It was Sixties' liminality for the last time.

That summer, after graduation, these impulses were pushed aside. With other communards, I traveled to Chicago for the convention that split SDS. New Left and PLP factions postured militancy in what was considered a "prerevolutionary" time. Crude slogans were created, and scripts chanted in competitive counterpoint by militants on both sides. The PLP faction kept time by waving Mao's little red books. Mirroring their sectarian militancy, the Weathermen emerged on the New Left side. "Days of rage" followed. Militants trashed the streets and clashed with police at Chicago's Democratic convention the year before.

Meanwhile, I had returned to Boston to participate in the Roxbury collective. We would provide collateral support to the Black Panthers in Boston's most impoverished neighborhood. These feelings of good will were not reciprocated. Our summer commune suffered several break-ins, one at gunpoint, when I was away. My friends postponed graduate school for the sake of the imminent revolution. Some went underground. The spirit of the Sixties took a dive. I decided not to stay.

Was it social conformity, good sense, or an increasing hunger for intellectual life that convinced me not to dismiss Berkeley's offer to train me in sociology? When I traveled out West to join the program, it was in some disarray. Even as I attended Neil Smelser's year-long lecture course in sociological theory, which was at once inspiring and intimidating, I began a countereducation in Marxist analysis. We formed a radical study group to explore alternative perspectives and to steel ourselves to raise critical points in class. I enthusiastically attended Richard Lichtman's courses in Marxist philosophy, which powerfully presented the Hegelian reading. I joined the junior wing of James Weinstein's radical new journal *Socialist Revolution*. Under the tutelage of John Judas and Eli Zaretsky, we studied *Kapital* intensely in the sweltering summer of 1970.

This radical intellectual education did not neatly articulate with the fragmentation and polarization of political life. Our sociology collective certainly did its part during street demonstrations, the rousing performances that unfolded inside tear-gas clouds. But we held back from the window breaking and systematic "trashing." We felt increasingly separated from the hardened members of the revolutionary vanguard. Driven by its own internal dynamics, but also by frustration with the triumph of backlash politics and Richard Nixon, the once New Left had become old. It was increasingly polluted by Stalinism and sectarianism. Desperate forms of militancy and acts of revolutionary terrorism displaced politics.

I watched this transformation with horror and fear. It drove me to try radical politics of a different kind. We engaged in more traditional organizing projects on our own. Our sociology collective traveled to Los Angeles to offer our services to the workers striking the Goodyear Tire plant. We confronted their trade union leadership and produced a wall poster that provided an alternative intellectual framework for their struggle.

We did not find any converts, and the first doubts about our radical criticism began to form in my mind. There were still some good days ahead. When President Nixon and Henry Kissinger ordered the bombing of Cambodia, in spring 1970, student groups organized massive demonstrations and a national strike. Berkeley was effectively shut down. Fred Bloch and I organized about one hundred sociology undergraduates, graduate students, and even a few scattered members of the faculty into the Fremont Project. For three months we canvassed this working-class community of General Motors workers. Our goal was to organize them against the war and to show them its connection to capitalism, whose exploitation they would be naturally against. While an hour's drive from Berkeley, Fremont was actually a universe away. The workers' evident and mystifying satisfaction with the American way of life deeply impressed me. Was commodification as alienating as the good book said? Or had capitalist culture brainwashed the workers in a hegemonic way?

I began to think more about culture during my second graduate-school year. Even as I continued to sophisticate my Marxist self, particularly with Antonio Gramsci and Louis Althusser, I exposed myself to the seduction of the classics of "bourgeois" social science. Leo Lowenthal's course on Durkheim raised big questions for me. I drew strained analogies between hegemony and conscience collective, but I began to worry about how collective culture could actually be. Was it plausible to link its origins, much less its effects, only to class interests and control? Was culture not more autonomous? Did it not have symbolic processes that exerted their own, specifically cultural effect? Robert Bellah's seminar on Weber sharpened these questions. Weber seemed the daring antidote for Marx. He suggested that the cultural superstructure of capitalism actually had preceded the base and that deep and abiding concerns about the meaning of life exerted far-reaching effects not only on culture but on social structure as well.

I spent the summer after that second year with *The Structure of Social Action*. I understood Parsons's great early work as providing an analytic framework that clarified the issues classical thinkers had raised in a more substantive and historical way. It was the idea of "voluntarism" that still compelled me. New Left Marxism had understood but hedged its bets with notions of ideology, false consciousness, and economic determinism "in the last instance." Parsons showed that you couldn't go home again. He was the bridge over which I walked from Marxism to sociology.

Such concepts as actor, movement, institution, and role had taken their initial meanings in terms of New Left Marxism. What I now understood was that classical and modern sociology could allow for their subjectivity but explain it in a more sophisticated way. My last piece of Marxist work, written during my third year, expressed this transition. It was called "Reproduction or Socialization?" I came down on the sociological not on the Marxist side. Faruk Birtek, editor of the *Berkeley Journal of Sociology,* decided not to publish this earnest confrontation of Marxism and sociology. I remain grateful to him for that.

I experienced the crisis of faith. I could no longer believe in the narrative of revolutionary salvation. The capitalism/socialism split seemed like a simplistic lie. Mao's cultural revolution now looked repulsive. Stalinism was something I began to understand generically for the first time. I became fascinated by Fabianism and social democracy. On election day in 1968 I had marched down Massachusetts Avenue in Cambridge to "vote with my feet" against formal democracy. On election day in 1972, I spent the chilly afternoon and the cold hours of dusk canvassing for McGovern. I was immensely disappointed at the scale of his defeat.

Which made Nixon's fall during Watergate that much more satisfying. It was also instructive in a theoretical way. This evil-doing, polarizing conservative, elected by a record landslide, was forced from power because he had acted like a political radical. He had stepped outside the rules of civil society, secretly deployed political cadre, and personalized power in an antidemocratic way. Public opinion forced him from office, fearful that the author of the "Saturday Night Massacre" threatened to pollute American democracy's sacred core. The discourse of American civil society had most powerfully expressed itself in a vivid secular ritual, the Senate Watergate Hearings in the summer of 1973. It was not material interest but civil interest "rightly understood" that, in the year following, fueled the massive but peaceful transfer of power to congressional Democrats, and to the Democratic presidential candidate two years later.

It took years of reading and thinking to find a way to articulate what I experienced during those critical years — more Parsons and Weber, the late Durkheim, semiotics, cultural anthropology, poststructuralism, and democratic theory. But social performance, civil society, and cultural sociology have remained my interests ever since those times. These ideas were planted by the seeds of the Sixties. The Sixties had to end before the plants could grow and bear fruit.

Antinomian Marxist

Michael Burawoy has taught at the University of California, Berkeley, since 1976. He has studied industrial workplaces in different parts of the world — Zambia, Chicago, Hungary, and Russia — through participant observation, from which vantage point he has tried to cast light on the nature of postcolonialism, on the organization of consent to capitalism, on the peculiar forms of working-class consciousness and work organization in state socialism, and, finally, on the dilemmas of transition from socialism to capitalism. He has developed theoretically driven methodologies, in particular "the extended case method," that allow him to draw broad conclusions from ethnographic research. Throughout his sociological career he has engaged with Marxism, seeking to reconstruct it in the light of his research and more broadly in the light of the historical challenges of the late twentieth century.

It is my impression that Mr. Burawoy is hampered intellectually by excessive and unrealistic preoccupation with what he regards as conflicts between himself and the prevailing trends of sociological analysis in the United States. He seems to think that he must struggle to prevent himself from being overpowered or seduced by "mainstream sociology." At the same time, I have not ever detected any originality on Mr. Burawoy's part in analyses which he has made from the standpoint which he regards as disfavoured in American sociology. . . . It might be that there is no spark of originality in him, or it might be that he is holding it in reserve. Since, however, I have known him for a long time and he has never hesitated to express his opinions to me on a wide variety of political and other subjects, I would incline toward the former hypothesis. . . . When I first met him, I was very much struck by his initiative. He knew nothing about sociology, and he knew nothing about India, but he struck out on his own, and that seemed to me to be admirable and worthy of encouragement. In the Department of Sociology he has done well in his examinations. . . . In seminars, I have been more struck by an obstinate conventionality and a fear of being led into paths which might disturb his rather simple view of society. It is a great pity because he obviously likes to do research and he is not inhibited when it comes to writing. He also has a very good I.Q. But somehow, either the security of sectarianism or a juvenile antinomianism seems to have got the better of him. I first noticed the latter in Cambridge. At that time he was an undergraduate and I thought it would pass. Thus far it has not.

Edward Shils (1975)

One is not born but, rather, becomes a Marxist. One becomes a Marxist, in part, through the damnation of others. As woman is to man so Marxism is to sociology—its excluded, marginalized, calumniated, fabricated, silenced, and mythologized Other. Just as man needs woman, sociology needs Marxism to identify itself, to give meaning to its own existence. Without its Other, sociology loses its reason for being, its originality, and its vitality. But Marxism is not just made by others, for others. It also makes itself. I made my Marxism not by abstention from the world but by entering its bowels—mine shafts, machine shops, steel mills, champagne distilleries, and furniture factories—in Zambia, the United States, Hungary, and Russia, under capitalism and socialism, colonialism and postcolonialism. I translated my experiences not into a party ideology but for an ongoing and open Marxist tradition, forged in the political trenches of academe. Within this field of domination, together with teachers and students, friends and enemies, lovers and colleagues, I have rotated between the reconstruction of Marxism and the critique of sociology. If my Marxism has so far been from the working class, now the question is whether it can also be for the working class.

Preludes to Marxism

It's difficult to know how one's social origins shape one's future. My mother's family fled Petrograd when she was thirteen, soon after the 1917 revolution.[1] My fa-

---

1. During World War I, St. Petersburg was renamed Petrograd, a more Russian sounding name. After Lenin died in 1924 it became Leningrad. After the fall of the Soviet Union the grandeur of the nineteenth-century city was recalled with the restoration of its old name.

ther, conversely, left earlier in 1912. He grew up in the Eastern Ukraine in Yeka-
tarinoslav, a city that would later become the huge Soviet military-industrial
complex of Dniepropetrovsk. Both families escaped to Germany, and my parents
met in Leipzig while they were university students. They fled the Nazi regime
for England in 1933. Before they left, they both had received doctorates in chemistry but only my father was to use his degree for employment in England. He became a lecturer in organic chemistry at the Manchester College of Science and
Technology. We lived a lower-middle-class life on the south side of Manchester.
As a foreigner and Jew, with a charming but immodest style, my father never
adapted to the English academic scene. His proclamation of communist sympa-
thies, perhaps prompted by his disaffection, only deepened his estrangement. As
long as my father was alive, my mother stayed at home to look after my sister,
eleven years my senior, and me.

When I was eleven my father died quite suddenly of a heart attack. My mother
found a job as a technician in a cancer hospital and then as a Russian teacher.
We had little money and so she took in lodgers — two at a time — so that our small
semidetached house was always overflowing. Mainly doctoral students, they came
from all over the world — from France, Italy, Germany, and a whole tribe from
Greece but also from much farther afield: Hong Kong, Israel, Pakistan, India, Japan, Brazil, Peru, and Poland. They were devoted to my mother, appreciating her
spontaneous and irresistible hospitality. She made a home for them and they became like family. Even if 22 Queensway was a veritable United Nations, I can't say
it cultivated my sociological sensibility. Perhaps, it made me curious about the
rest of the world. If the sociological spark was there it was latent, since in those
days I had only two passions — soccer and astronomy — and the rest could go to
the dogs. My mother cared only about my performance at school, and, under her
watchful eye, I flowered in mathematics. Trying to live up to her hopes and believing mathematics was necessary for a career in astrophysics, I worked hard.

All this changed when I took off for New York in 1965 at the age of seventeen.
In those days "America" was very far away, but remoteness was the appeal. I
found a place on a Norwegian cargo boat bound for Philadelphia, and thus began my six-month interlude between school and university. It was the era of civil
rights, of the free speech movement, the beginnings of the antiwar movement
and sit-ins. I watched from the sidelines but the American impression was deep.
It nurtured a restless optimism. I returned to face three dismal years of mathematics at Cambridge. I had so specialized in high school that I was fit for noth-

ing else. I did experiment with economics, but here, too, I found lectures tedious. After America, Cambridge was quintessentially irrelevant—removed from any engagement with a world I could recognize as "real." I could think only of escape. Four-month summer vacations and a short three-year degree were, therefore, Cambridge's saving grace. Convinced that education was the world's panacea (had I unconsciously imbibed this from my parents' sacrifices, their obsession with my own education?) and students its revolutionary force (had Berkeley, even at a distance, already rubbed off on me?), I ventured forth to South Africa in 1966, at the end of my first year at university. If university education was beyond their grasp, might black South Africans benefit from correspondence education? What about an Open University for Africa? These were the questions that lingered in my mind as I set off to hitchhike through the rest of Africa.

I devoted the next academic year to preparing for my trip to India in the summer. This time I would be better organized and more focused. For no other reason than it seemed important and practical, I decided to explore the question of the appropriate language of instruction in higher education. I had discovered the issue in a Fabian pamphlet. I could find no one interested in such matters under Cambridge's dreamy spires, except for a bespectacled, white-haired, podgy old man, ensconced in spacious rooms in Kings College. There, buried in books and papers, behind what were surely the thickest double doors, was the distinguished American sociologist, renowned anticommunist, and the most learned man I have ever met—Edward Shils. At the time I knew nothing of this. All I knew was that he was supposed to be interested in Indian intellectuals. Curious that an undergraduate would dare to knock on his door, he beckoned me to sit down and kindly listened to the lunacy of my project. He laughed at my tenacity and ignorance—where fools rush in, angels fear to tread. Still he gave me more encouragement than anyone else.

Armed with questionnaires, comprehension tests, and the chutzpah of an eighteen-year-old I traveled the length and breadth of India to see if indeed university students would be better off learning in English, Hindi, or the regional language. I wrote up a report—for whom and why I cannot imagine—that defended English medium education for elite universities and regional language for the lower tiers. Shils even considered revising it for his journal *Minerva*, but I didn't see the point. This was after all spring of 1968. Our relationship nonetheless continued as I had become one of his specimens—one of his antinomian students who were creating chaos in the university. Now that I was graduating, he thought I should pursue my interests as a sociologist at his own University of Chicago.[2] My passions needed disciplining if not taming. I laughed back at him and told him I'd had enough of universities and was off—back to Africa.

India left a deep impression—teeming, chaotic cities with the extremes of poverty and wealth mingling side by side, a world so utterly different from the sheltered suburbia of England. It was an existential watershed, so that now it is impossible to reconstruct life before 1967, uncolored by India. As to my project, if it taught me anything, it was that questions of education were questions of politics and that research detached from politics was a purely scholastic matter. I returned to South Africa in June 1968 less naive but unclear what I was about. Qualified whites were in short supply under apartheid and so, despite my clumsy English, I found a job that would have been beyond my reach anywhere else. I became a journalist with the then new liberal Afrikaner weekly, *Newscheck*, where I was given foreign affairs columns. I had no alternative but to learn to write. These were interesting times to be covering the international scene—the Biafran War, the Prague Spring, and student revolt across Europe. South Africa itself was ominously quiet and oppressively stable. The social movements of the 1970s—the Black Consciousness Movement, the Durban strikes, the Soweto uprising—lay in an unanticipated future. At the time it seemed as though change, if it would come at all, would percolate down through the liberalization of the regime. I had no inkling of the fires kindling in the belly of the beast.

Marxism Discovered: Zambia

South Africa was too regulated and confining for my adventurous instincts. After six months I decamped to Zambia. It was 1968, four years into Zambian "independence." I was still remarkably unclear what I was about. I talked with Jack Simons—longstanding member of the South African Communist Party, darling of the liberation movement and of his students at University of Cape Town, the closest to a true organic intellectual that I would ever meet, then in exile from South Africa and teaching sociology at the University of Zambia. He was skeptical of my (petty bourgeois?) interests in students and higher education. Hearing of my contacts with Anglo American Mining Corporation—I had camped out in

---

2. Little did I know what was happening in Chicago in 1968. I refer not just to the Democratic Convention but to student protest and the persecution of Dick Flacks and Marlene Dixon. Had I known about this I may never have gone to Chicago and my career would have been very different.

the garden of one of its chief executives two years earlier—he proposed that I investigate what the mining companies were up to, now that Zambia was no longer a colony. It was an important question since 95 percent of foreign earnings came from copper and the industry employed some 50,000 relatively well-paid workers, a considerable number in a population of 4 million. I needed the money anyhow, so I applied and received a job in the industry's Personnel Research Unit, located on the Copperbelt. I had never been trained as a sociologist, so this is where my career really began.

With my math degree I lodged myself in the Personnel Research Unit and made myself indispensable to management. I held the key to the industry's mammoth job evaluation exercise, which would integrate the pay scales of blacks and white—pay scales that had always been separated to reflect the colonial order. The leverage gave me access to the mines, and I launched surveys into the conditions of the working class. These were administered by Zambian personnel officers—amateurish surveys about job satisfaction, family background, labor and migration history, and above all attitudes to Zambianization. For I had secretly become interested in the question of the Zambianization, that is, the localization of the labor force, and particularly its managerial ranks. I was shocked by the persistence of the color bar. To be sure it was floating upward, so that shift bosses were already black and mine captains were increasingly black, but the racial principle obtained—no black should have authority over any white. I then began to study processes of Zambianization first hand, seeking out the broader forces at work in reproducing the racial order of the mines.

Enter class—the class interests behind Zambianization. White managers and skilled workers wanted to retain their monopoly of jobs—that was not surprising. African trade unions, which represented unskilled and semi-skilled workers, however, seemed equally uninterested in the upward mobility of a small elite from within their ranks. Instead, they wanted better working conditions and higher wages for their members who were equally unimpressed by Zambianization. As far as they were concerned, it was often better to be supervised by politically restrained whites than token blacks. As for the new Zambian state, it depended on its copper revenues and so did not want to rock the boat by threatening white expertise with displacement. Ironically enough, the copper companies were the most opposed to the color bar, most concerned to replace expensive expatriates with cheap black labor. But so long as the price of copper was high, they'd go along with the floating color bar, let sleeping dogs lie. In short, in postcolonial Zambia, the balance of class forces favored the retention of racism. *The Colour of Class on the Copperbelt: From African Advancement to Zambianization* was published in 1972 by the local Institute of African Studies. It caused more dispute and debate than anything else I would ever write. It was given wide coverage in newspapers and television and promoted by the government agency responsible for Zambianization on the mines. This class analysis, this Fanonite account, was used by corporate head offices of Anglo American against their own managers, instructing them to get their own racial house in order. Early on I learned that one has little control over what one writes, especially if one is so fortunate as to have it circulating beyond the academy.

Class analysis was not my invention! It was encouraged by my teachers — Jack Simons and Jaap van Velsen — at the University of Zambia where I enrolled for a master's degree in its fledgling department of sociology and anthropology. Week in, week out, I received a battering from these vigorous intellects who squawked over my slim offerings and those of two African students. I learned sociology and anthropology on the anvil of terror — healthy preparation for the University of Chicago but devastating for my ego! Jack and Ray Simons had just finished their classic of South African history — *Class and Colour in South Africa, 1850–1950* — a history from below, which brought class and race movements into complex relation. It became the definitive Marxist history of South Africa until it was displaced by new generations — those schooled in French structuralism (who would find the Simonses theoretically rigid) and those schooled in E. P. Thompson's social history (who would find the Simonses empirically limited).

My other teacher, and one who had a much deeper influence on my sociology, was Jaap van Velsen. Student of Max Gluckman, apostle of the Manchester school of social anthropology, student of kinship politics, he had already anticipated much that would later appear as novel in Pierre Bourdieu's *Outline of a Theory of Practice*. The only trouble was he seemed to have a perpetual writing block. His medium was oral, and I was the chief beneficiary. For hours on end I would listen to his booming intonement, meekly protesting his definitive critiques. It was a baptism of fire, permanently scarred into my sociological habitus. Jaap was no romantic anthropologist. He had long been interested in the system of migrant labor — the way colonial states had turned African territories into labor reservoirs to feed the various mining industries of Southern Africa. For him, too, like Jack Simons, no analysis could be complete without the consideration of class.

That, of course, was not everyone's view. Thus, the young American political scientist, Robert Bates, also spent time on the Copperbelt in the immediate years after independence. His dissertation and book, *Unions, Parties, and Political Development: A Study of Mineworkers in Zambia*, sought to demonstrate that the Zambian government had failed to elicit the cooperation of the miners in its development program. He deployed mining industry data that showed declining productivity, heightened turnover, absenteeism, strikes, and so forth—data produced by the very unit where I had worked. Familiar with its one-sidedness, I cut my sociological teeth in a long critical review of his book. He had, so I implied, been duped by the regime's postcolonial ideology that portrayed the working class as recalcitrant and indigent, an ideology that masked the class interests of state and capital. Bates's argument was also in line with then fashionable cultural explanations of backwardness—continuing despite independence. Mired in tribalism and primordiality (shades of Shils!), Africa was not ready for Western democracy or capitalism. At the time, modernization theory was just being challenged by underdevelopment theory. The refreshing and persuasive writing from Latin America, particularly the writing of Gundar Frank, argued that the development of the West had depended on but also continued to depend on the underdevelopment of the Third World. Liberating though it was, I had my doubts about this analysis of "neocolonialism"—all too convenient for the new ruling classes of Africa who could escape responsibility for Africa's slump by focusing attention on external enemies.

I was more influenced by Frantz Fanon's radical account of colonialism's class structure and its disabling legacies. *The Colour of Class* was intended as an extension of *The Wretched of the Earth* from Algeria to the very different context of Zambia. Even if there were few signs of a radical peasantry, there was a powerful labor aristocracy that sought to protect its relative privileges and a national bourgeoisie that collaborated with international capital. But what of the intellectuals, so prominent in Fanon's exposé—the conservative and the radical? I finally did what I had come to do. While at the University of Zambia, I undertook the study of students of which I had dreamed—making this my master's thesis. As one of a handful of whites, I immersed myself in student life, writing Fanonite columns for the student newspaper, setting up a sociological association, conducting opinion polls, inviting leading politicians to campus, and otherwise fueling student hostility to the government. In this case, my analysis was blinded by my participation. Identifying so unquestioningly with students, I was unable to see their distinctive class interests. I was unable to turn Fanon back on to this incipient national bourgeoisie. Instead, I succumbed to sociology, seeking to comprehend the precarious location of the university in terms of its contradictory functions and the rebelliousness of students in terms of their social and geographical mobility. My theoretical commitments were not strong enough to counterbalance my practical, nay incestuous, involvement with student politics. It was quite a lesson in participant observation!

Marxism Europeanized: Chicago

I had been four years in Zambia. It was time to move on, so I called on the avuncular Edward Shils once again. Could he help me find a place in an American sociology department? I applied to Chicago's department but *The Colour of Class*, then still in manuscript form, proved, not for the last time, to be a liability, sending me down the list of applicants. I just squeaked in but without any funding. I wrote to James Davis, then director of the National Opinion Research Center, to see if he had any research assistantships. He wrote back saying he didn't have any assistantships and, in a curt way, advised me against coming to Chicago. That settled it. I arrived in the fall of 1972 and poured all my Copperbelt savings into that first year.

After Zambia, Chicago sociology seemed enormously parochial. But as luck would have it William Julius Wilson arrived the same year as me. Bill's course on race relations looked the most interesting offering that fall. His lectures were based on his first book, *Power, Racism, and Privilege*. There I combined forces with Ida Susser, a fellow Mancunian and graduate student in anthropology, to shower Bill with a barrage of critical commentary. How could he reduce institutional racism to two monolithic categories—black and white? With my work on the class bases of Zambianization and Ida's parallel research on the class bases of ethnic and racial mobility in New York schools, we insisted on the broader political, economic, and especially class bases of racial conflagration. To his unending credit Bill took us very seriously. He was ready to hear our message as we know from *The Declining Significance of Race!*

I remember going to Bill's office one day to protest the idea of a midquarter in-class examination—I had not come all the way from Africa on my own money to be treated like an undergraduate! I emerged from his office some four hours later, having talked Bill's head off. By the end of it he had invited me to write a book with him on black workers. This was the high point of my first year, making it possible to endure what his colleagues were serving up. Under his stimulus, I recharged my interest in South Africa. Many a time Bill was to save my skin or find funding for me in those four and a half Chicago years. Still, I think I would have quit were it not for the sustenance I got from Raymond Smith in anthropology and, especially, Adam Przeworski in political science. Indeed, my second windfall was to discover Adam, just as he arrived in the fall quarter of 1973. I was wandering through the bookstore and to my disbelief came upon copies of Gramsci's *Prison Notebooks*, Ralph Miliband's *State in Capitalist Society*, Althusser and Balibar's *Reading Capital*, and Nicos Poulantzas's *Political Power and Social Classes*. These books, ordered for Adam's course, were becoming fashionable in Marxist strongholds across the country, but the University of Chicago? Adam had been in Paris for the year and he was now offering a course on Marxist theories of the state. Try as he might, he could not get rid of me from his seminar. Like Marx, Adam was infatuated by mathematics, and so in the end my math degree convinced him to let me stay. This was the most exhilarating seminar of my life, made up of remarkable students, with Adam pacing and chain-smoking his way through Gramsci, Poulantzas, and Althusser.

I was an instant convert. My Zambianization study had already taught me that the state is not an instrument of capital except in crisis situations, that for the most part the state does what capital needs without much prompting. It was much more effective for each to let the other get on with its business. But it was in Pick Hall that, for the first time, I began to appreciate the wonders of Marxist theory—a version of French structuralism that celebrated Marx's science and was thus perfectly suited to my contempt for Chicago sociology. During that year I grew intellectually by leaps and bounds. I saw Marxism as vanquishing sociology, and I sketched out the "definitive piece" on the end of sociology! At the same time I never lost an opportunity to irritate Adam by pointing to the parallels between Talcott Parsons and the functionalism of Althusser, Poulantzas, and even Gramsci. So, tired of my tirades, Adam proposed that we teach a course together on Marxism and functionalism, which we did, twice. At his side, I learned to develop a more sophisticated understanding of both structural functionalism and structural Marxism! From Adam I learned to teach, and from him I also learned the virtue of simplicity.

After all this intellectual sparring, I was ready for more practical engagement with the world. Determined to take on the Chicago school on its own terrain as well as earn my keep, I looked for and eventually found an industrial job in the environs of Chicago. Industrial sociology had been in remission for many years both in Chicago and in sociology more broadly—ever since the quiescence of blue-collar workers had put another nail in the Marxist coffin. Little did I know that studies of industrial work were about to enjoy a renaissance with the publication of Harry Braverman's *Labor and Monopoly Capital*. At this point, how-ever, I was more concerned with my daily battles for survival at Allied Corpora-tion. In the beginning, it was difficult enough to stand on my feet for eight hours, never mind making the piece rates. Then it became a matter of negotiating the human obstacles — fellow operators, the inspectors, the truck drivers, the crib at-tendants, my foreman — as well as material threats to life and limb in the struggle to "make out." It was the analogue of my induction into Chicago's sociology de-partment, and so I gave my coworkers the names of Chicago faculty — Bill, Jim, Morris, Ed, and so on. They were the dramatis personae in *Manufacturing Con-sent* as I revealed on one of my returns to Chicago, to the vast amusement of all those assembled.

My ineptitude as an industrial worker may have endangered my life but not my employment or, for that matter, my wages. As my dayman never ceased to tell me, "No one pushes you around here." But that was the puzzle: Why then do people work as hard as they do? Why do they bust their asses to make out? Money was only part of the story since marginal returns for extra effort were small and even negative. Industrial sociology, originating with management's concern to increase productivity, had always been interested in the opposite question: Why people don't work harder. Restriction of output had been the question of Chi-cago's great ethnographer of work, Donald Roy, who had coincidentally labored in the same factory thirty years before.

If industrial sociology asked the "wrong" question, Marxism asked the right question but gave the wrong answer. Marxists — from Marx to Braverman — in-sisted on coercion as the instrument to extract labor from labor power. Coercion did not make sense at Allied, where our employment and minimum wage were protected and where workers spontaneously consented to managerial expecta-tions. More than that, when managerial incompetence impeded workers, rather than sitting back on their laurels they would often invent some new angle to achieve managerial goals. Braverman's focus on the historical transformation of work through deskilling missed the subjective side of work. I argued that politics and ideology are not the preserve of the superstructure but are firmly rooted in the economic base itself. Gramsci's conception of force and consent, his notion of the concrete coordination of class interests, Poulantzas's conception of citi-zenship and the relative autonomy of the capitalist state, and Althusser's notion of ideology as lived experience all had their place there in the regulation of pro-duction. Marxism had located the organization of consent in the state, in civil so-ciety, in the family, in school — anywhere but production, which was presumed to be the crucible of class struggle. My experiences, by contrast, taught me how consent was manufactured in production. What I discovered and elaborated in my dissertation and subsequent book, *Manufacturing Consent*, was the hegemonic organization of work. Needless to say, my focus on the politics of production was also consonant with Foucault's insistence on the ubiquity of micropowers.

Many criticisms have been leveled against *Manufacturing Consent*, but the criticism I would level at it now is its static functionalism. For a Marxist, the functionalist question is a reasonable one: in an age of revolutionary optimism one wants to know what keeps capitalism going and why workers actively reproduce the conditions of their own exploitation. But there can be no final, unchanging answer to a functionalist question. I made the mistake of constituting the hegemonic organization of work as the metaphorical end of American history and turned, instead, to other parts of the world. I should have seen that hegemonic organization of work sowed the seeds of its own destruction. The effectiveness with which the "internal state" and the "internal labor market" demobilized class struggle and constituted workers as individuals with interests in capital accumulation would make organized labor easy targets of the Reagan offensive and of global competition. From then on, instead of capital making material concessions to labor, labor began to make material concessions to capital so as to simply hold onto jobs. Instead of hegemony, the working class increasingly faced despotism. The years 1974–75, when I was working at Allied, proved to be a watershed in the history of organized American labor, after which its decline has been continuous.

There are methodological lessons here, too: in constituting the macrofoundations of microprocesses, we should not forget that external forces are but shorthand for the effects of further, unexamined microprocesses. As a practical expedient, the ethnography of work may have to reify the state, but one shouldn't forget that states, too, can change as a result of internal (or external) processes. Similarly, in identifying the relevant external forces, one should allow new ones that had been latent to come into play. Perhaps global competition was not important when I was working at Allied but it surely became important very soon afterward. *Manufacturing Consent* suffered not only from the reification of external forces but also from tendencies in the opposite direction: the individualizing of social processes, overlooking the possibility that such processes could themselves congeal into a force, that individual consent could turn into a social movement, that making out could become making a strike. I had imbibed too much rational choice theory, forgetting that individual rationality was a contingent social effect! Rick Fantasia's *Cultures of Solidarity* would make this point deftly.

Marxism Historicized: Berkeley

But I am getting ahead of myself. Long before the dissertation was finished I started looking for an academic job. My penchant for kamikaze acts led me to call on my erstwhile benefactor Edward Shils for a letter of recommendation. What could be better than a letter from Edward Shils—sociology's éminence grise? Sure enough it arrived, damning me with faint praise, intelligent and hardworking yes, but also sectarian and antinomian. If my high school cramming had not snuffed out any imagination, then my mathematical training at university surely had. Through this thinly disguised red baiting, the message was clear: don't hire this adolescent. So unusual was this letter that it drew attention to my case wherever I applied and prompted a flurry of interviews. I found out about the letter from Erik Wright, then a graduate student at Berkeley, whom I knew to be a Marxist sociologist like myself. He said I'd better put a stop to Shils's letter as it had already destroyed my chances at Berkeley. Since I had been invited for an interview at the University of California, Los Angeles, Erik invited me up to Berkeley to visit with him. That visit was the beginning of a life-long friendship and joint commitment to Marxism. We discovered the first of our many Marxist complementarities—he the survey researcher of relations of production and I the ethnographer of the relations in production.

As I was to learn over the years, organizing is one of Erik's many strengths, and for my visit he'd already set up a little talk to graduate students as well as interviews with five faculty. They included the reluctant Neil Smelser, then chair of the department, who told me I was on a back burner. Next time I heard from him, some three weeks later, he offered me the job, the result of artful logrolling in a fractious department. Although I had assembled quite a few offers by that time, there was no doubt where I wanted to be! Still, I insisted on the real interview I had missed and presented my dissertation to an amazed audience, clearly divided into those delighted and those dismayed that I had somehow landed the job without a formal interview—surely the secret of my good fortune. I duly thanked Edward Shils for all his help and generous support. We would never meet again.

When it comes to self-education there's nothing like teaching, especially at Berkeley. Neil Smelser decided I should teach the required undergraduate theory course, and I've never stopped since I began in 1977. Then it was a quarter long, today it is two semesters. I teach it as a course on Marxism and sociology. The first semester plots the historical reconstruction of Marxism from Marx and Engels to Lenin, Gramsci, and Fanon. The second semester organizes a critical engagement with Marxism: Durkheim with Marx, Weber with Lenin, Foucault with Gramsci, de Beauvoir with Fanon. Over the years, the course has marched in tune with my own theoretical shifts — it has become a summation and repository of where I am theoretically. With ever more undergraduates, ever more poorly prepared by California's schools, ever more pressured by increasing fees and multiple jobs, and taking ever more courses simultaneously, it's ever more difficult to convince them to read difficult texts and write analytical essays. Still, so far, without fail they rise to the challenge. Whatever the class-size numbers, and now they are up to 220, I try to teach the course as an engagement with texts and with contemporary life — their own and others — as well as with me, with one another, and above all with Berkeley's dedicated teaching assistants. I think of teaching as I think of research, not as extraction or imposition but as dialogue, in which teachers, too, have to be taught.

When I arrived in 1976, crowds of graduate students were awaiting their token Marxist. But they thinned out quite rapidly when I announced that the first half of my Marxism seminar would be devoted to the writings of Talcott Parsons — a replay of the course I had taught with Adam Przeworski. Those who stuck with it gave me a hard time, quite hostile to the scientism of structural Marxism, having been schooled in its great rival, critical theory. This was after all Berkeley and the home of Leo Lowenthal. I was terrified of graduate teaching and still am. Fearing discussion, I would try to lecture straight through, but that never worked. I had to learn the hard way that student engagement was how learning occurred, and if this came at the cost of humiliating or derailing the instructor so much the better.

As to my colleagues, I was too intimidated and defensive to learn much from them. Besides, they were too preoccupied with their own battles to care much about their antinomian Marxist — except when it came to voting! But there were others, including the brilliant Margaret Cerullo, a visiting lecturer in 1977, who provoked me into taking critical theory and radical feminism seriously. At the time, this was quite a shock to my system, from which I only gradually recovered. Worldly, generous, passionate, and always challenging, she has been my unerring critic ever since. And there was Tom Long, subsequently a sociology graduate student, but at the time an undergraduate, giving his own courses on critical theory, Habermas, and Foucault. From him I learned more than from anyone else. There was also Carol Hatch, curriculum administrator, Marxist-feminist manqué, dedicated member of the *Socialist Review* collective, whose office was always a beehive of intellectual and political activity. She was usually the first and most exacting reader of my papers, indefatigable arguer in my courses, conscience of us all. She died in 1989—far too young to die—reflecting on the meaning of Tiananmen Square. Thus, it was from the "margins" of the department that I learned the most.

Berkeley forced me to confront a plethora of Marxisms, all of which had something to say about my twin areas of interest: production and politics. So my sanitized scientific Marxism took a historical turn as I tried to grasp Marxism's self-transformation, following one historical challenge after another. This historicized view of Marxism congealed in the undergraduate theory course but it also gave new impetus to my research. I became especially interested in the challenge of communism or, as I would call it, following Ivan Szelenyi, state socialism. Some, such as my friend Erik Wright, could never take real communism seriously, regarding it as a form of statism unrelated to Marxist communism. Erik refused the bourgeois provocation that associated actually existing socialism with Marxism and instead has sought out alternative "real utopias." I, however, always took the view that we have much to learn from communism's remarkable detour in history, which was undoubtedly inspired by Marxist ideas. We cannot afford to ignore it.

My teacher Jaap van Velsen used to pose the challenge as follows: Marxists are always comparing some ideal typical notion of socialism with actually existing capitalism, but who of them dares to deal with actually existing socialism? Of course, there have been great Marxist scholars of actually existing socialism, from Trotsky to Deutscher, the young Kolakowski to the Budapest school, and there have been a host of scholars on the borderlands of Marxism, including Rudolf Bahro, Ivan Szelenyi, E. H. Carr, and Moshe Lewin. Still, I agree, run-of-the-mill Marxism has not worried enough about the significance of state socialism. It should be said, however, that anti-Marxists are no less guilty of "false comparisons." In trying to discredit communism as inefficient and totalitarian they compare the realities of communism with ideal typical notions of capitalism. The conclusion is the same: we need to compare like with like: reality with reality, or, in more sophisticated analyses, the relation of reality to ideology in one context should be compared with the relation of reality to ideology in the other context.

There was yet another reason to turn to state socialism and that was the sociologist's critique of *Manufacturing Consent*—how do I know that the features of hegemonic production politics are a function of industrialism rather than capitalism? Only a comparison with noncapitalist industrial production might settle that issue. But how was I to garner information about the state socialist workplace—communism's most heavily guarded secret? After stumbling around in a literature of innuendo, propaganda, and speculation, my work took a leap forward when I discovered Miklos Haraszti's, *A Worker in a Worker's State*. Lo and behold, this was a participant observation study of a machine shop in Hungary, very similar in technical make-up to the one I'd done at Allied, yet the differences in our experiences were stark. Haraszti was slaving under a relentless norm that required running two machines at once, a piece rate system that offered no guaranteed minimum wage, and a political regime of production that promoted arbitrary, despotic interventions from a conspiracy of party, trade union and management. This was a bureaucratic despotism that contrasted so vividly not only with the hegemonic regimes of advanced capitalism but with the despotisms of early capitalism and colonialism as well. Based on existing case studies and primary sources, *The Politics of Production* reconstructs political regimes of production in these different societies, as a function of state interventions, workplace-community relations, and market forces. My goal was to understand how workers not only produced things, relations and experiences but simultaneously produced themselves as a class actor.

Although the notion of production politics was taken up, my account of class formation persuaded few. Yet, ironically, my analysis of production politics in state socialism—bureaucratic despotism—anticipated working-class revolt in Eastern Europe even before Solidarity took to the stage of history. Once it appeared, Solidarity only quickened my interest in state socialism. I schemed to go to Poland, but the academic world doesn't permit rapid transplantation. We are always following history at a distance. Before preparations could get under way, Solidarity's self-limiting revolution had been hijacked by Jaruzelski's military coup.

If truth be known, my own tenure at Berkeley was also being hijacked, which was providing distraction enough. My survival looked as unlikely as Solidarity's, since the old regime decided to turn my tenure into a resolute battle to defend "standards" and a "politically free" academy that, in its view, had been eroding ever since the 1960s. These defenders of neutrality and objectivity pulled every stunt in the book, from rigging committees to rigging letters of recommendation, from discrediting my teaching as pandering (despite being the only person in the department to have received the university teaching award) to dismissing my writing as ideological (despite articles in the two premier professional journals, the *American Sociological Review* and the *American Journal of Sociology*). A determined Robert Bellah, then chair of the sociology department at Berkeley, combining a legal brief with supportive external letters and unknown defenders in higher places, made my enemies look like the ideologues they were. With my future uncertain I went underground like Solidarity, taking up exile at the University of Wisconsin–Madison.

Just as Solidarity proved to be the beginning of the end of communism, so the struggle over my tenure was the beginning of the end of Berkeley's old guard. Through the 1980s, with the writing on the wall, the rump of the old guard took flight to other departments or to retirement. I returned from Madison with tenure to participate in rebuilding the sociology department. I had similar hopes for Eastern Europe — that the return of Solidarity at the Round Table Talks of 1989 would prefigure the reconstruction of state socialism in a more tolerant, democratic form. I was right about the reconstruction but wrong about the direction.

Marxism Challenged: From Hungary to Russia

Exile or no exile, Madison, of course, was attractive in its own right. It was an altogether calmer place with a deep professional ethos, proud of rather than threatened by Marxist resurgence. In that enormous department, in 1982–83, I was effectively the lone ethnographer. In the eyes of those graduate students who were dissatisfied with Erik Wright's analytical Marxism, ethnography became *the* Marxist method! This was an exciting year for me, simultaneously teaching the history of Marxism and participant observation, forcing me to reflect on their interrelation. On top of that I was able to enjoy Erik's constant companionship. Madison also offered me Hungarian sociologist, Ivan Szelenyi, who had recently arrived from Australia. What a breath of fresh air that was!

I had already benefited from Ivan's generosity the previous summer. When my Polish plans collapsed, he offered to introduce me to Hungary to where he was returning after seven years of forced exile. I went to Budapest for ten exciting days in the summer of 1982 and would return there regularly for the next seven years, finding manual labor first in the rural areas in a champagne factory and textile shop, and then in the summer of 1984 I worked as a machine operator in a place analogous to Allied. Between 1985 and 1987 I graduated to the Lenin Steel Works as a furnaceman for three successive stints, for about a year in all. In all these ventures I teamed up with local sociologist, János Lukács. His networking genius landed me in these impossible places.

What did we learn? First, Haraszti's experience was not at all typical. As a dissident and as a novice to the shop floor, he was ostracized by his fellow workers, leading to his overly atomized portrait. He worked in one of the first factories subjected to the economic reforms, which further intensified the despotism. On top of that, he had the dissident's eye for totalitarianism. Working in similar factories a decade later, I discovered a much stronger community on the shop floor, one that was mobilized to adapt to the exigencies of a shortage economy. Much to management's chagrin, Lukács and I proposed that leaving work in the hands of workers (rather than expropriating control) was necessary to get things done. Following János Kornai's theorizing, each system has its own rationality and irrationality, and each fashions workers who adapt to or resist those (ir)rationalities. Capitalist rationality called for deskilling, while state socialist rationality called for flexible autonomy.

The state socialist production regime had distinctive political effects. Mobilized by the state to promote communist ideology, the production regime ritualized the celebration of socialism as egalitarian, efficient, and just, which encouraged workers to view the poverty of their experiences in precisely these terms. State socialism had the paradoxical effect of manufacturing dissent to the socialist regime for failing to live up to its socialist claims. Solidarity-type movements were incipient to state socialism, but they are more likely to occur where civil society creates breathing space for movements (e.g., under the protective umbrella of the Church in Poland) and where avenues for individual advancement (as in the informal in Hungary) are less developed.

I was busy working all this out, with my attention fixed on the steel furnace rather than the political hurricane that was sweeping across Eastern Europe. The dissolution of the regime proved anticlimactic, at least on the shop floor — a ripple on the surface of working-class life. Then privatization followed, and workers saw their supervisors and managers pocketing fortunes while their own jobs were disappearing. Let out of communism, its inmates rushed headlong into capitalism, only to discover a prison of another sort. Lukács and I closed our socialist chapter with a book we titled *The Radiant Past*. It was a play on Soviet dissident Alexander Zinoviev's *The Radiant Future*, which dwelled on the absurdity of communist ideology that nonetheless embedded itself in everyday life. We turned his satirical novel on its head arguing that from the standpoint of many, but particularly its working classes, communism even with all its flaws would look unexpectedly rosy when seen from within its capitalist successor. As communism recedes into history, the truth of *The Radiant Past* becomes more palpable. Nostalgia for the guarantees and security, even for the communalism of communism, is an open secret. Still our book sunk without trace — too soon to capture postsocialist disillusionment with free markets and liberal democracy. A critical intelligentsia has yet to appear that would dare to recover the emancipatory visions and hopes lodged in the interstices of the past.

When it became clear that the Hungarian working class was nowhere to be seen in the crisis that beset state socialism, that the latter would be transformed from above not from below, and that the outcome was to be the radiant future promised by capitalism and not the promise of democratic socialism, I took off for the Soviet Union. In 1991, in what proved to be the twilight of perestroika, Kathie Hendley, then a political science graduate student at Berkeley, and I launched into a case study of a major Soviet enterprise in Moscow. After long exploratory talks, we bargained and bribed our way into Kauchuk. Starting in January 1991, we were there almost everyday and sometimes weekends for two months. Kauchuk had become an open book, a microcosm of the Soviet Union, caught between past and future. Arrayed on one side were the technicians from the Komsomol who defended Yeltsin, Russia, and the market. Arrayed on the other side were the old guard, heads of department with links to the ministries who defended planning and the Soviet status quo. Civil war divided management in all its collective rituals, fostering conspiracies behind closed doors, paralyzing production from within just as parallel battlefields disrupted supplies from elsewhere in the Soviet Union.

When our time was up, I accompanied Pavel Krotov to the Komi Republic, in northern Russia, where I found a job, once again as a machine operator in the local furniture factory that made wall systems for the entire Republic. Here in the periphery, life was quieter and the factory was making handsome profits as planning directives relaxed and management could exploit the proximity of raw materials (timber), its regional monopoly of the production of a basic commodity, and its cozy relation to the Komi Republican timber conglomerate. It was here and in Moscow that I learned the real meaning of Soviet enterprise — the end-of-month rush work, the work stoppages, the down time we spent playing cards and dominoes. In those months from April to July, Pavel and I mapped out the dynamics of the timber industry in the emerging market context where managers, with ever-shorter time horizons, were investing not in production but in windfalls from trading wall systems for food and liquor, for holiday places in the sun, for apartments, and most important for needed factory supplies.

The Soviet Union disintegrated soon after I left, when the August counter-coup of hardliners failed. Yeltsin assumed power, and the transition to the market economy began. It was planned like the communist economy to be accomplished in record time. The ideology of shock therapy was shipped in from the West — any transition to the market would have to take place at lightning speed, disarming any opposition before it could regroup its forces. It is a classic war of movement that converged with Bolshevik ideas of revolution. Destroy the old command system, and the new market system would magically appear. Accordingly, prices were immediately liberalized with the result that inflation sky rocketed, impoverishing populations overnight. Privatization vouchers were distributed to every citizen, effectively handing over enterprises to managers who concentrated capital and dispossessed workers of their jobs, wages, and means of existence. This was a caricature of Marx's description of nineteenth-century capitalism.

Pavel and I have been watching the disintegration of the Soviet economy in Komi for ten years, studying the timber industry, the coal industry, banking, and construction in turn. Markets spread to be sure, but at the cost of accumulation. Resources flowed from production into the realm of exchange, along networks of trade, mafia, and finance that spontaneously arose across Russia and beyond, rushing into the vacuum created by the receding planning apparatus. The working class, once so mighty, was destroyed overnight as its leverage power was pulled from under it. Workers and their families tightened their belts, made the most of the trickle of government support, relied ever more on subsistence production. Dispossessed of their jobs, men were made superfluous to the household while women took up the slack, reorganizing the domestic economy. To paraphrase Walter Benjamin: the wreckage has been piling up to the sky, as the capitalist storm from paradise sends the angel of history, hurtling involuntarily into the future.

How could one make sense of this tragic drama? This surely stretched the Marxist imagination that had never been equipped to consider the transition from socialism to capitalism. The focus on the power of the market, the dogma of neoliberalism called to mind Karl Polanyi's critique of nineteenth-liberal creed, how market utopianism could lead right back to extreme forms of state regulation (fascism, communism) Institutional economists were skeptical of shock therapy and the overnight creation of capitalism, favoring slower processes, which would build an adequate legal system, a financial infrastructure, and retain the power of the state. The evolutionists took China as their model, where the party state, rather than being destroyed, incubated market forces. The revolutionaries claimed Poland as their success story. But Russia was another story altogether. Neither revolutionary nor evolutionary, it was involutionary, with market forces generating a self-destructive economy, the realm of exchange parasitical on production. This was not England's nineteenth-century Great Transformation but Russia's twentieth-century Great Involution.

Marxism Defended: Rapprochement with Sociology

With the demise of state socialism, the 1990s forced me to ponder Marxism anew. With the last holdout against market capitalism defeated, neoliberalism took hold of the world by storm. I saw it in South Africa most vividly and most surprisingly. Once the African National Congress boycott was over, I renewed old ties and began to visit South Africa regularly. It was always refreshing to be dropped into the cauldron of South African politics after Russia's political desert. But for all that, the trajectory of South Africa was no less antisocialist even though it started in a different place. The African National Congress came to power in alliance with the Communist Party and the labor unions. Within years its socialist program was in tatters, neoliberal economic policies were hegemonic, and demobilization of civil society became the order of the day. Liberated from the doctrinaire control of the Soviet Communist Party, the 1990s could have been a period of socialist experiment. If not in South Africa, where?

The new world conjuncture called for reassessing the Marxist agenda. I was floundering, losing my way in the storm of capitalism. Even as purified capitalism unleashed extremes of opulence and poverty, despotism and oppression, locally, nationally, and globally, resistance seemed paradoxically (for a Marxist) to have died down. The social movements that had nurtured Marxism in the past were in remission. I turned inward to the graduate students around me for inspiration.

Ever since I arrived at Berkeley I had taught a research practicum on participant observation. Unlike Wisconsin students, who thought it was the Marxist method, Berkeley students regarded participant observation as the antithesis of grand Marxist syntheses, which had to be garnered from historical and comparative research. I set about convincing them otherwise, by elaborating the extended case method that I had learned at the feet of Jaap Van Velsen. I sought to marry two Berkeley traditions — the ethnographic tradition of Herbert Blumer, Erving Goffman, Arlie Hochschild and others with the macrohistorical traditions of Reinhard Bendix, Seymour Martin Lipset, Franz Schurman, Philip Selznick, Neil Smelser, and Robert Bellah. At the end of one particularly successful participant observation course in the fall of 1988, I seized the moment and proposed we continue toward a book. The students were skeptical but sufficiently fond of one another to want to continue to meet — as long as it was over sumptuous meals. It turned out that they had quite a talent for culinary practice. After many trials and tribulations, the result was *Ethnography Unbound* — unbound from the micro, unbound from the present, unbound from induction. Rather than discovering grounded theory, the extended case method sought to reconstruct existing theory in the light of anomalies thrown up by the field. Rather than suspending "context," our theoretically driven approach allowed the incorporation of historical and contemporary forces beyond the site.

Work on *Ethnography Unbound* began in the fall of 1988 and finished two years later, in the fall of 1990. Those were moments of historical optimism, stimulated by the fall of the Berlin Wall. In 1996, a time of political retrenchment, I turned for inspiration to a new group students whose dissertations I was supervising. Their research, broadly ethnographic, was scattered the world over: from Hungary to Brazil, from Ireland to San Francisco, from Kerala to Pittsburgh. Could we stretch the extended case method to embrace a vision of the globe rather than being confined to the national context. Could we collectively develop a view of globalization from below? None of us, and especially I, had any idea where we would end up. We simply began by calling our project "global ethnography." Our task was to figure out what that might mean and what light it might shed on the world around us. Globalization was not of a piece, but how could we divide it up? After much thrashing around in the literature and our own studies, we decided on three approaches: globalization as supranational force, seemingly beyond human control; globalization as transnational connections that demystified the naturalness of forces, revealing them as the product of social processes that linked people across national boundaries; and finally, globalization as postnational imaginations that galvanize movements with alternative visions and possibilities. The further we extended from the micro to the macro, the more important it was to conduct historical explorations of our sites and utilize theory to connect local to global. Our ethnographies had to become ethnohistories.

This was as challenging a project as I'd ever undertaken. From start to finish, it took us three years of Sturm und Drang and then a year to get it published. If the value of intellectual products varies with the suffering it calls forth, then this was indeed a very valuable project! I learned how limited was my own Marxism, which, like sociology, had such great difficulty in thinking beyond the nation state — something that came so much easier to my collaborators. Thus, when I thought of Russia's economic involution, I thought of comparing it with China's economic expansion rather than seeing it as the product of globalization, whether this be the information society, the ascendancy of finance capital, or the expansion of consumer capitalism. Significantly my contribution to *Global Ethnography* was confined to the introduction and conclusion.

If *Global Ethnography* was not distraction enough, my colleagues had another surprise in store for me. Desperate for a chairperson, they chose me! I was flattered and seized the opportunity to apply the extended case method to my own department. After all, I had been a participant observer there for more than twenty years. The least I could try to do was to give the department a sense of its own mission. I had always been in awe of Berkeley's illustrious past — the amazing people who had taught there in the 1950s and 1960s. Indeed, in the 1980s I had organized courses to get students to interview senior faculty on videotape or those, that is, who were still alive. Writing in 1970, my nemesis Edward Shils doubted whether the Berkeley department would ever add up to anything more than a "pluralistic assemblage of eminent figures" bereft of a unifying "line." Now that the old guard had gone and with them the battles of the past, we could begin anew the dialogue about whom we were. If there was any identity to which we could all attach ourselves it was that of public sociology. Many of us actually engaged publics beyond the academy, and those of us who didn't, like myself, thought it was an important thing to do. Pummeled, prodded, and aided by Jonathan VanAntwerpen, I began to uncover the fascinating untold history of Berkeley sociology, a genealogy of its public engagements. After a life of importing "sociology from" the world I studied, I now embarked on a new venture — examining the possibilities and dilemmas of exporting "sociology to" society beyond the academy.

Fate decreed that I take my campaign for "public sociology" beyond the department. So it was that in the middle of my term as department chair, I became embroiled in a fracas with the American Sociological Association. I publicly resigned from its Publications Committee for what I regarded as high-handed action by their Executive Council. The president at the time sought my excommunication, charging me with unethical conduct. This came to naught except that, unknowingly, I had tapped a groundswell of popular resentment toward the association's governing body and its oligarchic tendencies. I was swept into an ascendant path, from professional office to professional office. Within three years, I found myself elected president of the association, an unimagined honor indeed, which gives an ironic twist to those graduate school days in the Regenstein Library when I planned the end of sociology. There are those, of course, for whom my election does indeed mark the end of sociology. Edward Shils would no doubt be among them!

My Back Pages

Craig Calhoun is president of the Social Science Research Council and professor of sociology and history at New York University. Calhoun received his doctorate from Oxford University and taught at the University of North Carolina, Chapel Hill, from 1977 to 1996, where he was also dean of the Graduate School and director of the University Center for International Studies. His books include The Roots of Radicalism; Nationalism; Critical Social Theory: Culture, History and the Challenge of Difference; *and* Neither Gods nor Emperors: Students and the Struggle for Democracy in China. *He has also been the editor-in-chief of the Ox-*ford Dictionary of the Social Sciences, *coeditor for international and area studies in the* International Encyclopedia of Social and Behavioral Sciences, *coeditor of* Understanding September 11th, *and coeditor of* Lessons of Empire? Historical Contexts for Understanding America's Global Power. *Calhoun works especially on issues of democracy and the public sphere, social movements, and social solidarity in the contexts of global technological and social change.*

I am of the right generation to remember air-raid drills in which my grade school classmates and I ducked under our desks, practicing what to do if the Russians attacked. Indeed, I remember talking quite seriously with my friends about how prominent a target the Ohio River bridge we crossed each day on our way to school would be. And as a junior high school fire marshal I was improbably given briefings in "civil defense" as well as where the exits were. Yet I was born late in that generation and knew of the ban the bomb movement only secondhand as history. I first heard of it, and learned what a peace sign meant, from Mary Elizabeth Branaman, sitting in a high school classroom in Henderson, Kentucky, around 1966. I was a freshman; she was a senior, cluing me in. She and her boyfriend were the only two seniors headed "back East" to college, not only the class brains but more or less the entire minimal gesture toward the counter-culture locally available. It was an odd moment, when one might listen serially to Bob Dylan and Herman's Hermits, the Rolling Stones and Petula Clark, Judy Collins and Lou Christie and not realize this meant inhabiting parallel uni-verses. Or be equally worried about the football game, a date for the dance, whether there could be racial justice, and what the hell the Viet Nam War was all about.

In 1967, my family moved to California. I didn't want to go, but that was be-cause of friends in Henderson, not because of any bad images of California. On the contrary, California was Mecca. It never occurred to me that I was leaving a more liberal place for a more conservative one.

We moved, however, not to San Francisco but to Orange County. This was the sort of shock to the system that might drive anyone to social science. And it cer-tainly helped drive me to leave high school early—in the fall of 1969. My first year at college was the year of *Easy Rider* and *Alice's Restaurant*—the movie, not the "massacree". It was the year of "Let It Be" and the Beatles' break-up, of "Bridge over Troubled Water" and Garfunkel leaving Simon to be an actor. It was the year of the Kent State shootings and the strike and the peak of protests that followed. It was the year the splintering of Students for a Democratic Society (or SDS) entered its terminal phase and the year of the first Earth Day. In short, things were going on, but "the movement" was peaking. It was fabulous to find it, a joy to join, and a considerable disappointment that it faded soon thereafter. My sense of the Sixties has always been tinged not just with the feeling of loss—which I think I share with many of those a little older than me—but also with a sense of missing out on a lot. And if I shared a little of the excitement that it could happen at all—the rush that pervades the retrospective engagements of some of my elders—its quick loss of steam also influenced my intellectual orientation. I thought we were going to change the world. And if we did, a little, it only deep-ened the questions about why not more, why the world was so refractory, and what did "we" not fully understand. Among other things, I became enduringly interested in the relationship between the proliferation of radical ideas and the social structural conditions for the production of genuinely radical challenges to the directions of social change. In other words, I asked such questions as, What allowed for so much of the Sixties "revolution" to be co-opted by Madison Avenue just as the Beatles' "Revolution 9" was co-opted by a Nike ad? And what enabled some struggles to sink deeper roots?

For me at least, most of the Sixties happened in the seventies. More generally, many of the innovations we remember the Sixties for became generalizations in the seventies. And there was new momentum on some fronts — notably environment and gender. But well before the seventies were over the radicalism of a disobedient generation was something to look back on. So, though it was weird it is perhaps understandable that one day in the early 1980s a campus political leader in Chapel Hill, where I was teaching, called out from across the quad, and came running up to introduce his girlfriend. "This is Dr. Calhoun," he said, "he was in the Sixties." I was. I still had long hair, though that was starting to mean country not counterculture. I was both a sociologist and a socialist, and the Sixties played some role in that.

. . .

Growing up as a preacher's son is a well-traveled path into sociology and hardly generationally distinctive. Possibly more specific to the "disobedient generation," my poor father, already not quite conservative enough for Orange County — he tried to hire a black associate minister only to be defeated in a congregational rebellion — found himself dealing with the high school principal who wanted me suspended for publishing an "underground" (read: unauthorized) newspaper. The principal, a man offended by most everything we remember the Sixties for, was convinced that Orange High School was next on the list of some international conspiracy that had already ruined Berkeley. He had suspended the first editor of *Infinity* (our little attempt at intellectual critique in a county not much interested in that). I was editor of the second issue partly because it would be harder to attack me — honor student, letterman, and above all, preacher's son. After all, the principal had already found that enforcing the dress code by stopping me from wearing a large cross over my Nehru jacket was poor strategy (though I wince that my challenge to authority involved such sartorial pretension).

The newspaper wasn't much, of course. And I don't think the episode in connection with it brought my father a great deal of suffering (though he certainly looked pained). It was less of a trial than, say, my puzzling perseverance in playing in a rock band despite lack of talent. It was not very radical, not very well thought out, and more than a little pretentious in its quotes from Voltaire and its pontificating on what education could be (and manifestly wasn't at Orange High School). It wasn't very far underground, either, though it certainly wasn't the school newspaper or the Santa Ana *Register*. And it wasn't sociology, though it foreshadowed my academic interests. So did rock music, I suppose, though eventually I learned I was destined to be only a consumer not a producer.

The move from small Kentucky town to posturban California sprawl may have been even more important. The contrast between a stronger community and a suburb with a strong ideology of community became one of my lifelong interests. The Orange county town into which I moved was hardly the most anomic suburb in the area. It was relatively old, it was not newly created, it had a sustaining handful of multigenerational families, and it had at least a few businesses to provide local employment, though commuting was increasingly dominant. But it was marked by a substitution of cultural conformity for webs of interrelationships, an ideology of similarity rather than interdependence.

It is an illusion to think everyone knows everyone else in a town the size of the one I left in Kentucky. But it is not without a grain of truth. The first time I kissed a girl, someone in my father's church saw the furtive embrace at the town tennis courts and my parents knew about it before I got home. Yet this was also a reflection of my father's social status. Not everyone's first kisses got equal treatment. My family lived on Main Street. There was an area literally "across the tracks" that I only occasionally visited. Henderson was riven by class inequality and racial division — schools had just been integrated, and the notion of a "colored" balcony at the one movie theater persisted even after it was rendered illegal (and the fact that it was well-suited to necking may have been more important than antiracism to teenagers integrating it).

At the same time, the girl on the other end of that first kiss, Charlotte, lived two blocks down Main Street, directly across from my grandmother, and I don't think our parents ever interacted. Her father was a prominent local businessman and part of a more cosmopolitan, cocktail party set than my biblically oriented family — Ray Preston was the first person I ever saw wear an ascot in real life. I flashed on him the first time I met Robert Merton — and I'm not sure I knew any other ascot wearers in between though I saw many in the movies. I knew Charlotte not just out of proximity but because our parents sent us both to a private school in Evansville, Indiana, across the Ohio River. I was a scholarship kid in used uniforms, raised for upward mobility, an aspirant to social status my folks could barely afford. But by ninth grade, recognizing that following private school friends to prep schools back East was not an option, I sought a larger social world by shifting to public high school.

At Henderson's City High (stereotypical counterpart to County High), I experienced the wariness of black and white students in a newly integrated high school but also the successful integration of the football team. Well, mostly successful. Every August there was a football camp to get us in shape before the season started. I was the butt of integration humor when I was the first white freshman assigned to be the "slave" of a black senior. All freshman served seniors, but this was only the second year of integration, and the first time around no one had dared this racial reversal. My "master" (improbably named James Brown) was a star halfback and not too hard to take. But I was obviously marked for some sort of special status not just because I was an outsider to the established football team and therefore vulnerable but because it enabled others to manage social change. In any event, football served multiple purposes. I liked it in itself, it meant fitting in, and there were always cheerleaders.

There was pervasive racism and sometimes open racial conflict in Henderson (though it was hardly the Deep South, the school's fight song remained "Dixie" until 1970). But at least there were black people there. Moving to Orange County meant confronting a much more militant right wing and surprisingly deep racial anxieties, considering that there were hardly any African-Americans around. People were more racist; they just had fewer occasions to express it in petty discrimination because blacks were sequestered elsewhere, mainly in the dread metropolis of Los Angeles (and of course, mainly only in a few communities there). In fact, discrimination was precisely spatially organized. During my last year in high school and first of college, I worked as a real estate title searcher. One of my jobs was to remove newly illegal covenants, conditions, and restrictions from recorded deeds—such as those regulating what race could live in a housing development.

To be sure, there were Hispanics (some of whom admitted to being Mexican while others minimized that association in pursuit of upward mobility). But perhaps the most striking thing about the significant Chicano minority in my high school was how invisible it was most of the time (to me), and how minimally an issue it was. The young woman who took on the role of the school's mascot, "Patty Panther," was played by Linda Eltiste. She was a middle-class kid like most of us and part of the school's social elite. When the race issue was raised, "race" meant "blacks." Being Hispanic ("Spanish" as some of the older families said) was not an issue as such, though Mexicans were a different matter if they were distinguished by class as well as ethnicity. And looking at an old high school annual years later, I was surprised how many there were. The town of Orange is a third Hispanic (and significantly Asian) now—and surprisingly ethnically stigmatized to many of my classmates who wound up affluent enough to move to the "whiter" beach towns. In a strange twist on both white flight and immigrant assimilation, however, a guy I had run track with changed his name to sound more Jewish when he went into real estate.

Questions of ethnicity and cultural belonging were opened up in the Sixties. The decade did not invent the politics of identity, but it put it on the sociological agenda in a way different from the earlier twentieth-century discussions of immigration and assimilation. It did so, however, in a way that left many paradoxes intact — especially the simultaneous claims to universality and exclusion. The same issues were present in opposition to the war in Viet Nam, among the defining engagements of the Sixties generation. This was played out equally in equal terms of universal rights and moral outrage at their abuses, of local self-determination, and of a claim to personal violation by specific policies of the U.S. government that implicated each of us as citizens. We have struggled since with the tension among these sorts of claims, and rightly so. We have struggled in ways not just intellectual but emotional, as many of us have sought to recover the sense of belonging to an encompassing movement.

. . .

Oddly, I am finishing this essay in Viet Nam. During the 1960s I was determined not to go to Viet Nam, and more important, to get the United States out. Yet here I sit sipping a Tiger Beer on the rooftop terrace of the Rex Hotel. Straight ahead looms the steel and glass Citicorp tower; a new Sheraton is just off to the left. So the United States is not out, despite losing the war. And I am here, staying in what was once a U.S. officers' billet, in a Ho Chi Minh City that in places still eerily resembles the Saigon imprinted in my memory from war-time film footage thirty-plus years ago.

Yesterday, I visited a 50,000 employee factory on the outskirts of Ho Chi Minh City. Built to a standard plan its Taiwanese corporate owners developed in the People's Republic of China and elsewhere around the region, it makes footwear for many of the world's most famous brands. Multinational corporations, mostly based in the United States, set the designs and market the eventual products. The top management is from Taiwan, middle management and supervisors come mostly from the People's Republic of China, a few Vietnamese are moving into the supervisory ranks. But the goal, said the Taiwanese spokesperson to vigorous nods from the Vietnamese union chief standing next to him, was full "Vietnamization."

I am sure neither had a clue why the word startled me. Yet I am equally sure the word has distinctive resonance for others who remember the Nixon administration. In Hanoi last week, my hotel window looked out on the "Hanoi Hilton," the famous prison once inhabited by a range of U.S. prisoners of war. I am here for a conference on "poverty alleviation." And because of the prestige of the Social Science Research Council as an international partner, I have my photo taken with politicians and party leaders, make speeches about the importance of science to mutual understanding among nations, and appear on TV and in the newspapers asserting the importance of social science to tackling the problems and public issues that come alongside much wanted economic growth. I discuss sometimes the dark side of globalization, but my very presence is affirmative. I assert the need for a critical perspective but remember also how modernization theory and the RAND Corporation version of social science figured in the war.

To whatever extent I can make sense of this, it is through the eyes of one who first took up sociology while performing his alternative service as a conscientious objector during the Viet Nam War, someone who studies nationalism and social movements, community and the public sphere, and the intersection of "globalization" with specific historical and cultural contexts.

• • •

I was in Manchester, England, when Saigon "fell" (or was liberated). I listened to BBC accounts of the American evacuation over a transistor radio in the room of a fellow graduate student, Peter Rushton. Peter was in fact one of several graduate students who helped to convert me from anthropologist to sociologist, having themselves moved into sociology from some other discipline. But that day in 1975, we weren't discussing theory but listening to history. Peter made coffee on a hotplate in one of those convenient French miniature espresso makers, the first I had seen, for I was not yet among the frequent travelers or in general very cosmopolitan. But I was studying anthropology and doing it in England partly because I wanted to be a sophisticate.

Being outside the United States in the waning years of the war and the wake of Watergate was one attraction; an Anglophilia nurtured on James Bond and the Avengers was another (however contradictory their Cold War spy games and my antiwar pacifism might seem). But more academically, Manchester was then the strongest center of a kind of social anthropology that I found compelling and exciting and that shaped my intellectual outlook enormously, though it has largely faded from contemporary anthropology. I went to Manchester to study with Max

Gluckman. I lived in his house, in fact, though he spent much of my first English year in Israel and died of a heart attack in the spring of 1975.

I had first met Max several years before, while an undergraduate in California. He was a somewhat demanding guest at the home of my main teacher, Sally Falk Moore. She (or perhaps her husband) hit on the strategy of entertaining Max by giving him one of the things he liked best: someone to listen. I was a happy conscript.

Anthropology was, among other things, helping me mediate movement involvements, moral outrage over the war, and my search for a career that would connect me to the larger world without sacrificing too much of my idealism — or perhaps it would be better to say a career in which I could be ambitious without being obnoxious. After the Kent State shootings in the spring of 1970, my freshman year in college, I attended the protest marches and joined the strike but also busied myself organizing teach-ins on themes like Vietnamese village life — about which I certainly knew precious little — and war in other cultural contexts. My declared majors were English and cinema; I wanted to be a writer but also thought of attending law school. In anthropology, though, I had found not just an intellectual engagement but a social context — including two wonderful teachers in Sally Moore and Barbara Myerhoff, and a clique of students who were not typical of Southern California. By my sophomore year I was a teaching assistant and in the summer a research assistant. This latter job actually involved me in sociology — studies of police and criminal justice reform, in fact — but I didn't really cross the disciplinary divide yet.

For one thing, sociology seemed focused too much on the United States, and when it looked abroad it did so through the lens of modernization theory. Though I was not yet engaged in the Marxist critique of this that came to dominate, I was sure that "modernity" was a confining concept and quite likely complicit in the war. The war was omnipresent. I don't mean simply the draft but also the daily accounts — and images — of brutality and the more positive goal of peace. In fact, though as a child I had imagined myself often enough in uniform, by this time I had no doubt that I was a conscientious objector, a CO. I didn't really hesitate to say so in registering for the draft when I turned eighteen the summer after my freshman year. I objected with my full conscience — that shaped by my religious upbringing and that which I was forced by the language of the Selective Service Administration to call "philosophical." This was certainly an intellectual (hence philosophical) objection, but it was also an emotional reaction to the way the world looked and felt to me, to a horrific war that made no sense, to the violation of human possibilities that permanent preparations for war seemed to entail. And the intellectual part was pretty half-baked, I know, however sincere (and however much I still agree with the main conclusion).

By personality pretty optimistic, I confidently sent off my registration and request for conscientious objector status—though under the regulations in place this meant forfeiting an automatic student deferment. Somewhat alarmingly, several months later I received a card declaring me 1A and available to serve immediately. I appealed and eventually had to try to explain my conscience to a draft board back in Orange County—home of the John Birch Society and Knott's Berry Farm (which boasted of its brick-by-brick replica of Philadelphia's Independence Hall, equipped with a carefully cracked Liberty Bell). J. Walter Knott was on the draft board as well as the county's Republican Central Committee. My father sat with me in the anteroom as we watched other appellants go in for their hearings, which never lasted more than ten minutes. The deliberation that followed never took more than five, and all were refused. My own case took the committee nearly an hour and a half. I was asked how a former football player could object to violence and war (easy). I was asked whether if my mother were attacked in the street I would defend her (yes). I was asked whether I considered myself a real American patriot (sure, at least by my definition). Somehow the fact that I was a University of Southern California (USC) letterman seemed evidence in my favor. So too, of course, the fact that my father was a minister. But most important seemed the fact that my convictions of conscientious objection were unwavering.

I was not asked to deepen my "philosophical" account, to substantiate my reference to Kierkegaard, or to clarify the fuzzy boundary between religion and more secular conscience. I was asked in a dozen different ways how long I had known I objected to war, whether I was prepared to sacrifice for this conviction if necessary, and thus how sure I was that I didn't just object to being drafted. Eventually they did ask me the one question that had been troubling me and about which my answer still troubles me—though I offered it to the draft board with confidence, I think. Was I prepared to serve in a noncombat capacity? I wasn't, I had decided. But this wasn't a stable, long-term conviction. This was a problematic and muddled question. On the one hand, serving as a medic seemed extraordinarily honorable and un-self-interested (perhaps a little too self-sacrificing from evidence of the mortality rates of medics). On the other hand, such service still seemed part of the war machine, patching soldiers up to fight again, saving "my side" but not the others. This last is what I told the draft board, that I could not be part of the larger socially organized war effort, even if I were not the one actually pulling the trigger. I was sincere, but it was a doubly troubling position. First, of course, I was still a part of the larger socially organized country waging the war and I derived benefits from that (though at least I was actively opposed to the war itself). Second, serving as a medic would mean I took my place in the collective generational sacrifice; not going at all meant that someone else would be drafted in my place. And that someone else would more likely have fewer of the advantages that enable conscientious objection (or at least the drafting of a philosophical argument to get conscience recognized). The someone else would be more likely working class, more likely nonwhite. But above all, it would be someone, and they might get killed instead of me. They might have to kill and I wouldn't. I was truly as worried about killing as being killed (though I doubt the two would have troubled me equally had I actually served in combat). I figured I might make a good soldier, but I didn't want to live with that on my conscience.

My personal draft drama took relatively little time — though eventually getting drafted took two years of time in alternate service. I had free days (and nights) in those college years for sex and drugs and rock and roll, experimentations embarrassingly timid at first, then growing pleasures, though I was not as prone to abandon myself to any of the three as some of my friends). I don't even recall the draft as much of an oppressive cloud hanging over life, the way I think it might have been for those five or six years older than me. For one thing, "Vietnamization" was under way — which meant that the U.S. military strategy involved more bombing and fewer ground troops. It had become perhaps even more immoral, but it was easier for young American men to think it might not become as personal.

By the early 1970s, movement and counterculture had become widespread and even partially institutionalized on residential college campuses. Few thought much at the time about how skewed the ostensible "youth" movement was in class terms, how much less the stereotypical Sixties of memory figured at commuter schools and for those who simply had to work. But in any case it was spreading. It had even spread to USC, which certainly was not in the vanguard.

· · ·

I had gotten to USC because I wanted to get the hell out of high school and out of Orange County. But I was young, and my parents didn't want me to go far (especially not to the University of Chicago where my father, who had been a chaplain and was convinced too many students were suicidally miserable). The new University of California campus at Santa Cruz revoked my admission when they figured out I wasn't graduating from high school. But the University of Southern California had a resident honors program (RHP) for high school students who would spend their senior year living on campus as freshmen. Terrific, I thought, being a young man in a hurry, just starting on a career of trying to be a little bit older than I was. The RHP program really was terrific — thanks largely to the sociologist Tom Lasswell, who ran it — though overall USC was a mixed bag. It was truly the Sixties, though that was not all counterculture. My roommate and I were awakened one night our first fall by shouts of "booze and broads" and pounding on our dorm door by Sigma Chi pledge recruiters. We went to the party, heard how pledging would provide us with fifty close friends for life, but passed it up anyway. I studied film and creative writing, wrote and performed musical comedy, shifted my sport to crew, and inhabited a vaguely artsy (largely arts industry, music- and film-centered) Los Angeles. And I discovered anthropology and later, trying to write on the experience of time (and drugs), psychoanalysis and phenomenology.

The University of Southern California had an excellent anthropology program (partly because with no graduate students all the faculty attention went to undergraduates). This was the creature of Sally Falk Moore and Barbara Myerhoff, two exceptional researchers anchored in Los Angeles largely by virtue of their husbands' careers (though Barbara was happier about it and inhabited the city more easily). Figuring this out made me perhaps more sensitive to gender issues and less sure about ostensibly meritocratic hierarchies than I might otherwise have been. In any event, each pulled me into anthropology in a different way. I worked with Barbara cobbling together a program on ethnographic film (as I sought to combine my initial idea of a film major with anthropology) that would become more institutionalized later — and indeed, she went on to win an Academy Award for one of her ethnographic films, *Number Our Days*, about elderly Jews in Venice, California. Barbara, who died tragically young of cancer, reflected something of the Sixties' opening of academia to politics and protest movements but, more than that, to attempts to be creative in new ways (and opening it to women as well). I'm not sure I've ever lived up to my early ambitions, but it mattered a lot as I began to decide on a social science career that I saw this as a project of cultural creativity. For Barbara, and through her for me, anthropological study of myth and ritual intertwined immediately with poetic appropriation, creation, and performance.

Sally Moore was an even bigger influence, with more emphasis on the analytic side of social science. I took her course in the spring of my first year and was her teaching assistant by the fall of my second. A lawyer, Sally had been driven to anthropology partly by her experience as one of the prosecuting lawyers at the Nuremburg trials — and by the puzzle of how to separate individual culpability from guilt organized at national or party levels. Law was one of the many fields in which I could imagine reconciling intellect and passion, ambition and moral outrage. But then I also worried I might just end up some middle-aged California lawyer, seduced by the money, only occasionally recalling youthful ideals. In fact, Sally encouraged me to go to law school, suggesting both that I was a bit romantic in what I imagined academic life to be like and that law might enable me to combine thinking with practical effect a bit better. But I was hooked on academia. I would probably have wound up an academic lawyer. Under Sally's tutelage I read the ethnographic classics, from Malinowski and Radcliffe-Brown forward, with special emphasis on Africa. I read them with the constant instruction not simply to absorb, or only to critique, but also to see whether I could produce a better analysis of the data presented.

Sally was also my entrée to the impressive range of social anthropologists who cast up for longer or shorter periods in Los Angeles during that period, mostly feeling vaguely in exile (and Sally herself managed eventually to end her exile by moving to Harvard for the latter part of her career). I was eager to learn from all these not-quite-Angelinos (and also eager to explore new territories). But for a couple of years, I inhabited Los Angeles more seamlessly than most of them. I went to the beach. I drove a 1967 Mustang into which I had personally installed a cassette-playing stereo (new technology back in the day). I had an apartment in Hollywood with a view of the Hollywood sign and a sociological subtext: it was near the bottom of a hill; below it was only a transient apartment building that housed divorcing men who arrived in a Mercedes and left in a Ford. But up the hill the apartment buildings gave way to the houses of editors, writers, and other secondary Hollywood figures; decaying mansions like that of my friend Charles Louis d'Accursi di Ravenna, aged friend of silent movie stars and realist painter in an era that didn't want realist paintings; and, eventually, renovated mansions, including that occupied by Jane Fonda and (some of the time) Donald Sutherland, who ran over my cat heading downhill too fast.

Benefiting from a discount film pass issued to USC cinema majors, I went to as many as three movies a night (well, three on only one occasion: they were all Bergman, and I nearly never recovered). I discovered popular culture before cultural studies made it fashionable (and didn't even know it was *déclassé*, perhaps because I was not very *classé*). I searched for the Los Angeles that the Doors had recently abandoned. I prowled record stores filling in gaps in my musical education (Miles more than Mozart; early Eric Clapton but also Eric Satie—because of the Blood, Sweat and Tears rendition of the *gymnopédies*; Johnny Hodges just because it was on sale cheap in a cut-out bin; a lot of baroque and early music on traditional instruments because I knew some of the local players through Barbara). I heard many of the major and not-so-major rock acts of the era live, from Jimi Hendrix (who died soon after) to the Who, Jefferson Airplane, and Jethro Tull. And I heard the small club and open air acts from Don McClean and Eric Anderson to James Taylor and Joan Baez (whose poster had hung over my bed for a year).

I went to tai chi lessons in a park on Saturday mornings with my crew buddy Eric Prinz (one of the six-foot-two blond Los Angeles Jews who left me ill-prepared to recognize ethnicity properly when I arrived later in New York). I went to canyons north of the city to commune with nature and lie talking for hours with my girlfriend (and once got a truly horrible, emergency-room level, case of poison oak from rolling about—ahem—on what seemed a lovely hillside). I went to peace marches, sought signatures on antiwar petitions in Los Angeles airport, and protested outside military bases. I went to Earth Day and became an earnest recycler (once carrying some trash for half an hour through ankle deep debris after a march, humming "A Working Class Hero Is Something to Be" and believing there was some exemplary personal virtue in finding a garbage can even if no one else did). Or was that the Rose Parade? I went there, too, though only because relatives came to town. Come to think of it, I went to the Rose Bowl game, too, though that was the year before and because of a girl. We listened to John Mayall for hours while stuck in traffic and talked about how hung up we WASPs were about expressing personal affection/physical attraction. We kissed so hard I chipped a tooth but never made love (I mention this for those who think sex in the Sixties was always easy).

For a time, I thought psychotropic drugs might be an important source of social change and enlightenment. I remember asserting this to Sally Moore, who politely didn't laugh but led me to try to argue a case as to why, while herself suggesting that the birth control pill might be of more historical consequence (possibly an overdetermined comment as I was dating her daughter at the time). I didn't enjoy beer or whiskey until later, but I did discover California wine. And influenced by Gregory Bateson as well as more straightforward academic teachers, I developed an interest in psychoanalysis, took copious self-analytic notes under the guidance of Karen Horney's *Self-Analysis*, read first the American "relational" analysts like Harry Stack Sullivan and Clara Thompson, then Freud, and finally (this was really after I left Los Angeles) the ego analysts and object relations folk. I thought for a time I'd be a clinical psychologist and analyst (ah, the discarded careers, some more wisely discarded than others, but also the megalomania of youth thinking all things possible in an era that encouraged it).

So LA. But I left, was even eager to leave, for the East Coast in 1972. My USC anthro department friends had gone to Chicago or England and, besides, my girlfriend was moving east too. We both got into Harvard but decided (via tortured, probably overdetermined logic) that this would put undue pressure on our relationship. So she would go to Yale and I to Princeton. (I think among other problems we didn't have a good grip on geography.) I hadn't finished my USC degree but had gotten into Princeton and decided it was a step up. Finished undergrad and started graduate school at the same time (much as I had finished high school and started college at the same time).

My Princeton career was short: one term, passed the French exam, just barely got to know my adviser, Vincent Crapanzano, and then I got drafted. I really had concluded that wouldn't happen, but there it was. A lottery number three places below the cut-off, and off I went, surprisingly and not very sacrificially, to New York. Under the influence of a combination of Erving Goffman, book-learned psychoanalysis, and the filmmaker Frederick Weissman, I asked to be assigned to a psychiatric hospital as an orderly. I thought I would write an ethnography. They sent me to Teachers College, Columbia—which among other things ran a program at a prison on Riker's Island where I taught English (after brief stints as a secretary and a program coordinator). Rikers was sometimes scary and always depressing, but all in all the assignment did not involve much self-sacrifice. It turned out I was eligible for university housing and free tuition to Columbia. And although the anthropologist Fritz Ianni (who ran the institute where Teachers College eventually settled me) got a kick out of the letter from the Selective Service that addressed him as my commanding officer, he found it useful eventually to put me to work in his research operation — largely as a writer. If it seemed that I had realized my earlier ambition, there was a twist, for I mostly wrote reports to government funders, hack work at which I proved more adept than I like to claim.

I also wrote my first grant application and got National Institute of Education funding for a conference on the anthropological study of education to be held just before the World Congress of Anthropological and Ethnological Sciences. This ended up being the basis for my first edited book but, more important, my ticket to the congress itself, a huge academic blow-out that had aspects of a farewell to the Sixties. Sol Tax organized it right over the top, with not one but fifty edited volumes, and even an opera commissioned from Giancarlo Menotti: *Tamu-Tamu* (The guests) polemically juxtaposed foreign war and domestic security. The Native American activist Vine Deloria was invited to give the opening speech. Drinking late one night, he told me he finally understood why anthropologists were always out bothering Indians: they didn't like to be with each other unless they were drunk.

I got a master's from Columbia's anthropology program without ever really connecting. I sampled all manner of interesting offerings around the university, from Jacques Barzun to Robert Denoon Cumming, and found myself drawn more and more to sociology. Indeed, when my alternate service ended, I briefly stayed on at Columbia as Peter Blau's research assistant, running many a multiple regression for the Comparative Organizations Research Program. I learned a great deal from Robert Nisbet and Ben Zablocki and even more from Robert Merton, with whom I started discussing a potential dissertation: making national differences in anthropology an object of the sociology of science.

Columbia was suffering a post-Sixties fatigue. Still intellectually rich, its older generation was wary of the younger ones and, relatedly, finding it hard to renew the faculty. Radical politics was receding: while I remember getting summoned away from beer and jazz at the West End for a "riot at the Sundial," streaking was displacing demonstrating. Nevertheless, a variety of political sects survived on the university's fringes. Lyndon LaRouche (then calling himself Lynn Marcus) had been expelled from the SDS but reinvented its Labor Caucuses as the National Caucus of Labor Committees. They sold *New Solidarity* on Broadway, attacked Leftists of other factions, and decried a conspiracy mounted by the Rockefeller family, the inventors of Muzac, and the Columbia anthropology department (where a former lover of LaRouche's had enrolled). Like all paranoids, LaRouche saw himself at the center; diagrams in *New Solidarity* graphically represented how nearly all of the global power structure was organized mainly to get at the National Caucus of Labor Committees. My friends and I wondered whether he was simply crazy or backed by the Central Intelligence Agency or both. But the real puzzle was that he had perhaps a thousand followers — some loyal enough that when one young woman tried to quit they took her prisoner for "deprogramming." One of the failings of the Sixties was that such people were taken too seriously by too many for too long.

I was still searching for something, perhaps a better connection among the intellectual, the political, and the personal. England and anthropology still had an allure, and Max Gluckman and I had stayed in touch. He taught for a term at Yale and this gave ample opportunities for visits. On one, we attended a memorable very-Sixties event, a performance of the Living Theater. It was Mary Gluckman who really wanted to go. Max was impatient from the outset (and in truth, the Julian Beck/Judith Malina formula had gotten a bit stale). So when, in one of the troop's post-Brechtian agitprop set pieces a young woman, wearing only some dirty rags, ran up to Max and shouted "Am I your slave?" Max rose to his full and considerable height and yelled back "No! I'm bloody well yours, but no longer." With that he headed for the door. Making one of the career changing decisions that seemed to come up a lot those days, I followed. Max said he would arrange funding for me in Manchester.

Manchester social anthropology was a somewhat more critical, conflict-oriented stream within the broad current of British social anthropology to which Sally Moore had introduced me. This which was just coming under attack for its complicity in colonialism and obscuring of the role of the colonial state in constituting the societies studied. The attacks had some purchase but not nearly as much as the attackers thought. If social anthropology had sometimes hypostatized the "peoples" studied — if, for example, Edward Evans-Pritchard's brilliant accounts of the Nuer made them seem more autonomous and self-contained than they were — it also produced substantial internal critical analysis of just this issue. Godfrey Lienhardt's study of the neighboring Dinka raised questions about that of E.-P.'s of the Nuer. Jack Goody challenged the idea of discrete "tribes" before that rejection became fashionable, showing how language, ritual, and identity varied along a sociogeographic continuum in Northern Ghana, free of sharp borders. And indeed, Meyer Fortes's extraordinary research on the Tallensi had at the least foreshadowed this point a generation earlier (and in doing so brought to the fore the concept of a social field). Social anthropology had also produced major studies of "premodern" states — S. F. Nadel's *Black Byzantium* and M. G. Smith's extraordinary series of studies of the Hausa-Fulani kingdoms, for example — and Gluckman had long stressed both the importance of historical perspective and the interrelationship of colonial state and local social relations. Indeed, he was in the forefront of arguing that anthropologists were concerned with contemporary societies — not archaic survivals — and even when their field sites were located at a distance from the centers of metropolitan power they should pay attention to larger-scale economic and political forces.

Gluckman was a socialist and encouraged me to consider myself one too — thinking my loose "peace and freedom" ideology of the time rather too Californian and not politically serious enough. Of course, by the time I came on the scene, Gluckman's socialism was rather attenuated. He paid his dues to the Fabian Society and insisted on going to the standing sections at Manchester United football matches (when his backaches permitted). But Max had also shaped a Manchester department that challenged the aristocratic character of most anthropology; it had its own internally egalitarian approach to intellectual debate (even if Max was usually dominant) and more than its share of working-class members. Like Lewis Coser (and to some extent Peter Blau, Alvin Gouldner, and indeed their teacher Robert Merton) in the United States, Max had drawn on Marx, a non-Parsonsian Weber, and Georg Simmel to bring conflict into focus within a broadly structural-functionalist theory.

More than Coser, Max approached conflict through empirical cases. Indeed, when I once told Max I wanted to do more theoretical work, he scoffed. That, he said, was for old age — when liver disease made it impossible to go into the field. In fact, by the standards of anthropologists Max was much more theorist (and probably less fieldworker) than most. Nonetheless, he thought the right training came from analyzing empirical cases, and he set me the challenge of reanalyzing Meyer Fortes's classic studies of the Tallensi of Northern Ghana — which I did at length, and with the result of my first significant journal article, a reanalysis of ancestor "worship" and lineage authority that appeared in *Man* (the journal of the Royal Anthropological Institute — an organization I had proudly joined as an undergraduate who had never set foot in Britain or, indeed, off the North American continent).

Originally educated as a lawyer in South Africa, Gluckman was especially taken with legal cases but also rethought the idea of case study in light of court cases with their adversarial arguments and focusing of social relationships in an event of contested implications. Analyzing a case entailed knowing what happened in an immediate, "objective" sense, but also the conditions that made possible what happened — including structures of social relations and the different perspectives through which social actors differently located in those relations saw what happened. It brought both custom and conflict into relief: both the shaping sociocultural context and the interplay of power and interests.

This perspective shaped a more complex notion of the case study than that typical in sociology (as Michael Burawoy has recently pointed out in the pages of *Sociological Theory*). It shaped work on the mediation of conflict through ritual performance (most famously by Victor Turner, Gluckman's most brilliant student). It shaped the development of social network analysis, though this has not always sustained the dialectic of event and structure with which it was initially centrally concerned, notably in the work of J. Clyde Mitchell and Bruce Kapferer. And it encouraged attention to the mutual constitution of subjective and objective perspectives, structure and action (albeit not always agency), functional integration and social struggles.

I loved it. And it prefigured my enthusiasm for the work of Pierre Bourdieu, which I first discovered in Manchester and which brought similar themes to the fore in a process of parallel discovery, as Robert Merton would put it (and indeed Merton himself had more in common with British social anthropology — including the label "structural-functionalist" — and, for that matter, with Bourdieu than they or most others recognized). Bourdieu stressed his distinction from Mancunian "situational analysis" (as often from those who might be thought close to his own positions) because he thought it remained locked in the opposition of rule and exception, identifying choice with the latter, rather that fully integrating the two in habitus. The distinction cuts both ways, though, as Gluckman provided more place for the analysis of contradictions within social situations, lines of conflict not readily resolved in any stable pattern of reproduction. Certainly, though, even the best Mancunian social anthropology had limits, many shared with the field more broadly (not to mention much of sociology) and brought into focus by the intellectual, moral, and political discontents of the times. It remained weaker than I wanted on historical specificity, clarity about its philosophical underpinnings and normative implications, and the relation of face-to-face society to broader culture and political economy — even though it did more than most of its competitors to bring these concerns into focus.

· · ·

While living in and around Manchester, I decided to study Manchester. The Department of Anthropology itself offered an inspiration — not simply in its intellectual work but in its location: it was housed in a former girl's school built on the site of the factory Friedrich Engels's father had sent him to help manage in 1842. I learned this from the visiting American sociologist F. V. Walters, whom Gluckman had invited to Manchester on the basis of his study of Shaka Zulu but who spent much of his time tracing the walks around Manchester that Engels described in *The Condition of the Working Class in England in 1844* — occasionally inviting Peter Rushton and me to tag along.

I lived at first in the Gluckman's house on the boundary between Bramhall and Cheadle Hulme, two sweet little towns near Stockport in the second ring of bourgeois suburbs that grew up around Manchester during the industrial revolution. When the Gluckmans decamped for Israel, I shared the house with a marvelous South African doctor who had entered their orbit by repairing Max's injured knee on Kilimanjaro years before and who now ran a medical charity with Mary Gluckman on the board. Eugenie introduced me to Roibosch tea, Scrabble before bed (I always lost), and the antiapartheid movement. It was broadening to be self-righteous about sins that didn't focus on one's own national complicity. Later Eugenie and I moved into the Victorian folly of a house that was slated to become the charity's drug rehabilitation center, though NIMBY-minded neighbors fought it off. Inhabited by a shifting commune of often eccentric characters, it became the English home to which I returned on holidays even after I moved to Oxford. Eventually the charity folded but Eugenie's new house and whole foods shop in Haslingden, one of the ring of mill towns that figured later in my dissertation research, was still home after a fashion.

I decided it made sense to bring an anthropological approach to community, work, and their transformations in the case of Britain during the industrial revolution. This "case" had of course informed generations of theorization about tradition and modernity, economic development, and class struggle. My thinking about it started with a paper I wrote at Columbia for Peter Blau, raising the question of what it felt like to workers when division of labor and related changes transformed their solidarity and whether there wasn't resistance as well as anomie. In England, I had begun to read Marx more seriously and systematically. And on the advice of Peter Worsley — former anthropologist turned chair of Manchester's sociology department — I read E. P. Thompson's *The Making of the English Working Class.*

Like many, I fell under the sway of Thompson (a very anthropological historian). Indeed, I more or less forsook my intellectual first love of anthropology as I fell for this new one of social history. But as readers of my *Question of Class Struggle* know, both my Marxism and my sociology made me doubt the theoretical argument implicit in *The Making of the English Working Class* even while I loved its rich empirical content. In fact, I thought Thompson's wonderful history underwrote another theoretical argument altogether, one informed by social anthropology, in which tradition and community provided resources and orientations to struggle against capitalist transformation. Equally, I thought a reading of the English case that focused too completely on class struggle missed (*a*) the extent to which incorporation into a growing capitalist economy gave "modern" industrial workers an option of reformism not equally open to those — like traditional craft workers — being displaced by capitalism, and (*b*) the extent to which resistance to displacement, destruction of traditional solidarities, and deprivation of local autonomy (without compensating equality of opportunity) figured in anticolonial national liberation and other third world — read: Vietnamese (or indeed South African) struggles. Marxism might be the official ideology of the Vietnamese national liberation movements, but class struggle by itself explained the Vietnamese revolution poorly. Indeed (as Pierre Bourdieu noted in the case of Algeria), even the attempt to unify the national struggle worked to the benefit of the dominant, and subordinated many others, including those moved more than anything by a desire to defend their local relations, ways of life, and ancestral fields. Yet, as in most revolutions, these were the mainstays of struggle even if the insurgents were not able to take the reins of power afterward when more elite and usually urban insurgents dominated.

Anyway, it was turning to history that took me out of social anthropology. And at the same time, though my liver was still intact (despite a good bit of best bitter), I was only growing more and more engaged with theory — both Marxism and classical sociology, and philosophy related to both. Redefinition as a sociologist seemed the best way to combine the three interests. There may be something generationally as well as personally disobedient in my difficulty understanding why people would think academic disciplines were divided by sensible intellectual boundaries rather than demarcations of convenience, social networks of familiarity, and institutional structures of power and resources. Indeed, it wasn't until I began to study nationalism (and the limits of cosmopolitanism) that I got a better grasp on how empowering such identities and groups are, especially for those lacking capacity to realize their projects or find their way as individuals. There was certainly something generational about the reinvigoration of historical sociology, then taking shape out of a range of scholarly trajectories.

In 1975, Max died and I moved to Oxford. I considered returning to Columbia and the United States but really liked England. And Clyde Mitchell (yet another anthropologist turned sociologist) had just moved from Manchester to Oxford and was willing to take me on as an advisee. The historians Angus MacIntyre and Max Hartwell and the sociologist Roderick Martin were my other advisers in a doctoral project constructed jointly between history and sociology.

· · ·

It takes a considerable effort to figure out the mixture of striving, and anger, and eagerness, and insecurity that drove me then. Twenty years later, I chanced to meet Angus MacIntyre's daughter Kate in Chapel Hill. She had been a small child when I worked with Angus, but she called home and told her father of the meeting. "Yes," she told me he had said, "I remember Calhoun well, thin, intense, and angry young man." I remember being thin most clearly.

Oxford had provoked a kind of class anxiety. It facilitated upward mobility but made clear the difference between that and being born to the place (or to Harvard and the American places that sent Oxford most of its Rhodes scholars and similar visiting student-dignitaries). Certainly, I had it much easier than English friends from comprehensive schools. I had no idea how to relate to servants, but an American accent was unclassed. Fortunately for the sake of my anxiety, I was at Saint Antony's, a very international college, and my closest friends were from Ukraine and Spain as well as England. Indeed, after Franco fell from power I joined my Spanish friends in their joyous return home. I was at a concert by the Orfeo Catala choral society the first time the Catalan national anthem had been sung for decades. I saw Santiago Carillo return from exile, weeping with emotion, and pull from his pocket the written text for a speech of true communist length, breaking the spell of the moment for most of the crowd. It was possible in the mid-1970s to think the denouement to the Sixties would be democratic socialism or at least social democracy.

I did like Oxford a lot, especially once I figured out that going punting and eating strawberries and cream did not materially betray the struggles of the working class. I reclaimed a certain American identity at Oxford—not an identity with the other Americans, exactly, but a sense that I was what I was. I got a reputation for studying hard (not unambiguously a good thing at Oxford, where genius is prized more than diligence) because I worked late at night in a room with a window facing the street. I read Marx more carefully, and then Hegel, and figured out I needed a lot of remedial education in philosophy and history, both of which Oxford offered in abundance.

If I remember a lot of anger—or at least angst—and moral outrage in the Sixties and early seventies, I remember also a lot of optimism, openness, and pleasure of exploration. It would be a mistake to recall the era solely through its politics, neglecting all the aspects of self-discovery, communalism, and social experimentation that were not explicitly political. The term "counterculture" suggests much of this but not quite all; it overemphasizes opposition and underestimates creativity and simple hope. It was an era that revealed one of the problems with Pitirm Sorokin's grand scheme of social and cultural dynamics. A single age could be simultaneously sensate, ideational, and idealistic, with none of these themes clearly ascendant.

That's Not Why I Went to School

Patricia Hill Collins is Charles Phelps Taft Professor of Sociology in the Depart-
ment of African American Studies at the University of Cincinnati. She received her
BA and PhD degrees in sociology from Brandeis University and an MAT degree
from Harvard University. A social theorist, her research and scholarship have dealt
primarily with issues of race, gender, social class, sexuality, and/or nation specifi-
cally relating to African American women. Her first book, Black Feminist Thought:
Knowledge, Consciousness, and the Politics of Empowerment, *won the Jessie Ber-*
nard Award of the American Sociological Association for significant scholarship in
gender and the C. Wright Mills award of the Society for the Study of Social Prob-
lems. She is also author of Race, Class, and Gender: An Anthology, *edited with*
Margaret Anderson, currently in its fifth edition, and Fighting Words: Black Women
and the Search for Justice. *Her fourth book,* Black Sexual Politics: African Americans, Gender, and the New Racism, *was published in 2004. She is currently com-*
pleting a book of essays titled From Black Power to Hip Hop: Essays on Racism,
Nationalism, and Feminism, *forthcoming in 2005.*

For African American social theorists, intellectual production encompasses much
more than playing convincing roles as competent academics either for tenure
committees within U.S. colleges and universities or as "public intellectuals" for
a racially naive American public. As an African American woman sociologist
who does theoretical work, I have confronted a series of contradictions that can
never be resolved, only continually negotiated. My scholarship has been honed
within these contradictions and reflects the dilemmas that confront not just Black

American intellectuals such as myself but progressive scholars from diverse backgrounds as well.

Continuing to do intellectual work that is honest, that aims to empower those who remain relegated to the bottom of intersecting social hierarchies of race, class, gender, sexuality, and nation, and that keeps its eye on social justice as a fundamental principle of democratic societies requires that I attend to my own survival. The social movements of the late 1960s were very important to me, but they were far from the defining moments of my life or my work. I do not see my scholarship as part of a simple career path where faculty mentors gave me nuggets of advice, wrote letters for me, or opened doors. I cannot look back on my college years from the comfort of a leather armchair in a posh faculty club, nostalgically celebrating my own student activism and bemoaning the seeming student apathy of today. Every day remains a struggle, and that fact is just as true today as it was when I was an undergraduate at Brandeis University (1965–69), a master's student at Harvard University (1969–70), or a teacher and organizer in the Black community schools movement in Boston (1970–76). Many people have helped me along the way, but I do not do Black intellectual work because of academia—I do the kind of social theory that I do in spite of it.

Both the content and the process of my intellectual work require keeping certain contradictions in play. For African American thinkers such as myself, negotiating these contradictions and shielding one's intellectual production from spinning off into meaningless directions requires continual vigilance. I have never had the luxury to be just a social theorist, the archetypal armchair intellectual who ponders and passes judgment on the issues of the day without taking any responsibility for his thoughts and inaction. Instead, I have had to devote energy to a complicated struggle that required me to create spaces where I could criticize existing power relations, imagine new possibilities, and, when necessary, try to bring them to fruition. I had to ensure my own survival first and hope that the rest would follow.

Beyond my family and community, whose unshakable support made all the difference, no one ever expected me to make it. In the Philadelphia neighborhood of my youth, normal African American women aspired for jobs as domestic workers or secretaries, certainly not college professors or social theorists. Early on, I had to create the space for my own intellectual survival—it was not readymade for me. I had to learn to appear to be obedient in order to be intellectually disobedient. My challenge lay in being obedient enough in order to gain the authority to be truly disobedient without being broken by the process. In this respect, my struggles to create a space for myself as a social theorist resemble those of so many African American women who also struggle to make a way out of no way.

What It Meant to Go to College

I went to college in 1965, shortly after my seventeenth birthday. Getting there had not been easy. I received no guidance in high school, save sitting in a gymnasium with five hundred other students and listening to a canned speech about how to pick a college. Brandeis University and I found one another through affirmative action. My SAT exam included an optional question to self-identify one's race. It also asked whether I wanted to receive materials from schools that were looking for Black applicants. I checked both boxes. Brandeis was one of ten schools that wrote to me. I applied, but my family could not afford a campus visit, so I arrived for my first day of freshman year on a campus that I had never seen and had only imagined through glossy recruitment materials. I was on an important path because if I succeeded I would become the first person in my family ever to graduate from college. There was a lot riding on my success. As a token, when I failed, all Black people failed with me. But my success would not mean that all Black people would be viewed in a more favorable light. Rather, I would be judged the "good Black" who wasn't like the rest.

When it came to race, Brandeis University was definitely a shock. There I faced an important contradiction that persists today. On the one hand, I arrived at a school with a liberal reputation concerning race.[1] I encountered no rednecks that tried to run me off campus, no death threats posted on my dorm door, and nobody at Brandeis ever called me "nigger." This was a school that recruited me before it was fashionable to do so. I was not a threat. Rather, I was welcomed with open arms. I had white friends. On the other hand, there were virtually no Black people to be found. To my surprise, my college of about 2,200 students had only seven Black students in my freshman class. Apparently, this was a bumper crop. The class before me was rumored to have two Black students, and the one before

1. My dedication to scholarship on race began in college and has continued unabated ever since. In this and the remaining notes, I link the themes in the text to specific sites in the corpus of my scholarship. I am not the originator of these ideas. Rather, my intent is that readers consult my works and review the extensive bibliographies that I cite. Here I describe my participation in the early phases of the "new racism." For a recent analysis, see Collins (2004a).

that only one. The absence of any kind of substantial Black presence on this campus meant that every Black student was hypervisible. I have since learned that this is the classic situation of racial desegregation, regardless of whether one is moving into a white neighborhood, school, doctoral program, or job category. Early arrivers may be warmly welcomed but are still under constant surveillance.

Despite the pressures of being on constant display, I also came to realize that social class mattered as well.[2] The majority of students at Brandeis University were from fairly well-off homes. They were not the richest of the rich by any means, but their families certainly had much more money than mine did. Fortunately, this social-class gap did not make me feel bad about my class situation. To this day, I remain proud that I come from a family where people earned their money through honest work. That's what "working class" means. But the class politics of Brandeis did highlight certain issues, for example, my white friends' sense of entitlement. Most had never thought for two minutes in a row that they might never go to college. Instead, during their entire lives they and everyone else had assumed that they were going to go to college. The question for them was which college would they attend. In contrast, I had spent the first seventeen years of my life hoping that someday I might get to go to college. To this day, my acceptance letter to Brandeis stands as a major milestone in my life. The class politics also affected how we could spend our time. I had to study hard to maintain my scholarship and work to pay for my education. Because my white friends rarely worried about money, they could indulge in pastimes that were off-limits to me. For example, they could engage in endless debates about the unfairness of the Viet Nam War or the backwardness of the rednecks in Mississippi. I often had to leave these discussions, headed for the library or my job. What irony.

Having to work, living on a budget, and seeing the labor force that was cleaning the dorms, cooking the food, typing the memos, answering the phones, caring for the grounds, and all of the labor that it takes to keep a college going gave me a different view of work and class politics than that of my white friends. For many of them, the actual people who did the work that made their educations possible were invisible. This is the hallmark of good service — invisible hands that anticipate your every wish, minimize possible inconveniences, and meet

2. Attention to social class has permeated virtually all of my scholarship, but it has not been the prominent theme. For works where I more directly tackle questions of social class, see Collins (1999a; 2000b) and, for a more comprehensive discussion of social class, globalization, and its effects on African Americans, see also my *Black Sexual Politics* (2004).

one's every needs. It's too tiresome for the students to stand in line to register—we must find a way to make it more comfortable for them (juxtaposed to the time I spent standing in line with my mother each week when she had to report in to receive unemployment benefits—no one cared whether she was comfortable or not, there wasn't any place to sit down). It's not that I had a better or privileged view of Brandeis than everyone else—I definitely had a different view that had important intellectual and political consequences.[3]

Much of my work on standpoint epistemology was catalyzed by these early experiences of trying to come to terms with the race and class politics that I encountered as a Brandeis undergraduate.[4] Standpoint epistemology links experiences with consciousness, power relations with the knowledge that explains social realities. In brief, where you stand will shape what you see and, often, what you stand for. I don't automatically assume that if you have a certain set of experiences you involuntarily develop a certain perspective on those experiences. I can name many people who have had similar experiences to mine who see the world very differently than I do and who have made very different choices about their lives. What I do believe is that having certain kinds of experiences predisposes you to ask certain questions and to see certain things.[5] For example, when

3. The class politics were far from monolithic because Brandeis also admitted white working-class students from South Boston. I clearly saw shared allegiances with white working-class students, yet our backgrounds made us routinely suspicious of one another in ways that did not exist with the liberal middle-class white students.

4. Two signature pieces exemplify these ideas. In 1986, I published my first piece on the "outsider within" titled "Learning from the Outsider Within: The Sociological Significance of Black Feminist Thought" and argued that Black women as a group had a distinctive angle of vision that might benefit sociology (Collins 1986). Twelve years later, I expanded this argument in *Fighting Words* to propose that Black women in sociology brought a distinctive perspective that had contributed to the development of race, class, and gender studies (Collins 1998a, 95–123). My work in standpoint epistemology is also evident in the initial 1986 article as well as a 1998 piece published in *Signs* titled "The Social Construction of Black Feminist Thought" (Collins 1989). These two journal articles became pillars of *Black Feminist Thought*, my first book, published in 1990 and reprinted with a revised tenth-year anniversary edition in 2000 (Collins 2000a).

5. For a discussion of standpoint epistemology that avoids some of the dichotomous ideas of my earlier thinking, see "Black Feminist Epistemology," chap. 11 of *Black Feminist Thought* (Collins 2000a, 251–72). This relationship between what one sees and what one thinks is far from straightforward. I have returned repeatedly to questions of the relationship between power relations and consciousness. For example, in *Fighting Words*, I include a chapter titled "Some Group Matters: Intersectionality, Situated Standpoints and Black Feminist Thought" that analyzes the ways in which standpoint episte-

I arrived at Brandeis University in 1965 and found so few African Americans, I questioned how the absence of Black students might affect the type of education I could expect. In contrast, all around me, my classmates were more likely to be thinking "how nice it is that I'm going to school with articulate Black students, maybe I can finally have some Black friends."

These differences of race and class epitomized my marginality as a Black student in an overwhelmingly white school and a working-class student attending school with children of middle-class and affluent patents. They also predisposed me to ask very different questions than the majority of my classmates. When it came to the prerequisite skills and motivation needed for success, I belonged at Brandeis (after a quasi-shaky start, I improved and graduated cum laude). I was an insider where few other Black students had gone before. At the same time, I perpetually felt like an outsider—I wasn't white, affluent, Jewish, or suburban. It was only years later when I wrote about the notion of "outsider within" positioning that I came to see how my own intellectual and political development had been so affected by my social location.[6] For example, my longstanding interest in studying the intersections of race and class, and later on gender and sexuality, reflect my efforts to reconcile these seemingly contradictory and virtually invisible factors in my undergraduate education. How could both race and class be so important to me yet so invisible to others? How could gender be so important to some of my white women friends and so unimportant to me? Why was I constantly encountering situations where I had to choose either race or class or gender as being more important than the other?

Getting an Education — Outside and Inside the Classroom

When I arrived at Brandeis, the major issue was the war in Viet Nam. My classmates were rising up because, for the first time in their lives, something had touched them personally. In contrast, I had just escaped from twelve years of public school education that was technically good to excellent yet mind-numbing to me because my intelligence had been questioned virtually everyday because I was Black. In my neighborhood, the war sent working-class Blacks, Latinos and

mology remains useful for African American women (Collins 1998a, 201–28). See also, my comments in a symposium on constructionist approaches to "doing difference" (Collins 1997).

6. For a comparison between my signature piece on the concept of the "outsider within" and my thoughts on how it had been weakened, see Collins (1986, 1999b).

white kids off to fight, and many of them did not come back. What was so new about that? Very little — everyone in my neighborhood knew that Black people's humanity was questioned, that Black men were expendable to the military, and that Black women often took up the slack. Virtually no one in my neighborhood went to college, and for the most part, few openly complained. If anything, they were attempting to be obedient in order to survive. They supported the military because they had few other options. They enlisted because they were trying to feed their families. Men and women alike worked in demeaning jobs to make ends meet. They had neither the time nor the space to be disobedient. Their children were killed, yet they had to keep waving the flag, at least in public.

When the war in Viet Nam touched the children of privilege because they were being drafted just like their poor and working-class counterparts, things changed. My classmates began to be "disobedient" but in ways that differed quite dramatically from my own forms of disobedience. I was being "disobedient" by going to school and excelling. In contrast, their disobedience centered on defying their parents, dropping out of school, and protesting the war. Despite our different social locations regarding schooling and the war, my classmates' antiwar political activity definitely had an effect on me. I decided fairly early on that I was opposed in principle to militarism and warfare, yet the complexities of race and class made Viet Nam a far more complex issue for me. This realization came to me during an antiwar march in Boston that my freshmen roommates dragged me to when an egg thrown by a spectator narrowly missed my ear. Initially, the march felt great — hundreds of college students were marching down the street, showing a collective power that I had never before experienced. But on our way to the church that was to be our meeting place, we were pelted with eggs by people who looked surprisingly like the working-class whites and some Blacks that I had left behind in Philadelphia. I wasn't hit, but I clearly remember sitting in that church during the rally and thinking, "If I'm going to be hit with eggs, it's damn sure not going to be about antiwar protests against Viet Nam."

That egg incident convinced me that other issues were higher on my list. During my freshman year, civil rights was a palpable force in my life. It wasn't that I was turning my back on the antiwar movement. I saw the connections between political activism and social change. But I also recognized that there is no one best way to work for social change and that, while the war in Viet Nam certainly affected Black people, it was one issue among many. My top priority was civil rights because it was clear that the struggle for Black empowerment was far from won. Unlike my mother, who never got to go to college because there was no social movement to open doors for her, the civil rights legislation resulting from the struggles of the fifties and sixties created unheard of opportunities for me. I was at Brandeis University not only because I studied hard in high school and was qualified but also because people whom I would never meet had marched, sang, sat in, prayed, held bake sales for scholarship funds, and filed countless legal briefs to get me there. If I were going to get hit with eggs, my agenda would be what I could deliver to those Black people who came after me. At the time, I may have lacked formal sociological training, but I did see the world in social structural terms. I wanted the racial rules changed and the inequality of racial opportunity eliminated.

In contrast, civil rights appeared to be a sort of personal politics for my white friends and for most of the white people whom I met. They felt that if they supported civil rights in the abstract and had one or two Black friends, then they were exempt from thinking about issues of race in their everyday lives. In their eyes, I was the acceptable Black person who made them feel that progress was being made. To them, civil rights struggles occurred in far-away places such as Mississippi and South Africa, not in Boston and most certainly not under their very noses with the racial desegregation of Brandeis University. Very few could conceptualize my struggle for a college education as part of a broader civil rights struggle to desegregate all aspects of American society. Obviously, this kind of gap in perception fosters misunderstanding and, in my case, alienation. For me, issues of civil rights and issues of social mobility were life or death decisions whereas for my white friends, they were topics for debate where they could practice analytical thinking.

In muddling through this undergraduate angst, attending Brandeis was a real blessing. The social dynamics of the school were strange, but for the first time I got a taste of intellectual freedom. Brandeis is a special school. As a Jewish institution founded in 1948, the early faculty, staff, students, and donors of Brandeis had living memory of the Holocaust. There was no need to convince anyone at Brandeis that anti-Semitism is a form of racism and that knowledge produced by elite groups could have a profound effect on power relations in society. They understood the tragedy of genocide, and, as a result, Brandeis at that time was infused with a strong social justice tradition. These themes would have shaped the ethos of Brandeis regardless of social movements for civil rights, Black power, Chicano nationalism, farmworkers' rights, feminism, antiwar activism, or any other social movements. In addition to this social justice tradition, Brandeis was also deeply nationalistic. I saw firsthand the benefits of funding and building institutions that reflected your own view of reality. In Europe, Jews had been assimilated and had played by the rules. In the end, no one had their own interests at heart more than Jews themselves.

This Brandeis ethos that recognized the connections between knowledge and power in a very visceral way, that was dedicated to social justice, and that also incorporated a staunch Jewish nationalistic ethos had an important effect on Brandeis sociology (and on my subsequent transference of these issues to African Americans). I majored in sociology because its focus on race came closest to my growing interest in studying Black people. In my program, we talked about race in very progressive ways. By today's standards, Brandeis sociology in the late 1960s was quite radical. I was taught by faculty members who either were Jewish refugees who had been forced to leave Europe in response to the Nazis or were influenced by European interpretive social thought associated with this group of intellectuals. Brandeis sociology lay closer to philosophy than science — for example, the critical theory of the Frankfurt school, Freudian psychology, Mannheim's sociology of knowledge and the materialist analyses of Karl Marx. To me, Brandeis sociology with its focus on philosophy, the sociology of knowledge, and critical analysis of society was "normal" sociology. As an undergraduate, I had virtually no exposure to functionalism or to the empiricism that has come to symbolize American sociology. I was taught by people who basically understood the horror of institutional racism and who believed that good sociology cast a critical eye on society. Racism was not an abstraction to them, a decontextualized social theory, or something that they could ignore and go about their business of just being faculty members. They knew the horror of it in their bones.

I am grateful that this is the sociology that I learned. My professors asked big, interesting, and important questions, assigned original works, and trusted in our ability to think. We were not only encouraged to criticize society — industrialization, poverty, militarism, the growing influence of the media, racial discrimination — but the social justice traditions of Brandeis also created space for those of us who wished to change society. There was no "group think" of having to memorize the "right answers" for the test but instead a sustained emphasis on developing sociology majors who were synthetic, analytical thinkers. I came to love the puzzle-solving challenges of doing synthetic, conceptual work, for example, speculating about the connections between Marx and Freud or, later on, between William E. B. DuBois, Booker T. Washington, and Frantz Fanon. After four years in an elite public high school for girls that trained us in obedience to prepare us for college, intellectual freedom was a breath of fresh air. I learned to be an eclectic thinker, to take the best from a range of thinkers, and leave the rest behind. Then as now, I was uninterested in shadowboxing with thinkers so that I could produce a virtuoso performance of what they got "wrong." Instead, I wanted to know what they got right and how we might assemble it in a new, functional way in service of ethical ends.[7]

This was the political and cognitive context in which I studied race. The theory was visionary, and ideas about social justice and imagining new possibilities were the hallmark of many in my generation. But to be honest, I wasn't simply studying at the feet of the masters and writing down nuggets of knowledge about European interpretive sociology. I was understandably suspicious of this very same established knowledge that held visionary ideas (primarily due to what it did and did not say about Black people). Pragmatically, I had to make it through school. Sociology was one important place where race was taken seriously so that seemed like the best fit for me. Yet another contradiction—how to combine the visionary stance provided by the social theories that I studied in sociology with pragmatism, namely, the actions needed to make them happen. This concept of visionary pragmatism constitutes another unresolved tension that cycles through my work.[8]

Just as the anti-Semitism targeted toward Jews and the forms of institutional racism targeted toward African Americans (slavery, Jim Crow segregation, etc.) are related but not the same, studying race is not the same thing as studying Black people. Fortunately, I was in a department that encouraged me to develop my own interests within a sociological framework, and my interests increasingly turned to the economic, political, and social conditions affecting African Americans. Race was inside the sociology department—the study of Black people often lay outside of it. It wasn't hard to locate courses on Black people because there were only two. I took both. One class covered politics in Africa south of the

7. I remain fascinated by the need to classify my work under predetermined headings. Am I a postmodernist, a functionalist, a critical theorist, a Weberian sociologist, a feminist, or an ethicist? Here I describe an alternative cognitive style, one of mining a range of diverse work in search of answers to the big questions that transcend each specialized field. Race constitutes such a big question. For a discussion of this type of theory, see Collins (1998a).

8. In *Fighting Words*, I link this concept of "visionary pragmatism," the necessity of linking caring theoretical vision with informed practical struggles, to the epistemological criteria of critical social theory (1998a, 187–200).

Sahara. It was a depressing but excellent course. The other was an introduction to African American experience taught by Laurence Fuchs through American studies. Because this course was the only course on African Americans, it was popular and typically reserved for seniors. Professor Fuchs's class was the first and one of the few times that I have seen a professor take diversity seriously. He decided to discriminate in favor of African American students, asking white students, "Does it make any sense to you for us to have a class about Black students that Black students cannot take? Can you see how having a more diverse class will change what you learn?" With that rationale, he declared that any Black student who wanted to take this class could. This was a pretty safe deal because there weren't many Black students. But his admission policy did impart a powerful lesson about knowledge, power, and diversity. Diversity talk can be cheap in situations that exclude the very people from the discussion who are the object of study.

I enrolled in that class during my junior year, my first and only undergraduate course on the African American experience. For that class, I wrote a paper on Martin Luther King by researching and reading everything that I could find that he had written. Not much of his voluminous work was in print, but I read what I could find. Because issues of racial integration and economic justice were key themes for me, my paper on Martin Luther King helped me think through these themes. Because the antiwar movement touched my classmates directly and was higher on their list of priorities, race and class were not as important to them. Martin Luther King's assassination changed all of this virtually overnight.

King's Assassination: The Fork in the Road

For me, Dr. Martin Luther King's assassination was a watershed event. Peak moments are those when your personal life, political life, and intellectual life converge. The events surrounding April 4, 1968, were like that for me. Coming to terms with King's death forced me to confront many of the larger questions that continue to frame my work: How do we bring about social justice? How are Black people ever going to be free? Can white people change their ways? How do we evaluate racial integration and Black nationalism as strategies for bringing about that freedom? How do we ensure that political agendas of the Black freedom struggle are inclusive of all Black people? In what ways, if any, can the community development strategies of Black nationalism be reconciled with broader agendas for social justice advanced within the civil rights movement? At the time, I saw these questions primarily through the lens of race and social class, but over time, I increasingly saw how intersections of gender, sexuality, age, and nationality (American citizenship) also mattered.

When it came to race, King's assassination revealed the contradictions of race relations and positioned me at a very important fork in the political road. Through April 3, I, like many others, was critical of the traditional civil rights agenda but still felt that it merited pursuing. The civil rights agenda aimed to dismantle Jim Crow practices and desegregate American society, yet it also focused on making Black people more presentable for integration with white people. Its major contribution was an unshakable belief in the humanity of all individuals and the struggle to bring about the social justice that would recognize this basic humanity. King's much quoted "I have a dream" speech taps into this legacy.[9] As King became more "radical" by arguing for structural change, especially concerning issues of poverty and militarism, he became much less acceptable to middle-class whites. But to me, he was beginning to make far more sense because his antiracist, civil rights agenda was becoming inclusive of class and global politics and was becoming attentive to social-structural causes of social injustice.

King's assassination not only supported the claims of his Black nationalist critics who argued that the civil rights movement was too little and too slow, it also challenged the strategies that I had been pursuing to get my own education. King preached that if the movement touched the conscience of white America, white America would come around. His critics argued that the majority of white America had no such moral conscience regarding Black people and that this strategy was doomed to failure. When a white man assassinated somebody who had a message of peace, a program grounded in nonviolence, who won the Nobel Peace Prize, and who tried to reach out to the conscience of a population that had ignored Black suffering for hundreds of years, I wanted to know what the hell else do you have to do to get white people to listen and change?

The immediate events in the aftermath of King's assassination shaped my in-

9. I see King's legacy in my scholarship on humanism and social justice. In *Black Feminist Thought*, I examine what I call the humanist tradition in Black feminist thought, one that does advance a view of the world where people can be different and equal. For discussions of these concepts, see Collins (2000a, 41–43). In *Fighting Words*, I use the search for social justice as a metaphor and as criteria for evaluating oppositional (critical) social theory (Collins 1998a)

tellectual and political development in ways that continue to affect my work. Most immediately, I wrote a letter to the *Justice*, the school paper, which had been named for Louis Brandeis who was a justice on the Supreme Court. I expressed how angry I was at white America and talked about how tired I was of a threadbare civil rights agenda that put Black people, one at a time, through the ordeal of racial desegregation. I was genuinely angry and profoundly tired of always being on my best behavior around classmates who couldn't have cared less about how I felt or what I really thought. When I walked into the dining hall after the paper came out, you would have thought that I had grown a second head. My classmates looked at me like they had never met me before. One said, "We didn't know you felt that way." They honestly didn't know because my survival depended on their not knowing. My anger started well before King's assassination. I was enraged about all the time that I had spent being careful and playing by the rules. The virulence of my reaction took them by surprise because they saw my reaction as one explosive and seemingly irrational act. They could not see the context of what it meant to grow up with persistent racial discrimination. For me, just knowing that I was not going to put up with any more shit was a freeing intellectual moment.

King's assassination also introduced me to the ways in which ideas really matter. After King's assassination, there were riots in many cities, including Washington, DC. The riots in Washington had been especially bad—Black people had burned down about ten city blocks relatively close to the White House. Virtually overnight, the little term paper that I had written for my African American studies class rose in importance because my professor was affiliated with an educational services corporation that provided curriculum materials for schools all over the country. Lo and behold, King was assassinated, riots break out all over the country, and no one in that organization knew much about Martin Luther King. To his credit, Professor Fuchs did not simply appropriate my little term paper. Instead, he asked me whether I would like to accompany a team of educational consultants who were using my paper to prepare materials that would be put in the hands of Washington, DC, public school children when schools reopened. What should children be told about King on their first day back at school after the riots? What should their teachers say to them?

A few days later, I found myself on a plane en route to Washington, DC. I was the only African American on the team, and that trip constituted one peak experience of my undergraduate education. I knew that I was Black window dressing, and that my Black hypervisibility was part of what made that curriculum legitimate, but I'm glad that I went. I can close my eyes and feel how that day felt. I got to walk to school with elementary school children whose new crossing guard was a rifle-toting National Guard member. I visited several elementary schools and saw my materials (vastly improved by professionals) put into the hands of African American children. They knew nothing about Martin Luther King, and my research had been folded into a larger project that taught them some of what they needed to know. To this day, I believe that every word that I write matters, even if I seem to be the only one who might ever read them. I also ate lunch in a high school where, through the cafeteria window, I viewed the staging area for the tanks that had been brought into the neighborhood to quell the riots. That image certainly affected my opinions about armed struggle against the government. White students could protest all they wanted, but the tanks came out when Blacks exploded. It was really quite an amazing experience when I think about it.

King's assassination also pushed me toward Black nationalist politics, a philosophy that I have grappled with ever since. After King's assassination, I went on a march that was billed as a King memorial march of some sort. This march was very different than the antiwar, egg-throwing march that I attended my freshman year. Past marches for racial equality often started in Boston's African American communities and headed downtown into white space. There was a scripted nature to the marches for racial integration as if to say, "We're carrying candles; we're singing 'We Shall Overcome'; we got some white folks with us so you know this is legitimate; and we're the safe 'we want in' Negroes." The geography and ethos of the King memorial march was entirely different. It started in white space and marched into the heart of the Black community, losing white people along the way. As that march proceeded, its tone changed from a somber eulogy for King to a festive street parade that reminded me of traditional Black funeral practices in New Orleans. During the march, a white couple in a car was momentarily trapped when the marchers surrounded their car because they were on the march's route. Nobody did anything to them; but when I passed the car and saw the fear on the faces of the white occupants, I realized the force of Black Power. I'm not endorsing scaring white people or engaging in unprovoked violence. There was none during that memorial march. But that march also reiterated the significance of Black solidarity. In the aftermath of King's assassination and joined with my firsthand experience of the efficacy of Jewish nationalism at Brandeis, Black nationalist strategies of self-help, community building, organizing, and advocating on one's own behalf made much more sense.[10]

This was a crucial time in my intellectual and political development. So much was in my mind. The civil rights movement's goals of striving for racial integration and social justice seemed worthwhile, yet its strategies of appealing to the moral conscience of the nation seemed impractical after King's assassination. I was analyzing the philosophies of Martin Luther King and Malcolm X; trying to get through school by stitching together work study jobs; searching for classes on Black people; writing editorials that scared my classmates; flying to Washington to tour a riot zone filled with confused and angry African American children; and participating in a reverse march that shifted from a eulogy to a festival—all of this during my junior year.

I look back on my senior year as being pivotal in terms of my coming to terms with the ideas that have defined my life's work. Then, as now, I see struggles for social justice as being everywhere and ongoing. There's nowhere to hide. Rather, it's more a question of choosing where you want to fight and with what tools. If you don't fight for social justice, you've chosen to capitulate to oppression. When it comes to social justice, despite what social constructionists might say, there is no ethical midground. My choices following King's assassination put me on a path where words and ideas were my weapons and where my writing, teaching, and public speaking became my forum to bring about change. I knew I needed to get myself out of school so I wasn't that free, but I did approach my senior year with a focused sense of what I wanted to study. I dedicated myself to being the best student that I could be.

Writing a senior honors thesis in sociology was my way of investigating the issues that were important to me. At that time, I wanted to know what a quality education for African American students would look like. What were the components of a good antiracist education that would empower African Americans to resist racism? I settled on the topic of community control of Black schools—what knowledge would be produced if Black people controlled the schools? I was committed to centering my work on Black students, but I also recognized that empowering Black students shed light on education for social justice for everybody.

10. I retain a healthy interest in Black nationalism, specifically, and in the literature of nationalism more generally. Rather than judging nationalism as inherently bad or good (the feminist vs. the Afrocentrist interpretations), I have systematically returned to nationalism to interrogate it. For works on these topics, see Collins (1992, 1998b, 1999a, 2001, 2004b).

Two important things came out of writing my senior honors thesis. For one, I asked Dr. Pauli Murray to be one of the three faculty readers on my committee. At the time, she was the first and only African American faculty member at Brandeis, and she was the only African American teacher that I had since the second grade. I was a student in her course Law as an Instrument of Social Change. At the time, I did not realize what a major figure she was in social justice causes. Mercifully, my ignorance enabled me to take risks in everyday conversations with her that did as much if not more for my intellectual development as reading the major court cases assigned in class. She was wonderful to me. No one can fully appreciate the pressures placed on senior African American women scholars than others who are in this position. The demands are incessant. I did not realize the scope of her life's work until I read her autobiographies some years later. Now that I am on the front line of moving through academic institutions, I have so much respect and appreciation for those African American women who came before me. What was it like to be Dr. Murray? I can only imagine.[11]

Another outcome of my senior honors thesis was that I realized that I could be a scholar. Because I was passionate about my topic, my paper was approximately one hundred pages long. This was shocking to me because I had no idea that I had so much to say. I discovered that doing my own research differed greatly from writing a paper for a professor. Consciousness really was a sphere of freedom. I had the opportunity to use that space of intellectual production to investigate the issues that I thought were important. I was fortunate enough to be in a school that encouraged me to do that, and it gave me the resources and confidence to excel.

Doing Social Theory, Roxbury Style

When I was an undergraduate at Brandeis and a graduate student at Harvard University's School of Education, theory (scholarship) and practice (activism) seemed to pull against one another. It wasn't until I went to work for the community schools that I began to fuse theory and practice in ways that began to work for me. During the six years that I worked in the community schools movement, I continued to juxtapose theory and practice but did so in ways that dif-

---

11. One hallmark of my work is that I read and cite the works of Black women thinkers. Despite the time that it takes to do so, I believe in providing extensive bibliographies in order to legitimate the work of thinkers who have not been in the inner circle.

fered dramatically from what others my age were doing who had continued on in graduate school. Freed from the stricture of trying to please professors or from the "publish or perish" professional socialization that plagues contemporary graduate students and untenured faculty, I was free to explore ideas. I didn't write one word of social theory, but I think I did some of my best intellectual work during my time with the community schools.

I was in the community schools movement, teaching, writing curriculum, and doing parent organizing in three kindergarten through eighth-grade schools in Roxbury, MA. I set out to explore the issues that I had written about in my senior thesis and to practice the craft that I had studied as a master's student at Harvard University. Ironically, I shifted from Brandeis's Jewish social justice traditions of critical thinking and scholarship to the secular humanism of Harvard's liberalism (lots of John Dewey and education for democracy and the common man), to the liberation theology of Catholicism that influenced global social justice projects. Because I was raised neither Jewish nor Catholic and have yet to embrace uncritically a secular humanism that rejects spirituality, drawing from the social justice traditions of these diverse settings in the context of working for social change was fascinating. During my times with the community schools, I tested ideas about race, class, gender, and social justice, not in the terrain of abstraction with people sitting around the seminar table reflecting on what might constitute a quality education for Black students. I tested ideas by doing. Along with others, I actually tried to provide such an education and, each day, could reflect about what worked and what went wrong.

I started off as a seventh- and eighth-grade teacher of a class that was overwhelmingly African American and working class. Their needs were immense, and because I wanted to bring the world to them, I read voraciously. Unlike my undergraduate and graduate school experiences, I had no assigned readings because I had a full-time job. I could assign myself what I wanted to read, and I did. I gave myself the Black studies education that I couldn't get in school and I shared it with others as I got it. I read pretty much anything I could find on Black people, for example, Harold Cruse's *The Crisis of the Negro Intellectual*, *The Autobiography of Malcolm X*, and many works by William E. B. Du Bois, including *African Slave Trade* and *The Philadelphia Negro*. I read many books that are now considered classics in Black studies, but because there was no Black studies at that time, I didn't know they were classics. Black fiction was fabulous then. I read everything from the fiction of the Harlem Renaissance to the trashy novels of Iceberg Slim. It was just a question of anything I could get my hands on that might be of use to me and/or my students. Toni Cade Bambara's edited volume *The Black Woman*, published in 1970, was a groundbreaking book for me, as was Toni Morrison's *The Bluest Eye*. Finally, here were writings by and about African American women and gender that seemed relevant to my life and those of my students.

My approach to what I read while I was a teacher had a profound effect on how I conceptualize and produce social theory today. During that period of time, I read extensively and distilled what I read not only for the seventh and eighth graders in my classroom but also for the diverse people with whom I worked. In the community schools movement, I worked with people who were very different from one another: African Americans, whites, men, women, nuns, laypeople, Harvard professors and graduate students, a few stray hippies, formerly incarcerated community residents, parents, closeted Black gays and lesbians — the works. We were all committed to quality education for the students in our school and to building an institution that was grounded in principles of social justice. I learned to translate ideas across age, race, class, and gender. I did not have the luxury of producing social theory in quiet library spaces. Doing social theory was not a solitary endeavor.[12]

I deepened my ideas about the questions that concern me now through lived experiences of thinking and doing. When I write about praxis, it's not an abstraction to me. When I argue that definitions of excellence need not be predicated on exclusivity and elitism, I'm not imagining some utopia. We built schools that were excellent and diverse. The majority of the ideas that I deal with now were negotiated through the community schools experience in some way. The ideas that I carried with me from my formal education into community politics certainly mattered, as did my style of testing those ideas through the crucible of trying to teach the very population that so concerned me. I did not pursue a passive model of finding an internship where one gains experiences as a commodity that can be brokered for future jobs. Rather, I enjoyed a recursive style of theorizing that involved thinking about important questions and principles, seeing one's own placement in those issues, reflecting on one's own and others contri-

12. This idea of translation and ideas that can travel across multiple communities remains one way that I think standpoint epistemology can approach the criticism of the privileged standpoint. I investigate this notion of "dialogical processes" as a new way of doing social theory that in turn should generate different types of social theory more suitable for actual social justice projects. See Collins (2000a, 33–39).

butions, and limitations concerning the common good, all the while trying to live life by certain principles. That's what the social movements in which I was involved in the 1970s did for me. Activism is not just talk. Activism is trying to make a difference in people's lives and taking responsibility for one's thoughts and deeds. That's what it's like to be in a social movement that is significant in people's lives. That's where I learned to do social theory that matters in people's lives. It did not matter that I did not write it down then. I have time to do so now.

Some Final Thoughts

The themes that permeate my work predate the events of 1965–76, the eleven-year period of time described here, but this period was critical in shaping how I view the world and how I choose to live in it. Puzzling over the connections between power relations and versions of knowledge that justify them (standpoint epistemology); trying to understand the mechanisms and ideologies that maintained racism (e.g., Black sexual politics); viewing racism through a lens of intersection (e.g., the initial intersections of race and class or the gendered racism that confronts African American women and men); studying the resistance strategies used by oppressed groups, for example, advancing alternative worldviews that grow from these intersectional spaces (outsider within theorizing); analyzing and legitimating the subsequent oppositional knowledge that oppressed groups produce (e.g., African American women's experiences and Black feminist thought as critical social theory); and examining all political and social theories in light of their ability to foster social justice projects (civil rights, Black nationalism, feminism, Marxism, and queer theory): these are not ideas that first occurred to me in college classrooms or through impassioned speeches of the antiwar movement. I needed to understand these ideas in order to survive.

When coupled with the intellectual freedom that I found as an undergraduate, what the social movements of the 1960s and 1970s did was encourage me to develop and nurture my own critical consciousness concerning the circumstances of my own life. The unshakable belief in my right to ask my own questions and test out my own ideas is fundamental to my social theory. I suppose I could have done social theory within domestic or clerical work that was the Black women's place waiting for me, but had I not taken advantage of the educational opportunities that were afforded to me, who would have cared what I thought? Grappling with issues of social justice during a time of immense social change created a powerful recursive relationship between my personal biography and the social conditions that I have worked so diligently to change and catalyzed my sociological imagination. Had I been in school during a time of political quiescence, I'd still have been faced with a similar struggle concerning the politics of race and social class. But in the absence of the catalyst of visible social movements dedicated to changing America, my individual struggle would have been profoundly different.

References

Collins, Patricia Hill. 1986. "Learning from the Outsider Within: The Sociological Significance of Black Feminist Thought." *Social Problems* 33, no. 6:14–32.

———. 1989. "The Social Construction of Black Feminist Thought." *Signs* 14, no. 4:745–73.

———. 1992. "Learning to Think for Ourselves: Malcolm X's Black Nationalism Reconsidered." Pp. 59–85 in *Malcolm X: In Our Own Image*, edited by Joe Wood. New York: St. Martin's Press.

———. 1997. "Comment on Hekman's 'Truth and Method: Feminist Standpoint Theory Revisited': Where's the Power?" *Signs* 22, no. 2:375–81.

———. 1998a. *Fighting Words: Black Women and the Search for Justice*. Minneapolis: University of Minnesota Press.

———. 1998b. "It's All in the Family: Intersections of Gender, Race, and Nation." *Hypatia* 13, no. 3:62–82.

———. 1999a. "Producing the Mothers of the Nation: Race, Class and Contemporary U.S. Population Policies." Pp. 118–29 in *Women, Citizenship and Difference*, edited by Nira Yuval-Davis. London: Zed Books.

———. 1999b. "Reflections on the Outsider Within." *Journal of Career Development* 26, no. 1:85–88.

———. 2000a. *Black Feminist Thought: Knowledge, Consciousness, and the Politics of Empowerment*. New York: Routledge.

———. 2000b. "Gender, Black Feminism, and Black Political Economy." *Annals of the American Academy of Political and Social Science* 568 (March): 41–53.

———. 2001. "Like One of the Family: Race, Ethnicity, and the Paradox of U.S. National Identity." *Ethnic and Racial Studies* 24, no. 1:3–28.

———. 2004a. "Black Nationalism and African American Ethnicity: Afrocentrism as Civil Religion." Pp. 96–117 in *Nationalism, Ethnicity, and Minority Rights*, edited by Stephen May, Judith Squires, and Tariq Madood. London: Cambridge University Press.

———. 2004b. *Black Sexual Politics*. New York: Routledge.

The Sociology of Power and Justice

Coming of Age in the Sixties

Karen Schweers Cook is the Ray Lyman Wilbur Professor of Sociology and senior associate dean of the social sciences at Stanford University. She is the coeditor of the Trust Series for the Russell Sage Foundation and the editor of two recent books, Trust in Society *and* Trust and Distrust in Organizations *(with R. Kramer). She is also the coauthor (with R. Hardin and M. Levi) of* Cooperation without Trust? *Other publications include* Social Exchange Theory *(ed.),* The Limits to Rationality *(ed.) with M. Levi, and articles in a number of journals on trust, social exchange, physician-patient relations, and power dependence in social networks.*

Personal Prologue

Growing up in Texas may have influenced me as much as coming of age during the Sixties, but both factors contributed significantly to the making of a sociologist interested in the topics of power and justice. Other more personal factors set the stage. I come from a solidly middle-class background, am one of four children, and have a twin brother—ten minutes older. My father and mother, both raised in Texas, were the first to become college-educated in their families. They met as undergraduates at Texas A&I University in Kingsville just before World War II and married secretly during my dad's officer candidate training for the navy at Columbia in 1942. Dad left on the Indiana for the Sea of Japan, and mother traveled to find work in San Francisco to await his return. Three months turned into three years. His ship finally returned, passing under the Golden Gate Bridge in 1945.

My twin brother and I were born in 1946 in Raton, New Mexico. My father, the former naval officer, gave up his dream of owning a ranch in Texas and took a job with the Bureau of Reclamation (Department of the Interior) as a soils scientist, moving from Texas to New Mexico, Colorado, Oklahoma, and then Austin, where Ken (my twin) and I entered the third grade. Gregg and Donna were added to the family in Oklahoma City in 1951 and 1953, respectively. Gregg's claim to fame was setting the neighbor's backyard on fire at the age of three. Donna was "the baby" of the family — still is.

Both sets of grandparents lived on farms, one set on a large citrus farm in Raymondville, Texas (the "valley"), the other on a small family farm in Hondo, not far from San Antonio but much closer to Quihi, a town of two hundred — except on Saturday night when the population rises to four hundred, filling the local dance halls. Summer visits to the farm provided a window into the Texas version of rural America that was the norm then — at least for those living outside of the suburbs I called home. My cousins (almost all male) taught me to drink beer, line dance, and shoot rabbits, deer, and rattlesnakes. They were cowboys and proud of it.

Two things seemed to matter most to those who framed my world as a child: education and religion, in that order. Pursuing the former led me to give up the latter during my college years, but some of the values I retain were strongly influenced by the Texas version of Lutheranism I was exposed to — a blend of social justice, social responsibility, and more than a touch of anti-authoritarianism. Growing up in Texas in the late fifties and early sixties meant that racism was a part of everyday life. Schools were primarily segregated by neighborhood. Employment opportunities were stratified clearly by race, class, and gender, in that order. The day laborers were Hispanic, the "help" was typically black, and the women who "worked" either typed or taught — I learned to do both. In fact, as a young girl I was paid to do both during the summers. I became president of the Future Teachers of America at Travis High and established a Saturday morning program to teach Hispanic five- and six-year-olds English before they entered kindergarten, a novel idea at the time. Summers also included typing the names and addresses of policyholders for the State Board of Insurance, the only job I, the valedictorian, and my best friend, the salutatorian, were able to get before entering college. (To my knowledge Ken was never given a typing test that summer.)

Traveling with a youth group by bus in the ninth grade from Austin to Miami in 1960 meant seeing the Deep South for what it was in person for the first time — separate doors, separate lines, separate bathrooms, separated seats, separate water fountains, deeply separated lives: some in the group more equal than others everywhere we went. Stopping at the church where Martin Luther King Jr. preached was the highlight of the trip for me and the rest of this group of young Texans, steeped in the teachings of Martin Luther as we were. I mark this trip as the most important step in my educational journey, with leaving the state of Texas for college being only the second most important. Close my eyes today and I see many of the images of that trip in vivid detail — nothing faded.

High school went quickly. Growing up in South Austin (now central Austin) was uncomplicated. School was easy — after all, they only offered three languages, two really: Spanish was not a foreign language in Texas. Latin was. I took Latin. Calculus was not offered, and the only equivalents to advanced placement classes were the hard science labs, which only about 10 percent of each grade ever took. Vocational education was important for most. I had to choose whether to join Future Teachers of America or Future Farmers of America. That was easy, too. My cousins would not have permitted the latter.

High school guidance counselors put students into two categories: college bound or not. If lucky enough to fall into the first category, you had only three options — (1) University of Texas at Austin, for many, (2) Rice University, for the mathematically talented, primarily male students, and (3) Southwest Texas State University or Texas State University at San Marcos for the rest — because the dean of "girls" had no catalogs for schools outside "the state." No one had ever asked for one. Fortunately for me, my dad's eldest sister had married a Lutheran minister and left the fold to move to California early in her life. Her two daughters ended up at Pomona College. Aunt Elvira had moved to San Jose from Southern California in the late fifties. She mailed my dad a course catalog and two applications to Stanford University in the fall of 1963 with a note attached: "The twins might want to apply here." They did, and so did Gregg and Donna several years later. All four of us graduated from "The Farm" (a.k.a. Stanford University).

My dad may not really remember the exact day he said you should leave the state of Texas to get educated. I do. He meant it, and fifty years later he views it as the best piece of advice he ever gave his kids. But this was not a popular piece of advice in the mid-Sixties. Most of my parents' friends warned that "the twins," if sent to California, might get involved with sex and drugs — or was it drugs and sex (it was California after all, not Texas). It was 1964. Kennedy had just been assassinated, Lyndon Johnson, a real Texan, had taken over, and the Viet Nam War was in full bloom. The early antiwar activities seemed to begin and end in California. Ken had joined the Naval Reserve Officers Training Corps to secure a scholarship to study engineering at Stanford. This enabled him to avoid Viet Nam by serving as an officer in Admiral Rickover's nuclear power program in Washington, DC, for five years before returning to Stanford for an MBA. My scholarships came from the Elks Club, the Daughters of the American Revolution, and Stanford's early efforts at "need blind" admissions. I ended up choosing teaching over typing and staying at Stanford to earn an MA (1970) and a PhD (1973) after completing my undergraduate degree in 1968. Living in California in the Sixties, among other factors, led me to sociology in pursuit of an understanding of the world I found myself in, like most students who were drawn to the social sciences then. What I found has sustained my interest for almost four decades.

Sociology and Social Reality

The brand of sociology I studied as an undergraduate seemed untouched by the complex political reality of the Sixties — proudly so. It was the early days of Stanford's bold programmatic move to create a department dedicated to the development of a real science of society (with the emphasis on "science"). Emboldened by the works of Karl Popper, Carl Hempel, and Thomas Kuhn, the Stanford "Big Five" — Joseph Berger, Bernard Cohen, Sanford Dornbusch, W. Richard Scott, and Morris Zelditch — together with many coconspirators along the way, such as Bo Anderson and S. Frank Camilleri, developed a range of formal, often mathematical, theories of social processes, including primarily status and authority relations and, subsequently, an early effort to analyze distributive justice. Joining them were John Meyer, a political sociologist (one who has always marched to the tune of his own drummer) from Columbia University and, in 1970, Michael Hannan, a student of Hubert M. Blalock from the University of North Carolina at Chapel Hill, who subsequently developed the subfield of organizational ecology. In addition, Nancy Tuma joined the faculty (originally also part-time at SRI). She was a methodologist who, with Hannan, developed important applications of event history analysis in sociology.

But Stanford in the Sixties, like many universities at that time, was an uneasy mix of radical politics and the natural conservatism of educational institutions (not to mention the political conservatism of many of its private donors). David

Harris was elected student body president in 1964, my freshman year. He became not only the campus spokesman for the antiwar movement but a public figure in the movement as well, subsequently married for a time to antiwar activist Joan Baez. In a widely publicized event, Harris's head was shaved in the fountain across from the campus bookstore by fraternity members who did not favor his antiwar politics or his "hippie" appearance. The university struggled with its role as a protector of civil liberties and free speech. It still does.

Campus politics entered an unprecedented period of ferment, and student activism spread as youth across California and the nation joined in what became perhaps the second strongest social movement of the time, building on the previous successes of the civil rights movement of the early Sixties and fanning the embers of the early feminist movement, marked for most of us by the publication of Betty Friedan's *Feminist Mystique*—a book that grew in popularity at the grassroots level more quickly than on the national scene. I, like many other females across the nation, joined a consciousness-raising group in the community—a group of women cross-cutting age and experience boundaries—to reexamine the meaning of being female in our society. Fortunately for me, growing up as the female half of a male-female twin dyad had already seared into my consciousness the many daily forms of differential treatment by gender, both small and large. It also meant that I had developed an extremely well-honed sense of fairness and equitable treatment—a fact that revealed itself most vividly in the form of a doctoral dissertation aptly titled, "The Activation of Equity Processes" (1973).

Scholars have written thousands of pages on the subject of the social movements of the Sixties, many sociologists and political scientists touched by that era. For me, the journey was more personal than professional. Teach-ins became a routine part of my college education, if not part of my formal training in sociology. The Viet Nam War ended abruptly as the tide of public opinion slowly shifted against what was ultimately viewed in retrospect as an "unwinnable" war. By this time, Lyndon Johnson had declared unexpectedly that he would not seek reelection, America had rejoiced in Neil Armstrong's "giant step for mankind," and Nixon had been elected for a second term. Along the way came the Cambodian War, more antiwar rallies, teach-ins, and confrontations on campuses across the country, some deadly. The National Guard and local police were called in to "protect" campus property. For me, the sight of police in riot gear lining the street in front of the quad marked a low point in the campus management of student antiwar activities.

Leaving a late-night study group and biking up the main campus thoroughfare near Encina, I encountered police nightsticks smashing in several windshields of cars trying to exit the campus. It was not clear whose property really needed protection that night. The riots at People's Park on the University of California, Berkeley, campus had set the tone in California, and Ronald Reagan was in charge of the state. Subsequently, during the Cambodian crisis, antiwar protesters set the attic of Encina Hall on fire, assuming the building held important administrative records for the university. Such records had long been removed. Instead, on the fourth floor of Encina was the Laboratory for Social Research and other research offices occupied by sociologists.

My officemate, Jean Warren, and I were called by graduate student friends and told that the building in which our office was located was on fire. That evening, the first undergraduates for my dissertation experiment had been scheduled to arrive at 7 p.m. Despite their persistence, the police and firefighters turned them away as they tried to make their scheduled appointments on the fourth floor of Encina. The laboratory in which my study was to be conducted did not burn but was damaged by smoke and fire. It was several months before I was able to actually collect my data in a makeshift lab in the Graduate School of Business. The dean at Stanford, a psychologist, was not able to get the psychology department faculty to open their labs for temporary use, even though many of the labs were unoccupied at that time. The dean of the Graduate School of Business was more accommodating.

Finishing data collection was essential since I had accepted a position at the University of Washington in the fall and had to complete the dissertation during my first year as an acting assistant professor. This was not the only way in which antiwar protests affected the lives of students and faculty at Stanford in the early seventies. Some faculty sympathizers were denied tenure. Other faculty left voluntarily. It was a time of unrest on a number of levels, and universities nationwide had difficulty managing the task of protecting property and also allowing peaceful civil protest and free speech. That same tension exists today but for entirely different reasons.

Just as on the national scene, politics and science primarily remained separate endeavors for me during the next decade. Coming of age professionally in the Sixties as a sociologist marked my studies in subtle but clear ways. I began with a focus on distributive justice and fairness and later moved to the topic of social power as a result of a long and fruitful collaboration with Richard Emerson (power-dependence theory) for a decade at the University of Washington, where

I began my career and served on the faculty for twenty-three years before moving back into the world of private universities. Little of my work has not focused fundamentally on issues of power or justice during the course of the past thirty years. I was often questioned early in my career about my orientation to feminism. This was not a difficult question to answer. For me, issues of power and justice were at the very heart of all of the social movements of the Sixties. I needed to understand not only the microlevel social interactions that embodied power inequalities but also the broader social, economic, and political dimensions of these processes in order to comprehend the social changes that enveloped me.

Power and inequality remain at the center of local and world politics in the age of global interdependence. The tools I learned as a sociologist, both theoretically and methodologically, were essential in my quest for understanding. Who or what determines who has access to which sources of power? Why does inequality persist? How do power shifts occur? How does social position determine access to resources and hence one's life chances? Who determines what is just? How is distributive justice assessed, by whom, and on what basis? Is redistribution possible, and if not, why not? How is a just society defined? Can a more just society be created? How and with what costs? In short, deep sociological questions regarding inequality reside at the root of my commitment to sociology as a profession — and, most likely, for many of my colleagues who were also compelled to enter the social sciences by the events of the Sixties.

Later in my personal life I came to be involved in causes that were rooted in the types of social justice commitments that were derived from the Sixties for many of our generation. As a young assistant professor I was married to a social activist and eventually had two sons, one born the year I received tenure (1978) — and the reason I remember the year so vividly — the other born in 1983 just after the university had finally created a maternity leave policy (based on disability law, oddly enough). During this time I was part of a community organization that was deeply involved in social justice causes, providing soup kitchens and shelters for the homeless as well as refuge for undocumented aliens, especially those deemed politically unacceptable for asylum during the Reagan era. Salvadoran and Guatemalan refugees became a part of my life for a while. When my son Brian entered kindergarten at five, he often escorted several refugee children from the school bus they rode on every day to their classroom in his elementary school in Seattle. Twenty years later, Brian is fluent in Spanish and is studying refugee resettlement, labor migration, and economic development at Oxford.

I sense in the current climate among undergraduates and graduate students a return to some of the same questions that motivated me to enter the social sciences under different times and circumstances. This is a good sign. And some in this generation are likely to demand the kind of relevance of sociological inquiry that we had hoped for during the Viet Nam era. What we got was a broad social scientific training that required a deeper theoretical analysis of social, political, and economic factors than was common at the time among those trained in fields more closely linked to social work when the distinction between "basic" and "applied" social science was much greater than it is today. Simple answers to complex questions rarely ever lead to good social policy. In addition, we were required to put our ideas to scientific test. Empirical examination is an essential requirement for a social science that aspires to provide insights into "how the world works," a phrase I often heard Herb Costner use in his methodology classes at the University of Washington where we were colleagues for more than two decades.

The Legacy of My Training as a Sociologist

The Stanford stamp that came with my graduate training remains important in my work today. It demands that sociological inquiry proceed from deep theoretical understanding of social reality. General theories of social processes and social structures are required if we are to come to understand the social realities that make up the worlds we occupy. This, in my view, is even more important as we confront the complexities of a vastly interconnected set of social, cultural, economic, and political systems. One way to do this is to take a slice of social reality and try to theorize about it in ways that make analysis of various settings possible. This is the value, for example, of the Emersonian approach to power-dependence relations that I came to adopt and extend in my own work over the years in collaboration not only with Richard Emerson (at the University of Washington) but also with a number of other student collaborators and colleagues over the years, including Toshio Yamagishi, Mary R. Gillmore, Karen Hegtvedt, Joseph Whitmeyer, Jodi O'Brien, Eric Rice, Coye Cheshire, Robin Cooper, and Alexandra Gerbasi. There are certainly other valuable theoretical approaches, many of them reflected in the biographies of other sociological theorists in this volume who were trained in different modes of inquiry.

As an example of theoretical work that alters the way we see the world, power-dependence theory is an excellent case study. Prior to Emerson's work on this topic in the early Sixties, power had been seen primarily as an attribute of an actor or a social unit. Political scientists at that time were intent on determining who had power when. Was it Congress? Was it the executive branch? Who had power in the legislature? Which president had more power? Emerson's theoretical work shifted the unit of analysis from the actor or some other social unit to the relationship between the parties involved. Power was, in his view, relational. An actor, A, was said to have power over another actor, B, if B was dependent on A for something of value and had few, if any, alternatives. This relational conception of power opened the way for structural inquiries into the sources of power, such as the position one held in a network of social relations or alternative exchange opportunities. This work led to the cottage industry of analyses of exchange networks. In addition, the conception that dependence was directly linked to power in a relationship opened inquiry into the way in which power could be more balanced in a relationship by, for example, finding alternative sources of valued resources or by reducing one's own dependence on another by changing what one values. Applications of power-dependence theory to organizations, individuals in relationships of all kinds (parental, familial, friendships, dating and romantic relations, economic relations, etc.), and even to nation states have opened new areas of inquiry. Because of the fruitfulness of this theoretical perspective, Emerson's original formulation, published in 1964, earned the label, "citation classic," in the 1980s. This is only one example of the kind of generalizing theoretical work that provides broad insights into social reality, cutting across time and place.

My years at the University of Washington (1972–95) were as formative of my professional career as was my earlier graduate training at Stanford. There are a number of significant ways in which my work at the University of Washington, especially early in my career, served to amplify and extend the training I had received as a graduate student. First, many of the faculty at the University of Washington had a similarly positivistic orientation to sociology, believing as did others at that time that sociologists were primarily engaged in the complex task of building a "science of society." The emphasis was not only on science as a perspective but also on standard methods of scientific inquiry and the development of new statistical methods and formal models.

To facilitate this work there were a number of faculty members at the University of Washington who were at the forefront of the development of methodologies for analyzing and interpreting data. Perhaps the two best known for this were Hubert M. Blalock and Herbert L. Costner (and, much later, Edgar Borgatta who joined the faculty in the eighties). Blalock and Costner were not only innovative in their use of methods, but they were also excellent teachers who had a significant impact for several decades on the quantitative training of graduate students in sociology, as well as in some of the allied social sciences. What distinguished both of these scholars, however, was that their craft was not divorced from deeply theoretical concerns and they admonished cohort after cohort of graduate students to conduct "theoretically informed" research. For Blalock the theoretical model usually consisted of some form of causal model, often quite complex. For Costner, it was often a much simpler model since he placed greater emphasis on parsimony.

This latter emphasis was consonant with the more theoretical training I had received at Stanford. To build my research skills I often audited classes taught by Blalock and Costner as a new assistant professor. I was not unique in this respect. Over the years a number of junior faculty members who joined the Department of Sociology at the University of Washington in the seventies were mentored in methodology by Blalock and Costner. What I appreciated most during this time of my career was the degree to which many of the faculty at the University of Washington at that time felt a part of a larger collective effort to produce a theoretically informed, methodologically sophisticated brand of sociological inquiry, a legacy of an earlier generation of sociologists that had created the department in the shadow of the University of Chicago. There were exceptions to this orientation, of course, but the common purpose was a boon to the careers of those who occupied Savery Hall in the seventies and eighties.

My UW colleagues, beginning with a number of social psychologists Philip Blumstein, Robert L. Burgess, Richard Emerson, Robert K. Leik, Frank Miyamoto, and David Schmitt—provided me with the environment to continue to develop my central interests in social psychology in a collaborative and very supportive environment. Other significant faculty members in the early days of my career were Hubert M. Blalock, Edgar Borgatta, Fred Campbell, Herbert Costner, Ed Gross, Pete Guest, Michael Hechter, Otto Larsen, Jim McCann, Sam Preston, Guenther Roth, Pepper Schwartz, Rodney Stark, and Wesley Wager. To many of them I owe a debt of gratitude for allowing me as a sociologist to pursue my own version of the field with little interference and often with encouragement.

Back to the Sixties

The editors of this volume refer to the group of theorists, the graduates of 1968, as part of the "disobedient generation." There is some truth in this label for me, but the disobedience, if that is what it was, took much more subtle forms. It was not the kind of disobedience that led to jail time in the Sixties or a lifestyle that marked me as particularly different in most ways from the generations that had preceded me, with one major exception. That exception was the choice to pursue, as a female, a lifetime career as a professor, something that was much rarer than I had been led to believe while I was somewhat cloistered in graduate school. The rebellion inside me that took hold of my professional life after the Sixties propelled me to make it in a profession that was and to some extent remains dominated by males, despite the fact that now over half of the new PhD's in any year in sociology are obtained by females.[1] This rebellion, fueled by the women's movement that took form in the Sixties and led to the first wave of affirmative action hiring for women and minorities in 1972, continues today with much less progress to show than I had ever dreamed possible. In 1972, there were three junior faculty hired at the University of Washington — one black male and two white females. There were three white men hired with tenure that same year. I somehow thought that once the gate was opened the flood would occur and the barriers mysteriously would be forever lifted.[2]

Well, for a sociologist, that was incredibly naive thinking. I had underestimated the extent to which the institutions themselves had become gendered from top to bottom, and not only because the occupants of most positions of power were male. The expectations for success were gendered. The expectations for teaching had been gendered, and the expectations of reviewers and even many university administrators, not to mention colleagues, were subtly if not blatantly gendered. One of my early students once claimed that she was shocked to find out that I was a professor. In her mind I had to be a teaching assistant. There

1. If I recall correctly, this number was at least 30 percent even when I completed my doctoral degree in sociology in 1973. Thus the graduate cohorts included many more females than were ever reflected on the faculties of most major universities at that time.
2. To bring the record up to date, at Stanford University in 2003, there was only one female full professor in the chemistry department, who was hired in the early 1970s, and only one full professor of economics, recently hired, who is female; the other one retired recently. There are no female full professors in statistics. Progress is slow.

was no category in her head for female professor. She had never had one. Come to think of it I had only had three female professors in four years as an undergraduate at Stanford. I still remember who they were: Eleanor Maccoby, a psychologist; Louise Spindler who taught anthropology jointly with her husband George Spindler, though he gave most of the lectures, and Mary Sunseri, a calculus professor who taught introductory calculus for almost four decades to legions of undergraduates. I had the same problem at the library when I asked for a faculty carrel. The librarian vehemently refused to give me an application since I had no ID with me and there was "no way" I could be faculty. There was no category for female faculty in her head either. (I later acquired a faculty carrel by written application.) The same was true of the parking attendant in the faculty parking lot where I tried to park on a daily basis and the faculty club where I quit trying to find food after awhile despite the spectacular view of the Cascades . . . and so on.

At one of the prestigious East Coast institutions where I was interviewed the year I went on the job market I was told very earnestly by the department chair that they would "consider hiring me and if I worked out in six years they would consider hiring another one." The hiring model reflected in this comment may be closer to reality than we would like to admit, one every six years or so. He also indicated that I was a more appropriate role model than the first two women they had interviewed for the assistant professorship because they were too old. Needless to say the decision to accept the offer at the University of Washington was an easy one in this context. There would be two of us on the faculty. Pepper Schwartz and I remain close friends today as a result of having survived in the trenches together.

Subsequently, I was the first woman hired as a beginning assistant professor to be granted tenure in that department, and one of the first women to be tenured at the University of Washington. Pepper was the second. Since that time I have spent a large portion of my career mentoring, in particular, female graduate students and junior faculty, hoping to leverage my seniority and the influence that occasionally came my way at various institutions to make the path smoother and wider for them. In my view, this was not really a form of disobedience. It was a mission. It was a deeply formed individual commitment derived from the Sixties to personal freedom of choice for women in all domains — the choice of career, of lifestyle and orientation, of having or not having children, of choosing to marry or divorce or not, of choosing how to be a professor, breaking the mold that was narrowly gendered and highly constraining. I count this commitment as the major legacy in my own personal and professional life of having come of age in the Sixties.

And thirty years later we are still in the throes of debates about diversity, affirmative action, parental leaves, tenure clocks, and work-life balance in the university setting. In my view, universities have too often abdicated their role as cutting edge institutions charged with the fundamental task of paving the way for new forms of knowledge and new ways of doing things. If ideas can't manifest themselves in change in institutions of "higher" learning, where can they be transformative? Understanding this process of change (or the lack of it) and its determinants is even more important to me as a sociologist, as one who understands the nature of the social construction of reality. Fostering, in universities, a climate of change and innovation is critical. If the Sixties were about change and the transformation of society as we had come to know it, the nineties seem to have been about conservatism and preservation of the status quo. In the current world setting, post 9/11 as we call it, I am more concerned than ever, as a sociologist, that we will let our fears re-create for us worlds of the past, in which difference is defined as something to be feared and in which common purpose is hard to find.

Sociology in the new century should return to the basic study of topics such as power and justice. Global social and political dynamics beg us to understand power globally and to figure out how it is used or constrained in new ways as a result. Inequality is also a global (as well as a local) reality. How should we think about global inequality? What justice principles apply, with what social and political consequences? The sociology I came to know as a graduate student and developed over my career still moves me to pursue fundamental questions of power and justice. For me there never was much distance between my interests in abstract, sometimes formal theories of power and inequality and the world in which these processes reveal themselves daily. Other theorists seem to view abstract theories as removed from reality or as inhabiting a "rarefied intellectual atmosphere," as one theorist put it. That depends on perspective. It takes many different tools to understand fully the complex social reality we study as sociologists. Debates about "one true method of analysis" or form of theorizing have never been persuasive to me. Sociology as a theoretical and empirical project is multifaceted, a major collaborative project that requires the cooperation of the best minds we can produce. Each of us may have a hand on a different piece of the elephant. If that is the case, we will need to continue to support different forms of inquiry and theorizing, even if they are not what we have been trained to do, and we will need to provide room for new hybrid forms of inquiry that supercede our own intellectual commitments and styles of work.

Concluding Remarks

It is often said that World War II put an indelible stamp on the social scientists trained just after the war, many on the GI Bill. These sociologists studied obedience to authority, conformity, nationalism, loyalty, social solidarity, immigration, the politics of consent, democratic versus authoritarian forms of governance, labor movements, the family, and religion. In contrast, the sociologists produced during the Viet Nam War era focused on social movements, nonconformity, the politics of dissent, oppositional parties, social inequality, comparative politics, divorce, and social change.

The next generation of scholars coming of age in a distinctly global era, now shadowed by terrorism and the U.S.-led war on Iraq, will have an even bigger task than these two large generations of sociologists marked so deeply by two very different wars. Hopefully, the sociological tools we have inherited and passed on, often passionately, during our careers will be up to the task.

Selected References and Relevant Work

Cook, Karen S. 1973. "The Activation of Equity Processes." PhD diss. Stanford University, Stanford, CA.

———. 1977. "Exchange and Power in Networks of Interorganizational Relations." *Sociological Quarterly* 18:62–82.

Cook, Karen S., and Robin M. Cooper. 2003. "Experimental Studies of Cooperation, Trust and Social Exchange." Pp. 277–333 in *Trust, Reciprocity and Gains from Association: Interdisciplinary Lessons from Experimental Research*, edited by Elinor Ostrom and James Walker. Trust Series. New York: Russell Sage Foundation.

Cook, Karen S., and Richard M. Emerson. 1978. "Power, Equity and Commitment in Exchange Networks." *American Sociological Review* 43:721–39.

———. 1987. *Social Exchange Theory*. Newbury Park, CA: Sage Publications.

Cook, Karen S., Richard M. Emerson, Mary R. Gillmore, and Toshio Yamagishi. 1983. "The Distribution of Power in Exchange Networks: Theory and Experimental Results." *American Journal of Sociology* 89:275–305.

Cook, Karen S., and Karen A. Hegtvedt. 1983. "Distributive Justice, Equity and Equality." *Annual Review of Sociology* 9:217–41.

Cook, Karen S., and Joseph Whitmeyer. 1992. "Exchange Theory and Network Analysis." *Annual Review of Sociology* 18:109–27.

Cook, Karen S., and Toshio Yamagishi. 1992. "Power in Exchange Networks: A Power-Dependence Formulation." *Social Networks* 14:245–65.

Emerson, Richard. 1962. "Power-Dependence Relations." *American Sociological Review* 27:31–41.

———. 1964. "Power-Dependence Relations: Two Experiments." *Sociometry* 27:282–98.

———. 1972. "Exchange Theory, Part I: A Psychological Basis for Social Exchange." Pp. 38–57 in *Sociological Theories in Progress*, edited by Joseph Berger, Morris Zelditch Jr., and B. Anderson. Boston: Houghton Mifflin.

———. 1972. "Exchange Theory, Part II: Exchange Relations and Networks." Pp. 58–87 in *Sociological Theories in Progress*, edited by Joseph Berger, Morris Zelditch Jr., and B. Anderson. Boston: Houghton Mifflin.

Molm, Linda, and Karen S. Cook.1995. "Social Exchange Theory." Pp. 209–35 in *Sociological Perspectives on Social Psychology*, edited by Karen S. Cook, Gary Fine and James House. Needham, MA: Allyn & Bacon.

Yamagishi, Toshio, Mary R. Gillmore, and Karen S. Cook. 1988. "Network Connections and the Distribution of Power in Exchange Networks." *American Journal of Sociology* 93:833–51.

Life in the Cold

John Hall was born near Manchester in 1949. His background made him familiar with "Manchestertum," that is, the provincial world, based on the cotton industry, of liberal middle-class politics and culture. But for family reasons he was educated in the south of England in the "public schools," total institutions in Goffman's sense. He studied modern history at Oxford, becoming attracted by 1970 to the potentials of historical sociology opened by Barrington Moore. An MA in the United States was followed by a doctorate at the London School of Economics and Political Science (LSE). Clarity to his intellectual life came in the mid-1970s when working at the LSE with Ernest Gellner and Michael Mann. Accidental circumstances took him to Harvard in the mid-1980s and to McGill in the 1990s, where he remains today.

I suspect that my British background might make this memoir stand somewhat apart from the others that comprise this volume. For one thing, "the Sixties" were rather different in Britain than in the United States. This is not difficult to explain, nor is it especially problematical. But something deeper and altogether more personal is involved. I have come to feel, within myself, a rather distinctive psychological propensity caused by a very particular British upbringing. Hence a character at least half formed reacted to the Sixties rather than being completely molded by the events of that decade. This is not to suggest any sudden descent here into self-psychoanalysis, for the trope in question has clearly identifiable social roots. What is at issue is a habit of being a nonjoiner and a counterpuncher, of standing outside in the cold. Probably this role was thrust on me, albeit I more or less choose it willingly now—for the opportunities it provides more or less balance the costs that it imposes. Still, the personal does affect my views of the political, understood in the broadest sense. Differently put, where some who rebel then establish a new order, I have tended to remain ill at ease, continually kicking against the pricks. The extent to which this is a dominant or even a relevant consideration is for the reader to judge—for writing about oneself is inherently distasteful, tending always to justification rather than truth.

Class Queasiness

It was and is the case that Britain is dominated by class in a more complete manner than is the United States, despite the prevalence of structures of social inequality within the world's Leviathan. Money can take you to the top more easily and more quickly in America than it can in Britain, a far more conservative society in which manners retain some power to create social distinction. An Arnold Schwarzenegger could not gain high office in the United Kingdom, albeit such exclusion is perhaps not wholly to be celebrated. What concerns me here is an odd, at times ugly, detail of Britain's class system in action, namely, the fate of those who are in but not of (or sometimes of but not in) the higher classes. What is at issue may as well be called the Orwell syndrome.

In a famous essay, Orwell described his experience of being a scholarship boy at a private elementary school, preparing, in fact, for admission to Eton—the foremost of all "public" (i.e., elite and private) secondary schools. Such schools were not completely centered on academic achievement, but a good academic reputation did gain them pupils and so ensure viability. Hence, poor but bright students were sometimes admitted so that their academic achievements could boost the prestige of the school as a whole. It was easy to discipline such boys— as Orwell, who was one of them, made clear. All that a teacher had to do was to expose the poverty of the scholarship boy to ensure the scorn of his fellows. The impact of stigmatization was enormous. British private schools are archetypical total institutions in Goffman's terms, in largest part because they are to a very great extent run by the students rather than by the teachers.[1] The in-but-not-of status certainly made Orwell a loner whose populism could not hide the fact that his primary emotion was that of hatred of his own class. And any peculiarities of

---

1. The power of these schools is brilliantly captured in William Trevor's *The Old Boys*, a novel that shows middle aged men effectively still at the mercy of their school experiences.

Orwell's case should not hide the fact that a pattern of behavior is at here at work. My guess is that this syndrome is present in Perry Anderson, perhaps made ill at ease at Eton by his Irish background and certainly, thereafter, driven far more by dislike of the British upper class than by love for the working class—although surely admiration at the very least ought to be present, given his allegiance to Marxism. More generally, it is not at all ridiculous to see this as the background for the Leftist intellectuals who spied for the Soviet Union. They were very much in but not of, with mutually reinforcing cycles of exclusion/reaction to exclusion leading to a world of brilliant, homosexual Leftists whose politics cannot be understood without an appreciation of their loathing for the establishment.

Even if some part of this is exaggerated and other parts merely speculative, I can bear witness to the veracity of its essence. My own queasiness within the class system resulted from being sent to private schools from a family riven by conflicts whose salience became central with ever greater financial decline. My father owned a small factory in Manchester, specializing in the dying of fancy yarns. While it was perhaps impossible to resist the decline of the cotton industry, my father's propensity for spending money certainly did not help with anything like capital reinvestment. He was representative of his time in cultural terms in a multitude of ways. He was educated in a genuine provincial world—chess playing, music loving, militantly secular, and rationalist. Importantly, this culture changed over time in one vital matter: the love of free trade on which Manchester had been founded was replaced by loyalty to the empire, not surprisingly since the freer the trade the more likely was the decline of cotton. This change was symbolized at home in the replacement of the liberal *Manchester Guardian* by the conservative *Daily Telegraph*. If the rationalism of this social world appeals to me still, it is only fair to say that it had another side. Liberalism was dogmatic, so sure of itself as to wish to exclude others. This mattered in my family, for my father married a penniless Catholic of Irish background, thereby ensuring much division at the heart of the family. But conflict only came to the fore during my school years. Money papers over cracks, and its presence ensured relative mental wholeness and unity for my elder brother. But an in-but-not-of status became ever more powerfully present in my own case. The paying of school fees was a near impossibility, and I knew that my mother and sisters at home endured real poverty—scraping and pinching, living off dreadful food or the scraps of others.

In one sense I am very grateful for this background. I realized early on that I could rely on nothing, that my fate was my own. Still, much confusion did result. I worried about my family and certainly did not fit into the easy certainties of the world of my schooling. It may be sensible to stress immediately the ambivalence involved in this sentiment, not least as it will continue to command attention. From one angle, there was a great deal to be said for criticism against the effortless ease of command bred by such "public" schools. From another angle, one wonders if rebellion was not fueled to some extent by envy. Whatever the case, family conflict was much increased by my trying—for inner direction led to good exam results—to get a school scholarship so as to ease the financial pressures on my family. The school was prepared to offer help, but my father wrote to my headmaster, undercutting me badly by saying that I was in effect making it up, that no help was needed. This was a formative moment, reinforced on many occasions and in many ways. My father ruled the family: he had the money and the power and the glory—in the sense that his standards of life, his fantasies of success, his refusal to curtail expensive tastes could not be challenged. I am quite sure that my long-term interest in states and in liberty, in domination and in the potential for curtailing it, feeds off these early experiences. On a minor note, this background made the ideas of Karl Popper an immediate and permanent part of my mental furniture. I read the first volume of *The Open Society and Its Enemies* on a train from school at age fourteen and was ready to absorb its message: no one has the right to be so certain about their ideas, everyone can benefit from criticism.

The Sixties

I gained a scholarship to Oxford when I was sixteen and arrived there after a year abroad—in North Africa and in Italy (to which country I owe everlasting gratitude since it provided my *education sentimentale*). The particular character of "the Sixties" in Britain can be explained immediately. Bluntly, there were limits to politicization. No one faced a draft that might get them killed in Southeast Asia, nor did they have the experience of a country being forced to face up to its racial scar. If these points distinguish it from the United States, equally important was Britain's difference from most European countries. British students were, and are, rigorously selected for higher education, making it almost impossible to fail once one has started. More egalitarian traditions in many European countries in combination with structural absurdities led to the overcrowding of classrooms and then to vicious exclusionary exam regimes—which, however, did nothing to prevent the overproduction of alienated lesser intelligentsia. If all this meant that real fuel for political mobilization was missing in Britain, this should not be taken to mean that political issues were not important. I remember famous demonstrations against Viet Nam (but not, I now sadly realize, against the Soviet invasion of Czechoslovakia) and against the racism encouraged by British politician Enoch Powell. Further, I went briefly to Paris in late May 1968 and was outraged by police repression but perhaps too much a British empiricist to feel comfortable with some of the revolutionary slogans of the moment. What was perhaps a natural allegiance to the Labour Party was, however, badly hurt in this period by disgust when Harold Wilson's government refused to allow East African Asians — placed there as part of an imperial policy of divide and rule and now facing ethnic cleansing — entry into the country despite their possession of British passports. Nonetheless, political action really was less intense, as I realized at the time when reading about students in Japan while participating in an occupation of a university administration building. While we took tea at night to the policemen forced to patrol outside the building, Japanese students were taking cannons to the top of Tokyo skyscrapers! But I experienced many of the cultural changes of the time. Differently put, I had a great deal of fun, going to London on weekends, wandering along King's Road, with passages in my life permanently marked by the music of the time.

Nonetheless, I remained very ill at ease. Oxford and Cambridge had, and to some extent still have, an air about them of finishing schools for the upper classes. Students from private schools were vastly overrepresented, and they set the tone in every way. The loud and braying voices of the English establishment, supremely confident and assured, could be heard at all times. Working hard was frowned on, for only effortless brilliance gained status. This did not suit me at all, and I now realize I would have been better served by going, say, to the London School of Economics. This was especially true because I studied history — and was too young and uncertain to switch to "Modern Greats," that is, to philosophy, politics, and economics, which might have suited me better. For history at Oxford was deeply conservative in intellectual terms, a record of continuity to be learned rather than of social processes to be explained. There was an exception to this, namely, the group of historians led by Christopher Hill, which sought to explain, in Marxist terms and with fabulous scholarship, the revolutionary politics of seventeenth-century England. Perhaps that made me open to Barrington Moore's *The Social Origins of Dictatorship and Democracy*. Here was a book that was at once historically informed, politically engaged, and concerned with utterly vital issues. My continuing but slightly troubled love for intellectual life was renewed and expanded, and I decided to go to the United States for postgraduate study, and in sociology rather than in history.

The two years I spent at Pennsylvania State University—deliberately chosen in preference to Chicago so as to avoid any American equivalent to Oxbridge—were both happy and productive. For one thing, there were inspiring teachers, notably David Westby in political sociology, and Carolyn and Muzafer Sherif in social psychology. For another, there was a real sense of political and social movement, albeit I arrived at the time when progressive movements were being curtailed. A long summer working for Model Cities in New York vastly expanded my horizons, but it also made apparent to me the horrible efficacy of two of the tricks that sustained the Nixon administration. First, the ending of the draft undercut the student movement, even given the invasion of Cambodia. Structures mattered quite as much as ideology, making it quite likely that an alliance of the student Left and of those facing discrimination would fail to gel. Second, it was all too easy to recognize the poison injected into American life by the way in which he played the ethnic card. Here was a prime example of "divide and rule" policies, a lesson in the immorality of power. I think these were early core insights into political sociology, early appreciations of the realities of power. And there was one further insight, remembered now because it led to some fierce arguments at the time. The neo-Marxist idea that the United States somehow needed Viet Nam, or some sort of hegemony in mainland Southeast Asia, was made nonsensical for me by even a naive consideration of basic facts of political economy. Perhaps it was a British background that made me feel so strongly that empires do not pay and that intervention was to be avoided—not because it is always necessarily wrong but nearly always, given the absence of means to translate desire into practice.

Despite learning a great deal, I was still not fully formed intellectually, with the debt to Moore still not quite repaid. Of course, the spirit of the time and a background in history made me critical of the consensual theories of Talcott Parsons and, consequently, much concerned with forces of social change. But it was the classical problem of progressive politics in Britain, that of the relation of intellectuals to a social movement, that dominated my own work at the time. Even though I worked on the ideas of Oliver Wendell Holmes, John Dewey, and Thorstein Veblen, the distance between intellect and power in the United States was so great, and its historical social portfolio so very different, as to make my key question seem all but irrelevant in the United States. Accordingly, I went back to Europe for my doctoral work at the London School of Economics.

Crystallization

It may be useful to some readers of this volume to highlight dead ends rather than avenues easily found. In my own case, a rather detailed thesis on change and conflict within the English intelligentsia between 1900 and 1920 did not quite bring me to what I now regard as the central part of my intellectual interests. There was enormous enjoyment in working in archives and in thinking about the sociology of intellectuals. Still, it became increasingly clear that some of my subject matter had become the province of intellectual history. The point may best be made by thinking about Max Weber. Sociologists need now to be careful in what they say about our great German ancestor, given the level of contextual scholarship beginning to emerge about his life and times. The general point in question is, however, rather different. Just as some avenues of research close, so, too, do others open. Scholars need to be sensitive to where they are and to be flexible enough to change to take advantage of new opportunities.

Despite some ambivalence about my doctoral work, final crystallization of my own intellectual interests did take place while at the London School of Economics. For one thing, the school was marvelously exciting; social scientists spoke to each other outside their disciplines, and interest in immediate political and social questions went hand in hand with a concern for empirical evidence. For another, I discovered nothing less than my *maitre-à-penser* in Ernest Gellner—whose work and influence is now much on my mind because, a little to my surprise, I am currently writing his intellectual biography. I had attended very few lectures in Oxford, not atypically as the emphasis there was quite generally on the importance of independent research. But I had heard of Gellner because of his no-holds-barred attack on the complacency of Oxford linguistic philosophy in *Words and Things*, a book that launched his career when a controversy followed on the refusal of *Mind* to review it, and so went to listen to a lecture when I arrived. I was immediately and permanently hooked. For one thing, there was brilliance, laced with delicious irony that made me laugh out loud. Here was someone for whom great figures of social theory were live presences, not least because the vicissitudes of European modernity—for he came from Kafka's tricultural world—were ever-present realities. For another, there was utterly fantastic ambition, nothing less than the desire to explain the structural constraints of modernity and of the options of belief that it allowed us. Perhaps most important of all was a personal link. I certainly felt temperamentally very close to someone who was an outsider, who distrusted warm and cozy meaningful unities, who insisted that life is difficult and bereft of ultimate consolation. Paradoxically, this very loneliness was linked to the creation of something like a tribe of his own: he treated his friends, of all ages and persuasion, in the same manner—sending them postcards, making them drink too much, showing continuing interest in their careers and lives. Gellner made me feel it was vital to be concerned with the fate of what were then the three worlds of modernity and to have opinions about philosophy quite as much as about sociology. He opened the world to me, and finally made it possible to bring together in a coherent manner the seeds that had been planted when encountering Moore nearly a decade before.

The immediate way in which connection bore fruit was in a weekly seminar at the London School of Economics entitled Patterns of History. Gellner's intellectual range was as huge as his reputation, and this was becoming equally true of Michael Mann who very soon became a co-organizer of the seminar. This resulted in a wonderful moment of intellectual effervescence. If the quality of the speakers was dazzling, what mattered quite as much was the fact that the seminar was not particularly popular. On many occasions the three organizers would probe and question at length and would virtually always ask for a specialized reading list. All three of us ended up writing works of philosophic history in part as the result of this collaboration. I still rely on the scholars who appeared here— most notably on Patricia Crone, the incisiveness of whose mind has to be experienced to be fully appreciated.

A little can be said about the intellectual consequences or findings of this particular world. Weberian themes and discoveries dominated. The historical record simply could not be understood without reference to power, to the impact of states and the consequences of war. To argue along these lines was unpopular at the time: the early 1970s saw something of a peak of interest in Marxist ideas, and I remember all too clearly being attacked as a militarist for suggesting that Carl von Clausewitz, Otto Hintze, and Raymond Aron were major theorists whom sociologists ignored at their peril. An appreciation of the role of coercion in history was instinctively present in Gellner, and it contributed to his very particular version of liberalism. These concerns equally led me to write normatively about the chances of liberalism, and Michael Mann's most recent work moves in that direction as well. Nonetheless, Weberian positions were not, so to speak, swallowed whole. Resistance was shown to an element in Weber that was much exaggerated by Talcott Parsons and by some of those influenced by him, notably Clifford Geertz and Robert Bellah. Human beings were not mere concept fodder, caught in such elegant and complete ideological systems that social life could be studied as a text. For one thing, most ideologies are messy, replete with options of dissent — making it requisite to understand why a particular option has salience at any particular time. For another, it is often the case that ideologies change as the result of political events — as was so obviously the case in the division of Europe at the end of the Second World War. This is not to say for a moment that intellectuals and ideological power could not at times be wholly autonomous, but it was a reaction against the dreadfully sloppy idealism that tends to dominate social science.

Beyond this general *prise de position* lay something more particular. The central question for much of British political life from the 1960s was that of national decline. Attempts to explain this tended, not least in practical politics, to concentrate on the role of the working class. Thinkers on the Left often suggested that giving greater salience to corporatist institutions would allow for greater economic growth; politically more important were voices on the Right insisting that the powers achieved by the working class were in fact blocking the developmental path of the economy. The truth of the matter surely lay elsewhere. An interest in states was closely allied to a realization that the way in which elites behaved often mattered much more than popular social movements — whose characters anyway so very often resulted from the nature of the states with which they interacted. The disease of Great Britain resulted very much from institutionalizing the moment of its success — or, differently put, from taking victory in two world wars as equivalent to some *welthistorischer* endorsement of its particular social arrangements. The working class had responded to decline far more than it had created it. I have no doubt but that my recognition of this had a great deal to do with dislike for the English upper classes, so comfortable in the possession of a world that they never sought to change much — as did other European elites, traumatized by defeat in war. Little has happened in contemporary Britain to necessitate much change of analysis. How can Tony Blair's slavish and embarrassing support for George Bush be explained other than in terms of the continuity of the elite — determined now, as before, to play Greece to America's Rome, to hang on to the illusion of grandeur rather than to accept its place within Europe?

Moving to North America

Not everything — indeed perhaps not much — in life is planned. After writing my own philosophic history, I became deeply interested in the comparison, then much in vogue, between the purported liberal hegemonies of Britain at the end of the nineteenth century and that of the United States after 1945. This brought me for a period of research at the Center for European Studies at Harvard. It did not take long to see that this comparison between Britain and the United States was all nonsense. Then almost by accident, I was led to a job teaching in the marvelous social studies program at that university. There were great pleasures to be had there. For one thing, I found myself in the midst of what I consider to be great period of development within social science. A generation of Americans that had come to distrust their state, because of Viet Nam and the civil rights movement, had moved from a Parsonian world to something like Weberian sociology—much of which, perhaps sadly, ended up in political science rather than sociology. The intellectual quality of the scholarship involved—think, to name but a few examples, of the work of David Laitin, Theda Skocpol, Tim Mc-Daniel, and Peter Katzenstein—was stunning, involving at its best nothing less than a rethinking of some of the basic concepts of social science. For another, there was much amusement to be had as an outsider. At an intellectual level, attendance at an informal geopolitics dinner taught me much when senior professors (whom I rather admired) talked about what should be done to various countries, taking for granted that they had the right to rule the world. At the level of academic politics, I could observe the horrors of struggling for tenure without participating in the race—for I was on extended leave from a British university and had no intention of staying.

But in the end I did stay in North America. There was a mild push factor, namely, the desire to escape the dreadful atmosphere of British universities when faced by cuts imposed by Thatcherism. But a considerable pull was exerted by Montreal. One element at work was genuine multinationalism. I had seen, and saw much more in the 1990s, of the twentieth century's work in Europe—that is, of the homogenization so central to Gellner's theory of nationalism. Where, say, Prague was beautiful but was made dull by being wholly Czech, bereft of Jews, Germans, and Slovaks, Montreal was vibrant with genuine nations. Any single issue of a daily paper made one understand the stakes of nationalism. I have to own up to pleasure in being at least in part a member of a formerly dominant minority fallen now on harder times, trying to come to terms with a different status. This is probably good for someone of English background, given the high status often unfairly accorded to the English in many parts of the world. One thing for sure is that I would do everything in my power to try to help avoid another episode of forced homogenization in Quebec—wishing in this matter to go against the pattern of the historical record. Another consideration was the benefit of life within an advanced but wholly dependent country, akin to a mouse next to an elephant, because this allowed one to see the world more clearly than when in the imperial center. Above all, one could see two dimensions of American power. First, the sheer size of its market and its extraordinary proportion of world military spending makes one realize that one lives less in a globalized world than one dominated as never before by a single power. Second, all the public worry as to the putative breaking apart of the United States was mildly nonsensical. What mattered in the United States was that everyone — with the appalling exception of African Americans — had the right to an ethnicity, as long as it had little substantive content. An element of American power, at once awesome and troubling, remains its capacity to homogenize those who come to its shores.

Historical sociology has sometimes seemed to me — happily so, at least some of the time — relatively esoteric and otherworldly. But events can make one relevant. A British background really does suggest insight into the imperial pretensions of the United States. But it is especially good to reflect on British experience from abroad. One huge intellectual development has been the realization that Britain is one of the last of the European composite monarchies, thereby placing the national question at the heart of its political life. The overwhelming impression in this matter remains that of the continuing salience of Dean Acheson's remark that Britain had lost an empire and failed to find a role. Devolution has been half-hearted, and misgivings about national identity, so obvious in the face of European integration, now dominate what had long seemed the most settled of European countries. This in turn inevitably draws attention to the future of the European Union, about which much could be said. One wonders if Europe can at last become an Austro-Hungary that works. How can the interests of Scots and Catalans be managed when they — with 6 million citizens each — have no voice in European affairs, compared to the independent but far less populous Estonians? These issues are mentioned merely to indicate that history has been kind to me, lending me now as pressing a scholarly agenda as at any point in my life.

Last Analysis

It is hard to escape the pattern of one's past, although there is something like development in being able to recognize the character of the web within which one has been placed. There does seem to be continuity to my life and career in marginality. The fact that this could have been avoided — I could have stayed in Britain, deliberately chose Montreal—has made me realize when writing this chapter that I want and need this. In my heart of hearts I tend to think that deep social involvement distorts one's freedom of thought; equally, moving from one intellectual world to another can clarify issues, even extend one's career. But I should not exaggerate, nor do I wish to do so—for I distrust mythmaking in general and romanticizing intellectuals in particular. To value freedom of thought is to belong to that virtual community that seeks the truth. Obligations come with this, from the protection of intellectuals elsewhere to making sure that intellectual values have priority above the bureaucratic demands of modern university life. To my amazement, the latter consideration led me to becoming dean of arts for a period. This suggests a final point. This is some way from the rebellious attitudes, themselves relatively tame, with which my early life began. Can something similar be said of the other contributors to this volume?

PAOLO JEDLOWSKI

Becoming a Sociologist in Italy

Paolo Jedlowski was born in Milan in 1952. He is married and has two children. He currently lives in the countryside nearby Cosenza, in southern Italy, where he is professor of sociology at the University of Calabria and director of the Course of Political Science. He teaches sociology of communication at the University of Lugano, Switzerland, too. He is the current president of the group on "everyday life" within the Italian Sociological Association and also consultant and referee for several Italian scientific reviews and publishers. He wrote handbooks on the history of sociology and edited the Italian version of Blackwell's Dictionary of Twentieth-Century Social Thought. He is also editor of some Italian translations of works by Georg Simmel, Maurice Halbwachs, Alfred Schutz, and others. He is the author of books and articles concerning communicative practices in everyday life, modern culture, and collective memory, mostly from the perspective of a critical phenomenology. Some of his articles have been published in French, Spanish, and Portuguese; a few of them in English: "Simmel on Memory," in Georg Simmel and Contemporary Sociology, edited by M. Kaern, B. S. Phillips, R. S. Cohen; "The New Class on the Periphery," in Hidden Technocrats, edited by P. Heuberger and H. Kellner; and "Memory and Sociology," Time and Society, vol. 10, no. 1 (2001).

Autobiography is a suspect genre. Whoever is writing guarantees he is going to talk about himself and what is written aims to coincide with the writer's life, but every self has many faces, and every story establishes an order that is not the same as in life.

However, a sociologist should be familiar with the autobiographical. Being a man or a woman, white or black, speaking a certain language, belonging to a generation or another one are all important: the background, what one is or has lived, affects the most rarefied theory, too. Saying "I" is not a symptom of narcissism for a sociologist: on the contrary, it is the recognition of his own being placed in space and time, of the specificity of his experience, of the necessary partiality of his own point of view.

In spite of this and the undoubted importance of belonging to the '68ers generation, I have difficulty in saying clearly what binds me to those years. I would have the same difficulty in trying to say what Milan, where I was born and grew up, means to me. The presence of the past pervades in both cases and makes both an analytical reconstruction and specific memories difficult. Like my city, 1968 was to me a climate, an environment. In the following years, I do not think I ever talked about it with particular emphasis, unless to friends. Somehow, I have not considered the experience of 1968 as something to refer to publicly with a loud voice but, on the contrary, have treated it as an inner deeply personal fact. However, this is a fact shared with many people who, I think, having grown up in the decade of the movements, will recognize each other as having shared something profound.

In 1968 I was sixteen; I took part in the movements, mostly, during the early 1970s. In Italy, 1968, indeed, lasted a long time. Based on the youth countercultures of the 1960s, the decade of the movements in Italy was first an anti-authority movement of students who wanted change in school, family, and sexuality. That movement exploded in several cities, more or less contemporaneously with the events in France of "May '68." Television made its diffusion easy. Images of demonstrations and early confrontations with the police appeared everywhere. The following year, 1969, the student movement joined a wave of workers' struggles that had their center in the big industrial cities of the north. This was probably the most crucial year in Italy. The movement rapidly became political, giving rise to the birth of many extraparliamentary groups that declared themselves the vanguards of the proletarian revolution.

Actually, the bonds between this New Left and the working class and its traditional struggle were complex. On one hand, one of the theoretical souls of this New Left had its origin in the work done in the 1960s by intellectual groups close to labor unions and working parties (Raniero Panzieri, the "Quaderni Rossi"), which had reelaborated Marx in order to understand "neocapitalism." On the other hand, the New Left was very critical of the Italian Communist Party, which, in turn, showed a certain distrust toward the movement. Moreover, the workers whom the student movement intended to address were of a new kind: they were the "mass workmen," without any trade identity, who appeared with the birth of big factories in the 1960s. They were mostly young immigrants from the south of Italy, often without previous experience of labor unions.

The international context was also a source of conflict between New and Old Left: everybody opposed the American engagement in Viet Nam, but the events of 1968 in Prague were profoundly divisive. They gave rise to a separation within the Communist Party itself, which came true when those among its militants, who were closest to the movement, gave voice to their clear dissent against the Soviet Union.

I began at the University of Milan in 1971 as a student of philosophy. Almost simultaneously, I joined the "Gruppo Gramsci," which was one of the New Left groups. It included several workers and some employees, but, as in all the movement groups, mostly students and intellectuals. Among them were Luisa Passerini (later, one of the leading spirits of "oral history") in Turin and, in Milan, Giovanni Arrighi (now at the Fernand Braudel Center in Binghamton) and Romano Mádera (now professor of philosophy and a Jungian analyst). Almost all of the members of the group have had successful careers: as journalists, university professors, school teachers, advertising agents, and psychologists. However, success in a regular career generally came slowly; for a long time, we thought that to find a steady job meant to betray our oppositional stance. Moreover, nobody was willing to identify himself with a profession: our grounding and work style have always been a little "eccentric" and, in a certain way, "excessive" in comparison with any professional identity rigidly defined.

The group dissolved in 1974 and, thus, gave up the role of supposed vanguard of the working class, decisively and autocritically. Memory tends to synthesize processes, with some scenes becoming emblematic: I remember a university assembly of students and professors, all militant, during which, at a certain point, I felt like a stranger. It was as if the subjects we talked about — politics, classes, "correctly revolutionary" points of view — disguised group dynamics, inner passions, and individual needs that were hidden behind, and in a certain way betrayed by, those words.

After dissolving the group, we did not stop feeling avant-garde but turned to experimentation with new experience, study, and forms of life rather than political revolution. Some members of the group gravitated toward the most radical fringes of the movement. Hence, some of the leaders later ended up in prison, paying with those fringes and, in some cases, for them. But, most of us, myself included, turned our engagement to more cultural and "social" than clearly political activities. From a certain point of view, it was the second stage of 1968 and more open and experimental—or perhaps a return to origins, that is, to what 1968 had been before its hegemonization by Marxist-Leninist thought.

Obviously, a free and just society remained our point of reference, as did the desire to put ourselves on the side of the humble, the least, and the marginal and our pursuit of participatory democracy and participation in antifascist demonstrations. But daily life became our field of struggle. This does not mean that daily life had not been affected until then: in the most political years, too, the decade of the movements had always been, first and foremost, dedicated to experimentation with new forms of community and forms of behavior. But later we obeyed the slogan The Personal Is Political, and acknowledged that change should occur in and through face-to-face relationships and in consciousness. False consciousness became an enemy within ourselves, as much as hypocrisy had been the enemy in the bigoted Italy of our first rebel youths in the 1960s.

Feminism played an important role in this change of direction. Feeling and sexuality became not just a discovery but also a field of struggle. I remember that, together with other young people, I took part in the attempt to set up some groups of "male consciousness raising," like those that our female comrades were beginning to set up nearly everywhere in Italy. Looking back, that imitation of the women's initiative makes me smile. But somehow it is true that those years changed my, and our, way of being male. Certainly, it happened under the stimulus of women but followed in the same direction as our wish to reject the virility clichés that we had inherited from previous generations and that we felt failed to characterize us. In the following years, all this had a great influence on my way of being a husband and father. Saying how much feminism influenced me as a sociologist is more difficult. Many topics I worked out later in my books—such as, for example, the attention to lived experience or to everyday forms of reason—were widely dealt with by women: but I dealt with them by referring to philosophers and sociologists who are predominately male. In any case, the public presence of women and their research encouraged me. I have been a reader of their books and they have been readers of mine.

In 1968 we studied a lot. In the militant period, we read Marx (*Capital, The Grundrisse*: but I personally have always most loved the *Manuscripts of 1844*): we studied history and the different developments in Marxist thought, with a particular predilection, in my case at least, for the Frankfurt School (even today, I think that Adorno's *Minima Moralia* is one of the most beautiful books I have ever read). We studied the third world and the transformation of factory work. We read Nietzsche and Freud, but we were also impressed by Ronald David Laing, David Graham Cooper, and Franco Basaglia's antipsychiatry.

In some way, we began making sociology. I took part in a research project on supermarket workers; a comrade took part in research conducted by Alessandro Pizzorno on worker labor-unionism. By supporting the movement, in ingenious but concrete ways, we became experts on social research and communication.

We neglected literature during these years. When I was young, I had read a lot, but after becoming politically engaged, I stopped reading novels and poetry. Memory, again, synthesizes and, perhaps, betrays me a little: but I remember a woman, before university, who gave me *A Hundred Years of Solitude* by Gabriel María Marquez as a present. That gesture was a precious call to return. I started reading again, more or less, when my political group dissolved, and I have not stopped. Now, I think that a sociologist who knows nothing about literature (who cannot enjoy it and use it to refine his concepts of what life and human beings are) suffers from a handicap that is difficult to compensate for.

Another woman, with whom I was in love, got me into psychoanalysis. Rediscovering in memory the joined traces of love affairs and lessons learned is not so strange. One grows up and learns in friendship and love affairs. Those years provided a context in which making friends and falling in love was easy. We talked about life to each other with passion and tried to understand it and, where possible, to change it.

Some friendships matured in those years and have survived. I also met the woman who later would become my wife. Perhaps, this is the strongest bond to 1968 that I keep with me. Since we met at that time, 1968 is part of our story, even its origin. Being faithful to the spirit of 1968 always has meant to be very self-reflective and willing to verify and renew our relationship. But it has been the basis of a bond that has the dimension of intellectual cooperation, too. My wife took her degree with Theodor W. Adorno, in Germany, and since we have been together, each of us has read almost everything the other has written. I think I learned most sociology with her. We have changed over twenty-five years, but each of us represents an important thread of continuity for the other.

The university was of course important, too. There were many excellent professors at the Statale of Milan during the early 1970s. I was first attracted to Ludovico Geymonat and studied philosophy of science. I then attended the lectures of Enzo Paci. Paci was the most important and original scholar of Husserl's phenomenology in Italy. I asked him to become the supervisor of my thesis, but he was ill and died shortly afterward. I continued my work with the group of his students who gathered round *Aut Aut*, the review Paci had founded.

I do not remember exactly the reason why I chose Paci. I was mainly attracted by his *Diario Fenomenologico*, a little book telling the story of his discovery of phenomenology, which was interwoven with meetings, life fragments, and aesthetic and personal notes. I remember that one night I took the train to Pavia, to be under the red towers, which he talks about in a certain passage, at dawn. Initially, I did not realize the influence his thought exerted over me. However, some years later, when I became a sociologist, being interested in phenomenological sociology was natural. Some aspects of Paci's thought proved important, such as the invitation not to make a fetish of thought categories, to inquire into what I take for granted, to use words every time as if it were the first instance.

My thesis concerned Henri Lefebvre. I went and met him. But while working on my thesis, I bumped into the works of Walter Benjamin, who more than anyone else became my life long love. Indeed, I still draw inspiration from his sentences in almost all my works.

But we learned everywhere. Beyond the university there was the cinema. We watched Rainer Fassbinder and Wim Wenders, new South America movies, retrospectives of French, Spanish, and Swedish movies. Obviously, *Easy Rider*, too. Frederico Fellini was making his last movies; Nanni Moretti was just starting. Ettore Scola, Bernardo Bertolucci, and Marco Bellocchio movies helped our maturation. At the same time, Dario Fo worked as an actor in Milan: every night, at the end of his performances, it seemed that a revolution was about to break out. Love for Fo is still lasting: when he received the Nobel Prize in Literature, in 1997, it was a day of joy. I pinned his laughing photo, taken in Stockholm, to my office wall.

A love of theatricality, irony, and desecration became an important component in the last stage of the movement, which reached its peak in 1977. By then, it was far from any reference to the traditions of the working class, and in Italy, the movement rejected every form of political organization. Marginality was sought as such: giving free play to subjectivity and overthrowing all cultural codes, with a grin, was the goal.

However, it did not last long. In 1978 the members of the Red Brigade kidnapped and killed Aldo Moro, who was then the president of Christian Democracy party. The goal of the Red Brigade and other small, but extremely dangerous, armed groups was to intensify and radicalize the struggle with capitalism by weeding out reformers. A very hard repression against all branches of the movements followed.

Actually, the historical stage had already changed, as was clear to everybody in 1980, when forty thousand white-collar workers marched in Turin (the city of Fiats, long the center of working-class struggle) to demand the restoration of previously large wage differentials and status, in comparison with the blue-collar workers. But the presence of armed struggle was the element that contributed primarily to the political defeat of the movement in Italy: it allowed many people to call these years, in retrospect, *anni di piombo* (lead years — from the title of a Margarethe von Trotta movie). The name has been used to both forget and deny what 1968 was. Though unsuccessful politically, 1968 transformed Italy. Under the stimulus of movements within ten years, workers' rights increased, public life was laicized, and family law, school and public services, and, most of all, customs and culture changed. In a certain sense, the decade of the movements was an important process of collective education, democratization, and modernization.

I had studied philosophy at university but had always considered philosophy strictly bound to social sciences, so I also had done exams in history, economics, and sociology. The first job I found was in 1978, teaching sociology in a school for social workers. This was an experimental school through which passed many well-known sociologists. I taught there for almost three years. From that experience, I learned how difficult it is to work as a social worker, as they are caught between the needs of a system to exercise social control and the needs of the weakest people; it is a kind of job that requires an uncommon mixture of theoretical competencies, aptitude for research, self-analysis and ability to communicate.

Since I was interested in subjects concerning corporeality, I invited some actors to help me in lessons. Theater attracted me: I took part in the seminar of some Jerzy Grotowski scholars and was stimulated by Tadeusz Kantor and Bob Wilson performances. (Recently, I have started again to write for theater: indeed, a too-defined professional identity — as already mentioned — is restrictive for me.)

At the same time, I began psychoanalytic treatment and signed up for a course to become a psychotherapist. But then, I changed everything. In 1980 I left the school and moved to Southern Italy. I had had a daughter and married, and my wife had obtained a job at a university of the south, near Cosenza. For a short time, I traveled up and down Italy, until love for my two women defeated love for my city.

After two years where I had several jobs, I started teaching at the University of Calabria, first with a contract for philosophy of social sciences, then as an established professor of sociology. The University of Calabria was born in the early 1970s and was modeled on American universities (with a big residential center, services, sport centers, and so on). It was part of a great program of public investments for development in the south; it attracted professors from all of Italy and abroad. At the beginning, especially, it was a very particular place. It was as if we did not live exactly in the south: it was as though we were in a separate world. My two children (I have a son, too) played in the botanical garden of the university and went to the nursery school together with the children of other professors.

The university is located in the countryside: relations with the city of Cosenza grew up slowly. Cosenza people were curious but also distrustful of these strange and somewhat hippie intellectuals; we criticized southern society severely and wanted to teach students how to transform it. Perhaps in the end, we were the ones who learned the most: that 1968 in the south had also meant the struggle against the mafia, for instance. Later, our sociology was also transformed: we discovered that not all classical categories suit the Mediterranean area equally well.

The south has been good for me. On one hand, it gave me freedom from the pressure of more competitive academic environments. On the other hand, it taught me that the world is more varied than what I could have imagined when living in Milan. The south, I found, is not like the one where great men of the previous generation (Danilo Dolci, Manlio Rossi-Doria) came to promote the redemption of semi-illiterate masses: during the last decades, the south went through an improvement, which was perhaps distorted but impressive and impetuous. But it was a particular improvement: I found myself before sociality styles and forms of development that are typical of peripheries and that people living in the center cities tend to underestimate.

My path into sociology was indirect. I had no academic grounding in this subject. This is not unusual: the first faculty of sociology, in Italy, was only established at the end of the 1960s, so all of the oldest sociologists, as well as many sociologists who are my age, graduated in philosophy, political sciences, law, or economics.

When I was a student, sociology was having a period of spectacular growth and regard. But it was actually still fairly recent in Italy. Its rebirth in the 1950s, after a break in the fascist era, was strongly influenced by American structural functionalism, on the one hand, and German and French sociology on the other hand. The effect of 1968 was to push sociology strongly to the Left. Some scholars, already famous, such as Franco Ferrarotti, Francesco Alberoni, or Alessandro Pizzorno, provided sociological explanations of the movements, but to many of the youngest scholars, the exercise of sociology and political militancy overlapped, for some years at least. Some journals, such as *Quaderni Piacentini* and many others, were at the same time a place for theoretical elaboration of the movement and a development center for new sociological ideas. However, to these young sociologists (and to me, too, as I enjoyed dining with them at the end of a seminar or demonstration) it was clear enough, early on, that sociology is a different thing: political engagement can give the direction to research, but sociology in itself is different from it.

I studied sociology seriously only after taking my degree. I was attracted by classical scholars, most of all Georg Simmel and phenomenological sociology. Simmel was translated into Italian nearly completely, and very well, above all thanks to Alessandro Cavalli. His concept of *Wechselwirkung* taught me how to avoid the traps of monocausal determinism; his analysis of modernity and the ability to connect the details of daily life to the deepest trends of an era were fundamental to me.

As for phenomenology, reading Alfred Schutz was the key to connecting my philosophical grounding to sociology. In the United States, the phenomenological approach contributed to the creation of a sociological alternative to functionalism; in Italy, it helped most of all to correct a certain positivist ingenuousness of the sociology inspired by Marxism. As for me, I have never been interested in Talcott Parsons very much (I loved Robert K. Merton, but this is another matter); and I already had a degree of distance from positivism thanks to my studies in philosophy. But the influence of Marxism led me to join the phenomenological sociology of "common sense" to the consideration of social transformations and conflicts that are absent in Schutz.

When I won a scholarship for going abroad, this interest in phenomenological sociology led me to go and meet Peter Berger. In 1987, I spent almost a year at his Institute for the Study of Economic Culture in Boston. I was surprised at his political positions, which were much more conservative than what his books had made me suppose. Anyway, this was not important. Berger was very kind. He is blessed with a great synthetic mind: able to identify fundamental matters quickly and search for the best concepts to confront them with. Then, on behalf of the institute, and together with Hansfried Kellner and Frank Heuberger, I carried out the Italian part of a research project about the culture of the new European and American middle classes, which is one of my few books written in English.

Meanwhile, I was learning a lot from many scholars. I shared many interpretations with the young sociologists I mentioned above and, more generally, the idea that sociology cannot be a mere description of reality but a means of comparing reality with the possible. When becoming a sociologist myself, my models were most of all scholars who were a little older, like Alessandro Cavalli or Arnaldo Bagnasco. I became particularly close to some of them, like Franco Crespi and Alberto Melucci.

Crespi is a sociology professor belonging to the first generation of postwar Italian sociologists. Though too little translated abroad, in comparison to his profundity and originality, he is the representative of an extremely noteworthy theory of social action inspired by phenomenology (or, better, by Heidegger's thought). Apart from his specific theoretical positions, Crespi's importance in Italy lies in his unremitting reflection on the philosophical and epistemological grounding of the social sciences, which reinforced its importance and legitimated its study in the eyes of younger researchers. Sometimes we worked together, other times we sat at the café in the cities where we went for a conference and talked about life with each other and contemplated what he calls its "indeterminacy."

Melucci is another matter. Ten years older than me, he died two years ago. He was the most famous Italian sociologist of his generation abroad, thanks to his work on collective movements and the transformations of contemporary identities. His job as a psychotherapist is less known. I met him about in 1978 in this capacity, when he had founded a research and cure center inspired by Gestalt psychotherapy, together with his wife and an older psychiatrist. Melucci was both sociologist and psychotherapist almost until his death. I think that he always met with a certain difficulty in making his academic colleagues understand the relationship between his two careers. But the profundity of his works (both his methodological innovations and his sensitivity to the subjective experience) cannot be grasped without knowing its source. Alberto interpreted social movements as attempts to conceive the world in new ways. Like Crespi in this respect, he realized that the meaning of action is not merely a cognitive matter: everyone's life initiates a search for meaning, with the solution to be found at a deeper level. He recognized the extent to which human beings are fragile and contradictory and that our experiences exist on many levels. His sociology is rich for these reasons.

Every time I went to Milan, after moving to Calabria, I spent an evening with his wife and him: and I miss those evenings.

·   ·   ·

Memory is a matter of continuity. Memoirs are made easy when they can rely on meanings within lasting social bonds. But they also have an exquisitely individual dimension: to me, 1968 is also Milan and my youth. It is an atmosphere of curiosity and desire, certain songs, the motorcycle I was riding when I saw a girl at night; it is the memory of the passionate will to experience the world and the sensation that changing it would be easy.

That particular year didn't change much, or not at least in the expected direction. I did not grieve over this: I accepted it as a philosophy of history lesson. History is much less a linear and progressive process than it is the interweaving of different processes, the course of events with uncertain results. No "necessity of becoming" replaces the duty to act and assert our own ethical convictions and to assume responsibility.

Classical sociologists, such as Max Weber and Simmel, helped me in learning these lessons. Indeed, I have devoted myself to the history of sociology with passion. My engagement in the history of sociology embodies a great respect for this discipline, which in some ways is a strange result. In the years of my intellectual forming I was not inclined to limit myself to a discipline. This was a collective attitude: we were critical of the "division of sciences." Moreover, we were critical of the notion of science itself and, even more generally, we were against almost every institution.

The idea of the absolute importance of interdisciplinarity is still within me; but my attitude toward science and institutions changed. The idea of science in itself has an ethical strength: it is the ambition to construct a disinterested and intersubjectively valid knowledge, based on methodical doubt. In the current climate, in which economic interests play the role of lord and master and, at the same time, every "truth" is thought by many to be equal to another, science is an ideal to be defended (obviously, as an ideal only: not the pretension to monopolize knowledge). Something like that is also the case for institutions. Our generation contributed to the disillusionment of them by showing their human and conventional nature; and thus, we understood their fragility. But we also learned that without them social life tends to dissolve itself, not so much into chaos as into the domination of brute strength (what Weber called *Macht*, in opposition to the mechanisms of conflict governing and order legitimating expressed by the concept of *Herrschaft*).

In the early 1980s, the Italian Association of Sociology was established. The first meeting in which I took part was the one where a section of the association named Social Reproduction, Daily Life and Collective Subjects was established. I became one of its members. Though I worked in other sections, too, this group of sociologists was the most important for me. The group is characterized by a strong female presence and a collective identity with a low degree of orientation to academic careers: mutual sensitivity and curiosity prevail. The generational affinity of many of its members is important: not a matter of belonging to the same cohort, but the fact of having been formed during the decade of the movements. Suggestions from the American sociology of daily life (Alfred Schutz, Erving Goffman, Harold Garfinkel, etc.) joined with stimuli from France (Henri Lefebvre, Michel de Certeau but also Fernand Braudel and the *nouvelle histoire*), from the sociology of culture, and from neofeminism. In general, daily life was thought of as the core of concrete social existence, where "micro" and "macro" categories are integrated, where the study of action and structure are not opposed but also where forms of social stratification, which are different from the forms traditionally taken in consideration by sociology, appear and where an investigation of the formation of identities is possible.

At the beginning, the primary object of analysis was collective movements; then, subjects became more diverse: from health to public services, conversation to media reception, consumption to the study of temporalities (perhaps, this last one is the field where the highest originality and importance have been reached). The group produced significant innovations for all Italian sociology: the attention to gender, ethnicity, and generations spread from its members studies; the practice of qualitative sociology made clear the dynamics of the relations between observer and observed; language and the mechanism of reality construction became primary.

I think that, from a professional point of view, my membership in this group is my strongest bond to 1968, not as a matter of nostalgia but because of our common origins in the movement. The sociology of daily life in Italy, in comparison with other countries, is characterized by a strong orientation to emancipation (it is studied to be criticized, improved, or, at least, reoriented), whose origin lies in the political and social engagement of those years. In a certain sense, the presence of this group was a defense against the pressures of the increasingly mercantile logic that characterized Italy and Italian university life in the 1980s and 1990s.

I do not know whether my make-up as a sociologist today comes more from 1968 or from having the good fortune to practice a little theater and psychology, from having studied philosophy, or from the love for literature. However, it is true that 1968 was a favorable context in which this very plurality of experiences could flourish.

Some of the protagonists of that generation are still bound to an economic and essentially positivist version of Marxism. I feel far from it. Since then, what I think I have learned is both how much reality involves the interacting of a multiplicity of factors and how much discourses are relevant in constructing reality. I have also learned the extent to which the effects of one's actions are often counterintentional. After all, we were mistaken, too, during 1968: a proletarian revolution was not plausible in Italy and the West, and probably it was not what we wished for in our hearts.

. . .

These thoughts lead me to the present time. In the early 1990s in Italy, the Christian Democratic Party, which had governed continuously from the birth of the Republic after the Second World War, was overwhelmed by scandals involving illicit finances and, thus, was dissolved. The same thing happened to the Socialist Party, which Bettino Craxi made the party of the rising middle classes in the 1980s. The new situation is dominated by the presence of the Northern League, which is a movement/party aiming at defending the interests of the small entrepreneurs and traders of northern Italy, with strong xenophobic inclinations; and Forza Italia, the party/firm established by Silvio Berlusconi. Both groups have a strong populist and anti-intellectual streak.

The decade of the movements has long since become an object of endless and livid envy to these people. The league rejects every principle of solidarity, in the name of differences and the local traditions that modernization dissolved long ago but without which its electors feel confused. Berlusconi's electorate includes middle classes that had absolutely nothing to do with 1968 or lived through it with hostility, nostalgic Christian Democrats and youth whom his television networks led to be devoted to the world of commodities, to the logic of market and advertising. The verbal violence, unscrupulousness, greed, and contempt for institutions that marked the rise of Berlusconi and his assistants took us by sur prise and disarmed us. Sometimes, I think that, paradoxically, they are perverse sons of 1968. We said that democratic institutions often concealed the violence of the strong; they seem to say: "Well, let us not conceal anything. Let the strongest one win, and that's all." However, there is more to it than this. Berlusconi is also able to misrepresent his policies through clever advertising strategies. His media empire shows how important the dimension of communication is in society. Our understanding of communicative means and processes proved to be outdated.

I am now interested in the sociology of communication for this reason, too. This is in part a new field for me, and I like it. During my intellectual life, I have been interested in different subjects. Apart from the history of sociology, I have written about collective memory, modernity, common sense, and narrative practices. I love beginning again every time and choosing the object of my studies, leaving aside academic considerations. Perhaps this has to do with the decade of the movements, too: though we were oriented to the creation of new forms of sociality, the decade of the movements also represented a strong stimulus to the individualization of each of us, to asserting the right and maybe the duty to obey our inclinations, listen to ourselves, and not betray ourselves.

·   ·   ·

The ideology of the New Right celebrates the triumph of market. Of course this is a misrepresentation: Berlusconi's position in mass media is largely monopolistic, and the policy of his ministers is often protectionist. The appeal to the market is most of all useful for the dismantling of public services, from health to education. Those who grew up during 1968 are still skeptics about the virtues of the market. Without a counterbalance, the free market causes unbearable inequalities. Most of all, the fact that the logic of market economy involves every field of social and cultural life is unbearable.

Under the pressures of the New Right and the logic of the market, life in Italian universities at the moment is difficult. Researchers have to justify their studies in terms of the economic utility; teaching is expected to legitimate itself as a means of enabling youth to enter the labor market. Lack of time and resources becomes the governing reality. We defend ourselves by remembering that we have studied, researched, and lived with passion and pleasure, and passion and pleasure are what we still try to defend and convey to our students.

We have been a lucky generation. Few of us saw war; we grew up while "history" seemed to be a synonym of "progress"; we wanted to break rules, but we lived in a social world where rules were strong. The present prospect is different. Many wars are being fought; progress is a myth that reality is evaporating (or showing its ambiguities, at least); rules have become uncertain. The future is also uncertain (even saying "uncertain" is a euphemism: it is easy to foresee a future full of inequality and international rivalries without precedent against the background of more and more wide and probable ecological disasters). Perhaps, there has never been as much need of sociology as now and, I would like to say, of a sociology like the one that 1968 contributed to building. Indeed, 1968 taught us to study reality but also not to be dominated by it: that is, to be critical.

A Pragmatist from Germany

*Hans Joas has contributed to the renaissance of American pragmatism and in par-ticular to its reception in social theory, especially through his books on G. H. Mead and on pragmatism. On the basis of these interpretive studies, he developed an ac-tion-theoretical approach that claims to be an alternative to models of rational and of normatively oriented action (*The Creativity of Action*). This action theory is the point of departure for his more recent work on the genesis of value commitments and on violence and war (*The Genesis of Values *and* War and Modernity). His current interests are focused on theoretical questions related to the "human rights" value complex and on a theory of social change. Joas studied at the University of Munich from 1968 to 1971 and then went on to continue his education at the Free University of Berlin. From 1992 to 1996 he served as president of the Research Com-mittee on Theory in the International Sociological Association. Besides teaching in Chicago, where he also serves on the Committee on Social Thought, he is the Max Weber Professor at the University of Erfurt (Germany) and director of the Max Weber Center for Advanced Cultural and Social Studies there. He also plays a role in the exchange between American and Continental European intellectual traditions.*

It is one of the fundamental insights of George Herbert Mead's social psychology that our identity develops out of the interaction with others and that each at-tempt at self-presentation depends on the anticipation of the image others might have of us. If I follow these insights in an autobiographical reflection on the de-velopment of my scholarly work out of its conditions, I must start with what I take to be the dominant image of my work. I assume that I am frequently seen as an outpost of American pragmatism in Germany. Sympathetic commentators emphasize the original theoretical achievements I have developed out of the reception of American pragmatism. Less sympathetic commentators see my work as a mere contribution to the interpretation of an intellectual tradition that had been developed in all its main features by others, the import of which to Germany had already been initiated by Jürgen Habermas and Karl-Otto Apel. Their estimation of the merits of such work is then determined by their views on the significance of pragmatism in general.

As is often the case, this image contains some truth. Since my student days, pragmatism has indeed been the unbroken guiding thread of my work. Without exaggeration, one can say that I "fell in love" with pragmatism in the year 1970. At first it was only one of its important thinkers, perhaps the most obscure of the classical quartet, to whom my attention was drawn: George Herbert Mead. But soon my feelings of love expanded and extended to the other three (Charles Sanders Peirce, William James, John Dewey). Their company has, since then, remained for me a continuous source of inspiration and deep intellectual satisfaction.

Trivial explanations for this development can be excluded. I did not encounter pragmatism in an American high school or college or in any contact with academic teachers. Moreover, pragmatism does not apply to the conditions under which I grew up. Nobody denies that pragmatism is deeply American, deeply philosophical, deeply influenced by its Protestant background. Now I am not American or a philosopher or Protestant. The object of desire with which I had fallen in love was hence, under these conditions, rather exotic, and I have never ignored the differences between it and myself. How then could this relationship become so stable and fruitful?

Every explanation of such a process is, of course, a reconstruction or, in even stronger words, a retrospective construction produced in a specific new situation. Decades later, it seems to me evident that I encountered pragmatism in a biographical constellation in which I felt simultaneously attracted and repelled by three intellectual worlds. These three worlds were all massively present, in the culture in which I grew up. But their combination appeared to be as unlikely as would be a simple choice between them. Therefore, confusion or mere eclecticism was threatening. I experienced the encounter with pragmatism as the sudden revelation of a way that could allow me to keep what is valuable in all three intellectual worlds but also to get rid of what had to be rejected and thus advance to an intellectual synthesis. This constellation has characterized the generative core of my work up to this day. With pragmatism, I had encountered one of the most important articulations of American culture, leading to a lifelong interest in the United States and to a balancing between German and American culture. The United States became for me an Archimedean point from which I could hope to realign the depreciated German traditions.

What are the intellectual worlds that contained such unbearable tension? A first glance at my biographical point of departure will make this clear. A short-hand formulation for it would be: I grew up in a Catholic milieu as the son of a Nazi father and a Social Democratic mother. The family apartment in Munich where I was born in 1948 (after my sister, born in 1944) was part of a Catholic worker's cooperative founded in 1909 by Catholic workers and Christian trade unions. Even after war and Nazism, there was in this very modest framework, a spirit of mutual neighborly support and a shared careful attitude toward the green backyard and the playing grounds for the children. On Sunday, everybody went to church — those who didn't could count on being asked for the reasons of their absence. After conflicts, people came to each other to apologize because the priest had asked them to do so in the sacrament of confession. No doubt there were also envy and calumny, even violence among the members of the coopera-tive society — but no anonymity. My grandmother was for me the incarnation of strong religious faith to whom an atheist was an exotic being.

But my parents did not fit well into this framework. My father (born in 1905) had, in an act of rebellion against his own also deeply religious father, joined the Nazi movement before 1933. He considered Nazism throughout his life to be the modern replacement of old-fashioned and narrow-minded Catholicism. Work-ing as a salesman for textile goods, he became, during the Third Reich, the Nazi speaker of the employees (Nationalsozialistischer Betriebsobmann) and a mem-ber of the Waffen-SS. Months before the war ended and, with it, the Nazi regime, he still entertained serious hopes for a further career in the power apparatus of the regime. The collapse of the Nazi regime and the unconditional capitula-tion of the German Reich were for him catastrophes he never could reconcile. Whereas innumerable "fellow travelers" of the Nazi regime and even many en-thusiastic supporters of it briskly turned themselves into democrats, at least in lip service, my father remained faithful to his convictions after 1945. Repentance he did not know; the rising democracy he observed without comprehension and with feelings of alienation; he had more sympathy for bolshevism than for the

West. His difficulties coming to grips with the new phase of German history were not only political. Economically, he tried to start his own business and founded a wholesale firm for textile goods. But this ended in complete shipwreck, and he had to declare himself bankrupt in 1954. This led to the seizure of almost all private belongings, too. One of the earliest childhood memories I have is how all of our bookcases were transported out of our apartment; my father only saved Nazi propaganda books from them. After this, he sank into a long depression. While West Germany experienced its "economic miracle," he remained unemployed or with only small temporary jobs for years. In family life, he nevertheless acted with what remained from Nazi vehemence as a tyrannical and authoritarian "leader." It was not until 1958 that he began working on a regular basis again, but a deadly stroke in 1959 ended this abruptly.

My mother, born in 1917 and thus more than a decade younger than her husband, had fallen in love with this older man who appeared to her (in the company in which they both worked before the war) as a radiating personality, a rhetorically, theatrically, and poetically highly talented man, as he was indeed. Politically, she had nothing to counter his Nazi convictions; she shared them, if at all, only in the most superficial manner. The war destroyed her loyalty to the regime completely. When, soon after the war had ended, the democratic parties were again allowed to become active in public, she came into contact with the Social Democratic Party (SPD), to which she became faithful for the rest of her life. My father considered my mother's newfound political orientation a source of shame, but he had less and less power in their increasingly difficult relationship, all the more so as his wife contributed more to the economic survival of the family than he did.

The death of my father in 1959 plunged the family into even greater poverty and absence of prospects. Without welfare from public funds, life would have become impossible. If we had not lived in the housing complex of the cooperative society, loss of the apartment would also have been likely. Poverty and exclusion thus became a fundamental feeling of my youth. But similarly characteristic was the extraordinary intensification of my religiosity after the sudden and shocking death of my father. Despite all the ambivalence of my feelings toward him—who was not an especially good role model and against whose political convictions and their horrible consequences my mother energetically cautioned her children—his death shattered me completely. Moreover, the fear that my mother, who had always suffered from severe depressions and toyed with suicide again and again, could follow him into death soon was a constant threat. Consolation from faith, escape into literature and, a little later, into nature kept my head above water.

A few weeks after the death of my father I entered the gymnasium (i.e., the selective German high school that starts at the age of ten). Neighbors and relatives, even the employees of the state welfare agency, outdid one another in the intensity of their advice that under our economic conditions an educational career for me and my sister would be ridiculously illusory. My mother, who had herself left school at the age of thirteen but became — like her husband — a passionate reader, held fast, against all advice, to the idea that only in this way could the future be better. During all nine years of gymnasium schooling, I was, at once, one of the poorest and one of the best pupils at the school, receiving many awards, even national ones. My central interests and best work was in mathematics and physics. I found it enormously attractive that problems could indeed be solved by research and calculation. My religious faith took on rather neurotic forms for some years. I read the Bible every day and attempted to interpret even the most difficult biblical texts — a task that overtaxed me completely. I experienced my social surroundings as disharmonious, totally interwoven with conflicts as they were. The idea of reconciliation, of true understanding, and of a transformation of people and interpersonal relationships by love and understanding — this I dreamed of and experienced as the radiant countermodel and authentic concretization of the Christian faith. But more and more I also became interested in politics. I found the Social Democratic convictions of my mother not radical enough, offering no perspective to the excluded. I started reading writings from Leftist Catholicism and increasingly also from Marxism — through publications I had received from a neighbor in our house. The close alliance between Catholic Church and political conservatism I found scandalous. When Franz Josef Strauss, the leader of the Christian conservatives in Bavaria, reproached the Social Democrat Willy Brandt with his out-of-wedlock birth, I protested against this so loudly that I remained hoarse for several days. For me Christianity should have nothing to do with a demagogical play on middle-class prejudices.

My religious and political attitudes made me an outsider in school for some time. Fortunately, my interest in soccer led to certain countertendencies against the threat of isolation. Toward the end of my years at the gymnasium, the atmosphere changed dramatically. When, on June 2, 1967, a student was shot dead by the police in Berlin after a protest demonstration against the visit of the Persian Shah, most gymnasium students suddenly expressed solidarity with the nascent movement; that turned me—who had already been in contact with Leftist radical groups—from an outsider into the spokesman. In activities against so-called emergency state legislation in 1968—activities driven by a hysterical fear of the return of Fascism—this continued. During the tumultuous spring and summer of 1968 I had to take the *Abitur* exams, the end of gymnasium education. I witnessed the climax of the student movement at that time in an intense way—but not as a student yet.

In addition to the three languages taught at the gymnasium (English, French, and Latin), I had also learned Italian. Italy is not far from Munich, and during several hitchhiking trips, I had gotten the impression that a Leftist Catholic would learn a lot there. In the exams at the Italian Cultural Institute, I gained a place in the summer course at the University of Florence in 1968. On August 21, the Soviet military intervention in Czechoslovakia took place during my stay in Florence. Florence was crowded with Czech and Slovak tourists; the Italian political parties, including and particularly the Communists, protested vehemently against the violent Soviet repression of the experimental "socialism with a human face." Since these tourists often understood German, but not Italian, I translated the texts of flyers and special editions of newspapers to groups of devastated people on Cathedral Square in Florence. The disappointment, if not the horror, in the reactions of these people is perhaps my most important memory of 1968.

I remained quite ambivalent toward the student movement proper. It had helped me to overcome political and personal isolation, and it soon revolutionized my erotic life, too. But I never lost the feeling that its main activists acted out of completely different experiences than I did. The spokespersons and leaders often had a rich bourgeois or even aristocratic family background and were, behind a thin Leftist facade and often kitschy idealization of the "proletariat," full of pride of place. The numerous friends I found during my student days were—as if determined by some deeper law—social outsiders in academic life like myself. The overheated character of my religiosity decreased at that time; it partly shifted to a radical alienation from the Church.

Because of my increasingly strong political interests and certainly because of the atmosphere of 1968 (frequently perceived in Europe as an epochal rupture), I decided, during my last year of school, not to study mathematics or physics but, instead, a discipline better suited to serve my political interests. My teachers recommended law, but nothing was further from my concerns at that point than a career on a fixed track. I vacillated between history and sociology. To make sure that if far-reaching hopes were to fail I could make a living as gymnasium teacher, I also studied some German literature and philosophy. One of the hotly debated topics cutting across disciplines at that time was sociolinguistics. How language and social origins were connected held great interest for me, for scientific and extrascientific reasons. In this field of study, I encountered the writings of George Herbert Mead because they were mentioned by authors in educational studies and by Jürgen Habermas.

The three intellectual worlds between which I had moved until this encounter took place were Catholic Christianity, Marxism, and the specifically German intellectual traditions of historicism, hermeneutics, and philosophical anthropology, which had to some extent played a role in the intellectual formation of Nazism or at least not resisted it. All three intellectual worlds unmistakably shared a deficiency: they were insufficiently permeated by the spirit of democracy. Although German Catholicism had kept a greater distance from Nazism than had German Protestantism, the motives for this distance were ambiguous and largely defensive, not determined by an offensive plea for freedom, democracy, and human rights. This changed during the 1960s, symbolized by the Second Vatican Council, beginning in 1963, which I followed with greatest suspense. But the Catholic milieus in Bavaria often remained quite unaffected by this and, in many respects, predemocratic. Against the idealization of "actually existing socialism" in East Germany and in the Soviet sphere in general, I had become immunized by my experience with the end of the Czechoslovak experiment. Although Marxism appeared to me, when I was a student, as it did to many others of my generation, as a promising program for the social sciences, I was convinced that even as such it was deeply in need of correction because of a lack of its understanding of democracy — and this not only with respect to politics but also to theory construction. And my fascination with the hermeneutic tradition that had set in very early from my inclination to interpret texts, biblical and otherwise, was again and again irritated by the nationalist and antidemocratic attitudes in many of the most important proponents of this impressive tradition. In Mead and the pragmatists I seemed to have found a potential for the "democratic correction" of Catholicism, Marxism, and hermeneutics and for a combination of elements from these traditions.

At first this was, of course, not much more than a hunch, a suggestion. At the University of Munich, where I spent the first five semesters of my studies, I did not find much inspiration in my academic teachers. The strongest impression I got came from a historian, Karl Bosl, an expert on Bavarian history; because of this specialization he seemed a bit marginal, but his writings and sweeping lec-

tures offered a comprehensive social and cultural history of my native country—
and I have always found local or regional history very interesting. In the spring
of 1971 I changed to the Free University of Berlin because I wanted to be in the
center of intellectual and political life. I consciously decided against Frankfurt,
because Berlin promised to be more pluralistic than the Frankfurt School that I
had always associated with bourgeois pride of place, and against Marburg, which
I perceived to be under the control of Marxist intellectuals with leanings toward
the Soviet Union. In addition, Berlin had been an almost mythical place for me
since my childhood days. My father had spent several months there at the end of
the 1920s and kept his rapture forever; as a pupil and as a student I had read Alfred Döblin's novel *Berlin Alexanderplatz* several times—one of the fateful books
of my life. During my only visit to Berlin before my move, I found it fascinating
to live in a city that allowed close contact to both democratic and communist
world systems in all their mutual hostility.

My first experiences as a student in Berlin were disastrous. Out of the student
movement, several political sects had developed that took the Soviet Union or
Maoist China as their points of orientation. In some classes at the university, serious discussion was impossible. Even on academic questions, for example, theories of language, the speakers of Leftist radical groups took turns to propagate a
kind of official standpoint on the question at hand. An important reference author for them—oddly enough—was Joseph Stalin. Habermas's name, in contrast, was taboo because of his criticism of tendencies toward a "Leftist Fascism"
in the student movement. Whoever mentioned his name, nevertheless, as I did,
had to reckon with the same fate of being shunned. In other classes, the exegesis
of Marx's texts dominated over all substantial problems. Although most students
had not read much Marx, they were guided by the conviction that in his writings
the key to the solution of all questions could be found. The only open question
then was whether Marxism-Leninism or some other version of Marxism would
result from these efforts. Many professors, who experienced this type of university life as a lunatic asylum, had moved to calmer universities or resigned. Others attempted to defend small islands of serious work.

I was fortunate enough to be able to save myself on such an island. If I had not
met Hans Peter Dreitzel, Dieter Claessens, and the young Wolf Lepenies as
academic teachers, I would have left Berlin in full flight after one semester. All
three saw themselves in the German tradition of philosophical anthropology.
Dreitzel's inspiration was his teacher Helmuth Plessner; for Claessens, it was Arnold Gehlen; and for Lepenies, a student of Claessens, it was also French an-

thropology, after Claude Lévi-Strauss. Gehlen's work, which I had already begun reading while still in Munich, became extremely important for me; in retrospect, I see that my attempts to cope with it were a silent struggle with my father. I thought Gehlen a genius, who, after having been attracted as a young man to the modernist aesthetic revolt, later became one of the philosophic stars of the Nazi regime. His books were of enormous plasticity—both in their anthropological aspects and as cultural criticism; he was the first in Germany to draw attention to G. H. Mead and Lévi-Strauss. But he was, although no vulgar racist, an intellectual Fascist of the first order and remained, after 1945, an antidemocrat of the Far Right. Personal encounters with him, in 1973 and 1975, mediated by his student Karl-Siegbert Rehberg, confirmed my feeling that his work, but not his objectives, could be used as an important starting point.

Within academic Marxism and the Leftist subculture, there was also room for serious discussion and fair interaction. As in all things human, moral and political orientations did not always coincide. One of the leaders of the German student movement, in a certain sense its second-in-command after Rudi Dutschke, was Bernd Rabehl; in numerous discussions with him and his circle, I developed an ever-deeper understanding of Russian and Soviet history, the origins of Stalinism, and the possibilities of an alternative. For some time I believed with them that Leon Trotsky had represented a revolutionary but democratic socialism. I started to learn Russian and spent several weeks of the year 1975 in Leningrad. I had the ambition to become a truly contemporary mind, and that meant, for me, to understand both world powers—the United States and the USSR—out of their respective conditions.

One of my most important intellectual encounters before I wrote my master's thesis was Agnes Heller. A Hungarian philosopher and an important student of Georg Lukács, Heller came to the Free University of Berlin in 1972 as a visiting professor. In her classes, for example, on Marx's *Grundrisse*, she demonstrated her superior knowledge of that author. In my conversations with her, she also made clear how enormously difficult the situation was for intellectuals, even Marxists, in "actually existing socialism". She and her friends and colleagues (like György and Maria Markus) soon experienced exclusion from the party and were prohibited from publishing. At the end of the semester, when Agnes Heller invited me to visit her in Budapest at my convenience, I took advantage of her offer within weeks. During this and several later visits, I met more Hungarian dissidents. I also became the German editor of a great book by Heller on everyday life. Unfortunately, our relationship ended after several years for reasons that had to do with pervasive distrust of the dissidents. I studied the writings of Lukács intensely in those years. His critiques of the German tradition, which he censured as the "destruction of reason" on the path that led to Nazism, paradoxically had the opposite effect on me and served as a guide to discover what authors like Wilhelm Dilthey, Georg Simmel, and Max Weber—who Lukács distorted ideologically—truly had thought and intended. But his question of the intellectual prehistory of Nazism and the Holocaust remained.

In the classes taught by Dreitzel and Claessens, my focus was on sociological role theory. I found this approach attractive because it offered instruments for the analysis of interaction processes but also because of its potential to spell out what the idea of democracy means in the micro- and macrosociological realm. At that time in Germany, role theory was mostly criticized and interpreted by means of ideology critique. I was asked to write an extensive protocol of a class that, after further enlargement, became my master's thesis and first book (published in 1973 as *The Present Situation of Sociological Role Theory*). The book had three editions and sold seven thousand copies—an astounding success that can only be explained by the wave of public interest in sociology at that time. On this basis, I was offered a job in the Berlin sociology department. I soon developed the plan for a doctoral thesis in which I intended to describe the history of Marxism from a critical viewpoint. The idea was to uncover the constant failure of Marxism regarding the idea of human intersubjectivity—from Marx's early and unfair critique of Ludwig Feuerbach's philosophy (of "altruism") via the deficiencies of Marx's economic and historiographical writings to Lukács's concept of reification and the present. There is no doubt that this project was kicked off by Habermas's epochal essay "Labour and Interaction" on Georg Hegel's writings from Jena in which I found the emphasis on interaction very attractive but found the reconstruction of Marx's "expressivist" concept of labor in the concept of "instrumental action" less than convincing. I was able to develop parts of this project, but I also soon discovered that the positive reference point for my critical argumentation in each one of the chapters was the thinking of George Herbert Mead. What I knew of Mead at that time was not much more than *Mind, Self, and Society*—a book full of grandiose ideas but still a bad book because it leaves much to be desired in the sense of argumentative rigor, due to the fact that it is the posthumous publication of a compilation of students' and other notes taken in Mead's classes. Mead, whom I called then the most important philosopher of intersubjectivity between Feuerbach and Habermas, seemed to me to surpass Habermas in several respects: his understanding of intersubjectivity was less language-centered and thus better connected to human corporeality; all types of action, including our action toward physical things (in which Habermas never has shown much interest) became the subject matter of his analyses; and discourse remained in a functional relationship with action in a much clearer way in Mead than in Habermas.

But if every chapter of the planned dissertation were not going monotonously to end up with the same criticism and if my real motivation was the development of an adequate social psychology and macrosociology using the ideas of inter-subjectivity and democracy, it seemed necessary to change directions. It was more attractive to write a monograph about the thinker who had become a positive reference point, and that is why I decided to write about Mead. From that point on, my interest in Mead almost became a mania. I read every title in the bibliography of his writings and all the secondary literature I could obtain. I even studied books Mead had reviewed or mentioned in his writings and a large number of works in intellectual history and the history of science to contextualize his thinking. The current state of research at that time on the topics he had pursued became important for me. I undertook vast bibliographical searches, and I succeeded in discovering many publications by Mead that allowed a reinterpretation of his intellectual development.

My book was intended to differ in three respects from existing work on Mead, including the excellent book by David Miller published in 1973. In the first place, it was to be a genetic presentation, not the imposition of an allegedly atemporal systematics on his work. My models for this approach were Karl-Otto Apel's reconstruction of Charles Sanders Peirce's intellectual development and also Dilthey's biography of Friedrich Schleiermacher and his work on Hegel's early "theological" writings. Second, my dissertation intended to demonstrate the enormous importance of classical German philosophy (Immanuel Kant, Johann Gottlieb Fichte, Hegel, Friedrich Wilhelm Schelling) and of German hermeneutics for Mead — against the ridiculous misunderstanding and simplification of Mead as a behaviorist, which was due to his idiosyncratic use of the term "behaviorism." When I found out — in the archives of the university in (East) Berlin — that Mead had indeed studied with Dilthey, this was for me a triumphal confirmation of my original intuition. Third, I wished to do justice to Mead's achievements in the whole spectrum of his work and not only in the small section popularized by the symbolic interactionists. Mead's writings on the definition of the psychical, the constitution of the "physical thing," on moral and temporal consciousness should be discussed extensively, not to speak of the contextualization of his work in terms of intellectual and social history.

At that point I realized that I would not be able to reach my goals in Germany because many publications were not available there and because Mead's remaining papers with letters and unpublished manuscripts were in Chicago and Austin, Texas (in the possession of David Miller). But a trip to the United States appeared to me then like flying to the moon. Due to Peter Dreitzel's encouragement and to Wolf Lepenies's help in getting a scholarship, however, I was able to take that trip in 1975.

During the trip I was not completely alone. In the fall of 1974, good luck would have it that I meet Heidrun, a teacher working for the Protestant church in Berlin, with whom I fell in love (even more than with pragmatism . . .). She became my girlfriend and has been my wife since 1976. Three days before our departure to the United States, we learned that she was pregnant. The following months in Washington, DC, Chicago, and Austin were an extremely intense time for our personal and my scholarly life. In terms of scholarly pursuits, I found the Library of Congress in Washington, DC, and the Regenstein Library in Chicago to be paradise. I realized more and more that my plan could indeed be successful. With Mead I felt increasingly sure that his conception of intersubjectivity—what I called "practical intersubjectivity"—was indeed the transformation of fundamental Christian assumptions into social psychology and ethics. "Transformation" was an ambiguous term here, as it could mean secularization or a contemporary articulation of belief.

But we also experienced other facets of the United States during this trip. I don't think we had arrived with a completely idealized image of American democracy. The influence of Leftist critiques of America since the Vietnam War had been too strong for that. But we were shocked when we first saw the inner-city districts, with their poverty, crime, and decay, in Washington, DC, and Chicago. How was it possible that such a degree of social inequality and tolerated decay could exist side by side with outstanding educational institutions and in a country with an uninterrupted democratic tradition? This question increased my interest in the United States far beyond the question of how pragmatism could emerge.

Soon after our return to Berlin, our son Christian was born. His childhood years did not help accelerate my ambitious dissertation project, and it was not completed until 1979. The resulting book on Mead, published in German in

168 | HANS JOAS

1980 and in English, on Anthony Giddens's initiative, in 1985 received considerable attention.

Its long maturation was worthwhile for another reason, too: it allowed me to accumulate material for other writings. It was in my mind to demonstrate the significance not only of Mead's work for contemporary sociology and philosophy but also of the whole development of a sociological research tradition from the philosophy of pragmatism. A book on Mead was not the right place for macrosociological or methodological questions. My research in this area did not lead to another monograph but, rather, to articles that were much later collected and published as *Pragmatism and Social Theory* (1992 in German, 1993 in English). In 1980 I had met in person (in Paris) a Chicago sociologist who was to become one of my greatest sponsors, particularly in this area: Donald N. Levine. The visiting professorship in Chicago he initiated for me in 1985 strengthened my relation to this department, which led, in 1998, to an offer to teach there and become a member of the Committee on Social Thought.

Moreover, the conclusions I reached in my book on Mead gave me the feeling that I would now be able to determine the precise relationship between my own conclusions so far and the traditions of German philosophical anthropology, Marxism, and historical anthropology. For this project, I invited a friend to become my co-author—a friend I had first met in 1974 and who for many years was my closest intellectual discussion partner: Axel Honneth. We went through decisive phases of our intellectual development together, in constant exchange of ideas. Unlike me, he learned a lot from Theodor Adorno and the whole Frankfurt School and from structuralist authors like Louis Althusser and Michel Foucault. He thus kept me from making superficial refutations and from harboring a lack of interest in these types of thinking. We shared an admiration for Jürgen Habermas, toward whom we nevertheless took a very different attitude. Whereas Axel Honneth strove to improve Habermas's theories by means of immanent criticism, I marked more rigorously where my own ideas and those of Habermas seemed to differ in fundamental ways. The oral presentation of my critique of the Theory of Communicative Action brought me the sharpest disapproval of the master and years of cold distance. Axel Honneth is now the successor to Habermas in his Frankfurt philosophical chair and director of the glorious Institute for Social Research.

The anthropological book Honneth and I wrote together, a book not fully mature in many respects, was published in German in 1980. An English translation

(*Social Action and Human Nature*) appeared in 1988 — with a preface by Charles Taylor, another thinker both Honneth and I have admired enormously.

Professionally, completing my dissertation was an important turning point. I became research assistant in an empirical research institute, the Max Planck Institute for Human Development and Education in Berlin, and assistant to its sociological director Dietrich Goldschmidt, incidentally also a student of Helmuth Plessner's. My task was empirical research on the labor market for young scientists in Germany, the social origins of academic faculty, and the sociology of professions in general. This research, largely oriented to the present but partly also historical, led to numerous articles and the book *Science and Career* (published in German in 1987). The coauthor of the book was Michael Bochow, who later became a leading sociological researcher regarding male homosexuals in Germany. Years of empirical research with quantitative methods for the collection and analysis of data were an extremely useful but also very hard school for me. I learned the tools of research in this practice that I had not acquired as a student. Frequently I felt in the wrong place. When I read in Elias Canetti's autobiography how he kept longing for literary writing when he worked as a chemist, I saw myself in that description, since my strong theoretical interests constantly had to be neglected or put in second place, and combining them with predetermined empirical questions was not easily possible.

From the early 1980s and onward, a new peace movement began to develop in Europe and particularly in Germany — for fear of a new intensification of the Cold War that might jeopardize the mitigations of the situation achieved by détente policy and that even lead to a nuclear inferno in Europe. These problems occupied me enormously. The invitations to give talks on "peace congresses" in German universities triggered a project I pursued at first only on the side, namely, to study what knowledge sociology had produced in its history regarding the explanation of war. In the beginning, I had a suspicion that this knowledge did not amount to very much. If this proved to be the case, it would be of interest to investigate why sociology had a blind spot here. Even before that, I had found it attractive to study the potential of pragmatism in establishing connections between democracy and peace and creating institutional mechanisms for the peaceful solution of international conflicts. Moreover, this topic was ideally suited to pave the way for closer scientific cooperation with colleagues from East Germany and the socialist states in general. This cooperation led, after many difficulties, to the publication of a volume in 1989, which I edited together with

an East German Marxist sociologist, Helmut Steiner. This same line of work ultimately led to the book *War and Modernity* (published in German, 2000, and in
English, 2003); in its introduction I sketched the political context more extensively. Initially, however, it was not the cooperation itself that was of greatest
importance but the intense experience of how little latitude for intellectual freedom in socialism existed, how humiliating the forced adaptation to political control was, and how little authentic belief in Marxism one could still find. These
experiences corroborated my commitment to German social democracy to which
I had felt close for a long time before and which I joined as a card-carrying member in the early 1980s. Against the mood of the times I also had a strong desire for
the reunification of Germany. After my move from Bavaria to Berlin, I had trans-
ferred my hobby—interest in local history—to Berlin and Brandenburg (the
area around Berlin). Although I had doubts that I would live until reunification,
I had no doubt that it would happen some day. When, after the sensational opening of the wall in 1989, a window of opportunity for reunification suddenly flew
open, I spent weeks in euphoria. I was relatively strongly integrated into the network of East German sociology. It was easy, therefore, to deal with the competing explanations for "the collapse of the GDR" in a volume of the same title I
wrote with my colleague Martin Kohli.

Alongside empirical research and these political and scholarly activities regarding war and peace, I continued my constructive work in social theory. No
longer did I want to speak mostly as an interpreter of pragmatist (or other)
thinkers; I wanted instead to develop in a systematic way what a theory of action
based on pragmatism would look like. For this purpose, I sharpened my theoretical instruments by critically discussing competing projects—not only, as already
mentioned, that of Habermas's *Theory of Communicative Action* but also Anthony Giddens, Jeffrey Alexander, and the Greek-French philosopher Cornelius
Castoriadis, who had belonged to the instigators of May 1968 in Paris but who
also was perhaps the most competent and rigorous critic of Marxism in all its versions. I was particularly attracted by his focus on the creativity of human action.
Castoriadis provided me with a catchword to characterize the understanding of
action in pragmatism—as a specific version of creativity.

The opportunity to carry out the plan to write a book on this topic did not
come until I left the empirical research institute. My first regular professorship
at the University of Erlangen-Nuremberg (1987–90) offered me a chance to elaborate many aspects of this project in my classes. But I could not finish this most
ambitious and, as I believe, most important of my books until the early 1990s.

The fundamental idea of this book, *The Creativity of Action*, is that sociology and economics have, as far as their understanding of human action is concerned, moved constantly, since the end of the nineteenth century, between the poles of rational and normatively oriented action. In this regard, Durkheim's critique of Herbert Spencer in his book on the division of labor, published in 1893, Parsons's critique of utilitarianism in his *Structure of Social Action* of 1937, and Amitai Etzioni's critique of modern microeconomic theorizing in his *The Moral Dimension* of 1988 turn out to be strictly parallel. I do indeed think that Parsons's earliest book is a definitive critique of the rational model of action. But pragmatism, being just as critical of the rational model, nevertheless launched a very different critique of it and cannot simply be subsumed under the model of normatively oriented action. The pragmatist understanding of creativity makes possible the solution of two problems that had remained unsolved in Parsons. It allows a new perspective on the question of how norms and values are transformed into action orientations within specific situations of action and how norms and values emerge after all. Other developments in sociology have pointed in the same direction, above all in ethnomethodology and symbolic interactionism but also in the work of great sociologists I admire very much like Shmuel Eisenstadt and Alain Touraine. My idea was that these approaches could be elaborated in a more systematic way by going back to pragmatism.

Today I would still defend the first three of the four parts of the book or write them in a similar manner; the fourth part, however, appears to me in retrospect to be insufficient. In the first part of the book I attempted to trace, following studies by Donald Levine and Charles Camic, the logic of the marginalization of the model of creative action in the history of the relationship between the disciplines of sociology and of economics. In the second part, I dealt with different ways to conceptualize creativity, paying particular attention to the limits of expressivism, Marxism, and *Lebensphilosophie* in this regard. The most important part of that book is the third section, in which I investigate the ability of actors to set goals, dominate one's own body, and differentiate one's own self from the others and in which I bring to light — and introduce in a reconstructive way — the dimensions that are tacitly presupposed in the models of rational action. Part 3 should be seen as an attempt to present the fundamentals of a neopragmatist theory of action. But the book does not end at that point, although this might have been better. I feared, when I wrote the book, that such a revised theory of action for macrosociological theory construction could potentially be completely be ignored if I did not add anything to the action theoretical aspects. Then again, I was not really able, at that time, fully to redeem my vision of a neopragmatist macro-sociology. That is why I could not truly offer more than fragments of such a theory at that point and, mostly, critical arguments against functionalism and differentiation theory. To offer more than that is still very high on my agenda today.

The book has been translated into several languages (English, French, Korean), but its fate is very different in different national contexts. In Germany, the area of theory in sociology was so completely occupied by Habermas and Luhmann that it proved to be very difficult to find attention for a rather different project. To my disappointment, both these authors completely ignored my book. More fruitful was the reaction of Wolfgang Schluchter who recognized some overlap between his own Weberian and my pragmatist research program. In France, in contrast, where the book came out with a preface by Alain Touraine, it found considerable interest at a time when many intellectuals and social scientists turned away from structuralism and poststructuralism toward a "rehumanization of the social sciences" (Dosse 1999).

A difficult point in the German reception of the book lay in a frequent misunderstanding of its normative dimension. I was partly praised, partly censured for having declared creativity itself to be the highest value. But this was totally misguided, both with regard to my own reflections and with regard to historical pragmatism. But mere repudiation of this misunderstanding would have reduced the book to nothing more than a contribution to a highly abstract academic discussion. That is why I decided to approach this normative challenge from the offense in another book, *The Genesis of Values* (1997; published in English, 2000). The debate about communitarianism also played a major role in this connection — a debate that had started as a philosophical discussion about the limits of John Rawls's *Theory of Justice* in the 1980s but had been transformed into a concretely political debate since around 1990.

In 1990, I received and accepted an offer to join the faculty from the Free University of Berlin. I thus returned institutionally to the place where I had studied. Fortunately the position was not primarily located in the sociology department, which still suffered in sometimes odd ways from the aftereffects of 1968. My main affiliation, instead, was in the interdisciplinary John F. Kennedy Institute for North American Studies. At the Kennedy Institute — where I served as director from 1993 to 1995 — I could follow my inclination to do comparative work about the United States and Germany (or Europe) in a congenial atmosphere. In the period of turmoil in East Berlin, I also taught classes at Humboldt University. In the sociology department of the Free University, I became responsible for teaching classical and modern sociological theory — against manifold resistance from colleagues who were either opposed to the formation of any sociological canon or opposed the specific canon out of their late-Marxist or postmodernist motives. I first met Amitai Etzioni in person as director of the Kennedy Institute. His book *The Active Society*, vastly neglected in sociology, had for a long time already appeared to me to be an important anticipation of later theoretical developments and one of the few serious alternatives to Parsons. After our personal encounter, I became more and more involved in the international communitarian network. I interpreted Etzioni's communitarianism as a new version of antiutilitarian and anti-individualist American thinking — and thus quite comparable to certain features in John Dewey's works, for example. Journalistic work in this area led to innumerable invitations to speak to political parties and big churches, reaching to the highest levels, for example, in a panel discussion with Mikhail Gorbachev.

These public discussions were, as I mentioned, one of my reasons to write a book on the question of how values can arise out of action and experience. The book was written in 1996/97 during a one-year stay in the United States, in close contact with my friend Charles Camic in Madison, Wisconsin, and with the leading pragmatist Richard Bernstein in New York. The book deals partly with a philosophical discourse on the question of the genesis of values that took place between 1887, when Nietzsche's *On the Genealogy of Morals* was published, and 1934, when John Dewey's *A Common Faith* came out. Against Nietzsche, whom I have never been willing to acquit from having played a destructive role in German intellectual history, the book poses the magnificent phenomenology of religious experiences in William James. This move again shows my constant attempt to overcome certain limits of German thinking by a detour through America. The response I give in that book to the question of the genesis of values lies in the proposition that value commitments arise out of experiences of self-formation and self-transcendence. In hermeneutical manner this response is elaborated by ever more comprehensive interpretive efforts. It offers a rich phenomenology of experiences of self-transcendence, from prayer to love, from the shattering of a person by the other in compassion to the experience of fusion with nature. The book is intended also to offer the basis for a historical sociology of value change. Religious motivations in my social-theoretical work can be more easily discerned in this book than in any preceding one.

In the German public outside of sociology, this book was a sort of breakthrough for me. The echo from philosophy and theology is strong and persistent. In the English-speaking world I received several rather polemical manifestations of complete lack of comprehension — from a proponent of rational choice to the postmodernists. This, of course, does not include those I consider fatherly friends and my true academic teachers although I never was their student: In addition to Bernstein, Etzioni, Levine, and Taylor, whose names I have already mentioned, I mean here Robert Bellah, Philip Selznick, and Edward Tiryakian. Their works, but frequently also their personal encouragement and help, have been for a long time an important stimulus for my efforts. In this regard (and in many others) I am certainly not mostly a "man of 1968"; their writings are more important for me than most of what came later.

In my present work, I continue along the lines of *The Creativity of Action* and *The Genesis of Values* in various ways. My book *War and Modernity* is partly devoted to the strange inversion of the features of value-constitutive knowledge in the experience of violence, be it as a perpetrator or as a victim of violence. My scattered attempts to do justice to the dynamics of religious experience in sociological theory will soon be published as a collection of articles. The title of this forthcoming book, *Does Man Need Religion?* stems from a talk I gave in April 2003 to an audience of more than five thousand people in Berlin — in the context of an event that can only be called historical for Germany, namely, the first common church congress of Catholics and Protestants in Germany. In addition, a very lengthy new book has to be mentioned, a book with the immodest title *Social Theory*. Based on years of teaching and written together with Wolfgang Knöbl, it offers the most comprehensive overview of the development of social theory after 1945 in English-, German-, and French-speaking areas; there is nothing comparable on the book market. Despite all efforts to be fair in the presentation of theoretical approaches, the book is not written like a neutral textbook: it is itself part of the long-term theoretical project of its two authors.

Two new projects are currently keeping me busy. The first is an attempt to concretize the "genesis of values" in a study on the history of human rights and the idea of universal human dignity; the second is an attempt to further develop the pragmatist approach in macrosociological theorizing in *The Creativity of Action*; this will be presented under the theme of "contingency," initially in the area of the sociology of religion. For these historical-sociological works, the writings of Max Weber have become progressively important to me over the past decade. I had never been able simply to take my stand on the shoulders of this giant — probably because of my persistent reservations concerning German traditions in general and also because of Weber's deep-seated nationalist and anti-Catholic attitudes. I think I have only recently been able to spell out what the continuation of his work should look like — and what it should not look like. In the year 2002, I resigned from my professorship in Berlin because of the deteriorating work conditions there. Since then, I have split my time between a new small advanced-study center, the Max Weber Center, in the city where Max Weber was born, Erfurt, and the much-admired University of Chicago. As director of the Max Weber Center in Erfurt, I am the successor to Wolfgang Schluchter, the great expert on Max Weber. We share the program of an interdisciplinary, comparative, historically oriented and also normatively interested social science. If I am indeed healed from a life-threatening disease (of which I learned in 2002), as it presently looks, I hope to be able to continue those projects I have begun. But only few things in life, I think, happen according to our expectations. The experience of contingency and the hope of a creative solution determine my feelings of life continuing.

Bibliography

Camic, Charles, and Hans Joas. 2004. *The Dialogical Turn: New Roles for Sociology in the Postdisciplinary Age — Essays in Honor of Donald N. Levine.* Lanham, MD: Rowman & Littlefield.

Dosse, François. 1999. *Empire of Meaning: The Humanization of the Social Sciences.* Translated by Hassan Melehy. Minneapolis: University of Minnesota Press.

Etzioni, Amitai. 1968. *The Active Society.* London: Collier-Macmillan; New York: Free Press.

———. 1988. *The Moral Dimension.* New York: Free Press; London: Collier Macmillan.

Honneth, Axel, and Hans Joas. 1988. *Social Action and Human Nature.* Translated by Raymond Meyer. Cambridge: Cambridge University Press.

———, eds. 1991. *Communicative Action: Essays on Jürgen Habermas's "The Theory of Communicative Action."* Translated by Jeremy Gaines and Doris L. Jones. Cambridge: Polity Press.

Joas, Hans. 1985. *G. H. Mead: A Contemporary Re-examination of His Thought.* Cambridge: Polity Press.

———. 1993. *Pragmatism and Social Theory.* Chicago: University of Chicago Press.

———. 1996. *The Creativity of Action.* Translated by Jeremy Gaines and Paul Keast. Chicago: University of Chicago Press.

———. 2000. *The Genesis of Values.* Translated by Gregory Moore. Chicago: University of Chicago Press.

———. 2003. *War and Modernity.* Translated by Rodney Livingstone. Cambridge: Polity Press.

Culture of Life

Karin Knorr Cetina is visiting professor of sociology and anthropology at the University of Chicago, professor of sociology at the University of Constance, Germany, and a member of the Institute for World-Society Studies, University of Bielefeld, Germany. In addition to her three degrees, she has received several honors, including Vienna University's Fellowship for the Gifted; she was a Ford Foundation Post-Doctoral Fellow, a member of the Institute for Advanced Study, Princeton, and president of the International Society for Social Studies of Science; and she is a future member of the Center for Advanced Study in the Behavioral Sciences in Palo Alto, California. She has published numerous papers and books, including Epistemic Cultures: How the Sciences Make Knowledge, *which received two prizes. She is currently working on a book on the global microstructures of financial markets.*

Vienna, the Matrix

If there is a place that both fostered and mediated my participation in the student rebellion of the late 1960s and early 1970s, then this was Vienna. Vienna had, in the view of many, become a somewhat wilted garden of creativity after its hothouse years from the turn of the twentieth century to the 1930s. And it was wilted. There were no counterparts to the major philosophers (Ludwig Wittgenstein and the Vienna Circle), writers and poets (e.g., Robert Musil), architects (Adolf Loos), composers (Arnold Schoenberg, Gustav Mahler), painters (Gustav Klimt, Egon Schiele, Oskar Kokoschka), radical political thinkers (Leon Trotsky), and physicians (Sigmund Freud) who had been concentrated there earlier. Nevertheless, Vienna remained a distinctive milieu that had what I still regard as a spe-

cial ambience and blend of traits. It continued to be the Center, if you could ignore what it was the Center *of* after Austria lost its empire in 1918. Its inhabitants
still cultivated the cynical wit, the morbid attitudes, and the rhetorical brilliance
in the local idiom that had so captivated earlier writers. The Viennese still ap
peared to be obsessed with spectacles, whether of a "beautiful funeral," a nicely
laid out corpse, or an articulate play staged in the Burgtheater. The Viennese enjoyed scandals — in which Viennese public figures regularly got themselves embroiled. They created scandals; for example, they would keep on gossiping about
the city's various artistic directors, supported by a notorious press, until these
figures found it too much and left, which they regularly did. They staged their
own lives — I have never seen so many "characters," failed geniuses, and sensual
blondes, playing their roles with great panache while going about their mundane
daily business. I never had so many friends and colleagues whose lives seemed to
come directly from a Schnitzler play, given the way they talked, dressed, and
comported themselves. It is not so much that the Viennese engaged in the Goff-
manian presentation of the self in everyday life. It seemed rather that Vienna's artistic past and present inundated regular life and the Viennese fitted their lives
into the expression of this art.

The medium in which all this thrived was an ongoing public conversation in
which many seemed to participate. The relative inclusiveness of this conversation was in no small measure due to another Viennese characteristic: the close
interlocking of its cultural and political classes. Politicians, artists, and intellectuals crossed one another's paths on numerous occasions at all manner of venues,
many of them institutional, others provided by Vienna's still important cafés, its
wine pubs (called *Heurigen*), and its cultural scene. Like Vienna's theatrical dimension, interlocking elites were not a new feature. Edward Timm, the Cambridge biographer of Karl Kraus, who edited periodicals from 1911 to 1936 and was
perhaps Vienna's most articulate satirist, comments on the circles that had
formed around the dominant avant-garde personalities of that time and the striking fact that they all intersected (1986, 7–8). The circuits of the 1960s and 1970s
were no longer personality-centered but they still intersected. The circuits created a social grid through which talk flowed — and through which many other
things also passed. Vienna, the matrix for the cultural performance of life, was
also a matrix for the social distribution of goods and favors that many needed and
that were scarce.

The powers that had inserted themselves into the grid at the time when I began my studies at the University of Vienna in the mid-1960s were the large polit-

ical parties, the social democrats and the conservatives, which often ruled as coalitions. They were an additional dimension of the grid, the factor that gave the matrix of circles and connections its imposing quality. The parties secured their power and the loyalty of large populations by mediating market and merit-based processes of resource allocation. Market processes, for example, were not just reined in, as they were in Germany, with the help of state regulations but shaped through the mediating role party members played in market outcomes and processes. There were large socialized industries and public sector bureau-cracies—all receiving state support—in return for which they kept an open ear to requests for favors filed through their party members. These industries and bu-reaucracies were also a rich reservoir of votes—employees were expected to be-come party members and vote accordingly. There was, also, the role party mem-bers played on the boards and councils of public and private organizations, in committees, interest groups, and so on. To obtain a position in public institutions and agencies (e.g., universities and schools), in state-run industries, and in the media, and the like, to obtain affordable housing in a real estate market in which not enough was being built, even to get a phone line fast, it helped to have a party affiliation and to go through party contacts. The parties played the role of facili-tator and interest broker. They cared for the population, and they were benevo-lent. But one had to pay a price. The price was party loyalty and membership and the willingness to lubricate and cultivate the relevant contacts.

The population played along. Many wanted, it seemed, in this long postwar era, job security and stability. The problem was not a lack of initiative or entre-preneurial guts. Even after many years of watching Austria from a distance, my impression is that of a state that lost a large multinational playing field along with its empire but that is still producing at full speed the intelligentsia and sophisti-cated public servant class it would have needed had the empire survived. The problem was not an unskilled or unmotivated workforce, as perhaps in other countries; quite the opposite. It simply suited the Austrian psyche (or perhaps just that of Vienna, where I was) to be cynical about life's possibilities and to take a certain pleasure in undermining the very future one did not dare to believe in. Anyone could be an optimist and ostentatiously pursue ambitious ends with an eye to being appropriately rewarded for one's achievements. It befitted the so-phisticated, however, to see through life's promises and facades, to expect re-wards not to be forthcoming or to be diverted, and to work through systems of ob-ligation, indebtedness, and membership that were joined with systems of merit and market. The parties worked the membership systems and infused the latter with affiliates that gave things the appropriate spin, when spin was needed. The population went through the necessary motions; it joined the parties and acted sympathetically. But it also kept its mental distance from what it was doing. One sustained the parties by joining them because one thought they would reciprocate the favor when it was needed.

Vienna provided a matrix for turning everyday life into a forum of cultural performance and discussion. But it also provided a matrix for conducting one's life in the shadow of political groups and their ways of defining and mobilizing social power. Both aspects of Vienna's matrix for conducting one's life were sociologically interesting. The parties had set up a machine for creating and reproducing social power that worked smoothly, that included the political opposition — through coalitions, systems of distributing offices proportional to party membership, and the device of "social partnership" — and that somehow managed not to prevent a welfare state, low levels of unemployment, and economic growth.[1] Everyday life had its own wellspring of sociality and collective life: more than in other places, it seemed based on the observation and awareness of others and on conducting one's life — with gusto, rather than with existential dread — under the gaze of the other. Both forms of sociality infuriated me once I had become a full participant. I liked the charming ways of the Viennese, but I also thought one should be less submissive to the other and true to oneself. I viewed the parties' ways of subjecting market and meritocratic institutions to a social overhaul that channeled things through party affiliation as fundamentally nonobjective and unjust. Both forms of Viennese and Austrian society delivered the concrete reason for a concrete disgust with a particular culture and environment. While the Viet Nam War and the widespread suppression of the rights of "minorities" (such as students and women) fueled the discussion and the student movement from afar, the concrete Viennese experience shaped it from close by.

A Sensual Think Tank

Becoming a participant had its sensual aspects. The late 1960s and early 1970s were a continuous Harold Garfinkel experiment, an experiential makeover of things. They forced one to confront the taken-for-granted conventions of bourgeois and university life by going through habit-breaking experiences. They

---

1. Social partnership involves regular direct negotiations between capital and labor; for many years, these defused most labor conflicts and prevented strikes.

forced one to develop an attitude. They were perhaps "liberating," but liberation had to be accomplished—by overstepping rules, breaking codes, colliding head-on with the smooth and accommodating habits of Austrian daily life. This was strenuous work for someone who had been brought up conventionally and harbored no particular radical and some anticommunist feelings (there was one member of our extended family who was reputedly a communist and was abhorred for his "proletarian" habits; my grandmother tried to rescue his son from the proletarian milieu by making us play with him). There were the icons of student protest, imported in spirit from the United States and France, the physical disturbances of lectures and political and administration meetings. We called them sit-ins. At one point some of our more display-oriented male students turned one into what could only be called a "shit-in"—they defecated in the lecture hall. They were expressing their opinion on the issue of where we were at, at that stage of high capitalism (despicable), and what the university was doing about the sorry state of world affairs (nothing) and for student rights (denying them). One had to get used to this sort of insubordination and to quashing one's own embarrassment. There were also other strange breaches of norms that were physical in nature. I remember once going to a lecture by a younger instructor and finding a black room where everybody was sitting quietly. Then a young female, clad in largely transparent cat suit stepped forward, positioned herself on top of the desk that stood in front of the room, and started to perform slow and at times sexually suggestive dance movements to perfumed candles and Indian music. The instructor had the reputation of being one of the failed geniuses (in physics and mathematics) of which Austria had so many. He was, I think, a niche player who got a kick out of designing his own brand of antiestablishment happening. Reality took on an event structure. It consisted of happenings and interim periods during which we anticipated new events and discussed the old, as bystanders and participants.

I was, when things started happening, close to beginning my dissertation and was more of a bystander. My contribution to the movement had so far consisted of personal counterculture statements, like marrying all in black rather than white. I was holed up in the university's library, struggling with texts and suffering from a lack of competent guidance. Things improved when I changed institutions, moving from the university to Vienna's Institute for Advanced Studies in the fall of 1970. The institute was the postgraduate training ground for the future Austrian economic and social science elite. Those who passed the entrance exam felt themselves a select crowd; they were rewarded by a reasonable stipend, exposed to weeks of lectures by renowned American, British, and French social scientists, and had to undergo some training in mathematical and statistical modeling — the dominant discipline at the institute (and that of most institute leaders) was economics, and the curriculum was laced with quantitative methods. The institute was also something of a think tank for the Austrian government. The ruling party at the time was social democratic, and it believed in state intervention. To help it intervene, the government wanted economic and social science research — and financed it lavishly. The institute was a favorite place for conducting some of this research. The research was fundamental and autonomous, but given the spirit of the times one wanted it to be "socially relevant." It was never tied to any particular political decision or plan. In fact, I cannot remember a case where the government actually implemented any suggested or implied research recommendations. Nonetheless, the social democratic government seemed to like the idea of financing a center of excellence whose participants were by nature, discipline, and generation inclined more to liberal and socialist rather than conservative ideas. It understood the institute as a breeding ground for an intelligentsia that it vaguely hoped it might use in some distant future — or perhaps that it thought was better contained at the institute than left on the street.

The institute was a think tank of an inward-looking kind: it was above all a center of thinking and discussion for participants among themselves. I came to the institute together with a notable portion of Austria's most outspoken student movement leaders and participants, who were all roughly my generation, and various other recruits who also happened to be strong characters. My student movement colleagues had several years of political activism behind them, and some were the daughters and sons of Austrian political and philosophical leaders (one pair of recruits was the Austrian chancellor Bruno Kreisky's son and daughter-in-law). The institute has to be credited for recruiting and nourishing us. It did not have a policy of closing its doors to challengers and nonconformists. It understood, I think, those who are difficult to be the more interesting spirits and wanted to try its hand at their cognitive refinement. It branded itself elitist and lived up to its image by recruiting those who stood out — never mind the political, bohemian, or other beliefs they stood out for. The institute did not quite expect, I suppose, to become itself the subject of contestation at the hands of its students. The years after the arrival of our generation were strewn with conflicts between the administration and the student body over questions of directorship, curriculum, participation in decision making, and hiring. The administration's position usually prevailed, but it also gave way on occasion, and it continued a policy of accommodation rather than rejection. It hired most of us into assistant professorship positions after the two-year postgraduate training.

As a consequence, my generation of "scholars," as we were benevolently called, spent not just two but often six and more years at the institute, most of which were intense, exciting, and formative. Unlike my more fortunate colleagues, I was not yet properly politicized when I came to the institute in 1970. My student movement classmates enlightened me as to world politics and instructed me about what I ought to be battling. They also often corrected other of my opinions they deemed strange. For example, I found the econometrics and mathematical modeling courses interesting but was undecided on the virtue of these subjects. The movement practitioners, however, had already come to a verdict on these courses, and it was negative. I wasn't especially successful at holding my own when defending the potential value of mathematical models against them as I did not know enough about modeling and couldn't match their argumentation skills. Such verbal attacks by the movement's architects were at times somewhat personal, as if one was guilty of immoral behavior. I reacted defiantly to this treatment by later doing one of my first pieces of empirical research as an exclusively quantitative study that involved Lisrel models and long nights with fast computers. But for the most part I accepted their political knowledge as superior. Also, I had made emotionally stabilizing alliances of my own. Attractions of various degrees of were common between members of the student body but while I quite liked some of my student movement colleagues, I did not get involved with them. Instead, among the incoming students in sociology, perhaps half of whom had played no active role in the student rebellion and most of whom were men, I found my chief support in a hard-drinking, hard-smoking misfit who was not into politics but who was, as I understood him, into real knowledge. He was brilliant, and we struck up an intellectual relationship, which we later discovered to have other aspects as well. (Additional support came, in time , from an institute-mediated friendship with another brilliant and colorful character, a former priest.)

At the institute, a lot of energy went into discussions among ourselves. Some of us got involved in debates over the epistemological status of the social sciences, known as the debate over positivism, which was fueled by a controversy that Jürgen Habermas entertained with a philosopher who opposed him.[2] Some of us read and discussed Marxist ideas, and some enrolled in the various courses offered by distinguished visiting professors (those who stand out in my memory were Peter Blau, Aaron Cicourel, Jim Coleman, Paul Feyerabend, Rom Harré, and Gudmund Hernes [of Norway]). Much energy was also expended on relationships and relational issues. There were symmetric and asymmetric, fleeting and long-lasting attractions between the two sexes, some intensely felt but never fully consummated and still alive today, others not really felt but nonetheless consummated, still others that came into their own many years after our joint time at the institute. There were outbursts of jealousy and resentment, often on the part of our significant others who were not members of the institute and had come into our lives earlier. There were breakups of marriages twenty years later, breakups for which I now think seeds had been sown at that time. There was even a long period of time when several of us, all members of a couple, debated living together in a commune and attempted to work out the rules and attitudes that would help us do so. (Something indefinable happened, and we got scared.) There were group therapy aficionados among us who seemed, except for this purported childish pursuit, otherwise serious and intelligent scholars, and group therapy sessions in which it became fashionable to take part.

The institute somehow managed to be an intellectual and sensual place, a place where it all came together for some years and where energy appeared to be created rather than dissipated. It provided an endless stream of occasions for political dissent and activism, which we directed against its institutional structures, its directors, its links to politics, even its distinguished social science advisers (Paul Lazarsfeld and Jim Coleman, among others, were on the council of scientific advisers). It was elitist, which — I now think but did not then — helps create a stimulating environment. The institute emphasized reflexivity and articulateness; when I later moved to the United States, I felt that I had somehow been prepared, without quite noticing it, for seemingly any professional argument in seemingly any location. What also came together at the institute, I think, was the

2. The debate centered on the question of whether the social sciences ought to be understood as hermeneutic disciplines that basically belonged to the humanities, since they were based on people's meanings and interpretations, with all the implications this had for theory, research, and the epistemology of the social sciences. The alternative was that they belonged to the natural sciences in epistemological orientation.

end of an old era and the beginning of a new one. I associate the old era with the Enlightenment ideals we espoused and the belief in salvation by society. The new era anticipated our hopes for the individual perfectibility of life.

Culture of Life

The most severe challenge that emerged from the experience of the late sixties and early seventies was not that of questioning authority in the form of a hypocritical political establishment, our "conservative" parents, and the like. It was not the challenge of fighting against the discrimination and exploitation of the underprivileged and the struggle for civil rights. It was not even the struggle for the ending of an unjust and internally corrupt Viet Nam War. Rather, it was the challenge personally to lead a different life. Much of my experience of Vienna and its twisted ways of doing things suggested a simple alternative: straightforward ways. Its Catholic charms suggested the alternative of secular directness, its gossip culture the rejection of rumor and nosiness, its tactfulness the virtues of frank, if discourteous, directness. The massive strategic party affiliations of the population implied, according to the rhetoric of the time, that one had to refuse to join, except perhaps if one wanted to pursue a political career. The juicy little amorous intrigues that rendered life pleasurable in Vienna and supplied food for talk demanded to be turned inside out. If there was to be an extramarital affair, it had to be conducted, so we believed, in complete honesty and in close consultation with one's long-term marital partner. The requirements of fidelity were a form of possessiveness and implied the commodification of the relationship, since one treated the other like goods one owned. Such requirements had to be replaced by a pure love that made no demands on the other.

Many in my environment, myself included, attempted to implement these values. We discussed the difficulties involved on an abstract level, but when we failed to implement the new values, we found it hard to replace them with the old. Compromise was too entrenched in the rejected, surrounding culture to appear to be a way out of the difficulties we encountered. Over the years, the new lifestyle did get compromised, of course, and some of us consciously changed our beliefs and orientations. The one common outcome remaining from the whole experiment with alternative relationship models, I believe, has been the turn toward life. While the political significance of moving toward living one's ideas faded away, the taste for life did not: the taste for life and the rejection it implied of bourgeois and middle-class forms of sociality, of Vienna's off-putting "connection" — society and political appropriation of social power, tied in with the rise of new lifestyles that are more narcissistic, more individualized, more object- than human-centered, and ultimately postsocial. The end of youthful ideals also tied in with the rise of the life sciences and the promises they provide for individual improvement and solutions. The political outcries of the 1960s and 1970s were a last and dramatic attempt to insinuate the enlightenment values of equality, honesty, and objectivity into the general culture. But they also anticipated and perhaps were at the roots of today's culture of life.

I use the notion "culture of life" as a metaphor and anchoring concept to illustrate a cultural turn to nature that has replaced the culture of the social that was so manifest in Vienna. "Life" stands for an open-ended series of phenomenological, biological, economic, informational, and other significations and processes, but it does not stand for the expansion of Enlightenment ideals of the perfectibility of human society in terms of equality, peace, justice, and social welfare. In the second half of my institute years, we had, I think, already begun to shift away from these ideas when we began to focus on the conduct and realization of our individual lives. What has since emerged is a notion of the perfectibility of life whose symbolic territory has expanded; it now encompasses, among other things, life enhancement on the individual level, the biopolitics of populations, the protection and reflexive manipulation of nature, and the idea of intergenerational (rather than distributional) justice. One massive source of life-centered thinking has been the life sciences themselves. They replace the social sciences as a source of collective imagination. They produce a stream of research that inspires imaginative elaborations of the human individual as enriched by genetic, biological, and technological supplements and upgrades. Even in the social sciences today, the fantasized unit is more the subject than society — as manifest in individualizing theories that range from rational choice concepts to identity models.

My own post-Viennese days began when my husband and I moved for a year to Berkeley, where, on top of the Berkeley Hills, one could feast on breathtaking views of the San Francisco Bay, ride into dry, sun-drenched grasslands and woods (I found them cozy and comforting; our Austrian forests had always been green, moldy, and repellently wet), and enjoy the balmy air. I thought of this, at the time, as my rediscovery of nature. I knew then that the beauty of it all would spoil the experience of any other environment I might yet encounter. Berkeley was also immensely liberating — one cared little, it seemed, about any of the features that mattered in Vienna or the larger Middle European context. I was unable at first to distinguish professors from bums when I passed them on Telegraph Avenue — clothes did not seem to be a means of signaling social status. The elaborate little conversations of glances one had on Vienna's streets with those strolling past (first looking at the other's face, then sideways to the partner, then back and down the first person's entire frame to their toes, and back up till you met their eyes) did not exist. Even smoking a cigarette, which had always been a matter of reciprocity and social negotiation (would you take a cigarette if I took one?) in Vienna, seemed entirely a matter between tobacco and oneself. It seemed to me one could move in with a horse in this environment without anyone taking notice or finding it strange. I felt free: liberation somehow translated into creative impulse, and I embarked on my first "laboratory study," a piece of work that I might not have done in Vienna and that involved the study of natural science practice through the direct observation of scientists in the lab. I had been steeped in philosophy before coming to Berkeley; the university required philosophy courses, and we had read Habermas, Hans-Georg Gadamer, Willard Quine, Ludwig Wittgenstein, Karl Popper, Imre Lakatos, and later Thomas Kuhn in the context of the debate over positivism at the institute. I developed a great interest in the natural sciences from these discussions (as well as earlier ones at home in Vienna). But I had the most bizarre ideas about how the natural sciences worked — shaped by what I knew about the logic of scientific theories and the context of justification. It was unavoidable, I think, that I should get hooked on conducting a laboratory study with the first step into a lab — it was immediately obvious that things there were very different from what we all thought. No one, to my knowledge, had published such a work in the sociology of science before, and my earlier work on scientists in organizations had not captured my imagination. It had not even satisfied my sense of what it meant to do a social scientific study: correlations were low and explained less than 10 percent of the variance; they depended rather too strongly on what I did to them statistically, and some made no sense. Worst of all, the study was obviously not just a case of bad design but also exemplified what was to be expected, I feared, from survey research. The investment of time and money had been large (I headed the Austrian part of a six-country study), and I felt I had learned nothing theoretically interesting. I wanted to spend the year in Berkeley reading and developing a sense of what I should do next. The answer was there with my first step into a lab: what I saw was crying out to be studied. Researching natural scientific practice occupied me for the better part of the next fifteen years.[3] I also learned that the method of direct observation, if applied to the right setting, and if one wasn't chary of looking at things conceptually rather than merely descriptively, yielded the theoretically more innovative results — or let's just say the ones that I find exhilarating, as opposed to ones that are merely routine business.

The Berkeley experience was no less formative than that at the Vienna Institute for Advanced Studies, but it was the antithesis of it. The place seemed different in nearly all respects — climate, natural environment, way of life, intellectual context. If Vienna had been heavy on society and social mechanisms, Berkeley seemed the opposite. If there was any society at all in Berkeley at the time it was society light. At the Institute for Advanced Studies, we had surpassed Vienna's social ways of being by discussing and seeking collective problem solutions — in accordance with the enlightenment ideas of social justice and equality. Those who had been part of the Sixties movement in Berkeley on into 1976/77 seemed to have opted for and be living out individual solutions. Berkeley added models and ideas for realizing the personally different life we had started to implement in Vienna. But what these models reinforced was a new, postmodern era. The Berkeley models and ideas had one great advantage: they were livable. The difficulties we had had in implementing a new, more sincere, achievement-oriented life with fewer semantic layers disappeared against the background of a culture that seemed to know only one surface level, believed in a straight relationship between simple causes and desirable effects (e.g., between achievement and rewards), and gave individuals the right to do what they were likely to do anyway. Most important, perhaps, Berkeley added fun to the ease of life —Yosemite and the Muir Woods made environmentalism enjoyable, the ample health food stores and California's delicious vegetarian fare (available on campus) made it easy to opt for healthy things, Sesame Street had been up and running on TV for years and featured the antiracist, antisexist, multicultural fare we craved for our two-year-old, and specialty cafés, complete with an intellectual milieu — the one item I was sure I was going to miss outside Vienna — already existed. Even the continuous drought was made reasonably pleasurable —water conservation was dictated by the amount of water coming out of the faucet and could be taken off the list of things one had to bring oneself to pay attention to to act with moral propriety in daily life. For those who still craved political activism, excellent yoga classes were offered live and on TV.

3. Two monographs resulted (Knorr Cetina 1981, 1999).

The fun extended into intellectual life. The Berkeley campus and context provided a larger center of thinking than the Vienna institute and it offered more diversity. I learned my Heidegger in Berkeley, from Hubert Dreyfus, speech act theory from John Searle, and the ethnography of communication from both Jenny Cook-Gumperz's (1986; Cook-Gumperz et al. 1986) and John Gumperz's works(1982a, 1982b). I became briefly fascinated with Eleanor Rosch's cognitive psychology, Paul Feyerabend's breathtaking stories about the early history of science, and many student-organized activities. Aaron Cicourel, who had read my needs correctly, had advised me to go to Berkeley rather than somewhere else, and Troy Duster and his Institute for Social Change offered a home base—I have been grateful to both of them ever since. Both my husband and I went back to Vienna briefly after Berkeley, but it was clear that we wanted to come back to the States and we did.

Back to the Future: The Old Structures of the New

Like the Vienna institute, Berkeley happened at the right time. In its stimulating and liberating environment I was able to translate the obsessions we acquired in the late 1960s and early 1970s into another project that quickly became equally obsessive: research into the natural sciences. Research programs feed on themselves, they produce, from their own open questions and inadequacies, new research programs and obsessions. On that happily-ever-after note, one could end these reflections, were it not for another encounter with the Sixties and their aftermath into which I stumbled when—after some years in the States that I spent trying out postdoc and visiting positions and finally a full professorship on the East Coast—I returned to Europe in 1983, with my family trailing behind me. This time it was Germany rather than Austria and the small Northern German town of Bielefeld rather than Vienna. Bielefeld was not quite the culture shock one might expect it to have been after Vienna and Berkeley. The University of Bielefeld had the largest and, so I was told, the best faculty of sociology in the country. Sociology had Niklas Luhmann, Claus Offe, an excellent center for science and technology studies, and sociology of development. It had the Georg Simmel archive, Alfred Schutz's previously unedited letters, a phenomenologically informed microsociological tradition and a thriving macrosociological equivalent—systems theory. In fact, Bielefeld was a new "reform university" established in the late Sixties on the basis of the recommendations of a renowned German sociologist Helmut Schelsky—with Niklas Luhmann as its first professor (appointed in 1968).[4] Bielefeld had sociology in its genes, one might say, and this translated into the faculty's considerable size, rich course offerings, and manifold activities. Most important, perhaps, Bielefeld still had students interested in sociology — a first sign that the Sixties had carried over into the post-Sixties generation. During the late sixties and the seventies, the social sciences had offered the discipline of choice for many students. This love affair has now fizzled out, but it was still in full bloom when I came to Bielefeld. By virtue of my status as a professor I was now on the receiving end of the occasional classroom disruptions, faculty meeting breakups, and attacks on political posters that spiced up the disciplinary love affair for our students. I watched the goings on with some hidden pride in the anti-authoritarianism that had been bred and with sympathy for the issues students addressed.

There were other signs that the Sixties were not over, to which I reacted with less sympathy and pride — changes that had been wrought in the Sixties and brought forward. The political activism of the Sixties had been rather successful where German universities are concerned. It had helped to promote a complete overhaul of the university system. Senior faculty members no longer occupied "chairs" but held regular professorships, assistant professors were autonomous, student and entry-level faculty as well as researchers and nonfaculty had voting rights in most decisions, procedures and meetings had by and large become transparent (one could sit in on them or get the protocols of the proceedings), institutes with grants to particular chairs and endowed with their own budget were replaced by collective units (departments, working groups, centers, and the like), and the faculty "managed itself" with elected officials from within its ranks (there was no separate administrative hierarchy of deans). So far, so good. Against the background of the "authoritarian" university structures of before that we storied in our discourse, these reforms were an improvement. The changes in Bielefeld went beyond the modernizations and democratizations that were implemented elsewhere. Our founding patron, Schelsky, had wanted a research university that halted the fragmentation of the disciplines and truly nourished the traffic of ideas. Accordingly, Bielefeld was set up with its own institute for advanced stud-

4. Official planning for Bielefeld University started in 1965 and the first students were enrolled (in mathematics and sociology) in the fall of 1969–70. Schelsky's recommendations for this reform university can be found in Mikat and Schelsky (1966). Bielefeld was one of the universities created during a massive wave of university expansion that lasted from about 1965 to 1980, when nearly twenty new universities were established.

ies dedicated to interdisciplinary research; it offered the faculty the opportunity to switch between research and teaching on a term or annual basis, related disciplines were joined together in "faculties" to create synergy effects, and even the library had been reinvented—designed for total access (now twenty-four hours), it displayed its relevance and status by prominently occupying the gallery level in all parts of our sprawling, Beaubourg-like building. Some of these features might potentially have sweetened academic life, but some also got diluted over time (e.g., switching between research and teaching soon acquired the status of being "tolerated" only) and some were laced with constraints and transaction costs that made them unattractive to the more industrious faculty members. What counted in the end were the features that resulted from the general institutional reform. Here my enthusiasm waned. The problems concerned the form democratization actually took, the understanding of equality, and the failure to construe universities as producers of knowledge.

The form that democracy adopted resided in what the native idiom called the "structure" of the university. At the Commission Europeéne pour la Recherche Nucléaire (or CERN, as it is more commonly known) in Geneva, the European High Energy Physics Laboratory, where I studied the knowledge processes of particle physics, one also talked about "the structure" that one distinguished from "the science." By the former, physicists meant the administrative hierarchy and rules and, by the latter, what they did in their large experiments, which they controlled themselves. At CERN, the structure was the laboratory; it was the "bureaucratically" run facility and infrastructure in which research took place. The experiments were "democratic," meaning information was shared and decisions were taken consensually, if at all feasible.[5] At CERN, democracy resided in communication. In Bielefeld, it resided in voting rights and rules, in structures of organization prescribed on all levels of organizing, and in procedural requirements. Underlying the structure at CERN was the idea that a laboratory facility had to function in predictable ways to serve the science. Underneath the idea of structure in German universities lies a distrust of people. Structures are imposed to safeguard against the assumed tendency of people to seek power and use it against others. Scripted into the rules is an interest group model that assumes the existence of three categories of university participants that are naturally pitted against each other by virtue of the interests they share as classes of actors: students, entry- and midlevel faculty, and professors. The state's moral obligation is

5. This is further explained in Knorr Cetina (1999), chaps. 7 and 8.

to arm each natural class with voting rights and to set up a political process of interest arbitration (via votes) that protects each class against the potential assaults of another (German universities are state universities).

We professors did not, of course, share *a* common interest, nor did the members of the other two groups. The whole interest group model was a tremendous sociological construction that could have come straight out of a sociology of knowledge text, where such models are prevalent, but it had practical consequences. Its worst effect was that, to some degree, it actually created the classes it postulated. First, those of us participating in the structure had to become legally savvy—for example, we had to learn how votes were to be taken (e.g., written or not, with the option to abstain or not), with what majority, by what groups, on which issue, with what minute-taking necessities, etc. I have seen many a chair conducting these meetings with the several hundred-page-long code of laws governing universities by their side ready for instant consultation. Second, one had to acquire skills in the art of political debate, pre-and postmeeting coalition forming, mental record keeping and the like, as in a policy arena, at least if one wanted to win one's case. Third, one learned distrust; those in the lower classes in particular (pardon the saying, but this is how things were set up) started to distrust those in the upper classes, and such attitudes were reciprocated when they became apparent. Thus, those of us who did not distance themselves mentally (many did, including students) became reprogrammed on the information, performance, and trust levels. The whole process had other consequences; for example, it demanded time that had to be taken away of other activities. It had massive relationship costs. Relationships between students, professors, and mid-level faculty were strained by the distrust that developed on the basis of the assumed interest differences, and those within interest groups were somehow not improved by the interest bond that supposedly held them together either. It also had costs for the new generation. Many a young post-Sixties sociologist who believed in democracy and decision participation got caught up in the jungle of committees and paragraphs, only to reemerge too late for the pursuit of sociological excellence and perhaps even the advance of a career.

The frenzied structuring efforts of German universities in the post-Sixties era did, of course, arise from a disaffection with the past, which one sought to eradicate. But one can also discern in these efforts the desire for purity, objectivity, and semantic and moral clarity that engaged us in personal life. How was an institution—as opposed to an individual—to live democracy transparently, correctly, securely? The answer, the political system engineers thought, could only be found in the legal prescription of organizational design down to the level of each unit and decision. When the law did not work or had unintended consequences, new rules were invented to repair the old ones. This kept happy rounds of law makers and administrators busy in several locations: newly elected ministers of science dabbled with system, universities warily implemented the reforms, faculties and students shrugged their shoulders and complied, and the misimplementations eventually got back to the ministries, where they rekindled the process. No one ever seemed to have gotten the idea that democracy and self-governance could also be based on a model of autonomous individuals of whom one could expect that they would exercise their judgment independently and perhaps even reasonably. No one was willing to try American or Swiss models of democracy, which place greater faith in the individual. Institutions in Germany, unlike persons, were never thrown off track when it came to implementing the social imaginaries of the Sixties. When it became possible, as it did during the time of wild university foundations in Germany in the late Sixties and seventies, these imaginaries were simply put into practice — thoroughly and durably. The institutions that were created contained the seeds of the culture of life that emerged on a personal level. What one wanted to implement, I think, were institutions whose life was perfected. But perfection meant something that did not break away from the reflexive models of industrial society that started off the Sixties. The seeds did not germinate into a new institutional nature.

The beliefs of the Sixties, with their desire for purity and semantic simplicity, could also be discerned in another message that the system beamed out: its distrust of the symbolic. The twisted ways of Vienna against which we rebelled had included public-private and frontstage-backstage distinctions, layers of semantic nuance in most utterances, elaborate rituals, and bendable systems of rewards. Bielefeld knew no frontstage, it rejected rituals, and it balked at reward systems. Among these rejections, distrust in symbolic rewards is perhaps the most counterproductive, no matter what the realm of endeavor; but it is particularly deleterious in academic work, where one needs to maintain one's enthusiasm and motivation—usually without commensurate financial compensation.[6] The post-Sixties' universities had another model scripted into their structure, that of the

6. German universities do not offer financial rewards on the basis of merit; everyone in a particular category and age group, etc., receives the same pay. Pay raises can be obtained in connection when a position is offered by another university, but they are small and they tend to be temporary; also, they often do not carry over into pension benefits.

purely self-motivated actor. In private life, we had wanted to salvage the idea of pure love from the polluting components of possessiveness, jealousy, display behavior, even sex. Post-Sixties universities seemed to want to salvage the idea of pure knowledge from the polluting effects of rewards, recognition, and incentives. It was somehow contemptible and at the same time embarrassing to engage in the rituals that one devotes elsewhere to honoring excellence and achievement — even on a student level. This second transcendental construction also had practical consequences — it deepened participants' feeling of detachment and alienation from the institution that evinced so little interest in their work and achievement. In some cases, for example, in the case of Luhmann, who had already become internationally renowned as a theorist in the 1980s, one needed to make an effort not to notice the glory that was bestowed on him elsewhere. Bielefeld's sociology lived up to the challenge. Almost to the end, it refused Luhmann any special treatment. When Luhmann retired, he revealed that he felt hurt by this attitude — he wanted to be meaningful to the place that, decades before, had made him its first professor.[7] When the lessons that emerged from the frustrations of the Sixties were institutionalized, things sometimes took a fiendish turn. In the land of Max Weber, meaning, the symbolic values of life, were now banned from institutional embodiments and realizations. One had finally recognized, I suppose, the symbolic for what it mostly was, a mere simulation.

There is a third attitude that strikes me as a possible carryover from (or as reinforced by) the Sixties: the notion of university management as pure administration. Universities in Germany, when they are well run (which Bielefeld was) provide the necessary administrative services, from the care of buildings to hiring and accounting.[8] These services act as guardians of the rules and regulations that are imposed on them and as stewards for the budgets they obtain. What they do not normally do is see themselves as institutional producers of knowledge. The model I have in mind is that of the arts and other areas where there are, on the one hand, the makers of artworks (e.g., a painter) and, on the other, producers of art who enable, facilitate, and to some degree direct the making of artwork.

7. An unaddressed issue in Germany is the fear of elitism. To maintain equality, apparently, it is necessary to neutralize, disregard, or play down achievement and dismantle reputation.
8. The University of Bielefeld was long run by a mathematician, Karl-Peter Grotemeyer, who combined professional authority and personal integrity with political savvy and assembled an excellent team around him. He was admired even by his enemies and was, when he retired, one of the longest-serving university presidents in Germany.

This is a more constructive and creative role than the one I see allowed in German universities, where the action one gets out of administrations is often negative, preventive, or regulative and oriented to accountability — at the expense of activities that would stimulate ideas, develop the institution, or think ahead (I am talking here of roles, not persons, who are often heroically battling their constraints). The top, it appears, is not the place for visions or long-term objectives, let alone some Schumpeteran competitive elimination of old forms of the organization of production. We would not, of course, have liked the idea of a university to be associated with entrepreneurship in the Sixties. But we did not yet think in terms of a knowledge society or link producer roles to knowledge. Even an unreconstructed Marxist might agree that the sort of producer role that I imagine might serve knowledge has nothing to do with that of the exploitative capitalist or the morally tainted neoliberal CEO. Uncreative, sullen institutions are not an asset in a knowledge era: they are a negative force. Such institutions cannot simply be sent to Berkeley to acquire a taste for a culture of life. Or could they?

One has to be brave to try and reverse the institutional consequences of ideas one once shared through local work on a day-to-day basis. I was not very brave; I took to spending summers in the States and seeking sabbaticals there to take leave of my culture. My student and young adult rebelliousness had not started, I should add here, with the movement of the Sixties. It started with the distaste I developed at the age of eight or nine for my countrymen's habit of cooking their Sunday roast from early morning onward — the smell pervaded the streets and ruined the morning's freshness — and I experienced the first assault of alienation from my own culture (or at least the first I can remember). The repugnant odor came back to me later, at least metaphorically, though it often originated from institutions and those who acted as their committed keepers — it continued to affect me despite the nourishment that it also often signaled and delivered. The one consistent strand of my rebellion, I fear, over the years, is not the rebellion against a particular politics or injustice. It is not even the rebellion against structures and matrices of the sort described, though I still do not like them. It is the rebellion against what I see as obsolete modes of culture and attempts to prevent openings to new forms of life.

References

Cook-Gumperz, Jenny. 1986. *The Social Construction of Literacy*. Cambridge: Cambridge University Press.

Cook-Gumperz, Jenny, William A. Corsaro, and Jürgen Streeck, eds. 1986. *Children's Worlds and Children's Language*. Berlin: M. de Gruyter.

Gumperz, John J. 1982a. *Discourse Strategies*. Cambridge: Cambridge University Press.

———, ed. 1982b. *Language and Social Identity*. Cambridge: Cambridge University Press.

Janick, A. 2001. *Wittgenstein's Vienna Revisited*. New Brunswick, NJ: Transaction Publishers.

Johnston, W. M. 1972. *The Austrian Mind. An Intellectual and Social History*. Berkeley: University of California Press.

Knorr Cetina, Karin. 1981. *The Manufacture of Knowledge*. Oxford: Pergamon Press.

———. 1999. *Epistemic Cultures*. Boston: Harvard University Press.

Mikat, P., and H. Schelsky. 1966. *Grundzüge einer neuen Universität*. Gütersloh: Bertelsmann.

Timms, E. 1986. *Karl Kraus, Apocalyptic Satirist*. New Haven, CT, and London: Yale University Press.

Dionysus and the Ideals of 1968

Michel Maffesoli has taught sociology at the Sorbonne (University of Paris V) since 1981 and is currently director of the Centre d'études sur l'actuel et quotidien (CEAQ), which he cofounded there in 1982. He has been highly honored for his work on the sociology of the quotidian and on the social imagination: he has been inducted into the French Legion of Honor, and his book La transfiguration du politique *won the Grand Prix des Sciences Humaines of the Acadèmie Française in 1992. Educated at the University of Strasbourg and the University of Grenoble, he has written extensively on the sociology of the quotidian and on the social imagination. His many publications include* The Time of the Tribes, *which questions the idea that individualism is a defining feature of modernity, showing instead that there are new tribal determinants of identity, and* The Shadow of Dionysus: A Contribution to the Sociology of the Orgy, *and many works in French, among them* L'instant éternel: Le retour du tragique dans les sociétés postmodernes; Le rhythme de la vie: Variations sur l'imaginaire postmoderne; La part du Diable: Précis de subversion postmoderne; La contemplation du monde; *and* Notes sur la postmodernité: Le lieu fait lien. *Maffesoli serves as director of the Centre de recherche sur l'imaginaire at the Maison des Sciences de l'Homme and is vice-president of the International Institute of Sociology.*

Everything surely began on the steps of my native village, Graissessac, with its paradoxical mixture of the noonday sun and the blackness of the mined coal, of

Translated by Paul-Philippe Paré; edited by Anne Sica and Stephen Turner.

the tribute daily paid to Prometheus by this duty-bound man who was my father, an underground miner, and of the collective festival that seized the village each year, feast of the Holy Beard.

"Here one could live, for here one may live, and here one can go on living because we endure and do not collapse overnight," said Nietzsche (*On the Use and Abuse of History for Life*, 1878). It seems to me that the source of my reflection is the astonishing mystery of social vitality, which I have called "sociality," the essential social force that resists the imposition of various powers, economic, political, and symbolic, that characterize everyday life.

I cannot forget that in contrast to many of my friends and colleagues of "68," I do not originate from the lower or high bourgeoisie but, instead, from the common people, the miners of the Cevennes, an area of modest mountains in the south of France. I cannot say if my background gave me any advantage as a theorist, but it certainly sustained an intellectual sensitivity that made me suspicious of any kind of power, any sort of abstract theory, and any kind of moralism. All of this is consolidated in what Max Weber called "the logic of the duty of being": a statement of intellectual sensibility that is in synchrony with a common untheoretical anarchism, the knowing in one's bones that, although the princes can change (ministers of either the Right or Left), they remain agents of power. Therefore, it is important to know how to resist, how to outsmart this power. This is the source of my hypothesis of the *quant a soi social* (as for oneself social), which connotes the invisible distance that one places between oneself and the "owners" of society.

Such *quant a soi* illuminated the structural and fundamental duplicity that we found in the writings on the Sorbonne's walls in May 1968, proclaiming that we should "hang the last capitalist with the guts of the last bureaucrat": a strong expression of a concept that I later called *bourgeoisisme* to better criticize it. This strongly linked technocratic economists, syndicalo-political bureaucrats, and college academics, all of whom used social engineering to construct an institutionalized status quo.

Like many others, during the 1970s I wanted to try my hand at critical analysis. My first manuscript was titled "The Technique of Marx . . . and Heidegger." Indeed, I remember how at the beginning of my studies, after two years of studying medieval philosophy, I was attracted (me, a man of the south, Italian paternal grandfather, Arab grandmother, and my mother from Cevennes) to the border of Germany, very close to Freiburg, Heidelberg, and Tübingen. The winter mist and frosts, the long walks on the island's shores, encounters in the woods, led eventually to Heidegger himself. In 1969, in Heidelberg, in a hiding place of my friends of the Sozialistischer Deutscher Studentenbund (the German version of Students for a Democratic Society or SDS), my professor, Lucien Braun, and I went to listen to Heidegger's last lecture.

It was necessary, however, to pass beyond criticism, to exhaust "the logic of domination." My intuition was that the ideal of control, which I called the logic of domination, had become obsolete and unusable when analyzing the life of "the man without qualities," as Robert Musil had called him. My intellectual source, besides treatises of medieval philosophy and theology, was literature. Novels, indeed, constituted my base of reference — my window on the world, one might say. The novelist's perspective had more impact on me than all the economics textbooks, statistical studies, or official surveys together.

Why? We can observe everyday life in the novel. Life, indeed, is found in the novel but also in urban traffic, the effervescence of bars, the crowded marketplace, and in many details of existence. Later in life I would tell my students that above and beyond "book knowledge," it is important to know how to "drift" in the streets, and how to "waste time" in bars. These are the best places to experience sociality, the places where dreams, utopias, phantasms, and other fantasies—which are the true substrate of any society—are expressed. In many memoirs of May 1968, everyday life occupies a prominent place. We said then that "someone who speaks about revolution without changing everyday life has a corpse in his mouth." Paradoxically, Heideggerian and Marxist perspectives provided a bifocal vision of social complexity and all the small utopias that interstitially constitute everyday life.

But against philosophical or sociological orthodoxies, that of the "notaries" of knowledge, the street, and its manners taught us the complexity of things, in short, the polytheism of values. It is in this way that the novel is instructive for the sociologist. The novel expressed in popular speech (in contrast to the antiseptic language of scientists, their Latinization) shows the richness and sweltering heat of everyday life. This idea was and still is an "obsession" of my intellectual work.

I started my academic career in the small town of Grenoble at a time when municipal socialism had become gangrenous due to many years of holding power over both paving stones and people. The ideals of Marx had been transformed into farce (*theatre de boulevard*). The vacuity of the great universal values, which inspired political speeches as well as the analyses of the social sciences, was obvious. I developed this idea in my book *La violence totalitaire*, in which I argued that the real totalitarianism is the one of interpretative systems because they reinforce every social and political institution.

It was a time for drifting around the city at night, for denouncing all those who claimed to speak in the name of others, to make people happy against their will. I have always been true to this "anarchistic," "situationist" sensitivity. For some of my friends, pushing critical thought to its extremes led to a denunciation of oppression as well as to the temptations of liberation and, thus, led to a generalized skepticism, a description of a world coming to its end. I do not believe that the end of a world is the end of the World. The extreme attention and sympathy I have paid to everyday life, to the "men without qualities," to ordinary people, have led me to be more and more interested, not so much in the end of great systems, and in the decline of values from which productivism and rationalism were born, but instead in new values and methods of being and of understanding the world.

One must always be attentive to the present moment. The *Conquest of the Present* (1979) is my first positive book, my first attempt at "contradictory thought," and set a course I will never abandon. Its message: no more waiting for pleasure, no more of tomorrow's promises, but instead invest in the present instant of everyday life. One can see here the influences of Ernst Bloch (e.g., *Thomas Münzer and the War of Peasant* [1985]) and of George Bataille (*The Accursed Share* [1988–91]), which stress the importance of excess in social life. Rebellion and revolt can be thought of as anthropological structures: as part of what it is to be human. This is the meaning of Dionysus in emblematic form, protagonist of orgies, whom C. G. Jung called the "trickster." The instinct for turbulence is a dynamic component of social life.

I pointed out that in *The Elementary Forms of Religious Life* (1965) Émile Durkheim showed us the importance of anomie and effervescence, key concepts that I later used to understand many kinds of crowds, the *affoulements*. In the forward to a pocket edition of this major work of Durkheim, I should say that I first discovered the importance of these things in the works of the surrealists and the situationists. And although I later distanced myself from it, the work of Henri Lefebvre is in this respect paradigmatic, in that it well underlined the subversive character of everyday life. I must add that its prospective aspect makes me believe that "the anomie of today is the canonical of tomorrow."

Durkheim showed well in his analysis of the Australian aboriginal corroboree festivals that in anomic effervescence "the community reinforces its sense of itself" (178–79) With this in mind, I have always believed that revolts and daily excesses were the school for any durable sociality over time over. Yet tragedy is also a part of everyday life. Death may come at any time. In my childhood, the sound of the bell brought every woman, dressed in black, to the coal mine to organize immediate funerals. This led me to propose, in my book *Ordinary Knowledge* (1985), that thought is rooted in everyday life. In French, the etymological source of know (*connaître*) refers to birth.

Meanwhile, even when I had become a professor at the Sorbonne, my academic knowledge was enhanced by the experiences of living with different social classes and groups. I rejected an abstract sociology describing the world as it should be or as seen by those who project their own psychological distress on a bland world. I wanted a sociology of taste and culinary practices, of feelings and sex, of drunkenness and festivals, music and artistic inspiration, and so on — a sociology of the present instant, of the body, and of dance.

But I also wanted an imaginative and rooted sociology. We should remember that Max Weber, speaking about the logic of the duty of being, relied on systematic representations that were to some extent ideological. To take note of "what is" seems to me to be a true epistemological revolution and, to some extent, ideological as well. Recalling Antonio Gramsci, I could call it organic knowledge as opposed to mechanical knowledge, the kind of abstract knowledge contained in the quiet certainty of various orthodoxies. I retained my taste for audacious thought from my wild childhood and younger days as a situationist — thoughts from the high seas that know how to recognize essential boldness, integrating academic work with topics that seem frivolous or of little importance from the orthodox point of view.

In this spirit, untouchable due to my status as "holder of the chair of Durkheim," beginning in 1968, I was able to organize at the Sorbonne the first research group on homosexuality. At that time, research on homosexuality was very rare and I was consequently criticized by many of my colleagues. In the same mindset, I contributed to the development of research on online sex, on the body in its various forms, on prostitution, and on astrology. In 1981 I was accused of promoting homosexuality at the Sorbonne! And in 2002 I was reproached in the same way for promoting astrology.

In fact, *la connaissance ordinaire* supports the idea that every "social fact" can become a "sociological fact" and object of sociological inquiry, and we must not be afraid to examine the ubiquitous elements of our common life. From this point of view, Edgar Morin showed in his "sociology of the present" that there is no reason to stigmatize popular culture as "less important," for it is an expression of the whole that we share as our common being (the "social entity"). For myself, I have always believed that we must free ourselves from scholarly dogma, especially if it has become a lazy and cowardly prejudice. Knowledge makes us knights of the mind. We should be afraid of nothing, limited by no taboos, and unafraid of the powers that try to tell us what to study.

In France, I must say, few dare to challenge mainstream dogmas. They sidestep the weight of political thought among intellectuals friendly to the French Communist Party, which has not been reevaluated, though it is no longer in the majority. The sociology of the imagination — continuing the thought of Gaston Bachelard and developed by my master, friend, and thesis director Gilbert Durand, whom I replaced as head of the research center on imagination that brings together multiple international teams — seldom succeeded in placing its graduates in academic positions. And yet, after more than twenty years of teaching at the Sorbonne and the creation of my Research Center on the Present and Everyday Life (through which more than one hundred doctoral students have passed), I am convinced that this is the right path.

This approach, beginning with those elements that are closest to the way people live and feel, proved itself in research: the study of celebrations, musical styles, practices of the body and sex, new "religious" movements, and the practices and beliefs of magic and the spiritual shows that new values are being born right before our eyes. To use an apt Marxist saying: "It is necessary to know how to hear grass growing." And I am sure that our intuitions regarding social effervescence have been empirically confirmed. The young researchers of the Centre d'Études sur l'Actuel et le Quotidien (CEAQ), very often themselves protagonists of techno music or Goths, illustrate these intuitions precisely.

I have always held that these intuitions are an operating system, an epistemological-methodological lever, with perfect congruence with the spirit of the time. I owe this claim to the phenomenological tradition, to Edmund Husserl of course, but also to A. Schütz, P. Berger, and T. R. Luckmann (for whom I wrote prefaces for the French editions of their works).

Going beyond the representations back to the things themselves, as Husserl said, where the "things" were shocking or even illegal, produced a sulfurous aura around my work in France that still surrounds it. But, as I have said, moralism and its correlate, conformist thinking (i.e., political correctness), have nothing to

do with intellectual reasoning. The spirit of 1968 still remains relevant in its lib-
ertarian aspect, its freedom, and its existential function of nonconformism to
fight positivism and comfortable certainties.

Since the 1960s (1964 in the United States, 1968 in Europe), a profound
change has taken place. One cannot grasp this "change of skin" with the elaborate analytical categories of the past. We can still try to use the texts of the "founding fathers," but it is useless to set them up as abstract dogmas. We must use them
to their full potential in order to cast light on the present situation. Thus, for example, concepts of "anomie" or "effervescence" of Durkheim and "nonrational-
ity" of Max Weber can help us understand the phenomenon of crowds (in sports
or music). They can also support the international aspect of radical thinking in
sociology. Indeed, as borders are crossed by interactive communication systems,
"national" theoretical perspectives are free to travel internationally.

I cannot pass over in silence my bonds to various places in the world, to various intellectuals, friends in Brazil and Mexico, Japan and Korea, Italy and Fin-
land, to list only the countries that I visit several times each year. I am a voyeur.
My thinking is made fertile by experience — the world, the streets, trains and
planes. I lose myself in books, Heidegger, Jung, Meister Eckart, Georg Simmel,
Weber, and Tarde, to list only my favorites. I am fond of saying that Brazil and
Mexico, Japan and Korea are the laboratories of postmodernity, mixing the archaic and the technical, traditional and televisual culture. Empirically we observe that the old categories of political economy, relevant when analyzing the
world of the Enlightenment that I have called the modern epoch, started with
the *philosophes* and undoubtedly ended in the 1960s. Nineteen sixty-eight was at
the same time its acme and its end. These old concepts do not allow for a realization of what I called, following Jean-François Lyotard and Jean Baudrillard,
postmodernity. This phenomenon, which is sometimes heartily denounced, at
least in France, certainly originated in the effervescence of the 1960s. I believe
that from this moment one sees affirmed, with force, the characteristics of a nascent sociality.

My true intellectual birth certainly dates from this period. The new coherence of the social bond is no longer founded on the monotheism of a single value
(God, individual, state, work) but rather on relativism, best described by Simmel's notion of plural values. It is this polytheism that one finds in "architec-
tural postmodernism" (as elaborated by R. Venturi) and its illustration in societal postmodernity.

Above and beyond Judeo-Christian onto-theology, the effervescence of the

1960s led us to think about a structural polythesism that has its own dynamic, multicentered, and anomic. The effervescence of the 1960s' forces beyond the onto-theology that originated in Judeo-Christianity, and into a structural polytheism that features its own dynamic, is multicentered and, in many respects, anomie. Without fail, it produces disquiet for conformist, mainstream thinkers. Empirically, we see that new elements come into play, especially regarding practices of the young, elements that rest on latent hedonism, on the body, and by accentuating the present moment. These are the great characteristics of postmodernity on which all agree, however differently people evaluate it. This is what I proposed in my book *Eulogy to Reason* (1996), in which I try to show that it is possible, as a scholar, and without abandoning this spirit, to analyze emotional communities, what I have called postmodern tribes and the culture of feeling that tends to prevail in our societies. Indeed, since I realized that society was not finished, that the world was not at its end, I started to develop an analysis of what is, of the world as it is.

First, I developed the topic of neotribalism, perhaps because of my love for my work as a professor and the affection I have for my students. The century of the Enlightenment "invented" the modern individual, master of himself and the universe, banishing the gods and enchantment from the world, and set in their place scientism and historicism. This individual is bound to others in a rational and utilitarian manner, by a contract — the social contract. We can see here the crumbling of communities and the preeminence of politics and economics: work, nation, and the solidarity of democracy regulate social relations. In contrast, in the postmodern epoch in which we live, and that I observe, in particular, through my young researchers, the world is reenchanted, and there are new forms of solidarity that I call tribes. These are not based on communities of origin that imprison us but on transitory groups with fluctuating emotional ties and versatile identities. Rather than identity assigned by sex, professional stature, or political choice, we have a mask that we call a person, diffracted into successive identities. Such people are not bound to one another by stable relationships, a contract, or a history, but solidarity is made and demolished according to time and place. Solidarity is built and then disappears, based more on emotions than on reason and utility. This is what I have called an ethics of aestheticism. With the romantics of the nineteen century, surrealism in the interwar years, then situationism in the 1960s, one sees clearly the progressive emergence of these alternative values.

Rebellion against the established order is certainly the common denominator

of these existential "postures." They are now part of lifestyles. They are the cap-
illaries of the social body. They constitute its flesh. And one is a "scientist" to
want to give a theoretical account of it. There is in fact a red thread that leads
from the critical thought of the 1960s to the radical thought of the present—
which penetrates more deeply and grasps more strongly the basic forces that an-
imate our societies.

For my part I retain my fidelity to this red thread, this theoretical trajectory. I
refuse to exchange, as it has been written, "the Mao collar for the Rotary Club."
It is this faithfulness that provokes unthinking condemnation from the conventional scholarly mind. But it is also this constancy that enables one to return to
the lasting ideal of 1968: "change life."

Bibliography

Bataille, Georges. 1988–91. *The Accursed Share: An Essay on General Economy.* 3 vols. Translated by
Robert Hurley. New York: Zone Books.

Bloch, Ernst. 1985. *Thomas Münzer, als Theologe der Revolution.* Frankfurt am Main: Suhrkamp.

Durkheim, Émile. 1965. *The Elementary Forms of Religious Life.* Translated by J. W. Swain. New York:
Free Press.

Maffesoli, Michel. 1979. *La conquête du present, sociologie de la vie quotidienne.* Paris: Desclée de
Brouwer.

———. 1985. *La connaissance ordinaire: Précis de sociologie compréhensive.* Paris: Libr. des Méridiens.

———. 1995. *The Ordinary Knowledge.* London: Polity Press.

———. 1996. *Eloge de la raison sensible.* Paris: Grasset.

From Switzerland to Sussex

William Outhwaite, born 1949, studied at Oxford and Sussex and is professor of sociology at Sussex, where he taught in the School of European Studies from 1973 to 2003. He is the author of Understanding Social Life: The Method Called Verstehen; Concept Formation in Social Science; New Philosophies of Social Science: Realism, Hermeneutics, and Critical Theory; Habermas: A Critical Introduction; *and the forthcoming* Social Theory, Communism, and Beyond *(with Larry Ray). He edited* The Habermas Reader; The Blackwell Dictionary of Twentieth-Century Social Thought *(with Tom Bottomore);* The Blackwell Dictionary of Modern Social Thought; *and* The Sociology of Politics *(with Luke Martell).*

> As Jean-Pierre Le Goff says, the question posed by May 68 is whether people can still hope to find "a meaning which sustains them, words and action which really engage them."
>
> Daniel Cohen, Nos temps modernes

Prologue: My May 1968

In May 1968 I was on what had not yet come to be called a "gap year" between school and university. I had spent the previous four months at a German language school in the Black Forest and was now working for the chemical firm Ciba, with which my father had business connections, in Basle. I was in what was

I am grateful to Trevor Pateman and Austin Harrington for comments on an earlier draft.

called the Literature Department (*Literaturabteilung*), listing registered patents and doing occasional translation work from my newly acquired German into English. In the office we spoke mostly French, as lingua franca and out of courtesy to a francophone Swiss colleague, our native languages being English (in my case), Swiss German, and Hungarian.

I had briskly become a Marxist at around the age of fifteen or sixteen, soon after dropping a rather muted Anglican Christianity and after a summer reading inter alia a small compendium called *The Essential Left*, with four classic texts by Marx, Engels, and Lenin (1960). In Switzerland, I do not recall whether I was surprised at the "revolutionary" outbreak in the universities in Paris (which had been preceded by a year of student protest in Germany) or whether I saw it merely as confirmation of the predicted beginning of the end of capitalism. At Basle University, where I attended various seminars after work, there were some fairly muted echoes of what was happening in France and Germany. At one mass meeting, we had been promised a visit from the legendary Daniel Cohn-Bendit. Unfortunately, the "movement" had decided to counteract the dangers of a perceived personality cult by restricting "Danny's" public appearances, and sent instead a sharply dressed alternative speaker who addressed us in French, where the bilingual Cohn-Bendit would have used German, and was generally less charismatic. A language barrier of a different kind arose at another political meeting, where the young Marxist academic Elmar Altvater, invited from West Germany, struggled to understand the Swiss dialect of a "real worker" participant. I should of course have tried to hitchhike to Paris or elsewhere on weekends to see things at firsthand but somehow failed to do so. I occasionally took the city tram to the French border, but with a protracted general strike there was nothing much to see apart from men playing boule. I was still in Basle when the Warsaw Pact invaded Czechoslovakia ("Die Russen sind einmarschiert" said Dr Goldstein when I arrived in the office) and when Bobby Kennedy was shot.

Oxford

When I returned to England in September, there was correspondence from Balliol College, Oxford, where I was due to go the next month to study politics, philosophy and economics (PPE). There was a letter from the student president (of the "Junior Common Room" of the college), saying that JCR at Oxford did not stand for Jeunesse Communiste Revolutionnaire — "yet." It was the boast of Balliol, which had long had a radical reputation, that not only was the master of the college, the historian Christopher Hill, a Marxist, but so was the president of the JCR, the future Leeds sociologist and Korea expert Aidan Foster-Carter, and even the captain of boats (rowing being another important activity at Oxford), John Gledhill, who has since become a leading economic anthropologist.

How serious were my politics? The historian A. J. P. Taylor's description of his own politics as "strong views, weakly held" is probably the best description. I certainly wanted the United States to lose its war in Vietnam and joined the mass demonstrations against the war on October 27, 1968, and other occasions, though I had learned German alongside friends from South Vietnam and had few illusions about the sort of regime that was likely to follow an American defeat. I did not want either side to win the Cold War; the balance between the two superpower imperialisms seemed the least bad alternative. I had been briefly to the Soviet Union and was again without illusions about it, except that I tended, for a long time, to present it in relatively neutral comparative terms rather than accept that it was not just much worse than the capitalist alternative but also more unstable. I probably did not seriously anticipate the imminent collapse of capitalism, though when a friend said she was taking out life insurance I felt there was something odd in expecting the capitalist insurance industry to last quite that long. I never felt impelled to join one of the revolutionary parties, but I was happy to participate in looser groupings such as Oxford Left and Oxford Revolutionary Socialist Students.

Revolutionary socialism, then, was an integral part of the Oxford experience. Demonstrations routinely began at 5 p.m., after tea in the Balliol Common Room, and our tutors responded with a finely tuned mixture of courtesy and condescension to jejune attempts to introduce dialectical logic or Heidegger into analytical philosophy tutorials or Marxism into classes on neoclassical economics. There were, however, more serious forms of intellectual critique. A radical North American economist, Sean Gervasi, who subsequently continued an important career as a critic of U.S. foreign policy until his early death in 1996, was invited by students to give a series of lectures in what would now be called global political economy, and these were a major event of the academic year 1968–69, packing a large lecture theater. John Birtwhistle and Trevor Pateman launched a series of intellectual broadsides in various journals and papers, and Trevor, who was later a colleague at Sussex until 2000, published in 1968 *The Poverty of Philosophy, Politics and Economics* — the title of course drawn from Marx's *Poverty of Philosophy*. The PPE program, set up in the 1930s, in part as a preparation for the civil service and related activities, was a multidisciplinary rather than an interdisciplinary program. The individual component courses were remorselessly and rather narrowly disciplinary, and it was mainly left to us to make connections between them—sometimes with the aid of tutors who had themselves been through this program or something comparable elsewhere. I benefited from two recent innovations: the introduction, after long struggles, of a course in political theory, and the opportunity to drop one of the three components. (Being innumerate, and believing the rest of it to be mostly bourgeois ideology, I dropped economics.) Sociology, which was and remains marginalized at Oxford, despite its considerable strengths in empirical social research, was available in the form of several courses under the PPE umbrella but not presented up front. (It was, after all, only a century or so old. . . .)

For all the criticisms that could be made of PPE, however, there was a superb intellectual training provided by dedicated teachers such as Steven Lukes, Alan Montefiore, and Bill Weinstein and wonderful events such as lecture series and seminars by Noam Chomsky (commuting home weekly in an attempt to dissuade MIT from supporting the war effort), Rom Harré (apparently solidly local despite his New Zealand origins), John Plamenatz (ditto but from Montenegro), and Leszek Kolakowski, recently arrived from Poland via Canada. Kolakowski's lecture seminars in 1971, later a major book, were on the philosophical origins of Marxism, and by the antepenultimate week of the term, when I had to abandon them to take my final exams, he had got as far as Kant. I graduated with a second-class degree (Oxford did not bother to differentiate between upper and lower seconds) in a year in which, one of the examiners said, there were too many second-class men (sic) trying to pass themselves off as first-class men.

Sussex

By then I had decided where to go next. The choice for me was between philosophy and sociology, which I had studied in place of economics. Philosophy suggested staying at Oxford, sociology a move elsewhere. I had heard of and read books by Tom Bottomore, who had recently moved to Sussex from a short period in Canada, and I had been to a seminar by Zevedei Barbu, another Sussex professor who had impressed me not only by his remarkable taste in clothes but also by the fact that he took the work of Georg Lukács seriously, without the dreary Oxford laments about whether it was value free, falsifiable, and so on. For Barbu, Lukács seemed to be a contemporary (he was indeed close to Lukács's disciple and his fellow Romanian exile, Lucien Goldmann). I duly traveled down for an interview with Zev and obtained a place and one of Sussex's generous quota of Social Science Research Council grants.

At Sussex I studied sociological theory and the sociology of knowledge with Tom, as well as doing some work in development studies with the anthropologist Peter Lloyd. A seminar paper on *verstehen* grew into an M.A. dissertation, and I followed Tom's suggestion that I might take concept formation as a topic for a doctorate. There was no pressure to continue from M.A. to a research degree but also no disincentive; funding was generous: for the ten students who were eligible by virtue of U.K. citizenship, nine grants were available. If we were a disobedient generation, then, we were also a privileged one by current standards of competition.

After a year of doctoral work, the first term spent on an exchange at the University of Grenoble, where I worked mainly on French philosophy and history of science, I had another lucky break when the Sussex faculty found it difficult to fill a post that had been advertised as requiring expertise in the sociology of science and/or on the Soviet Union. My interests in the philosophy of science and the sociology of knowledge intersected sufficiently to secure me the job as lecturer in sociology in the School of European Studies, where I remained until the abolition of the school in a reorganization in 2003.

All this sounds quite low key, and indeed it was. I had embarked on a career and a pensionable job without much drama. I now had an office and I had to teach — my previous experience being confined to a month teaching English along the coast to French children. My supervisor, already a friend, had become a colleague. We were to work together on a retranslation, published in 1982, of Karl Löwith's classic essay on Marx and Weber ([1932] 1993) and, later, the *Blackwell Dictionary of Twentieth-Century Social Thought* (1993), which Tom did not live to see in print. Tenure, that often terrible passage in North America, was, as normally the case in the United Kingdom, a formality. (At least one female colleague, however, had a more difficult time — probably largely because of her sex.) I had a set of research projects to complete — the transformation of my M.A. dissertation into a book for a series edited by Tom Bottomore and Mike Mulkay (Outhwaite 1975), an essay for the New Cambridge History commissioned by Peter Burke, then a few doors away (Outhwaite 1979), and of course my often neglected thesis, on which I spent more years than is normally allowed these days. I did not, however, have much sense of a career. When I agreed to take on an administrative task in my school, I was surprised when a colleague and friend suggested that I must be very ambitious, and when the university, in one of its occasional financial crises, was encouraging us to take unpaid leave and there was a prospect of my spending a year as a teacher in Paris of what is known there as "English civilization," I was surprised when my then head of department, Julius Carlebach, suggested that I should decide on the basis of whether this would be of benefit to my career. Although of course I had read a good deal of work in the sociology of the professions and the sociology of science, tracking prestige hierarchies, journal citation counts, and so on, it did not seem personally relevant in any interesting sense. At the time of writing, I have still only ever submitted one unsolicited article to a journal; this was politely rejected on the reasonable grounds that the material had been sufficiently discussed in earlier issues.

Where then was the disobedience? I had drifted into a peculiarly flexible intellectual and organizational structure (at Sussex) in a peculiarly open discipline (sociology) at a time of expansion and further opening up (the 1970s) in a country (the United Kingdom) in which academic faculty, pace Kingsley Amis's *Lucky Jim*, in which a young lecturer is under the thumb of the department chair, rapidly become autonomous in a way that often surprises colleagues from continental Europe or North America. Politically, I had drifted from revolutionary socialism through political inactivity to a period of service to the local Labour Party as a candidate at local elections (not quite a "paper candidate" but not much more than heavy cardboard) to allowing my membership to lapse, around 1998, out of disillusion at New Labour's attempts at press manipulation.

The contrast between the slightly chaotic but flexible organization of movements and the rituals of an official local party, where minutes and correspondence read out verbatim took up a good part of each meeting, was instructive. "Ah, you're a social democrat," said my host when I visited East Germany in 1983, when I gave my party affiliation as a shorthand response to his question about my politics. Though I could not deny it, it was another identity I felt somewhat uncomfortable with.

Role distance was an important consequence of the spirit of 1968. A distanced attitude to one's national, professional, or gender identities was de rigueur, whether or not, as Theodor Adorno suggested in 1966 ([1966] 1973, 363), it is a more pervasive aspect of intellectual life. "Thinking men and artists have not infrequently described a sense of not quite being there, of not playing along, a feeling as if they were not themselves at all, but a kind of spectator . . . the ability to keep one's distance as a spectator and to rise above things, is in the final analysis the human part." [1] There was undoubtedly a significant generational effect in intellectual life associated with 1968, though it was probably stronger in continental European cultures, with more of a discernable difference in attitudes and forms of behavior between pre-'68ers and '68ers. What Norbert Elias, in *The Germans* (1989), calls the gradient of politeness, the *Höflichkeitsgefälle*, remains sharper in Germany and other part of continental Europe than in the English-speaking countries, which also, of course, lack the heavily marked differentiation between *T* (*tu, Du*) and *V* (*vous, Sie, lei*) forms of address. In academic life, there may have been a tendency to use the more intimate or democratic form in seminar discussions and to revert to the more formal one outside, rather as I have sometimes noticed continental colleagues dressing down for their seminars from their normal style. How far formality and, more important, inegalitarian structures such as professorial domination have actually been modified is of course a topic in itself, and one requiring much more detailed study. It is clear, though, that a "long" 1968, stretching into the expansion half-decade that followed, was an important evolutionary shift. I felt for a long time that I was some sort of outsider who had penetrated into a professional world while remaining basically distinct from it. The rituals of teaching, examining, writing references, and so forth all seemed a little unreal. In terms of Le Goff's question, recalled by Daniel Cohen, I had no doubt about the value of academic research, while feeling somewhat detached from university ritual.

Social Theory

The rise of social theory as an explicitly designated activity and form of scholarship is more or less identical with this period. There are, of course, exceptions, but they are mostly, I think, to be found in the critical theory literature. Herbert Marcuse, for example, subtitled his *Reason and Revolution* (1941), *Hegel and the Rise of Social Theory*, and Adorno of course reflects continually on the relation between sociology and social theory. In the United Kingdom, it is remarkable how little serious attention was given to social or sociological theory until the 1970s.

Talcott Parsons, who died in 1979, was, needless to say, a pivotal figure. Parsons's first major work, *The Structure of Social Action*, published in 1937, was the embodiment of a particular conception of the history of sociological theory that

---

1. I was reminded of this passage by an article by Ben Day (2004).

was fairly dominant in the middle years of the twentieth century. In Parsons's version, the classics (his holy trinity is composed of Émile Durkheim, Max Weber, and Vilfredo Pareto) can be seen to converge into a general theory of social action that Parsons spelled out here and in his subsequent works. This theory could be systematized according to some, at least, of the prescriptions of mid-twentieth-century Anglo-American philosophy of science and was in principle open, Parsons, thought, to empirical testing and confirmation.

On this model, then, Parsons was the midwife of *modern* sociology as well as its leading exponent. Even sociologists who did not accept Parsons's own theory probably tended, in the middle decades of the twentieth century, to accept something like his historical conception, also stressing, for example, the advances in empirical research techniques or the massive expansion in the numbers of people working in the social sciences in the post–World War Two period. Whatever the future might hold for sociology and the other social sciences, it seemed that they had definitely come of age. Marx, Weber, Durkheim, and the other founding fathers were, as the B-movie gangsters say, "history."

This triumphalist vision was called into question in the late 1960s. First, the revival of social conflicts in many of the advanced capitalist countries encouraged a revival of Marxist social theory. This had hitherto been marginalized in the "free world" with the beginning of the Cold War and perverted, in the socialist countries, into the official state doctrines of Marxism-Leninism and "scientific communism." Marxism came back in a variety of forms, ranging from dogmatic orthodoxy to various neo-Marxisms. Other classical social theorists benefited from a resurgence of interest in the history of social thought. This was marked in the English-speaking countries by Anthony Giddens's influential *Capitalism and Modern Social Theory*, published in 1971, with its very detailed discussion of Marx, Weber, and Durkheim. Tony presented a summary version of it at a seminar I attended in Oxford, and I was enormously impressed by the seriousness of his creative engagement with the classics. Durkheim was himself the subject of what remains a definitive study, published in 1973, by my former tutor Steven Lukes; another Oxford academic, John Torrance, was working on Marx (1977). Tom Bottomore had worked, initially with the French Marxologist Maximilien Rubel, on critical editions in English of Marx's work. Julius Carlebach's Sussex doctoral thesis and book *Marx and the Radical Critique of Judaism* (1978) was a pioneering work in the historical study of the relation between Marx(ism) and Jewish thought.

Alongside the revival of interest in the classics, contemporary sociological theory, too, had became more ambitious and speculative in the 1970s, with a shift of hegemony from the United States to Europe and an explosion of interest in Althusserian Marxism, Frankfurt School critical theory, British Wittgensteinian philosophy, and French structuralism and the work of Michel Foucault, Pierre Bourdieu, and others. What Quentin Skinner (1985) called "the return of grand theory in the human sciences"—in a series on BBC Radio 3 and an edited volume to which I contributed and that documented this shift—meant that "the classics" seemed less like remote ancestors and more like older contemporaries.

Generally, then, the time perspective of sociology changed. Its substantive concerns once again became a little more historical, in a partial reversal of what the great historical sociologist Norbert Elias had attacked in 1983, a few years before his death, as "the retreat of sociologists into the present" ([1983] 1987)—in other words their excessive concentration on contemporary social phenomena. Sociology's sense of its own past also shifted. Giddens (1972) had attacked what he called the "myth of the great divide" that had been set between the more or less unformed or chaotic prehistory of sociology and the subject in its modern "scientific" form. This conception, he argued, involved both a lack of sensitivity to the work of the classical sociological thinkers and an undue degree of confidence in the scientific credentials of "our" social thought. Others came to share this more nuanced account of the continuities and discontinuities in social theory. Substantively, sociology shifted its theoretical focus from industrialism or industrial society to capitalism or late capitalism (Spätkapitalismus), and then to a broader focus on modernity (and also what Lyotard and others called postmodernity), in which it addressed dimensions of power (including state power in its international dimension) and culture, which had previously been somewhat marginal to its concerns.

This partial return to earlier traditions in social theory can, of course, be evaluated in very different ways. Many sociologists and other social scientists would see it as, at best, a diversion from and, at worst, a threat to the pursuit of genuinely scientific knowledge of society that would be disciplined, systematic, verifiable, and cumulative. Divergent evaluations of this kind reflect not just different conceptions of the proper role of sociology and the other social sciences but differing conceptions of the way in which we can come to know social phenomena and, even, of their very nature.

The past thirty years have seen, then, a parallel and convergent process in both the philosophy of social science and the social sciences themselves, in which the somewhat simplified scientistic conceptions that were prevalent in the middle decades of the twentieth century have been replaced by conceptions that, though no doubt more sophisticated, are yet at the same time closer in many ways to those that we find in the early decades of the twentieth century. Max Weber would, I think, have felt more at home, though probably no less irritated, in many recent debates in English-language philosophy of social science than in the middle of the twentieth century, when his brother Alfred died. By 1968, things were changing intellectually as well as politically.

This, then, is roughly where I came in, jumping on to a newly moving bandwagon, when I first started teaching at Sussex. I was soon to be joined by Gillian Rose, who became a close friend and ally and whose work and intellectual passions I followed with constant admiration up to her tragically early death in 1995. After publishing her first book, on Adorno, she constantly surprised us with new activities: after Hegel, it was learning law for her critique of poststructuralism, then learning Danish for her work on Kierkegaard, and finally steeping herself in Jewish and Christian theology.

Outside Sussex, the main influences on my thinking were Jürgen Habermas and Roy Bhaskar. I had read a little of Adorno's work while in Germany and, at Oxford, become fascinated both by Lukács and by Habermas, who was beginning to be published in English but was still not very well known. My book on *Verstehen* substantially followed Habermas's approach in *On Logic of the Social Sciences* (1988) and *Knowledge and Human Interests* (1971). In 1974 I was able to meet him, when Roy MacLeod, then head of the interdisciplinary graduate program in history and social studies of science that I had been partly hired to teach on, took a party of us, graduate students and faculty, to a conference organized near Munich by a group of researchers at the Starnberg Institute that Habermas codirected at the time with C. F. von Weizsäcker. Habermas was not closely involved with this project, on the "finalization" of science, but he encouraged those who were, as we visitors justified our presence by picking holes in the finalization conception.

I had known Roy Bhaskar at Oxford through my friend Martin Wainwright and his sister Hilary, one of the leading figures in post-1968 socialist feminism. I read Roy's *Realist Theory of Science* when it came out in 1975, and realism provided a much-needed conceptual focus to my doctoral project on social scientific concept formation. I met Ted Benton by chance on a train when I saw him also reading Roy's book; he and I, along with Andrew Collier and others, met Roy increasingly frequently and we set up a regular conference series on realism and the human sciences that has continued uninterruptedly to the present. Roy, who had been at Edinburgh, spent a year at Sussex in 1979–80, where we discussed realism with Roy Edgley, the Marxist philosopher who, with Giddens, had examined my doctoral thesis, in a lively seminar series. It is a continuing generational fact that most realists have been interested in and sympathetic to Marxism, and although the prominent examples of Rom Harré and, more recently, Margaret Archer make it clear that the relation is not one of entailment, it makes sense to see Marxism as one prominent example, among others, of a realist theory.

Further afield, my main intellectual links at various times have been with the British Sociological Association's Theory Group, which Peter Halfpenny at Manchester and I organized for some years, with a very innovative research center on social work at the University of Caen, with Michel Maffesoli and Véronique Havelange in Paris, and other friends in Freiburg, Oldenburg, Leipzig, Berlin, and Moscow. Editing the International Sociological Association (ISA) journal *Current Sociology* in the late 1980s reinforced many of these links. The ISA met several times that decade in Eastern Europe; the old regimes were weakening, as I also experienced firsthand on two exchange visits to East Germany in 1983 and 1988, but when the ISA executive committee met on the Bulgarian coast in July 1989, we did not expect what followed in the autumn. If anything, the mood was rather somber, in the wake of the Tiananmen Square massacre and suggestions by the German regime and others that they could be similarly severe. Six months later, of course, things were utterly different. Julius Carlebach, who by then had retired from Sussex and moved straight on to take up the rectorship of the Hochschule für jüdische Studien in Heidelberg, asked me sometime that winter what Marxists like me had to say now. "Business as usual," I replied, rather too flippantly. I did not, however, feel that the collapse of the state socialist dictatorships had any particular implications for Marxism as an explanatory theory, whose weaknesses had been well brought out by neo-Weberians and others, or even for Marxist political practice, which was anyway looking increasingly problematic. Fifteen years later, I think the lessons go a bit deeper than that. I do not (yet) think that the project of rational and democratic social management of production is impossible, though it has clearly moved back from science (as Engels misconceived it) to utopia — in the sense of a project that has to be justified in normative terms rather than as a consequence of historical necessity.

The kind of international involvement that I have enjoyed has, of course, become increasingly common in the social sciences worldwide, as they become genuinely global in their orientation and dissemination. Internally, they are marked by tendencies toward both unification and division. I have emphasized the trends toward the flexible cooperation between philosophy and the social sciences and between individual social science disciplines, so far as these still remain distinct. The United Kingdom has been a relatively good context for interdisciplinary work of this kind, as I argued in a hubristically upbeat response to Peter Weingart's rather pessimistic diagnosis in a German discussion journal. Among other countries, Poland deserves special mention as a center of work such as that by Edward Mokrzycki on the interface between philosophy and sociology. The revival of the classics and the seminal influence of a number of social theorists across a wide range of disciplines has been an important unifying force, as has the rise of social theory itself.

Running against this trend, however, are pressures toward specialization and the division of labor familiar from the example of the natural sciences and similarly reinforced by funding opportunities and by disciplinary structures petrified along the largely obsolete divisions between academic departments. (My own university has followed Essex, Keele, and others in moving toward a more departmental structure, while hoping to preserve the traditions of interdisciplinarity for which it is best known.) The United Kingdom's Research Assessment Exercise, a centrally organized and incredibly expensive monitoring process, lies like a dead weight over the country's academic life and has driven out some of its most productive researchers. It has also reinforced disciplinary divisions and safe, mainstream research and publishing strategies within them. It is not just that that ambitious social scientists may prefer to be large fish in small ponds, presiding over a strictly limited area of inquiry; they will tend to find it easier to obtain funds, for themselves and hence for their institutions, for clearly circumscribed projects. The relation to the past remains contentious: many social scientists, not just empiricist researchers but even sophisticated and original theorists such as Niklas Luhmann, deplore the frequent reference back to the classics of social theory and to traditional problematics. What C. Wright Mills denounced in the Parsonian era as the coexistence of grand theory and abstracted empiricism remains an equally possible future for the social sciences in the twenty-first century.

The strength of social theory lies elsewhere, I think: in the sensitive attempt, as Hegel put it, to capture its time (broadly conceived of course) in thought; Karl Mannheim (1943) and, more recently, Axel Honneth (1994) have advanced the idea of "diagnosis of the times" (*Zeitdiagnose*) as an important area of activity. Although social theory, and particularly sociological theory, were generally slow, for example, to address issues of race and gender and of international conflict or the environment, they responded relatively promptly to the theoretical and practical challenges posed by ethnic minority, feminist, peace, and environmentalist movements in the last third of the twentieth century, just as the social theory of the late nineteenth and early twentieth century responded to the crises of liberalism and the rise of socialist and communist movements. Often the issues are the same, but the frame of reference radically reversed. Many of us, for example, are concerned again, as our predecessors were at the last turn of the century, with issues of ethnic or "racial" conflict or with nationalism, but few, thank God, would now describe themselves as scientific racists or nationalists.

This suggests a more general conclusion. To paraphrase a remark by the German philosopher J. G. (or Johann Gottlieb) Fichte, what kind of social sciences we choose to have depends primarily on what sort of societies we are. Societies that want, and that want their universities to want, social science departments whose output and social utility are as quantifiable as that of departments of applied science will derive less benefit, I suspect, than those that allow social theory to develop in relative freedom from institutional constraints and that leave it free to address what it, rather than its paymasters, identifies as important issues for investigation. A major threat to this approach lies in the attempts to revive and enforce conceptions of specialized academic professionalism and performance in a half-baked extension of a science policy that was developed in relation to "big science" and is of dubious application in the domain of the humanities and the social sciences.

I have argued, here and elsewhere, that the thinkers who have been retrospectively canonized as the classical social theorists of the last turn of the century were not just asking the right questions but were asking them in roughly the right sort of way. Such conservatism (with, naturally, a small *c*) requires justification of a kind that I have only been able to provide indirectly here. Let me summarize my claim in three theses.

First, to borrow an older formulation, no Newton for the social sciences. There has not yet been one, and the long sequence of unsuccessful candidates makes one think that there probably won't be one. It is not so much sour grapes as prudence born of experience that suggests we should stop looking out for one.

Second, we don't need one anyway, since we already know a good deal about the social world by being members of it. We're not beginning our ascent from sea level (which is what makes mountain climbing on the Isle of Skye, for example, even more strenuous than it would anyway be). We can build on the tacit knowledge we already possess as more or less competent members of society. The most helpful theories in the social sciences are those that do this explicitly, rather than repudiating this initial understanding or knowledgeability at the outset and then smuggling it in later.

Finally, it is worth reflecting on the way in which some of the principal themes of social theory often become truer as time goes on than when they were first formulated. The Protestant ethic of self-surveillance, for example, surely comes into its own in the era of psychotherapy, management theory, performance appraisal, and so forth, as do Marxist theories of fetishism and reification in the age of electronic money and intellectual property in cyberspace. Less dramatically, the theories of postindustrialism and technocracy, including critiques like E. P. Thompson's of the technocratic and commercial debauching of universities, which looked rather overstated in the late 1970s, have again taken on a new bite.

This is, obviously, where 1968 came in, with somewhat parochial concerns about local university arrangements in Paris and elsewhere escalating, in a way in which no one would have predicted, into more fundamental movements of contestation, set against the background of war in Vietnam and the rise of a counterculture in the West.[2] As Trevor Pateman (1972, 55) noted, "A gap existed between college political activity and extra-institutional politics—a gap bridged over by thick rhetorical planks: 'We must see our struggle against the Bursar in the context of the struggle of the Vietnamese people against U.S. imperialism.'" It is an interesting historical exercise to read or reread some of the classic analyses of that period, such as the historian E. P. Thompson's *Warwick University Limited* or Stephan Leibfried's *Die angepasste Universität*, subtitled *From Ivory Tower to Knowledge Factory*. By the standards of the twenty-first century, the technocratic and commercial prostitution of universities and the degradation of university education had barely begun; looking back at these critiques, we were straining at gnats while trains of camels approached below the horizon, laden with bullshit. The process was also much slower in most of Europe than in the principal English-speaking countries; even in Europe it has not been homogeneous, with the United Kingdom and incipiently parts of continental Europe coming under state regulatory regimes undreamed of in the United States. On the positive side, I think that universities, and academic discourse more broadly, have become more open and egalitarian; the Internet and e-mail have opened up possibilities of exchange between the intellectual superstars who have Web sites and

2. Looking through some old documents, I see I contributed to this sort of reflection with a talk at a day school in 1969 titled "The University and Society."

chat groups devoted to them and ordinary surfers and subscribers. The playfulness that was a crucial element of 1968 is something that we need to hold onto in the aging societies of the "west."

Contemporary intellectual life, and social life more broadly, take place under the twin signs of globalization, which we must now take to include not just economic and interstate processes but also the globalization of culture, and democratization — the democratization, in a broad sense that includes, in particular, the exposure to the need for discursive justification, of social relations of all kinds. The interrelations between these processes and states will shape our future. As Giddens and others have argued, these processes of democratization may give rise in turn to new fundamentalisms — not just of religion but also of gender, nation, "race," and so forth. Globalization may open up new democratic possibilities, as explored in theories of cosmopolitan democracy, or may undermine them, in removing the possibility of democratic control of economic processes. Whatever has happened to the generation of 1968, the moment remains an important evolutionary shift in ideas, practice, and institutions with consequences in the rest of the twentieth century and beyond.

Bibliography

Adorno, Theodor. [1966] 1973. *Negative Dialektik.* Translated as *Negative Dialectics.* New York: Seabury.

Bhaskar, Roy. 1978. *A Realist Theory of Science.* 2d ed. Brighton: Harvester.

Carlebach, Julius. 1978. *Karl Marx and the Radical Critique of Judaism.* London: Routledge, 1978.

Cohen, Daniel. 1999. *Nos temps modernes.* Paris: Flammarion.

Day, Ben. 2004. "From Frankfurt to Ljubljana." *Studies in Social and Political Thought,* no. 9, 1–20.

Elias, Norbert. [1983] 1987. "The Retreat of Sociologists into the Present." Translated by Stephen Kalberg and Volker Meja ("Über den Rückzug der Soziologen auf die Gegenwart"), *Theory, Culture and Society* 4, nos. 2–3 (June): 223–47.

———. 1989. *The Germans: Power Struggles and the Development of Habitus in the Nineteenth and Twentieth Centuries.* Translated by Eric Dunning and Stephen Mennell. Edited by Michael Schröter. Cambridge: Polity Press, 1996. Originally published as *Studien über die Deutschen* ([Frankfurt am Main]: Suhrkamp, 1989).

Giddens, Anthony. 1971. *Capitalism and Modern Social Theory.* Cambridge: Cambridge University Press.

———. 1972. "Four Myths in the History of Social Thought." *Economy and Society* 1:357 ff. Reprinted in *Studies in Social and Political Theory* (London: Hutchinson, 1977).

Habermas, Jürgen. 1971. *Knowledge and Human Interests.* Boston: Beacon Press.

——— . 1988. *On the Logic of the Social Sciences.* Cambridge: Polity Press.

Honneth, Axel. 1994. *Desintegration: Bruchstücke einer soziologischen Zeitdiagnose.* Frankfurt am Main: Fischer Taschenbuch Verlag.

Le Goff, Jean-Pierre. 1998. *Mai 1968, l'héritage impossible*. Paris: La Découverte.

Leibfried, Stephan. 1968. *Die angepasste Universität*. Frankfurt: Suhrkamp.

Löwith, Karl. [1932] 1993. *Max Weber and Karl Marx*. Translated by Han Fentel. Edited by T. Bottomore and W. Outhwaite. 2d ed. London: Routledge 1993.

Lukes, Steven. 1972. *Émile Durkheim: His Life and Work*. New York: Harper & Row.

Mannheim, Karl. 1943. *Diagnosis of Our Time: Wartime Essays of a Sociologist*. London: Routledge.

Marcuse, Herbert. 1941. *Reason and Revolution: Hegel and the Rise of Social Theory*. Oxford: Oxford University Press.

Marx, Karl, Friedrich Engels, and Vladimir Lenin. 1960. *The Essential Left: Four Classic Texts on the Principles of Socialism*. London, Allen & Unwin.

Outhwaite, William. 1975. *Understanding Social Life: The Method Called Verstehen*. Controversies in Sociology, vol. 2. London: George Allen & Unwin.

———. 1979. "Social Thought and Social Science." Pp. 271–72 in *New Cambridge Modern History*, vol. 3 (*Companion Volume*), edited by Peter Burke. Cambridge: Cambridge University Press.

———. 1997. "Nachrichten aus Niemandsland." *Ethik und Sozialwissenschaften* 8:40.

Outhwaite, W., and T. Bottomore. 1993. *Blackwell Dictionary of Twentieth-Century Social Thought*. Oxford: Blackwell.

Parsons, Talcott. 1937. *The Structure of Social Action*. New York: McGraw-Hill.

Pateman, Trevor, ed. 1972. "The Making of a Course Critic." In *Counter Course: A Handbook for Course Criticism*. Harmondsworth: Penguin. For an updated version of this essay, see "1968: Student Revolt and the Making of a Course-Critic" (2004), http://www.selectedworks.co.uk/1968.html.

———, ed. 1968. *The Poverty of Philosophy, Politics and Economics*. Oxford: Oxford Revolutionary Socialist Students.

Skinner, Quentin, ed. 1985. *The Return of Grand Theory in the Human Sciences*. Cambridge: Cambridge University Press.

Thompson, E. P. 1970. *Warwick University Ltd: Industry, Management and the Universities*. London: Penguin.

Torrance, John. 1977. *Estrangement, Alienation and Exploitation: A Sociological Approach to Historical Materialism*. Basingstoke: Macmillan.

Weingart, Peter. 1997. "Interdisziplinarität — der paradoxe Diskurs." *Ethik und Sozialwissenschaften* 8:521–28.

SASKIA SASSEN

Always a Foreigner, Always at Home

Saskia Sassen is the Ralph Lewis Professor of Sociology at the University of Chicago and Centennial Visiting Professor at the London School of Economics. Her latest book is Territory, Authority, and Rights: From Medieval to Global Assemblages. *She has also just completed, for UNESCO, a five-year project on sustainable human settlement for which she set up a network of researchers and activists in thirty countries. Her most recent books are the edited* Global Networks, Linked Cities, *and the coedited* Socio-Digital Formations: New Architectures for Global Order. The Global City *came out in a new fully updated edition in 2001. Her books are translated into sixteen languages. She serves on several editorial boards and is an adviser to several international bodies. She is a member of the Council on Foreign Relations, a member of the National Academy of Sciences Panel on Cities, and chair of the Information Technology and International Cooperation Committee of the Social Science Research Council (USA). Her comments have appeared in the* International Herald Tribune, Die Zeit, Le Monde Diplomatique, Vanguardia, *the* Guardian, Financial Times, *and the* New York Times, *among others.*

In May 1968 my family was living in Rome. Rome was burning with rage against the U.S. bombing of Vietnam. The U.S. embassy, located on a stunningly beautiful stretch of Via Veneto, was a public rallying point. Day after day we marched, we chanted, we burned flags, we suffered teargas and police baton attacks, and we ran like we did not know we could. During one of the most violent attacks by the police — now that Genoa 2002 has happened we know something about what they are capable of—I remember running, arms locked with two tall friends, one on each side, who ran so fast that I was barely touching the ground as my short legs moved fast, faster, till I had the experience of taking off, my feet no longer touching the ground.

That experience of escaping attack, and in so doing, taking off in the sense of a new beginning, is one of two experiences that became organizing frames for me for what it meant to be political. It is one that has repeated itself, albeit in different vocabularies. When one brings passion and conviction to one's actions, being attacked does not necessarily transform one into a victim. Something else happens. This has held for me also in the academy. What we might call the life of the mind offers many different ways of blurring the act of escape with that of taking off.

The second experience is that of always being a foreigner but never an expatriate. There was no homeland out there for me. It is an experience that can take on different forms—being out of it, the stranger, or the borderland native, a vulnerability that contains complex potentials. I had already tasted this growing up in Latin America as a Dutch girl in a very Dutch household. It reappeared under many guises as my life proceeded in five languages and four different countries. Living my life meant strengthening the knowledge of my foreignness and simultaneously its difference from expatriacy. There is a peculiar clarity to that condition. It became sufficiently commonplace to me, that when my political and theoretical concerns put me at the margins of whatever was the "real" center in the academy, I was at home so to speak. I think being a foreigner, yet at home, must have allowed me to survive, without psychic injury, some of the potentially traumatic rejections I had early on in my academic life: having my dissertation rejected, or having my first book rejected by thirteen publishers, or being told by my first chair that I should not even bother to apply for tenure. As my academic life proceeded it somehow showed that rejections from the gate-keeping system, even thirteen rejections, do not necessarily mean that you are out. You can still cross that border, even if only partly "documented." The dissonance can be a source for politics.

These internal borders also captured the slightly binary quality of my political and academic life, the fact that each was sufficiently consuming to be a full-time life. Their considerable autonomy from each other, and to some extent their considerable incompatibility, meant that I rarely shared the existence of one with my coworkers in the other. I rarely elaborated on my political life with my academic colleagues and, vice versa, I rarely elaborated on my academic life with my political colleagues. I am still that way. One might retort that the University of Chicago might not be particularly hospitable to my types of politics, but it long precedes my coming here. The exception to this rule was when crossing borders could be put to good use: knowledge about a political issue enabling a struggle and, obversely, a political struggle becoming a good research object. In my experience, there are definite limits to this type of feedback. Mine were political engagements that did not intersect directly with my life as an academic, even though they did shape me and inscribed my research interests. But academic work was also an island for deliberative engagement with questions removed from the storm of politics, war, and death.

The political landscape that brought me to activism in Rome in the late 1960s was a specific one. As the decades rolled on, each brought up its set of particular versions of injustice around which to become engaged politically. One struggle led to the next. In my experience, it never stopped. As the account that follows shows, in crucial regards it was a two-track life rather than one where politics and academic work were deeply enmeshed with each other.

The Big Move: Going to the United States

When my family moved to Rome, my obsession was to become a terribly serious university student. Rome was not the place. I enrolled for the first year of political theory. No one seemed serious, and no one seemed to take my seriousness seriously. In the meantime, I had met various academics at one or another of my mother's dinner parties, where a basic rule was always to mix worlds and to bring in newly made acquaintances along with good old friends. There would be a cardinal (minus robes) along with an artist, and so on, besides some dear old family friends. Rome was full of cardinals, and so one or another wound up even at my mother's, a militant atheist; nor could one escape the Catholic circuit generally if one had a sort of salon atmosphere at one's social events at home. At one of these dinners, then, I got to know William D'Antonio who was then chair of the Department of Sociology at the University of Notre Dame and must have wound up at my mother's through the Catholic circuit. As I held forth about my sociological passions he urged me to consider applying for college at Notre Dame. I remember keenly saying, oh, no, not college, only graduate school. It seemed inconceivable to me that going to an American college was worth my time. I was deeply misinformed and strongly inclined to be dismissive toward U.S. institutions. That conversation however stayed with me, and not too long afterward I decided I would give the United States a try.

I wanted to leave home. The asphyxia of "proper society" in Rome was becoming overwhelming. Further, in leaving I did not want to be dependent on my family. So I took a job as a live-in nanny with, of all people, a top-ranking member of the U.S. embassy in Rome who was going back to the United States — that same embassy I picketed and that same country whose government I hated. There is a familiar ring to this type of tension; it feeds many a good novel. But it is also emblematic of something about the United States: the need to differentiate between, on the one hand, the power of the U.S. government and large corporations and hence the ease with which that power can be abused and, on the other, the relative openness of U.S. society to foreigners, the weight of neighborhood and city-level political work, and the proliferation of small group initiatives, all so different from Western Europe.

I cannot recall all the details of my state of mind when I went for that job interview in Rome, but there was for me an element of adventure and a taste of danger. So there I was. My future employer instructed me on how to conduct myself upon going through immigration controls — since he expected me to go on a tourist visa and was not about to go through the effort to get me a work permit. That was my first direct experience with the U.S. government. Very instructive on how to enter the country in violation of its laws, how to earn money there without paying taxes and, as I eventually came to understand, how easy it is to become a very low-wage worker in rich America. Clearly this experience did little to temper my critical stance toward power, how power is constituted, and how it indulges itself in many big and small ways.

But the United States was also the country where the generosity of one single individual made it possible for me to start a new life. After a few months, I had had it with my job as a nanny/cleaner. I had been studying for the Graduate Record Exam since arriving in the United States whenever I got a chance — at night, early in the morning. Taking care of a one-year-old and a two-year-old plus some cleaning was exhausting and left me very little time. I decided to leave for Notre Dame. I gave my employer a one-month notice. They stopped payment for that last month "for breach of contract." It could not have been about saving money — I made fifty dollars a month! I guess it was to teach me something about the law. How not to experience the little irony of the far larger breach of contract with his own government, for which he moreover worked! It was February 3, 1970, when

I left for Notre Dame — the middle of the academic year. I got my first taste of what was to come when a massive snowstorm in Chicago stranded us at the airport, and the only way to get to South Bend, Indiana, was via bus. I presented myself in D'Antonio's office, the chair of sociology. At the time I did not think of how he must have felt when he realized I was an illegal immigrant, did not have a college degree, had not properly applied, had made no arrangements for anything, and expected to be taken into graduate school. I was an adventurer: if this failed, there would be another adventure for me to try out. But to him I must have seemed a bit unreal. He did recognize me from the dinner party at my mother's, and I had written him long letters about sociology, neither necessarily positives in being considered for admission. In one of the most generous and supportive decisions I have seen a person take, he decided to become my legal guardian, which was no minor procedure, and to take me into the department's graduate program — much easier than taking me as an undergraduate into the college. I would be on probation for a year to see whether I could make it; after all, my high school degree, my year at the University of Rome, and earlier, at sixteen, a year at the University of Buenos Aires, having done several high school years in one, did not amount to any formal degree or, indeed, an education.

Going to the University of Notre Dame was a somewhat devastating experience after having lived in Rome; yet it was there that I got the instruments for critical analysis in U.S. social science. Several seminars stand out as being exceptional experiences that opened up the academic world to me, the world of deep scholarship rather than intellectual debate I had become familiar with in Buenos Aires and Rome. Andrew Weigert's advanced seminar for undergrads, which I was required to take not having a college degree, introduced me to Peter L. Berger and Thomas Luckmann's *The Social Construction of Reality*, to Thomas Kuhn's paradigm shifts, and several other classics. The experience was as dramatic as the one I had as a young thirteen-year-old in Latin America reading my first essay in social analysis, José Ortega y Gassett's *Rebellion of the Masses* — a somewhat peculiar text for me, as I had become a communist at the time and was studying Russian to live up to my ideals. I had the experience that the Greek had in mind when they used the term *theoria*: seeing what cannot be apprehended by the senses and hence requires a distinct construction to enable the seeing. I will never forget Weigert's seminar, even now so many decades, meetings, and courses later. I can still remember what we read and the excitement of discovery.

And then there was the person who would become a key mentor, Fabio Dasilva. I sat in his theory class and I really did not know what he was lecturing about. I only got glimpses into what was, for me, an otherwise hermetic discourse. I knew that there was something there. Some of us, all but one with a Latin American connection, began to gravitate around Dasilva: we were interested in theory, critical discourse, and politics. Dasilva was a grand mix: a theorist and great cook and wine connoisseur, definitely a civilizing presence in South Bend. At some point he invited the five of us to come to his house where, over good food and great wine, we had the first of our theory evenings. We met every Friday for about two academic years.

This was a somewhat unusual group, and all of us—the Latin Americans— had trouble getting our dissertations accepted. It was both bonding and illuminating to share this trouble. In each case, there was a specific reason, evidently persuasive to the decision-makers. But looked at from a certain distance, one cannot but sense something systemic, perhaps having to do with our foreignness and with a choice of dissertation subjects and driving theoretical concerns far too removed from the mainstream, even for sociology. For instance, one of the members was Jorge Bustamante, an already somewhat renowned lawyer in Mexico, who decided to research Mexican immigrants in the United States. As part of his dissertation fieldwork, he entered the United States illegally, crossing the Rio Grande after leaving all his documents in Mexico. This was a harrowing experience but one extremely revealing about key migration issues. I remember him recounting it in full detail at one of our memorable Friday nights. This was not the type of experience the academy was comfortable with and Jorge, considered the most brilliant student in the department at the time, had to struggle to get his dissertation accepted. He went on to become one of the most distinguished immigration advisers to several Mexican presidents and to found the Colegio de la Frontera Norte, an institution specializing in border issues that is now recognized for its excellence and receives generous support from leading U.S. foundations. He has now also been named a distinguished visiting professor at the University of Notre Dame and returns there every year. Another member of the group, Gilberto Cardenas, who had grown up in the Los Angeles barrio, also ran into trouble with his PhD dissertation and wound up leaving the university without his doctorate and getting it elsewhere. As I will recount later, I also had my dissertation rejected and left without a degree (which often put me in the position of having to list a high school degree as my highest degree).

Politics in the United States

The passions that moved me in the 1960s did not go away, even as they changed content and objectives. It was always a politics against the abuse of power that stirred me, more so than power per se. I have never been a Weberian in my conception of power. I see power as a capability that gets constructed and cannot be reduced to something one has or doesn't have. From there, my concern is with the complexity of the condition of "powerlessness," with how the practices of the excluded have been one factor, historically, in the eventual formalizing of new inclusions — rather than such inclusions simply being granted by enlightened or civilized power.[1] This matters to my theorizing, as does the fact that no formal system of power has lasted forever — except, it would seem, the Catholic Church. I am more interested in detecting abuses of power that are lawful, rather than fraudulent or illegal, because it allows me to understand something about the construction of power and the problematic character of the rule of law, with its frozen inequities and hidden rules of permission for those with the power to seize on them. I found the United States to be an extraordinary "natural experiment" for understanding these various issues.

But these questions came later. It was in fact the protopolitics I evidently already had as a child that shaped my decision to become a sociologist — a word that when I first heard it at thirteen I immediately understood to name a particular passion for a juster world that I had discovered in myself years earlier. I proceeded to create a kind of fantasy around the term "sociology," which I saw as a nonutopian project for social justice. The word remained a bit incomprehensible to me (as it does, I find, for many of the students I teach today). The earliest incarnation for this protopolitical passion in me was provided by the inevitable book all children in English schools at the time had to read: *The Lady with the Lamp*. Yes, I wanted to be Florence Nightingale and I thought of this as a profession: Florence the reformer — the nurse part being of little interest to me. At age eight I was not picking up on the imperial subthemes in the story.

The early 1970s were years of intense antiwar activity in the United States. At Notre Dame, antiwar struggle contained a high dose of spiritualism, both generic and particular. I remember the Catholic Charismatic Renewal movement

1. The best long in-depth interview I have had on these types of issues is "Space and Power," in The Future of Social Theory, ed. N. Cage (London: Continuum, 2004), 125–42.

organized a huge antiwar rally very much centered on Christian values. Buddhism was big. The less spiritual among us threw ourselves also into the McGovern campaign — even though I was an immigrant, by now legal, and could not have voted.

The other political struggle I joined with brio was the Cesar Chavez farmworkers organizing. The Midwest is home to several migration streams from Mexico, some going back to the 1930s. One of our efforts was setting up a childcare center for the children of migrant workers. I remember receiving a Ford Foundation Minority Dissertation Research Fellowship and using most of the money to help set up such a care center in South Bend. I felt very good about it and was certain that the Ford Foundation, always in search of bringing about more social justice, would have been delighted. I did not ask them, however. At the time it seemed fair that since I was writing a dissertation on blacks and Latinos in the U.S. political economy I should use the money not to make them work more by answering questionnaires for my dissertation but should instead help them, who were so much needier than me. In other words, I had a rationale for this distinctive allocation of my doctoral fellowship.

A Summer in the Texan Desert

One of the memorable experiences that connected me to some rather specific political aspects of the United States happened after my first year at Notre Dame. I was invited to become part of a large research team directed by Bill D'Antonio that was going to be driving down to Fabens, Texas. This was a small town on the border not far from El Paso. We were funded by the Robert J. Kennedy Foundation and were meant to map the town in order to get at several issues concerning the relationships between Anglos and the Mexican-origin population. One of these concerned land taken by Anglo farmers from legitimate Mexican-origin owners. Other issues concerned migrant labor, undocumented immigrants, and police treatment of the Mexican-origin residents — in brief, matters that were not without their share of controversy. We were to spend two months there. We did such a good job of digging up the invisible history of this community and the land grabs by Anglo farmers that they took us to court and got an injunction against the study ever being published.

That was a summer like I'd never quite had before or since. We drove down to Texas in a motley mix of cars, from an imposing, impossibly tasteless red Impala, or something along those lines, to a small Volkswagen. We drove for three days, and I got my first taste of that type of American experience. We distributed ourselves around several houses in the town. The one where the three of us stayed — soon referred to as the women's house — had the desert as its backyard. When you opened the back door, all you saw was an endless stretch of sand and bushes.

The team had students from several disciplines. Among them was Tim Mc-Carthy, an exceptional person, extremely active in the antiwar movement and the founder of a commune in South Bend that practiced Buddhism. The commune members were all pacifists, vegetarians, and, it seemed, many other worthy "isms." Tim was a mix of passion, spiritualism, and intelligence. I immediately fell in love but never told him or revealed this — he was so spiritual, so consumed with his pacifism and his struggle for justice that it would have seemed an invasion. For those two months in the desert I loved him, I desired him, but I felt that any expression would violate the serenity that he seemed to construct around himself. A few months after we returned, he shot himself to death in front of the shop where he bought the gun, sitting on the street, in the middle of the day, in Berkeley. He had despaired of the world. The horror and desolation I felt at his death and at the absolute hopelessness he must have felt were almost unbearable. They had the effect of focusing my mind with an intensity that was a form of violence. I felt the loneliness, the deafening silence that Tim must have felt around him when he decided to kill himself. For many of us the struggle against war and injustice was — is — political. For Tim it had become existential.

But that summer in the desert, Tim's death had not happened yet, nor had the lawsuit against our study. I experienced that summer — my senses fully alert and my mind racing into whatever the surroundings or moment I found myself in. I felt like an investigative journalist tracking the dirty history of the town. And I felt suspended in time and place, my university life a vague memory. I remember one walk with Tim, the two of us alone climbing deep into the mountains to meet some healer who was to introduce us to peyote. Yes, we had all read Carlos Castaneda's *Teachings of Don Juan*. We walked and walked through the most stunning, edgy, solitary landscape, the sun setting on us. We did not see a single other human. We did not find the healer, but we did find what we thought was peyote. We sat till deep in the night high on a stone ledge. Getting back was not easy.

While in that desert Texan town I hooked up with some local activists, largely associated with liberation theology and *comunidades de base*, two radical movements within the Catholic Church that had mushroomed among the poor throughout Latin America. Tim and I went with one of the priests, a Jesuit, who was going to do mass in some remote community. It meant crossing the Rio Grande into Mexico and then, of course, coming back. It was not a routine operation even though a frequent one for the priest. There were risks, not only for himself but also for the communities he visited on the Mexican side — mostly because liberation theology was the enemy of power. The priest was a much beloved, respected, and honored figure in this community. A priest giving mass was a rare and precious event here. People from neighboring villages also came.

I will never forget arriving at the small cluster of huts at the other side of the river. It was an overwhelming visual experience: a mix of vast spaces, ample mud structures, and extreme scarcities; it was not the usual crowding of small shacks we associate with this type of poverty. Everything was the color of dry river earth — beige in my mind's vocabulary. So was the water they offered us. But the heat and thirst were unbearable; as I drank the water I clung to the thought that my growing up in Latin America had given me a healthy mix of immunities to diverse bacteria. No, I did not get ill. In a common practice, the water is held in a large vat so the claylike earth of the river filtered the water as it sank slowly over hours to the bottom. What was left was, indeed, water the color of light earth, but it had been filtered. As I travel around the world, I carry this experience as a reassuring fact. I confess, I think of myself as having an iron stomach, which is of course not true in any sense of the term.

The U.S. Academy: In Search of Political Economy

Reentering the academy after that strange summer in a Texas desert town was a slog. I decided that sociology was not getting me at the type of issues that I cared about — basically, critical political economy. I proposed to the dean of arts and sciences a program in political economy that would require taking one or two doctoral specialization areas in economics. This was in my second year. It was accepted after some lofty oratory on my side, and the promise to recruit students from the sociology department into my new "program." I recruited one: Gilberto Cardenas, one of my theory group comrades in arms. He dropped out after a few weeks. So the program had one student, moi.

Studying economics at Notre Dame included the history of economic ideas as taught by Stephen Worland, which meant you started with the *oikos* of Aristotle's treatise, arrived at the physiocrats, and finally waddled into neoclassical economics. The effect was, of course, to render problematic the category economy itself, to make legible the work of conceptually constructing a distinct and relatively autonomous domain in society—work that stretched over the centuries and involved many different schools of thought. Not since I had taken Weigert's seminar had I had the intellectual stir that Worland's course gave me. At that time I also got involved with the Union of Radical Political Economics (URPE). I recall Herb Gintis, one of the founders, giving a talk at Notre Dame, which convinced me this was for me. Those were heady days for URPE, a collectivized effort to produce a critical political economy about the United States, war, racism. When I moved to New York years later, the local URPE collective, especially the women's caucus, became one of my main intellectual homes.

My dissertation was an attempt at a critical political economy of the United States from the perspective of the condition of blacks and Latinos. It was neither sociology nor economics and evidently was a major irritant to just about every member of my dissertation committee. In individual discussions everything was fine. "Harvard civility" ruled. But when they met as a committee for my defense, the multiple detestations—between sociology and economics, between economics and my political economy stance—were too much. It got rejected. While shocking, it somehow was not devastating. When I think of a doctoral student today getting this type of rejection, I have the sense it would be far more traumatic. Well, perhaps my experience suggests it need not be.

The next stop was philosophy in France. Those were the days: Gilles Deleuze and Felix Guattari, Michel Foucault, Louis Althusser and Etienne Balibar, Nicos Poulantzas, all had exploded onto the intellectual scene, and all in France. At this time I had just married a radical political philosopher—a terror on the Notre Dame campus—who had gotten a Fulbright to teach in France. So off we went, life an adventure, and me barely remembering my failure at getting a PhD. (Though the practical Dutch side in me, one of the channels through which I experience life, made sure that all the requisite copies were safely stored in a friend's house at Notre Dame, just in case. . . .)

In Search Of Hegel

Now began a third phase in my *Bildung* and in my political formation. As usual, I had some idea as to what I really wanted to do, no matter that I might be unable to find it. Given the sharp dominance of the Althusserian reading of Marx—the "rupture epistemologique"—I was convinced there was time to delve into that reading. The Hegelian reading of Marx, in contrast, was threatened, espe-

232 | SASKIA SASSEN

cially when it came to the classical interpretation by Jean Hypolitte, the great French translator of Hegel. I found out that Jacques D'Hondt, one of the leading Hegelian interpreters of Marx and the last living student of Hypolitte, was teaching in Poitiers. He had founded the Centre de la Recherche et Documentation sur Hegel et Marx. The center had been a destination for many of the Hegelian Marxists from Italy, such as Lucio Colletti. Further, having grown up in Latin America, very much in a Marxist intellectual milieu as a student, we all knew of Jean Garaudy who had spent many years in Latin America, especially Brazil, and who was also a professor at Poitiers. So Poitiers it was for me, not glamorous Paris. I was in search of what was at risk of loss rather than what had burst onto the scene with enormous vigor, and glamour, with the promise of a future. Indeed, being a student in Poitiers and sitting in Jacques D'Hondt classes were constant reminders of this.

D'Hondt taught a required class for all students in their final year of graduate coursework in philosophy. His was not a fashionable perspective. And the students in the class (about fifty) let him know: they continuously chatted and made noise, very openly not listening to him. He walked back and forth lecturing, no matter the level of noise, no matter the absence of attention. I found myself progressively moving forward till I was sitting in the front row in order to listen to him. The first class, I thought the students had not understood that he had started lecturing and I tried to shush them down. Well, did they let me have it! I had managed to construct myself in an instant as a somewhat weird student — no matter my Latin American credentials in all of this, and no matter that I of course was much closer to Althusser's reading. The students were all eager to get the Althusserian reading but were stuck with a Hegelian one. I had experienced the intensity with which students could reject a professor in the name of ideas as a first year philosophy student at the university in Buenos Aires (where I had wound up at sixteen having finished my high school early by combining years and was, hence, young enough to be surprised at how students handled their professors). Still, Poitiers was a shock.

Given that the students had sent D'Hondt into internal exile, I had great access to him and was invited to be a fellow at the center. It became my library, my office, my intellectual home. I was typically the only student there. I did my thesis with D'Hondt on the possibility of methods centered in dialectical logic. I got to read the mathematicians and logicians Jean Piaget had gathered around himself to explore issues of formal and dialectic or, more generally, "nonformal" logic. And I got to read East German logicians, such as Ivan Narsski—yes, in German! It was easier than reading Kant in German at fifteen in Buenos Aires, though that had definitely been good endurance practice.

The defense of the thesis was with Jacques D'Hondt and Guy Planty-Bonjour—a highly regarded Heideggerian scholar with whom I had done one of my specialization areas—and a third person who I avow I cannot recall. One of the comments of the jury, even as they gave me highest honors, was that while written in French this was an Anglo thesis: very analytical and frugal, no French-style meanderings in the groves and crevices of erudite knowledge. I can still see them arrive at this observation, the struggle to articulate it and to put their finger on what it was that struck them as foreign, even as they expressed their admiration for the work.

The defense was held at 7:00 a.m. or thereabouts, not the usual time for these professors. They were so gracious to do this; I was taking off that day back to the United States, seven-months pregnant, with my husband waiting at the train station to take the train to the airport in Paris. As I left the beautiful medieval building where the Faculté des Sciences Humaines was housed at the time I had the sweetest feeling: I had completed this project and it gave me a very precise sense of what can best be described as possession.

Writing this thesis was an extraordinary experience. In many ways I had buried myself in a world that, while real, was not one I belonged to and was not of the moment, the moment being marked by very different types of questions and passions. I was an illegal immigrant so to speak, certainly undocumented. It was exhilarating writing this thesis on dialectic logic, so radically different from what I had been doing. It had a profound impact on my way of thinking as a scholar, as a researcher. But it is an invisible, unregistered link in my academic/intellectual life: the thesis is filed in the French library system, but I never refer to it, never cite it, and have never tried to get it published though I have received inquiries over the years from people who happened onto it.

Going to the United States, Round Two

Going back to the United States felt strange. I knew I was going to the new world, once again. And what awaited me was a new project that had been initiated unbeknownst to me many months earlier. After I had left Notre Dame it seems all hell broke lose because of what had happened at my defense. I never had written to anyone at Notre Dame or complained. I had just left. But the matter went up to the dean of arts and sciences, partly because my doctoral exams in both disciplines, economics and sociology, had been considered one of the best "ever" (whatever that might mean) and hence the rejection of my dissertation was questioned. The dean found that at least part of the fault lay in the conduct of the committee. Shortly before that defense, urged on by my husband D. J. Koob, I had circulated one of my papers, part proposal, part essay, on the growing importance of cross-border migrations in the constructing of transnational relations. I vaguely remember, though not with certainty, sending it to the Consortium for Peace and World Order — it had sounded like my kind of place. The end result was that I had been given a postdoctoral fellowship, no matter my lack of a doctorate; even more amazing, the offer found its way to me in Poitiers after meandering through the U.S. academic network in search of its addressee.

The postdoc was for Harvard's Center for International Affairs. Several Harvard scholars — Ray Vernon, Joseph Nye, Robert Keohane, and Samuel Huntington — had been working on identifying and measuring the existence of cross-border relations that did not involve national states as key actors: multinational corporations, tourism, religious organizations, and so on. My proposal on international migrations as an instance of transnational relations added what was at the time a novel instance for this list.

That I should have wound up there of all possible institutions is, depending on your taste, funny or ridiculous. This was a generous offer at an assistant professor's salary level, difficult to reject at that moment in our life. But I did not have a PhD. I wrote to Norte Dame, and given the fall-out after that committee's rejection, they were ready to more or less mail me my PhD. Julian Samora played a crucial role in securing this. I never went back; I got my PhD through the mail.

Winding up at the Center for International Affairs was, to my European's jaundiced eye, ironic. By then referred to as CFIA, to avoid all confusions, it had been a key target for antiwar activism. One of its prominent members, Henry Kissinger, had served as secretary of state during one of the most tempestuous periods of U.S. history. The fellows were mostly enormously distinguished men from various walks of life: former governors, former publishers of leading newspapers, as well as academics. Among us, the junior types, was Dan Yergin, who went on to write the bestseller *The Prize*, and Enid Bok — the only other woman.

The first lunch was hosted by Henry Rosofsky, the much admired dean of arts and sciences. I went with my husband — an oversight on my part since we had been instructed not to bring spouses. I was very pregnant, and must have looked unusually round in that setting and in that roundness much younger than I was. I was greeted by the center's hosts, and it was clear, though unspoken, that they assumed my husband was the fellow. I may misremember or be projecting my own wonder at why I was there, but when I shyly clarified I was the fellow, I swear there was, for a few seconds, a silence as pregnant as I was. So that was the start of my new life in the new world, second round.

D. J. Koob and I decided that the only place to live in "America" was New York City. I got one offer from New York—at Queens College of the City University of New York (CUNY), where else!—and I took it. Harvard had had the effect on Koob, the radical philosopher, of convincing him that international banking was his only option to make a living. His brilliant dissertation on Heidegger, language, and politics was not well received by academics in position to offer him a job. His were subjects that had an as-yet-precarious foothold in the U.S. academy. Further, his treatment of these subjects entailed a critique of Hanna Arendt for not being radical enough—in the sense of failing to get at the foundational aspects of politics, at the roots of categories for analysis—at a time when she reigned supreme, at least in some circles. And Heidegger was still mostly seen as a Nazi theorist/apologist. Too many rejections had led Koob to a radical departure into a radically different world, one transparent in its foundational premises. When banking can become a relief to an intellectual, we are looking straight at the horrors of narrow and self-indulgent academicism. It sent shivers through my body as I prepared to start a life as a professor.

The Inevitable Move: New York City, the Only Place . . .

New York pulled me into a world of thick and enmeshed presences. Of all the CUNY colleges, Queens was perhaps the one with the highest concentration of orthodox Jews—professors as well as students—and Latinos, largely students. Each of these two presences was enormously distinctive. My university life oscillated between these two worlds: clearly an outsider to one of these, I was deeply pulled in by the other. So began my life in New York—not a cosmopolitan route into this extraordinary city.

A year after arriving in Manhattan I decided to go up to MIT in Cambridge and join a six-week seminar run by Nicos Poulantzas and Manuel Castells. It meant leaving behind my eighteen-month-old son and my husband. Going to the seminar turned out to be a significant decision intellectually in that working with these two European theorists reconnected me to a type of scholarship that was both theoretical and political. After my work in philosophy in France, I had found it difficult to reconnect to theory in the context of the social sciences in American universities—whatever passed for theory seemed so epiphenomenal or mechanical. So I had thrown myself into highly controversial subjects, such as immigration, urban poverty, police power, American imperial moves into Central America, and the meaning of being on the left in "America." Personally, I thought the seminar in Cambridge was great as I found myself with a mix of academics, mostly young professors or advanced doctoral students, who shared many theoretic-political concerns. A lot of trust could be built up among us. Some of the people I got to know there have become life-long friends, such as Maria Patricia Fernandez Kelly, now at Princeton University.

By the time I returned to New York, it felt like I had been away for a year. My little son refused to recognize me. And I could not recognize my husband—too much intense intellectual and personal history had happened for me in those weeks in Cambridge. I left my husband, baby under one arm and a suitcase full of anticipations on the other. I was an adventurer once again. I decided to live in a commune—this was a growing trend in New York City in the late 1970s, replete as it was of Lefties and of flower children. I looked in many different places. I remember a place in Borum Hill in Brooklyn, which was just beginning to be inhabited by white middle-class Lefties in search of alternative lifestyles. I almost went there, but then opted for the upper west side in Manhattan. I could barely get myself to say I was actually a professor: the others were all artists. But it was, how shall I say, top of the line as communes go, consisting of two grand apartments across from each other on the twelfth floor of a West End Avenue building, with a glorious view of the Hudson River. I lived there for five years and fell in love like I never had before with a wild, brilliant, crazy, politically passionate composer and performing musician named Rip Keller. Living in this commune took me, once again, far away from what the regular professorial life was meant to be. It did make it easier to keep doing political work and, eventually, to become a performance artist, specifically, a sound poet. This was my night job.

Having gotten involved with several Latino communities when I arrived in New York launched a new research phase for me and a new political phase. At Notre Dame there had been the antiwar movement, the McGovern campaign, and the farmworkers. In worldly New York, my political life was initially exclusively centered in the Latino immigrant community. It moved to labor-union organizing and, eventually, to the Central American solidarity movement. Given the larger events becoming articulated around Latinos, notably refugees from the bloody civil wars in El Salvador and Guatemala, inevitably one became involved with Central American politics. There was a sanctuary movement to receive the wars' refugees, the solidarity movement had begun, and the question of undocumented immigrants from Latin America had burst into the headlines.

My research on Latino immigrants led me to get involved with activist organizations and to connect with a group of organizers from the International Ladies Garment Workers Union (ILGWU) and the Amalgamated Clothing and Textile Workers Union (ACTU). At the time, the labor union movement in New York saw an emerging split between a new cadre of young organizers, who believed in spending money on organizing, and the top leadership, which—as I used to put it at the time—believed that real estate development was the best use for whatever the union's resources. Organizing workers in New York City meant dealing with immigrants, many of whom were undocumented. I intersected frequently with the brilliant lawyer and organizer Muzzafar Chishti of the ILGWU, from whom I learned a lot about what it meant to organize a whole new generation of immigrants, many Chinese and Latinos, who did not speak much English, who did not necessarily have the kind of political and organizing past that many of the earlier generation of mostly Jewish workers in the union had had. I was pushing for community-based organizing and for organizing workers regardless of status—whether employed or not, whether citizens or not, whether legal immigrants or not. This was one line of reasoning among some of the young organizers at these two unions. Gary Stephenson, an organizer with the teamsters, was a passionate, dedicated, and innovative organizer, and I recall many talks about his tactics and his frustrations with the leadership. My then five-year-old son adored Gary and listened to his labor stories with rapture—the political education of a young man. I had gotten to know Gary through Barbara Ehrenreich, also a fellow at the New York Institute for the Humanities, who became a friend and to whose house in Syosset, Long Island, I went sometimes with my son. There I got to know her daughter Rosa—always reading novels and today, one of the emerging lawyers in the human rights movement—and her son Benji, a freelance writer with quite a few great stories to his name.

Being in New York in the early and mid-1980s meant one could do solidarity politics with Central America. The Sandinista leaders were often in town, and there were frequent marches against the U.S.-supported Contras and the military regimes in El Salvador and Guatemala. In one famous solidarity march, we walked in a single line, each covered by a black shroud with the name of one of the dead or disappeared in the brutal Salvadoran war. In the square where the march ended, we each stepped up to a platform and read aloud the one name we carried on our body. No other words, no other sounds.

Artists got deeply involved in the solidarity movement. I remember doing events with the poet Carolyn Forché and the Salvadoran Claribel Alegría, whom I then also later visited in Managua, where she had moved from El Salvador years earlier. One of the most stunning marches was organized by a Salvadoran artist living in New York City who became a somewhat legendary figure in the city but also aroused suspicions as he was a man of exceedingly few words — not the norm in New York. Even as I developed a friendship and more with this man, I never quite understood who he was, what he did. His last name, I was told, was not real, a nonexistent name in El Salvador; how they established this who knows, but evidently someone had worked at finding this out, and that itself was telling.

I organized events at my home, a large loft in Soho, on Greene Street in the Broadway building just south of Prince, where I had moved in 1982. I remember organizing an event for Father Ernesto Cardenal, the legendary Jesuit who had become Minister of Culture of Nicaragua under the Sandinistas. A solidarity event, it had multiple purposes, one of them being to showcase the primitivist art community of Solentiname founded by Cardenal. As can be the case in New York — certainly was within the solidarity movement — a vast mix of people came, largely drawn to the legendary Cardenal. I had invited people from several of the worlds I was moving in, from undocumented immigrants to key political activists such as Cora and Peter Weiss, to more literary figures like Frankie Fitzgerald, the journalist and author of the stunning Vietnam memoir *Fire in the Lake*. They all came. I had also invited the members of my music group — my night life as a sound poet in the fringe avant-garde of Manhattan — and they made music. These types of events were happening all over New York City, besides the very chic affairs aimed at raising money.

At that time there was a sense of urgency around the events in Central America. The Sandinistas were in power and promising a new type of society: education and health care for all were becoming a reality in Nicaragua. The Salvadoran and Guatemalan militaries and the Contras in Nicaragua were all funded by the U.S. government. Everyday there were deaths, and every day there was Contra sabotage against the Sandinistas. I got involved with the *Nation*, then run by Hamilton Fish, who as publisher had transformed the magazine and the activities around it. With him, and the support of Victor Navasky, the deeply political editor, we organized a large multiday, multisited public conference, Dialogue of the Americas, as part of the broader solidarity movement. The organizing idea was that artists might be able to communicate and break across the ugly political divides that were tearing Central America apart. We brought together leading Latin American artists and intellectuals with their North American counterparts. From Latin America, we had Ariel Dorfman and Luisa Valenzuela. I remember being in charge of getting Susan Sontag and Edgar Doctorow to participate, whom I knew vaguely because we were all fellows of the New York Institute of the Humanities. (The institute, founded and run by Richard Sennett, was at the time one of the most exciting and cutting-edge places in the city of New York, bringing together intellectuals from many different backgrounds.) Out of organizing this dialogue came a very special friendship, rooted in shared political concerns, with Doctorow. Many people in New York City, who were not necessarily young fervent Lefties but had a keen sense of justice and a critical stance toward the abuses of power, participated in the dialogue: Rose Styron, Arieh Neier, Alfred Stepan — they were all of great help. Hamilton Fish was brilliant at putting it all together. The event was sensational.

There was, for me, a strong political character to life in New York at the time. Even my young son was caught in it, in the sense that he developed his own sense of initiative. In first grade he organized a "musicians for political action" group; he designed beautiful little posters around various issues that he would put on the (very few) trees in our Soho neighborhood. I recall a dinner at our home with June Nash — I was continuously doing dinners even though I really did not know how to cook, but it seemed ok, as it was not about the high art of domestic living. At one point she was talking about the debate as to whether there are still peasants, and my then three-year-old retorted, "there are still peasants in the world," a line he had clearly picked up from some other dinner. At yet another of my dinners — this time, as it happened, with people who not only were there for the first time but also were not quite the artsy/hippie crowd I often invited — my son, then about six, left and soon returned with a street musician, an old colorful familiar figure in our Soho neighborhood. We were still having drinks and thus conveniently seated to function as audience. He introduced the musician. After a couple of tunes, he informed us that the musician now had to leave because he had to go back to perform on the street. He took one of the funny, strange colorful cloth shoes he was making at the time to collect coins. He really took me by surprise: he had never quite done something like this before, and I admired his sense of time, the way he did not let it stretch on too long. The guests — Aric and Vera Zolberg, Tony Heilbut, and Ronald Steel — handled it all in a manner that suggested this was routine at Manhattan dinner parties. My son is, in fact, today an artist and a deeply political person. I do think that growing up in that time and place helped him arrive at both of these.

I had other involvements. In New York City it was easy to wind up in the wrong or, at least, an odd place. There were the all-too-familiar encounters with the aggressive organizing and recruitment by Lyndon LaRouche and his followers. I did resist that one. But I managed to hook up with some no less unusual political efforts. One of these was headed by a somewhat obscure and dubious figure who called himself Vince Ramos, clearly a play on Venceremos — the brigades to Cuba, where he had spent time. He had definitely had an underground Weathermen connection as well. I will never forget the day I was deemed ready to meet him — after having dealt with some of the "subalterns." I was picked up, blindfolded, put in the back of a car and driven a distance to what they described as a "cell." I never found out where I went though I surmise it was deep inside Brooklyn. When we arrived and they took off my blindfold once inside the building, I was reassured, but only partly, to see some faces I knew — Franny Moulder was one of them, at that time still a professor at Rutgers, who eventually, if I recall correctly, left the academy and joined yet another organization headed by yet another "unusual character, Marlies. There was one struggle I cared about in this strange organization, and that was what had brought me there and kept me involved for a while; it was an effort to organize the most destitute and powerless workers: migrant farmworkers on Long Island, janitors and home workers in Los Angeles, and so on. This was long before Justice for Janitors became the organization it now is with recent victories in New York, Boston, Los Angeles, and Chicago. In the long-term symmetries one can construct in a somewhat politicized life, I recently found myself at the opening event of the countersummit to the World Information Geneva Summit in December 2003, on a panel with a key United Nations organizer for the Justice for Janitors, Valery Rey Alzaga.

And then there was my music group, the Ocarina Orchestra (yes!), a group of musicians who were political in their own way. We rehearsed, we performed, we participated in international festivals, and we recorded. It had unknown performers such as myself. It had some known performers, such as the percussionist Glen Velez, at the time with the Stephen Reich group, and composers, such as Charlie Morrow. Morrow was an institution in that world and was someone who also had produced some famous, or infamous depending on your taste, musical ads. These provided him with a comfortable living. One of these jingles was the highly successful and deeply irritating "Take the train to the plane . . . " —familiar to any New Yorker, it announced the arrival of a dedicated subway line that took one to the airport, more or less. Our group had some flower children who had never sold out to the establishment and were terribly poor yet fulfilled, a kind of spiritual completeness emanating from them. I remember one of these, very radical politically, with a very long pony tail, who lived in a one-room place, on the ground floor in the east village, so elementary the room and so poor/radical he, that the place only had cold water.

Every Tuesday night we would get together for rehearsals, typically in Charlie Morrow's place or in Richard Hyman's place above the Ear Inn. The Ear Inn, on the far west side of lower Manhattan, was a great place, owned by Hyman, also one of our orchestra's members. The downstairs public space was a real hang out for all kinds of far out, fringe avant-garde artists. It was for many of us a home away from home: on lethargic Sunday afternoons, or a lonely night, I could always count on the Ear Inn as a place to run into someone, start making music. Sometimes we rehearsed in the old core of Wall Street, deserted at night—where it turned out there were quite a few artists living, especially musicians. I always thought this was a great use for Wall Street.

All of this was going on while I was also an assistant professor going through the obligatory steps to get tenure. My work as a sound poet remained largely unknown to my academic colleagues, and vice versa. I did not really elaborate on my life as an academic trying to get tenure with my political and musical coworkers. I remember reaching a point when I knew that I could no longer sustain having both a day and a night job. I basically never slept.

Exits

New York City, with its many engagements, was all-consuming. Even when I left on my multiple lecturing trips, part of me remained in the city. But I do remember three major exits from the New York City mindset.

One was a long trip to China, led by expert sinologist Mark Selden and sponsored by *Monthly Review*. That was yet another education for me. The group consisted largely of a certain kind of New Yorker—mostly Jewish Lefties of an older generation, not necessarily in age but in their politics. Ann Weiss and Anthony Heilbut, two exceptional figures, were on that trip. It was a memorable experience. Mark Selden's erudition about the Chinese revolution and his familiarity with present-day China made all the difference. I will never forget our arrival in Beijing. I was a fervent admirer of particular features of the Chinese revolution—the barefoot doctors, the enabling of village economies. I felt exaltation. And then I hit the smog wall. It was in many ways a continuation of my education.

The second one was a trip to Medellin, Colombia, in the late 1970s, for a conference on immigration and refugees in Latin America. It was organized by Lelio Marmora, an Argentinean who had long worked helping immigrants and refugees in the decades of dictatorships in the Southern Cone. He set up a system, under Peron's second presidency, to grant papers to Chilean refugees escaping the Pinochet butcheries so they could move on to safe countries; there was the daring move of bringing in thousands of them on a Sunday and giving them papers, no questions asked.

I was flying in from Venezuela where I was doing research on a postdoc from the Social Science Research Council. My flight to Bogotá was delayed, and I missed the connection to Medellin. Against the advice from just about everyone I asked at the airport, I decided to take an overnight bus from Bogotá to Medellin. The first step was to get to the downtown bus terminal, in itself a major proposition given widespread kidnapping and the uncertainty of who was actually driving whatever taxi one took; the second step was to survive the dangers of the bus terminal itself, where I might have to wait for several hours for a bus. I made it live to the terminal. There I had to wait, indeed. It was a suspenseful couple of hours since roaming bands do not hide their intentions and indeed flaunted their dangerousness. Being fluent in Spanish, I chatted quietly with the women next to whom I had seated myself. Perhaps my fluency in Spanish saved me, because there was certainly no way that I could blend in; at any rate, I was not accosted. Then came the tricky moment of having to get up and leave the oasis of womenfolk and walk across the terminal to my bus. I knew I was vulnerable. I had put my passport and cash in one of my pockets and basically emptied my handbag of valuables but made it look all puffed up with goodies and carried it so it was easy to grab from me without injuring me. I stooped a bit and made myself look frail but not scared. I did not want to provoke by walking like some kind of Valkyrie. Somewhere I hoped this would make it cowardly to attack me, but if it came to that, matters would be confined to grabbing my handbag. I was so busy figuring out how to protect myself through these tactics that I could not quite feel fear, my mind engaged in a little calculus of their intentions versus my chances. When I entered the bus, I felt quite exhilarated at the sense of having arrived safely. Somehow, I had not quite thought about the bus itself. It took a second as I climbed in to understand I was the only woman, and a foreign-looking one at that, with no business traveling at night, alone in this bus for the next ten hours. I kept my cool and quietly sat down as close as I could to the driver's seat. Very discretely I took my passport — my most valuable instrument, I felt — and sat on it. And, in case I needed a weapon, I took the thick report I had just gotten from the Venezuelan government — spelling out their labor recruitment policies, including drawing in workers from Europe (those were the oil rich days and they needed and could buy it all). The bus was what-is-today a typical school bus in the United States, promising maximum discomfort. Eventually, a woman with a baby came in, and we both clustered close to the driver's seat. I thought the worst was over and allowed myself to feel a delicious calmness, sitting on my passport.

We departed. We were deep in the *barrios populares* of Bogotá, and the drive allowed me to see areas of the city where I would never have wound up, no Colombian being willing to take me there and guarantee my safety. Bogotá was at the time, as it is today, a city pretty much in a state of alert, with a horribly repressed and abused people, an ever-present army, and roving bands of paramilitary in search of guerrilla supporters. So there I was, taking it all in. Suddenly the driver stopped to talk with another bus driver going in the opposite direction. They were both clearly extremely agitated. We took off again. The driver was now going as fast as the bus would allow, and it felt like it would fall apart. I sensed that something was not right in the situation. We turned a corner and onto a broad street — too late to avoid the trouble. All I could see was the large crowd on the street. The stones began to hit the bus. These were no pebbles; some were actually cobblestones. The massive report I was carrying came in handy: I put it against the window to protect my head from the rocks. I caught a glimpse of turned over and burned out buses, several. The driver was trying to move through as fast as possible. But suddenly he screamed, the bus swerved out of control, came to a standstill. (He had gotten hit in the head; later when I saw him, there was blood streaming down his face.) There was screaming inside and outside; I couldn't get the woman and the baby out of my head, horrible images. Then it really began. My report was no longer enough. I threw myself on the ground in the aisle — not forgetting my passport, which felt like my one ticket out of the nightmare — pure nonsense, of course. Everything was covered with shattered glass — the floor, my hair. A man threw himself on top of me to escape the rocks, thereby protecting me from the worst hits. The crowd was also rocking the bus, it swayed from one side to the other. The screaming outside was infernal; inside we were huddled, and I vaguely recall a kind of terrified silence.

It must have gone on for five or ten minutes, and my feeling was it could only get worse. It did get worse, and it felt dangerous. And then the rocking stopped. Something had changed outside, it was not clear what, but there was no more screaming. Whatever had happened, the crowds seemed to be leaving, running away. Some army trucks had arrived, as it turned out. The broad avenue outside was empty except for the trucks: the crowd had vanished. All was silent except for the army people instructing us to leave the bus. People in the bus got up and out. I saw bloodied faces. I got up, my passport still clutched in my hand, and grabbed my things, and as I was descending the bus steps, it happened. I vaguely knew I was beyond fear: I was terrorized. Terror, unlike fear, is disabling. Fear makes you run faster than usual; the adrenalin strengthens your survival instinct. I could barely stand, so intense was the trembling of my body. But as I made it down the bus steps I was pulled out of this terror as I saw the other passengers disappear into streets and alleyways. In a flash I understood they were all somehow of that world of the *barrios populares* and that I was really alone, with nowhere to go and no one to ask. There was no taxi to hail. I guess this moved me out of terror back into fear because I found myself running behind the column of army trucks, which were moving on. I ran and called out to them. One truck stopped and the leader explained that they could not take me on, they had work to do, and the city was exploding into violence. I pleaded. I cannot recall the exact sequence of events, but they put me onto another bus, a small, open vehicle, with all the windows shattered, and a terrified driver trying to get out of the danger zone. That was a frightening ride, as we passed destroyed, turned-over buses. I was crouching, again in glass, but there was little protection from possible stones since it was wide open. We made it to the bus depot. Arrived safely! Rescued by the Colombian army and a bus driver! There was no way of getting to the airport — which now seemed a far away haven. I was told there was too much violence on the main road to the airport. The men in the bus depot pointed to a couple of seedy hotels in front of the bus depot — I was not allowed to stay in the depot, my preferred choice, because of the state of emergency.

A man in his forties or so showed me to a dingy room. I double locked the flimsy door. I began to deal with my multiple wounds, to clean up the blood that was, it seemed, everywhere on my body. Then I heard a key turn in the lock, and there stood the guy looking at me, already attacking me in his mind, or so it seemed. I knew I only had a second to turn the situation around. I think at that point all the fear and tension and terror of the past several hours mutated into *desafío*. I looked him straight in the eyes and said with enormous contempt: "So this is how you show your *hombria*" (there is no good translation, since "manhood" in English has collapsed into an elementary meaning) as I pointed to the blood on my body, on my face, and in my hair. I told him to get out. He did. I put all kinds of furniture against the door and waited for the morning to arrive and get out of there. The bus depot people helped me get a taxi, and I did get to the airport; on the way I saw several cars turned over and burned out. It had indeed been a night of violence. Throughout all of it I had not understood the why. The taxi driver explained the poor were protesting the newly hiked bus ticket prices.

I took the plane to my meeting. I did not talk about my night, though the newspapers were full of headlines about the violence. But none at the meeting even surmised that I had actually been in the midst of it, with my body safely covered, no wounds on my face, and those on my scalp covered by the hair, those on my knees by my skirt. I managed the morning, getting drawn into the academic discussion, one that, moreover, was more engrossing for the participants than commenting on the newspaper headlines. Then came lunch at the side of a pool in our luxury hotel. I leaned back in my chair, crossed my legs, and suddenly the bloody wounds on my knees were visible. I noticed several people sitting close to me looking with, I guess, something like horror or incomprehension. It must have been a shocking sight in that setting. I said very quietly and quickly that I had been caught up in the violence, kneeling in glass. There followed the briefest of silences. Then the conversation moved on, not one question asked. It struck me as amusing.

In that moment I saw the closing of the academic mind to an event so far fetched that it was best left alone. I think we function like that, we humans, vis-à-vis much of the misery and the pain in the world. Thus, even this highly mediated experience of what had happened was better left unaddressed. I never brought it up either during the meeting. I also learned something about how terror need not be traumatizing. I suspect that if the horrors, the relentless series of escalating tensions and fears of that night, did not leave me traumatized, it is because I knew there was an exit. (Though some dear friends tell me it is yet an-

246 | SASKIA SASSEN

other indication that while my spiritual life is rich, my psychological life is a bit thin.) But how does it feel when, as is the case with the masses of those persecuted in the world, there is no exit?

A Summer in Central America.

The third exit was going to Central America as part of a Faculty for Human Rights mission in 1984, sponsored by Senator Christopher Dodd, an open critic of U.S. policy in Central America and one of the most enlightened members of the Senate on this subject. We were meant to be an objective investigative and reporting team looking into human rights abuses in Guatemala, El Salvador, and Nicaragua, the latter thrown in to ensure neutrality in our mission. George Vickers and Barbara Epstein were among the group's members. That trip turned out to be one of the memorable events of my life. I met known killers, such as the Salvadoran general, Carlos Eugenio Vides Casanova, in charge of the country during the worst mass murders of civilians suspected of collaborating with guerrillas. He talked to us about the military's efforts as if this was an enlightened struggle. There was not an ounce of discomfort in him when confronted with our increasingly direct and aggressive questioning and invocation of known facts about military abuse and the participation of top-ranking officials like himself. In Honduras, we were invited to have lunch with John Negroponte at his home. Yes, this was the Negroponte of Vietnam fame, Bush's man in Iraq, and now the newly appointed head of Homeland Security. We went to the places where some of the largest massacres had happened and talked with the local villagers. I had for years been filming and did so here as well on each occasion possible. Being behind the camera gave me a peculiar liberty of movement in whatever place we were being received.

The most moving experience was getting to know one of the Jesuits who was a leader in the *comunidades de base* movement in El Salvador. He was one of the group of Jesuits, of whom six were brutally murdered later that year by paramilitary forces in El Salvador for their work helping the poor. He took me and one other member of our group to visit one of the camps for the internally displaced, housed in a vast old crumbling multistoried and multiunit structure — once, perhaps, an old palatial building occupied by one or another government bureaucracy, now too obsolete for reasonable inhabitation. He told us the people there rarely came out; rarely saw the light of day. They were, in fact, prisoners: whole villages had been moved to the city and put in these camps to isolate them from the guerrillas whom they had been suspected of supporting and to clear whole areas for military operations, including bombing.

Perhaps because we had spent some time together speaking and because of some of my past connections to the liberation theology movement in Latin America, he trusted me. He took me to see a couple of residents who had kept evidence of napalm bombings in their villages: the hard shiny black stuff that remains after the bombing and the fire. They told me harrowing stories: yes, of course, they used water to squash the flames on the bodies of people who had been hit, not knowing at the time that water feeds napalm flames, one of the more perverse versions of something akin to misinformation one can imagine. They showed me the back of one surviving child, deeply scarred where the flames had burnt, fed perhaps by the child's own blood.

I filmed their testimony, and the priest asked me to take the pieces of evidence with me to the United States. It meant smuggling them out of El Salvador, a country where we had already been marked as troublemakers, and into the United States, where we were possibly also marked, given the heightened tensions at the time and an emboldened solidarity movement challenging U.S. authority. But it was important to get this evidence out. At the time, Congress was holding hearings as to whether the United States had passed napalm to the Salvadoran military. The administration kept denying it even as the evidence mounted. So it was crucial to get that evidence to Congress, though it was clearly not definitive, as far as I could gather, insofar as the location of its use might not be clear. The age of the piece, however, might signal that it could not be from Vietnam and, hence, could be from El Salvador. I took it and managed to stay calm when exiting immigration and customs control in El Salvador and then again when we entered the United States. I passed these pieces and the film to a highly trusted friend, at the time working at a high level in the America's Watch Committee, as I thought he would be a credible channel, though I won't give his name for obvious reasons.

In El Salvador, we were also received by José Napoleon Duarte, who had just been elected president in an attempt to bring democracy, even though his top military man, Vides Casanova, was known to be the real power in the country and was protecting and allowing the paramilitary forces to continue their brutal murdering and kidnapping. Many were convinced that Vides Casanova operated with the tacit approval of the U.S. government. We saw Duarte as a tragic hero, who had been deposed by the military, fought for the return of democracy, and then, allowed to run, was democratically elected by a people who saw him as a real alternative to the murderous military in control of the country. Many on the Far Left objected to him because they felt he was a de facto intermediary between the military and the U.S. government in El Salvador. It was an uncomfortable place to be in, sitting there in his drawing room. It had been easier, in a way, to ask Vides Casanova tough questions — one could feel one's full hatred. Duarte was more complex as a character: he had been a strong defender of democracy and of people's interests but had then, by some estimations, at least, succumbed to power and the desire to run the country again and accepted the terms of the military. And then came one of those little incidents that captured the pathos of Duarte. I had been filming our *audiencia,* at times moving in for a close-up. Duarte was the kind of person who comes across as the opposite of anal: a sort of *campesino* simplicity à la Nikita Khrushchev. So there I was, in on a close-up, and I saw through the camera that his pant's fly was open. It was all pretty discrete, but it captured something about Duarte's disheveled presidency. It is still not clear, I think, whether his return to the presidency was the better of two evils or a tragedy, in that it camouflaged the continuing butchery and complete abuse of power by the military, protected only by the thin screen of a democratically elected president — and we know how the U.S. government can use a nominally democratic election to its advantage, even as it continues, say, to enable a country's military in multiple small and big ways. This collusion with the military can't have been a secret, either: one only had to look at the U.S. embassy in El Salvador, surrounded by béton blocks and tall wired walls, to know that the United States was not a simple bystander.

Nicaragua was fantastic. It was such a difference, after the oppressive atmosphere in El Salvador and Honduras. We were invited just about everywhere and met with all high-level officials. We learned a lot. We also met with the opposition. We ran into many foreigners doing their thing. Managua had become a somewhat international space. We stayed at the Intercontinental Hotel in front of the vast empty space that was left by the big earthquake at the time of Somoza, which had destroyed a big chunk of the city's center and was never rebuilt, no matter the foreign aid sent. Besides all the other things it was, Managua also had an air of bohemian excitement at that time. There were too many artists and musicians from all over the world for this not to happen. I knew some of them from New York and visited them: some stayed in what were basically neatly stacked mostly open-air beds for rent at a minimum charge, with collective bathrooms and kitchens. I started an affair with an American painter, a strong believer in Sandinismo. We made love in one of those open-stacked beds in the middle of the day. It felt all so alternative lifestylish, so flower childish, so very unreal as out in the countryside there were dead every day, courtesy of the U.S.-supported Contras. Though unreal, this bohemian aura was not indulgent. It was a reassertion of life in spite of U.S. military power and complicity. I imagine there must have been such moments and spaces in cities or countries today and in the past where a war aimed at killing a somewhat utopian project that may have captured the imagination of many not necessarily part of it. Managua then was such a city, a distinctive time/place equation, one that is difficult to describe in a few words. These are the kinds of situations that need to be lived to be understood, I think. Or you must know how to write, which I don't.

Toward the late 1980s, the Central American situation had calmed down in some ways, at least in part because the U.S.-Contra alliance had succeeded in throwing out the Sandinistas and reinstituting at least some of the "good old days": universal schooling and healthcare were out, the food stations that had been located everywhere in poor areas were out, the smallholder export-oriented locally owned agriculture that had given a livelihood to many peasants and farmers, out, replaced increasingly once again by large landowners and foreign agribusinesses. Seeing the familiar alignments return must have calmed the anxieties of the U.S. government: the reassuring centralized control of the economy by a few local oligarchs and a few foreign companies, the reassuring sharp income inequality and growing poverty, no access to politics for the poor, and so on. The late 1980s also saw some positive developments — in particular, emerging peace negotiations in Guatemala and in El Salvador.

It Never Stops . . .

Toward the end of the 1980s, it did feel like there was no immediate urgent political circuit in my life — though there were of course plenty of causes around the world. I had had to give up my night life as a performer, unable to sustain that double life. It seemed that once the intensity of 1980s' politics subsided, my adrenaline went back to normal levels, and I suddenly discovered that I also had to sleep. My academic career was humming along nicely. I had overcome a little contretemps: the same year, in parallel but totally separate tracks, I had Columbia University recruiting me and my chair at Queens College telling me not to bother even to apply for tenure since I was not going to get it and that they had already hired someone on my tenure line — a very nice person, whom I really liked and respected. I was a bit dazed. At that point, a dear and special colleague,

Dean Savage, insisted I apply for tenure anyhow. I did. Not only did I get tenure, but I was ranked at the top of the college's list of newly tenured faculty for the year, according to the president of the college. Funny.

After having followed his work for years, I got to know Richard Sennett at the New York Institute for the Humanities in the early 1980s. In retrospect, my two homes away from home in New York were the institute and the distinctly different Ear Inn. Richard and I married in 1987, the beginning of a great and lasting love. Marrying Sennett meant discovering a whole new world in the city, one that inhabited some of the same streets and buildings as my prior worlds but was so patently different. Intellectual debates arriving from France, the new magical realism in Latin American novels, Susan Sontag, Joseph Brodsky, John Ashbury, Rose and Bill Styron—they all became part of my life and they helped shape my thinking. This was, once again, a world that rarely intersected with my academic life.

But before I knew it, I was again involved in some intense politics. It was 1991, and Saddam Hussein had invaded Kuwait, the first Gulf War was being prepared, and I found myself speaking at a public rally at Hunter College with Edward Said and Robert Lifton. I was asked to address the question of migrant workers in the Middle East, and Said talked about the Palestinians being thrown out of country after country in the Middle East. That was how I met Said, and we immediately communicated: different vocabularies, different focuses, yet we understood each other politically. We knew we were both uttering a call for the same justice.

At that time, I had also become involved with some of the new media activists, largely a European rather than North American crowd. In the world of digital media, the Lefties in the United States were either techies doing free software or, mostly, techies doing utopian scenarios. Emblematic of this was Perry Barlow, the founder of the Electronic Frontier, a great person, with a great project, who really believed the Internet represented a zone of freedom and absolute possibilities, all well captured in his Declaration of Independence of Cyberspace. I got involved in this world through a specific channel. Beginning in the mid-1980s, my research had taken me to global financial markets. I was also tracking the extent to which the financial industry was pushing software development along paths of its own interest. Two issues emerged for me as crucial, and both of them led me to a set of interesting debates and exchanges with new media activists, landing me in a new kind of activism. One of these was the underutilization by civil society organizations of the capabilities of these new computer-centered interactive technologies compared with finance, which not only used these capabilities to the hilt but was also pushing their subsequent development. The second issue was the emerging cyber segmentations — as I called them — which included for me, crucially, a battle for bandwidth in which finance was winning, hands down. The matter, then, was not only the much talked about digital divide, the digital have and have-nots, but also a second divide inside digital space.

I hooked up with a group of digital media activists who founded an organization — and created a great T-shirt — called Bandwidth 4all. Geert Lovink was a key actor in this effort: I got to know him when we were both speakers at a plenary session at Ars Electronica in the mid-1990s organized by its then head, Peter Weibel, a deeply political artist. Lovink is a new media activist and theorist, one of the founding members of Ditigal City Amsterdam, who helped in setting up e-community and resistance networks in Central and Eastern Europe in the early 1990s. I found myself in what was emerging as a strong network of activists and theorists, a driving force in Europe that included the group around De Ballie in Amsterdam with Eric Kluitenberg, V2 in Rotterdam with Andreas Broekman (who today heads the Berlin Transmediale, a key organization for new media art and politics) and Florian Schneider of Nobody Is Illegal. In the 1990s, much of my political energy began to focus on issues connected to new media: it was the beginning of today's onslaught by large corporate actors on cyberspace via the mantra "intellectual property rights." The work continues.

The effect of it all on my academic work is unclear beyond the brief allusions throughout the text. Perhaps the reader might think otherwise.

LAURENT THÉVENOT

The Two Bodies of May 1968

In Common, in Person

Laurent Thévenot is directeur d'études at the École des Hautes Études en Sciences Sociales, Paris, and senior researcher at the Institut National de la Statistique et des Études Economiques, Paris. He coauthored, with Luc Boltanski, De la justifi-cation (forthcoming in English), which analyzes the most legitimate repertoires of evaluation governing political, economic, and social relationships. It has been in-fluential in the new French social sciences and in the so-called convention theory, a strand of institutional economics. He also coedited two books concerning new approaches to action, the practical engagement of objects and social cognition: Les objets dans l'action *and* Cognition et information en société. *More recently, he developed collaborative and comparative research (in Western and Eastern cul-tures) on the political and moral grammars of making things and issues common, and he coedited with Michèle Lamont* Comparing Cultures and Polities: Reper-toires of Evaluation in France and the United States. *He has just completed a book on the architecture of forms of life, agencies and the ways of engaging with the world:* L'action au pluriel: régimes d'engagement. *He is coeditor of the jour-nal* Annales, Histoire, Sciences Sociales.

We are invited here to confront two kinds of history: one is history because it concerns events lived in common; and the other is a story that is a history in

I am grateful to Ariane Zambiras for her substantial help in writing the American version of this text.

person. I will use this tension between "in common" and "in person" as the main thread for this text. This tension was heightened during the events of May 1968 — referred to in France simply as *Mai* 1968 — and it left a deep print in the path my research was to take. It can be reduced neither to a question of scale nor to an opposition between macro and micro. Indeed, you can engage "in common" with unequal extension: within the closest intimacy of love, within the bonds of friendship, within a militant community oriented toward an ideal, within cultural, ethnic, or national membership, within the common of the entire planet. But the scope of engagements in person is also unequal. *Mai* 1968 and its aftermath paved the way for numerous attempts at experimenting with this tension between in common/in person, through a great variety of behaviors: the inquiring and passionate exploration of strangeness, the cheerfulness of play, the social criticism targeted at the powerful and the irony turned back against oneself, the unveiling of injustice, the unyielding confrontation of arguments, the blind violence or aching humiliation resulting from careless gestures.

The conflicting interpretations of *Mai* 1968 find their root in this tension between communal and personal concern. Whereas some commentators have acknowledged the primary evidence of collective demonstrations and social unrest, others have recognized the mark of a liberal individualism evolving from autonomy to independence (Alain Renaut) or to an exacerbated narcissism (Gilles Lipovetsky). While some authors wrote about an active solidarity (Cornelius Castoriadis) or about utopian communism (Alain Touraine), others identified a withdrawal into the private sphere. In the wake of "*Mai* 1968," two oppositions that structured social sciences were unsettled: the opposition between collective and individual, on the one hand, and the one between public and private, on the other — and this is not the least benefit derived from *Mai* 1968.

The narrative I chose stages the various opportunities I met to experience and conceptualize the tension between "in common" and "in person." A first act sets the scenery and the atmosphere of the time we are concerned with. It can be summed up under the idea of the challenge to a series of common goods that mainly oriented the French republican community. It presents the narrator, the actors, and their role — in particular that of sociologist. In the second act, the tension is presented through the issue of representation that was at stake in the crisis of *Mai* 1968: political, scientific, or ordinary cognitive representations. The third act focuses on various experiences of living in common, coping with differences and making one's way from personal attachments to public existence.

The passion of bringing personal experiences in common was undoubtedly at the very heart of May 1968.

Act 1: Confronting History with a Story

The first act is composed of three parts. The first part unfolds along a series of statistics that represent people in the context of society. The theatrical device I use here should lay out the entire series in different scenes that occur simultaneously. The second part deals with scientific work on representations and takes place in the laboratory of the sociology scholar. The stage is thus divided into separate areas, making it possible to compare the activities of each one, their interaction or lack of thereof, and the slamming of doors worthy of the best vaudevilles. The third scene brings into play agents often left in the dark by the traditional staging of social and political science: things. Thanks to the interplay of things, playful and ironical forces are added to the plot that consequently turn it into comedy.

The first act took place just before the events of May 1968. Against the backdrop of a country — France — that was witnessing the challenging of its basic "orders of worth," the narrator experienced "sociological objectifying" when he assumed the role of the interviewee for the first time.[1] The statistical perspective transforms the personal landmarks into general forms and thus introduces History in our story. Not a harmless transformation. . . .

The Atmosphere and the Setting: The Challenged Orders of Worth of the French Republic The setting was that of a Parisian public high school. More precisely, the action took place in a *classe préparatoire* that trains students for the competitive entry exams to the *grandes écoles*. This setting is part of a very French higher education system that parallels universities and is designed to train a small number of highly selected students for occupations of senior civil

---

1. Introducing the atmosphere and setting, I refer to the theoretical framework of "orders of worth" (*ordres de grandeur*) that I elaborated with Luc Boltanski (Boltanski and Thévenot 1991, 1999, 2000). This is not the place for a presentation of these analytical categories, therefore I only mention basic terms, taking the risk of misunderstanding. Thus, people and things qualify for industrial worth in reference to the common good of technical efficiency and investments for the future. Industrial worth is no more limited to industry than domestic worth, grounded on entrenched trust, is restricted to family. All orders of worth are highly generalized forms of legitimate evaluation. Criticism and compromise are related not to individuals or collectives but to the plurality of orders of worth.

servant or large company managers (in particular, public facilities). One of the top *grandes écoles* is the École Polytechnique, which produces "state engineers," who both qualify for the technical/scientific "industrial" worth and for the public "civic" worth. A selective part of these trained engineers enter the so-called state bodies (*corps d'État*), that is, organized bodies of senior civil servants. This strange French invention smacks of the ancien régime, while aiming at the modernization of the country through the kind of civil engineering that is intended to contribute to the public good. The hierarchical authority of these bodies draws on a third order of worth that Luc Boltanski and I named "domestic" because it extends the kind of providential authority that has been associated with the traditional paterfamilias. This hierarchical, entrenched, and customary order was involved in ancien régime sovereignty but it is still implemented in contemporary French society. However, it lacks the official recognition that both the industrial and the civic orders of worth share. This domestic worth supports embodied hierarchies and maintains the centralized compromise between technical expertise and the civil service that was still the keystone of the 1960s' French state.

On the eve of *Mai* 1968, how were these three orders of worth regarded? The domestic worth was the first to be denounced because of unbearable personal dependencies and heavy hierarchies and the kind of allegiance that it involved. From family fathers to nation fathers, embodied authorities were to be the favorite targets of antiestablishment activity. By contrast, the civic order of worth was not disputed, and *Mai* 1968 activists would contribute to its dissemination throughout civil society, outside the state apparatus that was criticized for unduly monopolizing this worth. This civic worth equipped demonstrations and public meetings for the critique of social inequalities. Suspicion toward undue civic qualification nurtured the demand that every elected representative should be regularly put to the test of civic qualification. The industrial worth was also targeted by the criticism of the power of experts, technocrats, and corporate managers who failed to meet the general interest. The market order of worth was at that time foreign to the French state and sharply criticized in reference to consumer society and "one-dimensional man" (Herbert Marcuse). Commentators insisted on the desire for liberty and individual emancipation as the motivations for criticism. I rather bear in mind the efforts to aggrandize in common the kind of expressiveness and personal experience that qualifies as the order of "inspiration" worth. The body offers appropriate equipment for such an aggrandizement in inspiration. It fully contributed to the expansive exuberance of the 1960s. Criticism used to be grounded on a compromise between civic solidarity and in-spired expressiveness. "Imagination in power" was not the absurd catchword is-sued from an insane political utopia but the canonical investment formula of the inspired worth. Anticipating the continuation of history, I shall observe that the remnants of this inspiration worth were transformed into market commodities along with fashionable signs that were aggrandized through the worth of "fame." Semiotics, the science of these signs and of their power, blossomed during this period. In this regard, and only in this regard, one may say that the market and marketing expansion in France in the 1980s and 1990s continued the experi-ments of *Mai* 1968.

Action and Acting: Two "Bodies" Coming into Play, One for the Benefit of Instituted Common Forms, the Other for the Ease of Personal Use I have al-luded twice already to the word "body," each time with a different meaning: first, that of a common form, collectively acknowledged (in the sense of an organized body of civil servants or of a body of doctrines); second, that of the place for an intimate and familiar experience. I observe that the critical tension mentioned before is actually encapsulated in the two meanings of the word "body," a body that enables us to switch back and forth between a way of being in common (the organized body) and a way of being in person (the experiencing body). I associate this double body with a primary—if not primeval—scene. In fact, the discovery of these confronted bodies, and the tedious learning of the circulation between one and the other, are part of an ordinary experience of biographical aggran-dizement, that is, of adolescent transition from childhood to adulthood and thus participation in a public space. Far from being reserved to the king's two bodies (Ernst Hartwig Kantorowicz), this necessary experience is the cornerstone of adolescence.

In that regard, *Mai* 1968 was an adolescent crisis, and not only because of the harsh confrontation between two succeeding generations. I associate this time of my life with the experience of an essential tension between the two bodies, and I encountered this tension in three different fields. The first one, to which I devoted most of my time, was an intensive training in mathematics. There, the formal rigor of bodies, or groups, of definition met the intensity of a repeated practice that was first bodily and sensual through the handling of familiar and do-mesticated mathematical formulas. The second field of ardent exploration was that of "contemporary" music—as it was called at the time—which was in full bloom then. This exploration also led me to bring together formal structures and sensitive responsiveness. The formal realm was that of the Vienna School, or the stochastic compositions of Iannis Xenakis, whom I invited to a give a talk to my fellow students and whose works I introduced in an incongruous presentation to the military body during my national service. . . . The sensual experience was that of the gorgeous luxuriance of timbres and concrete sounds, for instance, with the composer François-Bernard Mâche who introduced me to so-called concrete music in the high school where he then taught classics. The third field of experience where the two bodies were combined was the continent of Marcel Proust's literary work. My excitement was here again rooted in two bodies of experiments: the discovery of systematic social mapping, on the one hand, and the rapture of words, on the other, the close contact with things and bodies they caress.

These were the things that enlivened my life in this *classe préparatoire* until the day when we received a visit from a team of sociologists, who asked us to fill in a questionnaire for their survey. You will easily guess the motivation of this survey—as I did afterward, when I discovered my own filled-in questionnaire during my training in the sociology center of Pierre Bourdieu!—knowing that the survey had been designed in this center and was dedicated to exploring cultural capital legacy and social reproduction (Bourdieu and Passeron [1979] 1964). Christian Baudelot was in charge of this survey before he moved away from the master's clout and developed a sociology of the school system with Roger Establet, adopting a more Marxist and "classist" approach (Baudelot and Establet 1971). Christian Baudelot succeeded Bourdieu as the sociology chair in one of the *grandes écoles* where I studied. Throughout his life, he stayed deeply committed to the social criticism of inequalities, without defecting. He is the one I most often saw at political demonstrations or protests, always supporting the virtues of popular solidarity and "practice" in common. In the wings of this survey were the first two sociologists who would initiate me to the discipline.

One question on the survey was about parents' occupation and education. My father had sat on the same benches of the same *classe préparatoire* as me, thereby revealing my educational legacy. Even more striking, there was nowhere to indicate that my maternal grandfather was the son of a modest peasant woman who raised him alone after her husband died, thus benefiting from the French Republican school system that made it possible to rise socially as a result of academic merit. My unease was intensified by the fact that there was nowhere on the answer sheet to indicate the activities that were the core of my existence, or my keenest engagements, or eager pursuits. Worst of all was the question about the last book I had read, which sounded to me like the blade of a guillotine. I had to confess — red in the face — that it was *The American Challenge*, by Jean-Jacques Servan-Schreiber.[2] I was done for. . . .

Act 2: Playing with Representations

Let's put aside the well-known demonstrations of May 1968 in which I took part, like millions of other marchers, and let's stick with the generalizing view on my education and occupation ("Formation et qualification professionnelle") — which was the name of a statistical survey devoted to those themes and to the analysis of social and occupational mobility and which was the very same survey I was in charge of a few years later in the French Bureau of Statistics. Was I to follow the path traced by my forefathers and inflate the figures at the diagonal of the matrices representing social mobility? Was I to confirm "social reproduction" and the "closure" of French society?

At first, I nearly did replicate my forebears' paths, with the exception that I turned down technical engineering for "social engineering" — more precisely, for the production of information to guide diagnosis and social intervention. Instead of the rural engineering body (Corps du Génie Rural), which aimed to modernize rural France with reference to the industrial order of worth, to which my father, my two uncles, and my grandfather belonged, I preferred a "body" with civic worth. The most social body, that of statistics and economic studies, holds out a promise of links with social science and with the criticism of social inequalities. The irony of the situation lies in the fact that I ended up at the National Institute of Statistics and Economic Studies (INSEE), at the very heart of the classifying state that categorizes and sorts out social reality, and that this "disciplinary" state was constantly under fire from critics in 1968. But INSEE was also, at that time, populated with a host of double agents, who supplied information to the enemies of such an increasingly contested state and, among them, with sociologists occupying the first rank of this social criticism.

Representing Society: At Home, in the Midst of Socio-Occupational Representatives, with Statistical Employees, at the Interviewee's House My reflective experience of the whole sequence of statistics that depict people is at the origin

---

2. Jean-Jacques Servan-Schreiber founded *Express* magazine and was really popular among executives, inciting them to take up the "American challenge" and try to modernize France.

of the attention that I paid to the process of making equivalence among of persons or things and having them "qualified," an analysis that Luc Boltanski and I later developed in the theoretical framework of orders of worth.

My first experience of these statistics is from the 1968 French census, whose large statistical charts were spread out on the floor in different rooms of my apartment, allowing a spatial representation of French society, at home. Handling them for days and nights to visualize social grouping led me to the publication of a first article that displayed the statistical representation of France along socio-occupational categories. My second experience showed that these categories had an impact on how professionals were represented: it offered my first insight into the politics of statistics. Involved in the creation of a new classification, I ended up surrounded by representatives of different occupations, who, since they were consulted, energetically confronted one another about questions of the delimitation and the denomination of occupational categories and about their respective position in the state classification. My third experience took place with those INSEE employees who were in charge of coding the filled-in questionnaires. My interest in shop floor practices was in accordance with the kind of radical sociology of labor that developed in 1960–70, opposing the unrecognized skills of workers to the formal and incomplete descriptions of engineers and technicians. I therefore conducted a survey on the know-how and professional practices of coders. In my fourth experience, the inquiry circled back to the interviewees. I visited them in their homes to make a direct comparison between what they'd said on their questionnaires and their actual living situations. I met the same tensions as in Act 1. Instead of the errors or lies listed in handbooks, I felt the unease that stems from representation of a familiar situation given by the statistical survey, stressing the confrontation of discrepant formats of collected information and their relations with forms of evaluation that remain implicit in the process of collecting the information.

Representation and Social Theory: From Classification Struggles to the Test of Orders of Worth Each of the experiences I have described casts a different light on social representation, in every sense of the word: in social science, in politics, in the common sense. Each of them can foster a contestation of representations in full accordance with the atmosphere of the time — contestation of the statistical order, of political pressures, of the abstract knowledge of engineers, of discipline. In parallel to our work on the definition of social categories (Desrosières and Thévenot 1988), the research we conducted would offer the matrix for social constructivism, and it was in effect influential in this direction. However, as scenes of this second part unfold, we will see that the plot is taking another direction.

Pierre Bourdieu's sociology was the heir, in France, to a sociology of the forms of knowledge and classification established by Émile Durkheim and Marcel Mauss and passed on through the prism of the influence of Max Weber and Karl Marx. For someone who was working on classification and social representations, this extremely ingenious sociology—both subtle and systematic—was an ideal source of inspiration. To the cleverness of the analyses was to be added the charm of the "master," which held the disciples spellbound in such a way that the following scene was shrouded in the warm colors of blessed dreams. The captivating company of this virtuoso of the reflective deed (for he was a man of action as much as a man of reflection) was first made possible through my elder colleague and friend Alain Desrosières, who had opened up the way for research on social classifications at INSEE. Keeping company with Bourdieu proved all the more pleasant as it was emancipated, thanks to our extraterritoriality (Desrosières and I had our office at INSEE), from the constraints weighing on Bourdieu's research group in which operated an iron discipline often akin to that of a political party's cell. This first scene pictures laboratory life in Bourdieu's house (*maison Bourdieu*), in the same sense as a French manufacturer. There can be little doubt that it was the mother house, where most of our sociological training was acquired, although it eventually led to the foundation of a new enterprise that would not be a subsidiary company, like so many others. The phrase "father house" would be more appropriate, given the paternalistic flavor that prevailed. I remember meeting one of the group's researchers at a contemporary music concert, who made me swear to keep secret this compromising attendance at a concert hall. We would later endure more totalitarian forms of control, ranging from excommunication to censorship of the authorized list of references. But let's stay here with the benefits of this propitious learning and with justifiable disagreement. Desrosières remembers two of the mottos used in the teaching of Bourdieu at the school attended by INSEE's executives: (1) look at the father's socio-occupational category and (2) look at the lens that is used to look at this category. The conjunction of the two prescriptions was a source of tension—almost a source of "double blind"—resulting from the encounter between the Marxist positivity of a science that armed criticism, and the deconstruction bearing in itself the risk of disarmament: a puzzling encounter typical of *Mai* 1968. In the following episode, theoretical developments unfolded concerning overcoming this tension.

I first encountered Luc Boltanski through reading the writings he did with

Bourdieu — more precisely, their text on class and classification struggles. However, Boltanski was not only Bourdieu's remarkably gifted student. His research developed in truly innovative directions. We first worked together when he was considering the statistical representation of the category "executives" (*cadres*) and the work of representation performed by its members and the institutions consolidating the category (Boltanski 1987). It converged with the experiences I described in the previous scenes, which had led me to approach representational work from a series of statistics and to develop a conceptualization of investments in forms, which are the base of conventions of coordination (Thévenot 1984). In both cases, we put in relation the operations required for political, scientific, and everyday cognitive representations, which we were about to integrate in a theory of "qualification" that transforms persons (as well as things) so as to insure their treatment in common — a theory of social art par excellence.

The relationship with Luc, who was ten years my senior, was first one of apprenticeship, in the literal sense of a learning process with a master of rigorous and generous craftsmanship. In that regard, it was not a symmetrical relation. However, the difference between our former training in different disciplines (I was first an economist) and between our trajectories soon enabled us to engage in reciprocity, which transpired with the elaboration of a new social theory. This time was characterized by a certain nomadism. The laboratory that was taking shape, as the experiments and games about social categorization inspired in part by social psychology succeeded one another, was first itinerant and then settled in a new joint venture: the Group of Political and Moral Sociology (GSPM), located at the École des Hautes Études en Sciences Sociales (Paris). It is thus difficult to locate precisely the next scene. In fact, the scene was reproduced in many places where classification games were played and where we drew the portraits of persons whose social identity was to be discovered. We had invented those games to explore the social art of categorization and qualification, and they were played by more than a thousand persons, both collecting data and contributing to the training of the coding employees for the 1972 census. This exploration also marked the distance taken from Bourdieu's theory — which was about to be a profound rupture — as we were taking seriously into account people's judgments and the plurality of underlying forms of evaluation that they involved (Boltanski and Thévenot 1983).

Represented Reality: The Irony of Things "Practice" was a highly praised category in those years. It took a new turn with the approach we developed, which, after Bruno Latour's other disobedient sociological innovation launched a few years before, took an interest in things. Previously, sociologists had taken little interest in the place of things among human relations and had left the analysis of a politics with things up to economists. Before the writings of Michel Serres, Michel Foucault's works had shown a certain inclination for things and their relations to words (Foucault 1966). Inspired by Gilles Deleuze, Bruno Latour went a step further and portrayed a fascinating world where human beings were "interested" in things, and—daring proposition—vice versa (Latour 1987). He was one of the very few in the new French generation succeeding that of Raymond Boudon, Pierre Bourdieu, Michel Crozier, and Alain Touraine to have the boldness and talent to embark on the adventure of a new sociological theory. *Mai 1968* gave their share to things as it did for the bodies through which we hold onto those things. The commodities that alienate people through consumption were denounced and sign objects were unveiled (Jean Baudrillard). Roland Barthes's semiotics was actually as fascinated with signs as it was concerned with their unveiling. Following the order of inspiration worth, things were strangely diverted from their original design. In a gesture akin to irony, creative uses disqualified the functional value that was relevant for the industrial order of worth and that engineers had bestowed on objects for the purpose of efficiency. Michel de Certeau has grasped better than anyone else those tactical diversions in the survey he directed on the arts of praxis (de Certeau [1990] 1998).

If human beings divert things, things, for their part, do not fail to divert human beings. Things distract humans' exclusive attention to actor's intentions or habits, an attention that overlooks the way things are disposed in *dispositifs* and the way they upholds human dispositions. There is an irony of things when their intervention betrays their alleged subordination to a human master. I do not have in mind the bitter and scathing irony of sarcasm but a more humble irony, borrowing Kenneth Burke's phrase. Relying on proximity and complicity, humble irony is opposed to "romantic" irony, the latter implying superiority, according to Burke's view on the seduction scene in *The Waste Land*—the poet appearing to be satisfied that he is not the hero of the book but, rather, a small infatuated employee (Burke [1945] 1969, 514). I would add that the lines Eliot suppressed at Ezra Pound's instigation expressed even more fiercely this sarcastic distance to "a touch of art . . . given by the false Japanese print, purchased in Oxford Street" (Eliot 1971, 45). The irony of things is humble from the standpoint that it reminds human beings of their common condition. Even when things do not betray human beings, they lecture them in the sense that they reduce their grand projects to concrete grounds. However abstract their construction may be, human beings will eventually have to lend a helping hand in their making and to engage not only their hand but also their full body and a concrete environment of things. This is what we call in French *la cuisine*, which points not only to Goffman's hidden backstage but to the most tangible aspects of human affairs as well. Thus, the third part of this second act faces up to things. It stages the irony of things in two *leçons de choses* that narrate the dissonant encounter between conventional forms and their mundane support.

The first scene exhibits investment in form, a category I created to relate the benefits of coordination to its cost and to the sacrifice of peculiarities that demands a general form of equivalence. The presentation first took place in Paris, in front of statisticians and economists from INSEE, and then at Harvard, in front of political scientists invited by the Center for European Studies. The talk was about the economy of conventional forms and foreshadowed the "economy of conventions" and the plurality of forms of coordination—which cannot be reduced to the competitive market (Thévenot 2001a). I discussed Spence, Stiglitz and Akerlof's research on the economics of quality together with an exhibition of a series of camembert boxes whose purpose was to make people understand the process of qualification of the product (the origin of the milk, its being non-pasteurized, and the ladling of the curdled milk are required for *appellation contrôlée*) and the plurality of orders of qualification (from "domestic" camembert to "industrial" pasteurized camembert). The empirical basis for this theoretical research on "qualification" drew on a comprehensive survey and included a final cheese-tasting blind test. The second scene also plays on the ironic distance between the conventional category and the tangible items, a distance where laughter originates, according to Schopenhauer. It was a more official scene that displayed the inauguration of the new state classification of socio-occupational categories. All the INSEE directors were there, with the general manager (Edmond Malinvaud) who is famous in economics and econometrics. After he cut the ribbon for the new code, we explained to him that he should move toward the buffet, which was also the fruit of our work since we had collected—and sometimes cooked ourselves—as many cakes as new "socio-occupational categories." The game we asked the august INSEE hierarchy to play consisted in guessing what cake was associated with what socio-occupational category. One of the pastries—it was purely white and spherical—left the audience perplexed. We finally revealed that it was a "meta-pastry," that is, a cake representing the conceptual model of all socio-occupational categories. Instead of being squarely shaped and suggesting the cross-cut of multiple criteria, it was spherical and it concealed a hardcore center (in *nougatine*) surrounded by a granular constellation (in meringue) of cases suggesting the extension of the category through typical cases (close to the core) and limit cases (close to the periphery). The buffet seminars of a so-called International Society for Culinary Epistemology thereafter provided several occasions for the confrontation between a series of tiered cakes representing the different orders of worth, with an outstanding inspired worth pastry homemade by Elisabeth Claverie (Claverie 2003) and a "Bavaroise des champs" (fields mousse) homemade by Michel Gollac (Baudelot and Gollac 2000) that allowed participants to taste a complete field structure with its different species of capital.

Act 3: Passions in Common:
From Personal Attachments to Public Existence

The second act has led us to the domain of the qualification of persons and things, from the qualifications imparted by the state, the institutions, education, and statistics to those imparted by everyday and informal judgments. The third act now approaches the story from a different angle, considering a person passionately engaged in the process of making common things rather than a person categorized for the purpose of administration and for science. In May 1968, discovering the personal experiences they had in common fascinated people. Even the passion for equality, which has been situated since Tocqueville at the heart of democratic individualism, came within the perspective of living together in solidarity and not within that of interindividual comparison. As for the relation to the self, it was already in vogue and was constantly put to the test of relation to others, through restless and sometimes hectic to-and-fro motions between the self and others. The first part of the third act brings together several scenes in which communities have to confront difference. The second part deals with the process of making common things and putting commonality to the test of personal attachments.

Experiencing differences in community In 1968, the most obvious portrayal of life in common was to be found in the various militant organizations in charge of offering or imposing such experiences. A whole range of those groups were present at my workplace, as well as at many others, and the groups fiercely confronted each other in meetings, on the job, in flyers, and in bulletins. But in order to set the first scene of these experiences of difference, I would rather not start with the most public space. This scene introduces us to a small work environment of about thirty people, the employment section at the head office of INSEE, which at the time was more akin to a commune than to an office. People would jump on any opportunity to challenge the explicit hierarchy of the managerial staff and the implicit hierarchy of gender relations. The grass roots had convinced the head of our section to take a day off work and spend it in the country to discuss, criticize, and self-criticize the way our unit operated on a daily basis. The aim of this kind of retreat was to question INSEE's practices and deeply transform them. The method used was to let employees speak since they were usually prevented from doing so because of the weight of the hierarchies. This small community intended to explore new models of life together. In our enthusiasm to intertwine various connections in order to overcome social boundaries, we thoroughly experienced the rich variety of political, professional, friend, or love relations.

In 1968, any work was to be done together. Students called for study groups and collective grades, denouncing the individual ranking that induced inequality by measuring them, according to the expectation of social constructivism. The second scene corresponds to an experiment of working jointly, in the closest form of collaboration, when the strength of a two-person commitment is combined with the power of friendship, and to the construction of a new sociology. Together, Luc Boltanski and I would revel in the ancestries of sociology, whom we found in the "grammarians" of the city — Saint Augustine, Jacques-Bénigne Bossuet, Thomas Hobbes, Jean-Jacques Rousseau, Adam Smith, and Henri de Saint-Simon — and in a comprehensive collection of political philosophy books, which we devoured in concert. But is it possible to think and write together? A passionate conversation does take place between two people, but in the end, isn't there just one hand taking up the pen? A four-handed writing process was made possible with the aid of an impersonal third party — the computer. It contributed to manufacturing a genuine common object. Each of us would in turn verify and complete the anonymous computerized text, ensuring the common goal of an anonymous result through the following rule: no personal mark should appear that would reveal one contribution or the other, and each of us would judge the text globally. We worked side by side, both on our computers, on the second floor of a country house lost in Orne County. Then, on the first floor, early in the morning, we would take care of another common object, more quickly prepared than our book: beef stewing all morning long, under carrots melting thanks to a veal's trotter (*bœuf mode*). For us, *gai savoir* intertwined with *cuisine* know-how.

It was legitimate, in May 1968, to discuss the differences rooted in social backgrounds, to which could be added the newly born category of gender. But civic universalism hardly left any space for the acknowledgment of other differences, be they expressed through attachments or membership of a community, and called in public "cultural" or "ethnic." The third scene combines several experiences of encounters with strangers and strangeness in work, offering the opportunity to differentiate one's own community. Two collective research projects have involved, for several years, a dozen researchers of two nationalities, American and French in the first case (codirected by Michèle Lamont and myself [2000]), and Russian and French in the second (codirected by Daniil Alexandrov and Oleg Kharkhordine, still ongoing). These projects have permitted intense empirical and reflective work on the grammars of communal life originating in contrasted political and moral contexts (Thévenot and Lamont 2000). The arrangement insured a cross-cultural approach, which did not come without the unease and the disagreements inherent in the confrontation between the foreigner's gaze and the native's conventional impression. The comparative perspective contrasted different ways of transforming personal and local attachments into something that could be made public. In a liberal grammar of the public, attachments must be voiced through the figure of the individual in public, with the risk that such attachments could be considered only as one among many other individual preferences, even in the case of cultural belonging. In a civic grammar of worth, where the emphasis is placed on anonymous solidarity within the general will, attachments are suspected of fostering dependencies. Any attached difference is suspected of corrupting the civic equality that is needed for the public, including the statistical and administrative categories pointing to ethnicity or culture, which would, however, be indispensable for the fight against discrimination. At the same time, attachments come first in the communitarian grammars of the "we," with the risk of preventing more detached conventions of the public.

This is not the place for the presentation of the results, and I will only hint at them through the following stylized performance of different actors (names have been changed). Let us observe that the American Mike started his lecture with an easy-to-grasp joke, to ease the tense atmosphere or, more precisely, to break the asymmetry between the person who talks and those who listen. The asymmetry is upsetting for a liberal constitution of the public for two reasons: the speaker is granted a de facto privilege instead of remaining one voice among others and there is no obvious individualization among the silent audience that listens. The speaker crafts the joke to reduce his possible arrogance and to allow individuals' expressive laugh. Thus, the joke restores, in an instant, a more liberal public space. By contrast, the French Michel's presentation was supposed to be devoid of any personal bias because of its high level of abstraction and potential universal validity. He even conceals one's inclination toward humor under the camouflage of a cold persiflage that alludes to hidden insinuations. Mike sharply criticizes Michel for the complex and elitist abstraction of his way of speaking and for the narcissism of his innuendos, which are all features that hinder the liberal process of making public one's individual opinion and prevent other participants from debating on an equal footing with him by expressing their own opinion. And the Russian Misha's style of presentation varies according to whether he is with "his folks" or in front of a foreign person. If he has managed to get closer to the person by any means, he will treat her or him to one of the hilarious Russian *anekdotes* that require familiarity with Russian everyday life to be understood, precisely because they jeer at the failings of this united life. By contrast to persiflage, this kind of brotherly and humble irony lies in a shared belonging to the community.

When the Conceptions of Life in Common Are Put to the Test of Personal Attachments In the preceding scenes, we grasped the variation in the scope of the common, ranging from friendship — not to mention love intimacy — to the common humanity aimed at by science or justice, without forgetting smaller communities. We have thus reached the last scene of this act, which focuses on how conceptions of the common are put to the test of personal attachments. This final development of my main theme articulates new theoretical conceptualization with original configurations of joint research. It results in an integrated picture of the tensions running across our society, a picture that offers a view of differences and pluralism that strongly differs from the stratified one we had at the onset of our story.

After shedding light on the plurality of the most legitimate forms of public qualifications, the theoretical framework has widened to encompass the plurality of ways of engaging with the world, showing the varying scope of commonality — from local and personal attachments to public involvement through individualized planned action — which cannot be subsumed under the public/

private divide. I can trace this movement back to tutelary figures. Whereas reading and discussing with Albert Hirschman had incited Luc and I to examine the political and moral plurality of involvement without reducing it to market exchange (Hirschman 1982), Paul Ricoeur's work pointed to several levels of involvement in relation to the enunciation subject (I, you, she or he): at the fundamental level is the maintenance of the self through narration; the second level implies the ethical consequences of the encounter with the other; and the third level includes the demand placed by a third party on justice and institutions (Ricoeur 1992). To cope with the diversity of models of action, strategy, practice, routine, and so on, I was in search of a more encompassing category. The idea was to characterize the variety of shared "regimes of engagement," which people rely on when they have to capture what happens in terms of agency to coordinate with each other and with themselves. Instead of the basic notion of "meaning" used in comprehensive sociology, I specified each regime by the formats of the good and of reality that are jointly engaged and put to the test (Thévenot 1990, 2001b, 2002, 2005a). I have tried to give more weight than usual to nonverbal tests, as they can be seen in the regime of familiarity: the nonverbal sustains a personality thanks to various attachments, without the explicit support of narrative and verbal promise. Research on democracy is limited insofar as it takes for granted that people have spontaneous access to the public state of individuals who voice their opinion. Such research fails to consider the preliminary requirement that a personality be maintained by close attachments.

This line of argumentation has been developed and implemented in a series of collective works on "politics with respect to closeness" (Thévenot 2005b).[3] The books in this series explore the extension of policies, and their resulting tensions, when the public and categorized treatment of populations is completed by additional devices that are intended to get the policy closer to the local context and even to the personal situation of the beneficent. This research program also considers the impediments encountered in the symmetrical transformation that the policy anticipates from the beneficiary. She or he has to temper personal attachments to engage in contracts and projects that test his or her individual autonomy (Luca Pattaroni). But this path to public existence is impeded when the

3. The later mentioned pieces of research by Nicolas Auray, Marc Breviglieri, Eric Doidy, Romuald Normand, and Joan Stavo-Debauge are presented in the edited collection already referred to (Thévenot 2005b); see also Breviglieri, Stavo-Debauge, and Pattaroni (2003).

person lacks the personal attachments that are sustained by a home and/or a job. Such a transformation is particularly visible in welfare policies that have been oriented toward the reintegration of disaffiliated persons. The policies that aim at the reduction of social inequalities and usually target limited social categories receive additional provisions that have been designed to accompany the reintegration of persons suffering from deficiency in terms of occupation or accommodation (Breviglieri, Stavo-Debauge, and Pattaroni 2003). Exclusion results from the lack of close attachments, and such attachments can hardly be publicly recognized as cultural or ethnic in a Republican model of integration that is henceforth blind to discriminations (Joan Stavo-Debauge) — those are the attachments of *jeunes issus de l'immigration* (second generations) who share the risk of growing up in nostalgic and enclosed communities (Marc Breviglieri). Political militancy is also put to the test of local and personal involvement when dealing with housing conditions or with the ecological environment, because the relation between the common cause and personal attachments is then strained (Eric Doidy). Education systems also aim at the aggrandizement of the person through the learning of a common knowledge and a common citizenship. The education crisis invites us to look for methods that are more welcoming to personal attachments (Romuald Normand). New epistemic communities dedicated to a learning process are based on the personalized use of information and communication techniques (Nicolas Auray). This research program was based on a common seminar, though several collective programs had full autonomy and were managed entirely by PhD candidates and young scholars. The politics and morals of this cooperative work echoed our scientific concern for the ways different levels of publicity, commonality, and closeness could be accommodated. We adopted a line of work in common that was largely open to familiar engagement, allowing for personal creativity and escaping the rigorous alignment with orthodoxy that I had experienced in my very first training in sociology. If I had to stage this adventure, the trouble would be to confine it to a determined place and time because of the different kinds of engagement involved in the projects, which were often relayed by e-mail or long-distance phone calls, as well as extensive face-to-face conversations. This joint production turned away from industrial or domestic types of organizations characterized by a hierarchical division of labor and responsibilities but also from a network management that is dedicated to a particular project (Boltanski and Chiapello 1999). Some might argue that deadlines suffered from such composite arrangements.

. . .

We started with a scene of French society in a stage of crisis. We end on another scene and a different kind of critical tension. In May 1968, power and the state were contested on the grounds of their authority, which embodied unbearable hierarchies. At the same time, the welfare state was shaken, and many of its components and compromises were questioned: both industrial and civic worth, which had been adopted as a way to secure solidarity based on profession, and ; the state organization akin to domestic worth, which contributed to a providential protection echoing monarchial paternalism. All these intertwining hierarchies (including the civic representative's authority) came under harsh suspicion because of the extended sense given to the notion of domination to which social scientists ardently contributed. But these social scientists could not easily grasp the new type of concern emerging at that time because of the collective substance of the social categories they used. I tried to stage this concern in this narrative and to suggest that the May 1968 crisis expressed a rising anxiety about the way to sustain oneself as a person while engaging with the world in common. In order to understand the move from one scene to the other, we followed a progression toward new conceptual frames. We experienced this progress through a series of encounters, moments of good or bad fortune in communities, searching for ways of being together and cooperative production that were neither too unfair nor too oppressive in regard to close attachments and to the consistency of the person.

References

Baudelot, C., and R. Establet. 1971. *L'école capitaliste en France.* Paris: Maspéro.

Baudelot, C., and M. Gollac. 2000. "L'informatique au travail." *Actes de la recherche en sciences sociales,* no. 134 (September).

Boltanski, L. 1987. *The Making of a Class: Cadres in French Society.* Cambridge: Cambridge University Press; Paris: Editions de la Maison des Sciences de l'Homme.

Boltanski, L., and E. Chiapello. 1999. *Le nouvel esprit du capitalisme.* Paris: Gallimard.

Boltanski, L., and L. Thévenot. 1983. "Finding One's Way in Social Space; A Study Based on Games." *Social Sciences Information* 22 (4–5): 631–79.

———. 1991. *De la justification: Les économies de la grandeur.* Paris: Gallimard. Forthcoming in English from Princeton University Press, translated by Catherine Porter.

———. 1999. "The Sociology of Critical Capacity." *European Journal of Social Theory* 2, no. 3 (August): 359–77.

Boltanski, Luc, and Laurent Thévenot. 2000. "The Reality of Moral Expectations: A Sociology of Situated Judgment." Translated by Jo Smets. *Philosophical Explorations* 3 no. 3 (September): 208–31.

Bourdieu, P., and L.Boltanski. 1974. "Le titre et le poste: Rapports entre le système de production et le système de reproduction." *Actes de la recherche en science sociales*, no. 2, 95–107.

Bourdieu, P., and J.-C.Passeron. [1964] 1979. *The Inheritors: French Students and Their Relations to Culture.* Translated by Richard Nice. Chicago: University of Chicago Press.

Breviglieri, Marc, Joan Stavo-Debauge, and Luca Pattaroni. 2003. "Quelques effets de l'idée de *proximité* sur la conduite et le devenir du travail social." *Revue Suisse de Sociologie* 29 (1): 141–57.

Burke, K. [1945] 1969. *A Grammar of Motives.* Berkeley: University of California Press.

Claverie, Elisabeth. 2003. *Les guerres de la vierge: Une anthropologie des apparitions.* Paris: Gallimard.

de Certeau, M. [1990] 1998. *The Practice of Everyday Life.* New rev. and augmented ed. by Luce Giard. Minneapolis and London: University of Minnesota Press.

Desrosières, A., and L. Thévenot. 1988. *Les catégories socioprofessionnelles.* Paris: La Découverte.

Eliot, T. S. 1971. *The Waste Land.* Facsimile and transcript of the original drafts, including the annotations of Ezra Pound. Edited by Valerie Eliot. New York: Harcourt Brace Jovanovich.

Foucault, M. 1966. *The Order of Things: An Archaeology of the Human Sciences.* New York: Pantheon Books.

Hirschman, A. O. 1982. *Shifting Involvements: Private Interest and Public Action.* Princeton, NJ: Princeton University Press.

Lamont, M., and L. Thévenot, eds. 2000. *Rethinking Comparative Cultural Sociology: Repertoires of Evaluation in France and the United States.* Cambridge: Cambridge University Press.

Latour, B. 1987. *Science in Action: How to Follow Scientists and Engineers through Society.* Cambridge, MA: Harvard University Press.

Ricoeur, P. 1992. *Oneself as Another.* Translated by Kathleen Blamey. Chicago: University of Chicago Press.

Thévenot, L. 1984. "Rules and Implements: Investment in Forms." *Social Science Information* 23 (1): 1–45.

———. 1990. "On Propriety; Conventions and Objects in a Theory of Action." Paper presented at the conference Conventions, Paris, March 26–28.

———. 2001a. "Organized Complexity: Conventions of Coordination and the Composition of Economic Arrangements." *European Journal of Social Theory* 4 (4): 405–25.

———. 2001b. "Pragmatic Regimes Governing the Engagement with the World." Pp.56–73 in *The Practice Turn in Contemporary Theory*, edited by K. Knorr-Cetina, T. Schatzki, and Eike von Savigny London: Routledge.

———. 2002. "Which Road to Follow? The Moral Complexity of an 'Equipped' Humanity." Pp. 53–87 in *Complexities: Social Studies of Knowledge Practices*, edited by John Law and Annemarie Mol. Durham, NC, and London: Duke University Press.

———. 2005a. *L'action au pluriel: Les régimes d'engagement.* Paris: La Découverte. Forthcoming.

———, ed. 2005b. "Les politiques au regard du proche." Forthcoming.

Thévenot, L, and M. Lamont. 2000. "Exploring the French and American Polity." Pp. 307–27 in *Rethinking Comparative Cultural Sociology: Repertoires of Evaluation in France and the United States*, edited by M. Lamont and L. Thévenot. Cambridge: Cambridge University Press.

The 1968 Student Revolts

The Expressive Revolution and Generational Politics

Bryan Turner is a professor in the Asian Research Institute and the Department of Sociology at the National University of Singapore. He was professor of sociology at the University of Cambridge (1998–2005). He has held professorial and research positions in Australia, the Netherlands, and Germany. He is the founding editor of the journal Citizenship Studies, *founding coeditor (with Mike Featherstone) of* Body & Society, *and founding coeditor (with John O'Neill) of the* Journal of Classical Sociology. *His research interests range over the sociology of the body, rights and citizenship, civil society and voluntary associations, and the sociology of religion. His early publications on Islam include* Weber and Islam: Marx and the End of Orientalism *and* Religion and Social Theory. *His recent publications include* Society and Culture *(with Chris Rojek),* Profiles in Contemporary Social Theory *(with Anthony Elliott), and* Classical Sociology. *He published (with June Edmunds)* Generations Culture and Society *and edited (with June Edmunds)* Generational Consciousness Narrative and Politics. *He also edited* Islam: Critical Concepts in Sociology. *His most recent publication is* The New Medical Sociology. *He is currently editing the* Cambridge Dictionary of Sociology.

The 1968 student revolts have to be understood within a broad sociopolitical context, namely, as part of the 1960s cultural and political movements. In turn, these movements were shaped by the rise of what sociologists have subsequently called postindustrial society. In retrospect, we can now see that the growth of consumer society, the decline of manufacturing, the expansion of the service sector, and the dominance of the mass media were associated with what I will call the decline of the class idiom in European politics. Because British sociology was so closely connected with the analysis of class structure, this transformation of society obviously had, from the 1970s onward, a significant impact on the sociological imagination. the Events are connected in important ways with the history of sociology in the late twentieth century.

My specific experiences of May 1968 and more generally of the 1960s were shaped primarily by my working-class background and, secondarily, by my simultaneous encounters with Christianity and Marxism prior to entering university in 1963. A biographical account is necessary in order to explain my skeptical response to the Events. Because I was the first person in my family to receive a university education, I experienced university education as a form of social mobility that would eventually take me out of the social class of my parents. University life was a tangible experience of social citizenship resulting from the expansion of postwar welfare and social Keynesianism. I am not aware of having read T. H. Marshall's *Citizenship and Social Class* (1950) before the 1970s, but I was deeply conscious of the importance of citizenship, given the poverty that was the lot of my grandparents and the burden of wartime struggle that had shaped the lives and expectations of my parents. On my mother's side, my grandfather was a coalminer. In later years I held negative attitudes toward the British Miner's Strike (1984–85) on the grounds that traditional coalmining should be terminated on humanitarian grounds. Mining meant squalor, sickness, and early death. My paternal grandfather was a sailor, and my father worked for British Railways as a waiter. Photographs of the poverty that my father and his numerous brothers experienced in Liverpool in the 1920s and 1930s have constantly reminded me of the injustices of the class system, and this background has been the experiential basis of my subsequent interest in the debate about citizenship and class (Turner 1986, 1993).

Childhood and adolescent experiences further reinforced this awareness of social class. I had the great fortune as a schoolboy in Birmingham to be taught French by a German refugee. "Dr. Sohn," as we knew him, did much to inform me in the middle of French grammar lessons about the rise of fascism, the tragedy of the Holocaust, and the importance of intellectual interests. He once took us as schoolboys to Amsterdam for a school holiday, where he tried, fairly successfully, to teach me about the involvement of the ordinary Dutch citizens in the transportation of Jews out of Holland to the gas chambers of Germany. He also, to my amazement, tried to explain prostitution by taking me on a tour of the "shop windows" of famous brothels of Amsterdam. It was not until I got to university about five years later that I discovered that Dr. Sohn was in fact the famous Marxist scholar Alfred Sohn-Rethel, who had participated in the revolutionary uprisings of 1918–19 and was the author of *Manual and Mental Labour* (1978b) and *Economy and Class Structure of German Fascism* (1978a). When I entered Leeds University in 1963 (at the age of eighteen years), I had as a result already read a considerable amount of Marxist literature, and my taste, as it were, for grand theory and large-scale issues had already been formed.

This intellectual exposure to the social sciences was reinforced by yet another peculiar accident. In 1962, at the invitation of a Jewish school friend, I attended the Communist World Youth Festival in Helsinki. This meeting took us by train with frequent stopovers through East Germany, Poland, and Russia. We had many meetings with communist youth in East Berlin, Warsaw, and Leningrad. This experience permanently influenced my view of the world. On the one hand, it made me deeply aware of the devastation that war had brought to the whole of continental Europe. East Berlin, which in those days was a military city, was a terrifying experience. It brought home the importance of Marxism both as a theory of history and as contemporary ideology. On the other hand, it illustrated how ignorant young communists were about contemporary Europe. Most of the young people I met appeared to understand England in the 1960s through the novels of Charles Dickens. One young person even asked me whether we still sent young boys up chimneys as chimneysweeps. Also painfully obvious was the high level of social control that was exercised over East Germany and the low level of infrastructure in the communist east. Young people were desperate to buy my jeans and T-shirts. The living conditions of the workers in Krakow looked depressing, but the political control of the party over the population was worse than the material squalor. This experience left me paradoxically with a deep suspicion about the claims of communism to serve the people and left me conscious of the fact that neither capitalism nor communism could necessarily provide the basis for a viable political democracy.

Because I was interested in both Marxism and Christianity, it was almost inevitable that I should become enthusiastic about the social philosophy of Alasdair MacIntyre who had been a lecturer in philosophy at Leeds and later became professor of sociology at Essex. MacIntyre brought a deep understanding of Catholic theology to the study of the social sciences, and his work has remained a source of continuous inspiration. My early faltering attempts to write about religion and Marxism were molded by *Marxism and Christianity* (MacIntyre 1968) and *The Religious Significance of Atheism* (MacIntyre and Ricoeur 1969). Reading MacIntyre finally killed off any residual theism in my personal philosophy, but my youthful engagement with Anglicanism left me with a long-term and deep respect for religious worldviews and a sociological awareness of how profoundly the modern world had been shaped by religion. In particular, I had a sympathetic feeling for the "tragic vision of the world," and in retrospect I assume this pessimistic view was drawn from reading Lucian Goldmann's study of Jansenism through the eyes of MacIntyre's sociology (MacIntyre 1971). At the time of the Events, I was more interested in long-term questions about how religion had shaped working-class politics and, more broadly, capitalist cultures.

At Leeds, my understanding of sociology was largely a product of my teacher Alan Dawe, whose "The Two Sociologies" (1970) had shaped the outlook of my generation of sociology students. Dawe made us feel that sociology was important and had powerful insights to offer into contemporary issues. His analysis of the sociology of action was intended to sustain political action in society and provided a critique of structuralism and determinism as epistemologies that were difficult to reconcile with political activism. Dawe had been supported by John Rex at Leeds, and from Dawe and Rex I developed my love for Weber's sociology. Rex taught my generation a deep hostility to racism and again showed how Weberian sociology could illuminate social and political issues, providing a powerful sociological insight into Apartheid. Our undergraduate program was founded on the sociological classics, and from the lectures of Dawe and Robertson I developed a fundamentally Weberian view of sociology and an appreciation of the scale and importance of the work of Talcott Parsons. At the time, this somewhat eclectic taste for Parsons and Weber was regarded as peculiar, but the connection was the sociology of social action as a critical reflection on classical economics as laid out in *The Structure of Social Action* (Parsons 1937).

The 1968 Events took place in the middle of my PhD program at Leeds, where I worked on a thesis on the decline of Methodism. Although the crisis in Paris was dramatic and unexpected, I was deeply unimpressed by the student revolt. There were three reasons for this lack of interest. The first, a largely trivial reason, was that provincial universities in Britain did not appear to have any significant involvement in the political disturbances, which were in any case of short duration. The main confrontations were in London and at radical universities such as Essex. Although Leeds had a strong tradition of student radicalism, the university union and the student body more widely did not become seriously involved in the Events. The second reason was more personal. My experiences of Eastern Europe and my reading of political sociology suggested that the middle-class radicalism of the universities was not serious and would not have long-term consequences. I was not convinced, having seen aspects of political repression in Eastern Europe, that "actually existing socialism" could provide effective solutions to the problems of economic growth and political freedom. The solution appeared to be more a question of transforming liberal capitalism through an expansion of citizenship and democracy. Obviously the student revolts were not simply socialist but involved diverse protests against authority that did not appear to yield solutions that could make effective political changes. Third, my proximity to working-class culture left me skeptical about what I saw to be the bourgeois protests of a rather privileged sector of society. While the Events were also protests against political authoritarianism, I remained unconvinced. At the time, I thought there were deep social inequalities between social classes that required radical economic and political solutions involving a systematic redistribution of resources rather than critique of bureaucratic authority in public institutions such as universities.

My reading of British society was influenced more by a tradition of British empirical sociology, such as *Coal Is Our Life* (Dennis, Henriques, and Slaughter 1962), than by romantic criticism of authority. It was this focus on the material conditions of everyday life in relation to consciousness that came eventually to influence the writing of *The Dominant Ideology Thesis* (Abercrombie, Hill, and Turner 1980). We were critical of the idea that there was "a dominant ideology" in capitalist society and that the apparent complacency of the working class had to be explained by the material conditions of their life world. Following the work of Peter Berger and Thomas Luckmann, we argued that to understand political acquiescence we need to look not toward ideologies or forms of consciousness but to how the everyday needs of mere survival exert a dull compulsion over the lives of ordinary people. Everyday life does not require a coherent ideological legitimacy; it does not "require additional verification over and beyond its simple presence. It is simply *there*, as self-evident and compelling facticity" (Berger and Luckmann 1967, 37). Student marches and street graffiti appeared to be far removed from this underlying social reality. In retrospect, much of my subsequent sociological writing, for example, about the human body, was an attempt to grasp sociologically what Berger and Luckmann had described as the brute facticity of this everyday world. I will return to this issue shortly.

The conflict on the streets of Paris looked more like a form of ritual effervescence, to borrow a phrase from Émile Durkheim's sociology, than an episode of serious political transformation. In retrospect, the politics of the 1960s, especially the student politics of Paris and London, were social manifestations of what Talcott Parsons (1974) would call "the expressive revolution." For Parsons, the counterculture represented a shift in Western values from the cognitive-rational to the affective-expressive axis. This new culture involved an emphasis on emotions, romantic love, and the glorification of the autonomous individual. Parsons's insight has in my view been completely vindicated, and more recent interpretations of the 1960s have followed a similar interpretation, albeit in a very different language. For example, Gilles Lipovetsky (1994) developed an interpretation of May '68 as a manifestation of what he called "transpolitical individualism." He notes that the May movement had no plan for society as a whole; it was, rather, an assertion of subjectivity over structures, of the right of everybody to speak out against authority. It was a "soft revolution," in which a poetic revolution was expressed through graffiti rather than attacks on property and policemen. The individualism of the May Events was not, however, simply a manifestation of bourgeois possessive individualism. It involved, instead, a fusion of the private and public, the existential and the objective, into a transpolitical individualism.

In writing this short memoir of May '68, I have reflected on an issue that has in recent years dominated my sociological thinking, namely, the importance of generations and generational consciousness as a social dimension of politics (in *Generations Culture and Society* [Edmunds and Turner 2002b] and *Generational Consciousness, Narrative and Politics* [Edmunds and Turner 2002a]). The May crisis represented the forging of a generational consciousness that survives over time through the periodic celebration of its founding events. Lipovetsky is correct to argue that the May Events were a response to a centralized state, ten years of Gaullism, and a generational crisis, but these conditions would not have been important were it not for the fact that the transpolitical individualism of May corresponded with deeper changes in the social structure. These structural conditions were the outcome of the growth of postindustrialism and the demands of new social strata for full citizenship (Touraine 1971). There was another important change, which was the development of "culture" as a field of conflict and contestation, especially in the United States where the cultural rather than political struggle became dominant (Hobsbawm 1973). The growing dominance of "the cultural" over "the social" can perhaps be dated from this period (Turner 2000). Daniel Bell's *The Cultural Contradictions of Capitalism* (1976) still provides the best sociological reflection on these changes. We can retrospectively say that the Events marked the beginning of a major social transformation of European society in which social class was no longer the principal division in social identity and attachment and, in particular, that the working class was no longer the vanguard of political radicalism. Here again, in attempting to understand these changes I have found my inspiration in classical sociology, namely, through a continuous reflection on Karl Mannheim's writings on ideology, conservatism, and generations (Turner 1995, 1999).

In the 1960s, I had not read the work of Pierre Bourdieu, but his analysis of the special relationship between sociology and social protest in *Homo Academicus* (Bourdieu 1988) is convincing. In the French case, he argues that sociology was a weak and indeterminate discipline, and it was low down the hierarchy of humanities and social sciences. It attracted students who were not engaged with the established disciplines, and furthermore sociology lecturers were also marginal to the academy. Given the overcrowding and congestion of postwar universities, the frustrations of students and staff converged in the late 1960s, and eventually this academic protest movement overflowed into the trade unions, which, for very different reasons, were antagonistic toward the French political establishment. In the 1960s, similar strains were apparent in British universities, where sociology also acted as ladder of social mobility for working-class boys like myself. We had at the time, I believe, a rather different set of intellectual leaders and aspirations. At Leeds, there were three very important texts that informed our undergraduate curriculum, namely, *The Uses of Literacy* (Hoggart 1957), *Culture and Society* (Williams 1958), and *Consciousness and Society* (Hughes 1959). The theme of the first two texts was the loss of working-class community, the rise of consumer culture, and the dominance of middle-class individualism. Both authors lamented the erosion of the cooperative tradition of working-class autonomy and the transformation of the culture of northern cities like Leeds and Sheffield by television and consumerism. Both Hoggart and Williams were grammar-school boys who had risen from the working class to positions of influence in English literature and cultural studies. William's sense of alienation from Cambridge was a common experience of socially mobile academics in this period. *Consciousness and Society* stimulated my interest in the social crises of the late nineteenth century and the origins of sociology — compare with the crises of the late twentieth century. Once more, these crises appeared to shape the imagination of a generation who were born in the period 1850–70 and who created the classical period of sociology from around 1890–1920.

The loss of working-class community was not an intellectual or ideological theme that was particularly compatible with the emphasis on subjectivity, autonomy, individualism, and critique of authority that informed the May Events. Here was another source of my sense of distance from the disturbances at the London School of Economics (LSE) and Essex. The tradition of Hoggart and Williams was probably in many respects nostalgic, and it gave a significance and authenticity to northern cities that was problematic. My student years had been spent in a working-class slum in Leeds just opposite the university. From that vantage point, I was not entirely convinced by Hoggart's analysis of the virtues of working-class community life. What appeared to be more important was the contemporary transformation of Britain through welfare reforms, access to education, and the expansion of democratic participation, namely, the extension of citizenship. My own sense of detachment from the Paris students was conditioned by my working-class respect for education and my own sense of good fortune in being at a university to study sociology. My political and cultural sentiments were at the time shaped more by Williams and Hoggart than by continental Marxism or by student protests, and years later when I came to read *What I Came to Say* (Williams 1989), I could fully understand and empathize with his sense of not quite belonging to Cambridge.

Having finished an undergraduate degree in 1966, I stayed on at Leeds and started my doctoral research on Methodism in England. This research often proved to be tedious, and much of my research time was spent in an old Morris van driving round the Yorkshire Dales talking to ministers about declining congregations. At the time, this research into the sociology of religious institutions was far removed from the heady excitement of Parisian street protests, Continental social theory, and student politics, and yet in retrospect I can see many continuities with my underlying interests in both Marx and Weber. The Methodists had been important because as E. P. Thompson (1963) showed in *The Making of the English Working Class* the Methodist chapels had had an ambiguous effect on the working class of the nineteenth century. Methodism had trained them, made them literate and hard working. These chapels were often sites of emerging proletarian radicalism, and yet at the same time Methodist theology diluted their secular radicalism. In my student days, the Methodist preacher Lord Soper in his opposition to Apartheid and nuclear armaments embodied the spirit of Methodist radicalism, but Methodism in the mid-twentieth century had lost most of these characteristics, and I found the conservatism of student religiosity increasingly unpalatable. I drifted further and further into an eccentric brand of Anglicanism, Marxist politics, and Weberian sociology. This

strange brew was another dimension that colored my approach to student politics. Durkheim says somewhere that religion is the serious life, and I was certainly a serious young man. Student pranks including rent-a-crowd politics had
no elective affinity with my version of "science as a vocation." In short, just as
Weber had said that the romanticism of the student disciples of Stefan George
would shatter on the hard rock of real social and economic conditions, so I assumed that student politics would evaporate into thin air, partly for the simple
reason that the student body is constantly transformed by its annual intake.

Although I have been critical of the political significance of the May Events,
it is very clear that the social and cultural movements of the 1960s profoundly
influenced my generation and had a lasting impact on our sociological imagination. The Events may not have been important for the economic and political
structures of European societies, but the 1960s epoch remains important because
they were culturally exciting. At the time, there was a distinctive mood of social
change and optimism — everything and anything were possible. The Sixties were
exciting precisely because the late 1940s and 1950s were drab, uninteresting, and
unimportant. The rise of popular culture, rock music, the consumer revolution,
and increasing prosperity created an atmosphere of progressive social and cultural change. However, what remains in my memory is that as a student body we
were deadly serious, committed, and engaged. There was little real sense of he-
donist experiment or playfulness in our actual lives, and the "sexual revolution"
always appeared to be taking place somewhere else. My research on the postwar
generation in Australia subsequently confirmed this sense that the student cohorts of the early 1960s were not significantly engaged in sexual experimentation,
drugs, or alternative lifestyles (Turner and Edmunds 2002). It was obvious that,
because we had fairly easy access to contraceptives, we were more sexually active
with more partners than our parents. It was obvious that some students had access to soft drugs, and at least in the student population there was tolerance for
homosexuality and lesbianism. However, student leisure activities were modest — the local pub on Friday evenings, the Student Union rock concert on Sat-
urdays, and a film at some smoke-filled dive in the middle of town on Sunday. In
the 1960s Britain was changing rapidly toward a postindustrial society, and my
generation was innovative. We were widely believed to be engaging in sexual experimentation about which our parents did not want to know. However, students, at least in provincial universities, were not necessarily socially rebellious.
Attitudes toward academic staff were still deferential, and professors were godlike
distant figures whom one rarely encountered. Students were not involved in de-

partmental committees, and lectures were never assessed or evaluated by students. The situation at the LSE, Lancaster, and Essex might have been very different, but there was little sustained political activity by students to change the authority structure of the university.

Politically active students had their minds fixed on larger issues than university reform, namely, the problems of nuclear disarmament, the real prospect of further military conflict in Europe, the confrontation between America and Russia in Cuba, the Viet Nam War, and the spread of military conflict in Southeast Asia. My tourist adventures in Eastern Europe in the early 1960s had convinced me that a hot war in Europe was a real possibility. In general, living through the 1960s had a profound long-term impact on my sociological imagination. These included the debate between Marx and Weber, the structuration issue, the sociological character of capitalism, and Weber's sociology of religion. Because one emerged from those changes with a distinctive generational consciousness, it is hardly surprising that my work in the past decade has focused on the aging of the baby boom generation.

Those of us born around 1945 got to fifty years before the end of the millennium, and looking back the major issue that struck me as a British citizen was that I had not, despite all my fears, had any direct or personal experience of modern war unlike virtually all of my male ancestors. My father served in Iceland in the Royal Air Force, and my mother had worked for Cadbury, the chocolate manufacturer, during the war. Had I been born in America or Australia, the story might have been very different. I never assumed we in Europe could avoid a nuclear confrontation, and hence social arrangements at the time always appeared somewhat temporary. These conditions produced important generational differences and a specific consciousness that existed over and above specifically gender or class differences. My generation was one whose mature lives, while always threatened by disasters, have been lived under conditions of (relative) peace. We missed conscription, and barrack room drills and sergeant majors did not interrupt our student lives. Aden, Suez, Kenya, and the Malaysian emergency were military episodes that marked the decline of military power. The Suez crisis of 1956 demonstrated that Britain could no longer operate as a great power without American support and approval, and Britain prudently withdrew from any further significant colonial adventures (until Mrs. Thatcher's defense of British interests in the south Atlantic). The paradox for my generation—and one we are probably reluctant to recognize—is that this relatively peaceful postwar environment owes a great deal to the political pragmatism of Harold Macmillan whose colonial policies (e.g., the wind of change speech) allowed Britain to avoid the confrontations that destabilized such colonial powers as France, Portugal, and Belgium in the postwar period. By contrast, the foreign policy ideas and racial assumptions of Enoch Powell received very little support from any quarter. Perhaps in our late middle age we baby boomers have to own up to the fact that we have "never had it so good." As a result, we have a generational responsibility to those who have come after us and whose economic and social expectations are far more constrained and whose political security is more uncertain. Their world may be filled with many September 11's.

How has all of this influenced my sociology? There appear to be three research fields that are associated with the Events and the Sixties. The first was an emerging interest in social citizenship and human rights. Although universities have been historically elite institutions, postwar reconstruction provided access for children from "ordinary backgrounds" to acquire an education that at the time was not obviously dominated by business interests. In the 1960s, university autonomy had not been extensively compromised. While the rapid and underfunded growth of university produced student unrest, it also laid the foundations for an expanding educated middle class. I was self-consciously part of that expansion, and it left me with a permanent commitment to the importance of social rights. This commitment has been expressed through the journal *Citizenship Studies*, which I founded in 1997. Second, my sense that student activism was a form of political froth encouraged me to look for more fundamental social conditions of action, and hence the practical constraints of everyday life became an important issue for my approach to sociological theory. After *The Dominant Ideology Thesis*, I became convinced that sociologists had missed the most important fact about social actors—namely, that they are embodied and that the human body places constraints and conditions on action that we should not and cannot avoid. The body is, to appropriate Berger again, the most significant dimension of the facticity of the everyday world. Having read Michel Foucault with admiration and excitement, I became interested in how the body and populations are managed by regimes of discipline and surveillance. I became interested, that is, in "the government of the body" (Turner 1982). With Mike Featherstone, I came to edit *Body and Society* in 1995 as a vehicle for promoting interest in sociological studies of the body. Although my interest in the body was motivated intellectually by reading Peter Berger, Maurice Merleau-Ponty, Arnold Gehlen, and Michel Foucault, it also has to be said that the general interest in the body in the humanities and the social sciences is also part of the legacy of the

1960s because it reflects new forms of consciousness and subjectivity that have been characteristic of late modernity. Finally, the defense of classical sociology can also be seen as a consequence of the 1960s and the Events. The youth protests of the period were often hostile, for example, to Marx and Marxist sociology. Marx had been scribbling in the British Museum while the revolution went on around him; academic sociologists were also just scribblers. By contrast, I have found the classics an endless source of inspiration for understanding the times in which we live, namely, for understanding the transition from national forms of Fordist capitalism to the late modernity of a global system. The crises of culture and consciousness of the 1890s (so wonderfully documented by Hughes in *Consciousness and Society*) remain in many respects the crises of the 1990s, and hence classical sociology constitutes a powerful framework for contemporary analysis but clearly not wholly and exclusively relevant. Sociology must continue to grow and expand if it is to remain relevant. It is this sense of preserving the tradition of classical sociology and remaining open to contemporary intellectual developments in sociology that has inspired me to start the new *Journal of Classical Sociology* with John O'Neill in 2002. These three journals neatly and effectively summarize my principal sociological interests, all of which can be traced back to the dramatic political excitement of 1968.

References

Abercrombie, N., S. Hill, and B. S. Turner. 1980. *The Dominant Ideology Thesis*. London: George Allen & Unwin.

Bell, D. 1974. *The Cultural Contradictions of Capitalism*. New York: Basic Books.

Berger, P., and T. Luckmann. 1967. *The Social Construction of Reality: A Treatise in the Sociology of Knowledge*. London: Allen Lane.

Bourdieu, P. 1988. *Homo Academicus*. Cambridge: Polity Press.

Dawe, A. 1970. "The Two Sociologies." *British Journal of Sociology* 21 (2): 207–18.

Dennis, N., F. M. Henriques, and C. Slaughter. 1962. *Coal Is Our Life*. London: Eyre & Spottiswoode.

Edmunds, J., and B.S. Turner, eds. 2002a. *Generational Consciousness, Narrative and Politics*. Lanham, MD: Rowman & Littlefield.

———. 2002b. *Generations, Society and Culture*. Buckingham: Open University Press.

Hobsbawm, E. 1973. *Revolutionaries*. London: Weidenfeld & Nicolson.

Hoggart, R. 1957. *The Uses of Literacy*. Harmondsworth: Penguin.

Hughes, H. S. 1959. *Consciousness and Society*. London: Routledge.

Lipovetsky, G. 1994. "May'68; or, The Rise of Transpolitical Individualism." Pp. 212–19 in *New French Thought: Political Philosophy*, edited by M. Lilla. Princeton, NJ: Princeton University Press.

MacIntyre, A. 1968. *Marxism and Christianity*. New York: Schocken.

————. 1971. "Pascal and Marx: On Lucian Goldmann's *Hidden God*." Pp. 76–87 in *Against the Self-Images of the Age*. London: Duckworth.

MacIntyre, A., and P. Ricoeur. 1969. *The Religious Significance of Atheism*. New York and London: Columbia University Press.

Marshall, T. H. 1950. *Citizenship and Social Class and Other Essays*. Cambridge: Cambridge University Press.

Parsons, T. 1937. *The Structure of Social Action*. New York: McGraw-Hill.

————. 1974. "Religion in Postindustrial America: The Problem of Secularization." *Social Research*, vol. 41; reprinted in *The Talcott Parsons Reader*, edited by B. S. Turner, Oxford: Blackwell, pp. 300–320.

Sohn-Rethel, A. 1978a. *Economy and Class Structure of German Fascism*. London: CSE Books.

————. 1978b. *Manual and Mental Labour. A Critique of Epistemology*. London: Macmillan.

Thompson, E. P. 1963. *The Making of the English Working Class*. London: Penguin.

Touraine, A. 1971. *The May Movement: Revolt and Reform*. New York: Random House.

Turner, B. S. 1982. "The Government of the Body: Medical Regimens and the Rationalization of Diet." *British Journal of Sociology* 33:254–69.

————. 1986. *Citizenship and Capitalism: The Debate about Reformism*. London: Allen & Unwin.

————, ed. 1993. *Citizenship and Social Theory*. London: Sage.

————. 1995. "Karl Mannheim's *Ideology and Utopia*." *Political Studies* 43:718–27.

————. 1999. *Classical Sociology*. London: Sage.

————. 2000. Introduction to *The Blackwell Companion to Social Theory*. 2d ed. Oxford: Blackwell, 1–18.

Turner, B. S., and J. Edmunds. 2002. "The Distaste of Taste: Bourdieu, Cultural Capital and the Australian Postwar Elite." *Journal of Consumer Culture* 2 (2): 219–39.

Williams, R. 1958. *Culture and Society, 1780–1950*. London: Chatto & Windus.

————. 1989. *What I Came to Say*. London: Hutchinson Radius.

STEPHEN TURNER

High on Insubordination

Stephen Turner (born 1951, Chicago) holds degrees in sociology and philosophy from the University of Missouri. He has been at the University of South Florida since 1975 and has had appointments at Virginia Tech, Notre Dame, and Boston University, an Honorary Simon Visiting Professorship at the University of Manchester, fellowships at the Swedish Collegium for Advanced Studies in the Social Sciences, and an NEH Fellowship. His writings in social theory beyond the time period of this essay include articles on charisma, Edward Shils, normativity, and experts and several books, including The Social Theory of Practices: Tradition, Tacit Knowledge, and Presuppositions *and* Brains/Practices/Relativism: Social Theory after Cognitive Science, *which are critical of a tradition represented by Bourdieu, and a response to Habermas,* Liberal Democracy 3.0: Civil Society in an Age of Experts. *He also writes on science studies and the history of quantitative social science, as well as various philosophical topics. Among the things that he has retained from the Sixties are several nonacademic friendships, his passion for Italian sports cars, his love of the* Miami Herald, *his devotion to the restaurants of New Orleans, and his loathing for academic snobbery. What he has enjoyed most about academic life are his long-term relationships with other scholars all over the world, whose many rewards are the best kept secret about the scholarly life. He lives in Pass-a-Grille Beach, Florida, with his wife and two sons, ten and eleven.*

I began reading the texts that I later came to understand as social theory and social science out of the most common of motives — to understand the existential contradictions of my own life. I had plenty of contradictions to deal with. From fifth grade, for reasons too complex to explain here, I was a student at the Laboratory Schools of the University of Chicago, an institution founded by John Dewey, which later had George Herbert Mead on its board and was nominally committed to the idea of experimental education and the freeing of the mind. In practice, however, the Laboratory Schools were a service to the faculty of the university, who could send their kids there at a reduced tuition, and embodied the ideal of academic careerism pur sang. The school also had, as students, a miscellany of others. Among them were many of the children of the black elite — several of whom were depicted in the high-society chronicler Stephen Birmingham's *Certain People* (1977), his book on black high society. Joe Louis's son, whom I occasionally sat with at lunch, was in the next class, and his half sister was in mine. Hyde Park, where the school and the university are located, is a white oasis in a million person sea of blacks, the result of the great migration from northern Mississippi. Race was a subject that was hard to ignore, but it was, scrupulously pretended away by people in Hyde Park. So was crime.

I never lived in Hyde Park. As a young child I lived in Woodlawn, the neighborhood to the south, perhaps the most studied of all neighborhoods. I was a familiar face in the shops on Sixty-third Street, where I was taken by Theo Suess, who, with his wife Sascha, cared for me while my parents worked. The Suesses were German Jewish refugees, and for much of my childhood the fact of the Holocaust could be read on the tattooed numbers on the arms of my friends' parents. Once I was in school, I lived in Marynook, a faux suburb built on a filled-in swamp in the middle of an older neighborhood of bungalows, Avalon Park, and across the tracks from Chatham, then a bastion of the black middle class, where I spent time as well. I lived through the change of both Woodlawn and Marynook from white to black. A joke at the time defined integration as the period after the first black moved in and the last white moved out. It was an accurate definition for both neighborhoods, and the period was not long for either.

The "integration" of Marynook coincided with the civil rights movement. I was delivering papers to both black and white customers in the summer of 1964, called Freedom Summer, and reading the reporting on the disappearance of James Chaney and Michael Schwerner on my break. Interest in Mississippi was intense in Chicago. Day after day, the *Daily Defender,* then the largest and most influential black newspaper in the world, ran headline stories on it. Civil rights was the great moral cause of the time. Images of blacks and whites with arms linked in brotherhood filled the papers. But day-to-day life never quite fit the fine speeches and lofty sentiments. Brotherhood was in especially short supply on the south side of Chicago. The black Muslim school bus, with its children in head shawls, picked up on my block every morning. The newspaper *Muhammad Speaks*, which declared that whites, or "blue-eyed devils," were the results of a failed science experiment by a black scientist, was sold by a man at a bus stop I used. Yet the Muslims were solid citizens, who preached and practiced sobriety, uplift, pride, and self-reliance. They were the Protestant ethic types in the black community. They ignored whites. But there were other blacks, my age, who took a special, hostile, interest in whites. I was often followed and accosted—and on one occasion pulled off my bicycle and beaten—and regularly called "honky" and taunted as I passed through other neighborhoods on my way home. Once, riding home on the Stony Island bus, two kids with knives cornered me, taunted me, pulled my shirt up, put the knife to my chest, and threatened to "cut my titties off." My parents' response to all of this was to say that I was insufficiently streetwise. In this, they were like other whites in the neighborhood. It was a form of denial. People went out of their way not to be racist and to pretend that the situation was normal. When a white kid was killed by blacks in a sidewalk confrontation in the early days of the process, an elaborate attempt was made to explain it away: the white kid was a hothead and provoked it, as though it was somehow acceptable to kill someone who failed to get off the sidewalk quickly enough. A campaign was organized to preserve the neighborhood, and white people pledged to stay to build an integrated neighborhood. It was a fantasy. After their bicycles were stolen, their kids threatened, their businesses robbed, and reality sank in, the whites gave up.[1]

I adapted. By the time I left for college, I had more experience with blacks than whites and was more comfortable around them. I worked with a mostly black crew of painters (with a Hispanic boss) during one summer and sometimes as after-school work. I had a substantial collection of Red Foxx and Pigmeat

---

1. There is a useful and accurate depiction of this process as it occurred in the neighborhood to the east, which was more Jewish and richer, in Rosen (1998). Rosen, a librettist and composer rather than a sociologist, spoke to both blacks and whites about this history, and the differences in their perceptions are very striking. For the whites, the personal experience of crime was decisive; for blacks it was largely invisible. The book can be usefully read against other writings on the South Side. William J. Wilson's *When Work Disappears* (1996), for example, mentions crime only in passing.

Markham comedy records and had the routines committed to memory. I knew a lot of black kid jokes, especially knock-knock jokes.[2] I was well-known in the neighborhood as Wino for my habit of riding around on my bicycle with a bottle of pop wrapped in a paper bag. There is film from my last birthday party, at eleven or so: most of the kids there were black. Yet at adolescence these relationships changed, or failed to deepen, and a strange, unspoken parting of the ways occurred. They had a social world to go on to. I did not. My parents were slow to give up. They were social idealists and staunch integrationists, motivated, so they said, by Protestant theology, who believed they had a moral obligation to stay in the city.[3] Their devotion was genuine enough. My mother volunteered as an obstetrician at a free clinic called the Maternity Center near Hull House — this is how the poor obtained medical treatment before Medicaid — and also practiced at Cook County Hospital, probably the largest charity hospital in the world. She later became a minor feminist icon, the subject of term papers in women's studies courses, for starting a rape crisis center. My father worked in the ghetto every day. He read the *Christian Century*, which was the mouthpiece of liberal Protestantism. I was a voracious reader, so I read it too.

It is fashionable nowadays to pretty up the religious sensibilities of the past and, especially, of the 1950s. I remember things very differently. Although they were theologically liberal, my parents were also puritanical in a way that was so petty but also so pervasive in its significance that it can barely be described.[4]

---

2. Such as this: "Knock, knock." "Who's there?" "Aunt Jo." "Aunt Jo who?" "Ain't yo' mama on the pancake box?"

3. The sensibility is well-captured in the novels of Sue Miller, which are based on her parents, Mr. and Mrs. Nichols, who were friends of my parents and involved with them in the First Presbyterian Church in Woodlawn. But Mr. and Mrs. Nichols lived in liberal Hyde Park and were socially liberal as well. My parents were not (see n. 4).

4. The most famous depiction of this paradox is in Gosse's *Father and Son* (1934), a book that explained to me a great deal of my own misery as a child. Of course Max Weber's *The Protestant Ethic* (1958) contains a more general depiction of the same thing and explained other aspects of this experience, but it fails to capture at a personal level, as Gosse does, the strange mixture of high-minded idealism and inhumanity that went into the parent-child relationship and the overwhelming power that these relationships exercised on a young child, who nevertheless could not fail to recognize that there was something fundamentally wrong. As with Gosse père, with my parents it was never clear what was a matter of their lack of generosity and punitiveness and what was a matter of sincere belief, and also, as with Gosse, there was a large gap between the child's and the parents' experience of the same events. Gosse's father, it now appears, had a more or less happy life. It was his son who suffered and had painfully to emancipate himself.

We had no television. Alcohol was never in the house. Anything that had the character of sport or pleasure, or cost money, was the object of suspicion and hostility. Coke was denounced as "sugared water"—a pointless excess. I was allowed to have a bicycle at age twelve, when I was "responsible" enough, and could use it to work, delivering newspapers. Nothing, it seemed, was too trivial for their censorious fury. The God of liberal Protestantism was terrible in his small-mindedness and able to find sin, construed in the high-toned theological language of "alienation from God," in every aspect of life. The much ballyhooed "social" significance of thinkers like Reinhold Niebuhr depended on this intrusive notion of sin, which could be made to serve whatever political ends they needed to serve. If Coke was a sin, why not add "collective sins" to the list? Niebuhr did. Thus did "social justice," and much more, became a Christian obligation.[5]

There is a kind of paradox of this theology that works like this: one is individually responsible to one's own conscience; but it just so happens that conformity to a particular set of social expectations is the expected result of the operation of one's conscience, so that any independent thought is a sign of a defective conscience. Where there are no social expectations there is simply a kind of free-floating moral vehemence that becomes merely arbitrary. Where it was convenient for them, they were permissive: no one cared where I went or what I read or brought home, and the city was open to me from an early age. Where it was not, there was a constant struggle over what I was to be allowed to do. Child-rearing manuals and the parenting magazines became central to this struggle. I pored over them like a pandit with the Upanishads. If they said that a fourteen-year-old should be allowed something, I made a case for it. But the manuals had about the same relation to life on the edge of the ghetto as the Upanishads. The one they used the most seemed to be obsessed with the question of how

5. The language is familiar from Weber, who commented in "Politics as a Vocation" ([1919]1946) on the very same "two kingdoms" tradition in German theology that inspired Reinhold Niebuhr. I will allow myself one theological comment. I hope there is a special—and very warm—place in hell for him. Weber wanted truth in labeling: an admission that in the end their goals were not of this world and that any consideration of harms done in this world counted for nothing against abstract ideas—or delusions—about justice and the like. What makes Neibuhr such a fascinating and diabolical thinker is his ability to substitute otherworldly moralism for responsible politics while insisting that he is not doing it and denouncing others for doing it. Niebuhr encouraged using "power to correct the injustices of power" (1960, 209) in the name of Christian obligation, but the fine print left ultimate responsibility for the this-worldly consequences of action to God, making his position no different from any other form of religious fanaticism in politics, albeit less honest.

many cashmere sweaters a girl should have — apparently a burning issue in 1950s' Scarsdale.

In self-defense, I became an avid reader of psychology — not academic psychology, but psychoanalysis, which was the basis for most of the advice books they read and which occasionally supplied some insight into their puritanical hostilities. The first book of "social science" I read was Vance Packard's *The Hidden Persuaders* (1958), a popularization whose significance I only later understood. Among many other things, it mentioned the work of Herta Herzog, one of Paul Lazarsfeld's wives, the director of creative research at the ad agency McCann-Erickson, and a serious thinker about human behavior in her own right. Packard made advertising seem like a fascinating career, though this was not his aim. I was deeply into Freud, absorbing *The Future of an Illusion* (1953) and *Moses and Monotheism* (1939) as inoculations against religion. I also read books like Robert Lindner's *Must You Conform?* (1956), which challenged the fifties' equation of mental health with "adjustment," a doctrine that my parents had imbibed from Harry Overstreet's appalling *The Mature Mind* (1949), a book that equated maturity with the voluntary acceptance of not only conformity but conformity to the mildly leftist social doctrines of the author, nicely turning Freudian psychology to the task of stigmatizing anyone who disagreed with him.[6] I soon graduated to Erich Fromm, and books like *Escape from Freedom* (1941) and *The Sane Society* (1955), which, as it happened, made the same equation but in a subversive and critical way. Of course, I had no idea that these books were part of the corpus of the Frankfurt School or that there was such a thing. To me, the books provided a way of understanding the escapes from freedom and social insanity I could observe around me.

High school conformism is characteristically absurd but, as W. I. Thomas would have said, real in its consequences. The Lab Schools were so strange that it was difficult to react to anything that went on there other than with bemusement, though precious little was amusing. I recall being ridiculed by a classmate

6. Parsons had more or less the same strategy — socialization was equated to conformity, which was equated to acceptance of certain doctrines, while those who objected to these doctrines were stigmatized as failures of psychosexual development. The whole line of reasoning was familiar to me because it was little more than a secularized form of the Calvinist paradox mentioned earlier. My parents deployed it, endlessly, as the following tautology: if you choose to do something other than what we want you to do, it is evidence that you are not mature and therefore shouldn't have the freedom to do what you want to do.

for wearing button-down shirts (or perhaps for not wearing button-down shirts). This would have been less weird if the fashion enforcers were not also enforcers of intellectual fashions, who prided themselves on their intellectual superiority. Many of these *Übermenschen*-in-training aspired to becoming Harvard professors. I learned to take their measure. I should add that although most of my time there was wasted, I learned some social theory. I got a strong grounding in Marx and Lenin (and even Karl Wittfogel's theory of hydraulic despotism). This was enough to enable me to begin educating myself. I attended speeches at the university by old Reds like Herbert Aptheker. My first hardback academic book purchase was Claude Lévi-Strauss's *The Savage Mind*, which I bought when it came out in translation in 1966 on the strength of a review in the Sunday *Chicago Tribune*. I picked up copies of the works of C. Wright Mills at used book sales, and, at some point, got my hands on *The Sociological Imagination* (1959). I read the classics on black life, such as E. Franklin Frazier's *Black Bourgeoisie* (1956), which could have been written about my neighbors, and a great deal on Black Nationalism. I read what Malcolm X was available, such as *Malcolm X Speaks* (1966), which I greatly preferred to the speeches of Martin Luther King. Before I left high school, I had taken a course in social stratification at the university with Terry Clark. The course was a good introduction to many theorists, and the mana of the great theorists came through in this course. So did the fact that there was a great deal of confusion about what sort of thing a theory was and what, if anything, Talcott Parsons was actually saying. It was also a good introduction to the power structure of sociology. Clark, newly arrived from Columbia and dressed in natty suits, told us that only three or at most four sociology departments counted. This was snobbery continuous with the snobbery I dealt with a few blocks down Fifty-ninth Street at the Lab School and was equally irritating. But it expressed a hard political reality: sociology was oligarchic.

I quit high school immediately after this course ended, one quarter into my senior year in 1967, and escaped to college as an early entrant. I wasn't worried about climbing the academic hierarchy. I just wanted out. The Chicago I had grown up in was a doomed world. It was clear that there was no future for me there and that when I left there would be no "home" to return to, even if I had wanted to. Growing up in the shadow of the ghetto also meant that I lacked the usual teenage experiences of life. I had no contact, except on the few occasions where I had been sent off to family friends for visits, with the kinds of suburban white kids that populated universities. My education had not included the kind of memorization and disciplined studying that they took for granted. What I knew about life, business, and practical affairs had little application outside of the ghetto, except, as it happened, in sociology courses, where it enabled me to judge what was taught about race and urbanism. But I knew my way around universities and was unintimidated by faculty. This proved to be enough.

The Sixties were the decade of the civil rights movement, which pervaded the atmosphere around me, at first as news from the south, later as an influence on the actions of people. The experience of living through it at one of its centers, and seeing it from the bottom up, had profound consequences for me. It was a focus of deep ideological puzzles. What is a "right"? What is justice? The realities of ghetto life had nothing to do with the high-sounding phrases of King. The problems of making sense of these realities were also omnipresent. Everyone had a theory. Most of the theories were obviously wrong. I went from being fascinated with ideological questions to being suspicious of them. When I encountered James Burnham's *The Machiavellians* (1943) in Clark's course, I could put a name to these suspicions. It was the beginning of a long interest in the theorists of the dark side—Donoso Cortes, Max Weber, Carl Schmitt. I should have known then that I was destined for the life of a scholar, but my desire to get away from all that was so strong that I would have laughed it off if anyone had suggested it.

Leaving Chicago and starting college was a tremendous liberation. It was an asset to have no real experience with ordinary white people and no familiar social world to return to. I was free from social prejudices about white people and open to the social diversity that was now arrayed before me like a grand smorgasbord. I took full advantage of my freedom, moving from university to university, making friends along the way, and encountering new types—pot-dealing farm boys, Baptist ROTC cadets, and refugees from the small town lower classes. To me they were all exotic, and I was exotic to them. I went first to Miami (where my father's family had roots reaching back to the 1920s, and which functioned for me as a sane point of reference), and from there to the University of Tampa in February of 1968. The Tet offensive, in which one of my public grade school classmates died, occurred as I was settling into classes. In March, President Lyndon Johnson announced that he would not seek reelection. I returned to Chicago for spring break in April. King had just been assassinated, and there had been major riots. In my neighborhood, a group of students had left one of the high schools and smashed store windows on the main shopping street. A black preacher and civil rights leader named C. T. Vivian, who lived a few blocks away, announced that no white people would be allowed in. It was bluster. The south side of the city was under the control of the National Guard, who patrolled in Jeeps with M-1 rifles. The main concern of the rioters — and the police, as it happened — was to steal color televisions and furniture. No one stopped them.

At the beginning of May 1968 I was still in Tampa. Exams were underway. The students, mostly from New Jersey and Connecticut, were working on their tans. My friends and dorm-mates who were flunking out were being drafted or choosing to enlist in something other than the army. I had escaped the shadow of the ghetto only to fall into the shadow of the war in Viet Nam. The war was well advanced by then. I read about it avidly, in *Ramparts*, the glossy magazine of the New Left, but especially in a magazine called the *Reporter*, which exposed the lies and confusion behind American policy. I read Bernard Fall's *Hell in a Very Small Place* (1966), on Dien Bien Phu. Although I was still two years away from the draft, the fact that I had started college early meant that I would be exposed. My attitude to the war was not especially high-minded. Robert McNamara, Maxwell Taylor, and McGeorge Bundy, the architects of the war, were obvious villains. Bundy and McNamara were proud of their intellectual prowess and didn't want to admit that they were wrong. Intellectual hubris was something I knew all about and disdained. Seeing them in this way made it difficult to see the war as part of anything so grand as "American imperialism."[7]

During most of May of 1968 I was in transit from Tampa to the University of Missouri, via New Jersey and New York City. I am not sure whether I even knew about the student uprising in Paris. Much more was going on. In early June, in New York, during the week of the Robert Kennedy assassination and funeral, I was meeting with the senior staff of "The New Majority for Rockefeller," the youth campaign for Rocky. Nelson Rockefeller was the only candidate with a "plan" for getting out of Viet Nam. I volunteered for, and was appointed, campaign manager for mid-Missouri. This meeting was my first, and last, brush with the American ruling class. The staff of Ivy Leaguers were as cynical as Chicago precinct captains. Their aspirations for themselves and their sense of entitlement, however, were at a far more exalted level. The campaign manager was a protégé of John W. Gardner and speculated that Rocky would appoint Gardner to RFK's senate seat, at which point the campaign manager would follow him as a staff member. Unfortunately, the plan that Rockefeller had for ending the war

---

7. This was also the diagnosis, incidentally, of Hans J. Morgenthau, the doyen of international relations (and, though I couldn't have known it at the time, a strict Weberian), who was persecuted by the administration for his antiwar views.

was Henry Kissinger's. When it was put into place, by Richard Nixon, it extended the war several years. I spent the summer doing things like organizing the manning of a table at the student union to give out bumper stickers. We gave out a great many. Rocky couldn't wrest the nomination from Nixon. It was his last campaign, and it was mine, too. I realized that I was too shy for politics and that I couldn't remember people's names. And I also realized that I could not connect on a human level with the eager and ambitious reformers that were entering politics, that is to say, the Bill Clintons and Hillary Rodhams.

I had originally gone to Missouri with the idea of looking at its famous school of journalism. I had been a paperboy for the *Chicago American* and a tear-sheet boy at the *Chicago Tribune* and knew a reporter neighbor, Marty O'Connor, whose questions at news conferences were famous for making Mayor Daley apoplectic. I shared this talent for making people apoplectic so I thought this might be an option worth considering. In the registration line, I began a romance, with a normal blonde from the heart of the heart of the country that eventuated in marriage two and a half years later. I was nominally an economics major, but I had never managed to get into an introductory class in economics. Because I had the prerequisites for sociology and psychology upper-level courses, I could get into those and then into graduate courses. By the spring of 1969 I was taking the most advanced graduate course in sociological theory, but I was still an undergraduate with a series of humanities requirements to meet. Whenever I took a sociology course, I wrote a theory paper that made metatheoretical comments, and I was routinely told that I needed to read something on theory construction, usually Robert Dubin's *Theory Building* (1969). I never read Dubin. Instead I went to the Philosophy Department and asked what I needed to take in order to master theory construction. I was told to take logic. I took a lot of it, and a lot more philosophy.

Like everyone around me, I was against the baleful influence of Talcott Parsons and positivism. One hardly needed a political motivation for this—both were clearly wrong. And there was a strong elective affinity between what was wrong with them and what was wrong with the war in Viet Nam. McNamara, the secretary of defense, was a quantifier, famous for his belief in statistics, and the war was run as an "operations research" project, in which commanders reported kill ratios that were then treated as evidence of progress. We know, from recent revelations, that generating numbers of Viet Cong dead was the motivation of the horrific war crimes perpetrated by the U.S. military in Viet Nam: in fact, much of the killing was not of the "enemy" but of ordinary people, who were then counted as enemy in order to satisfy the demand of the Pentagon for evidence of progress. The same mentality of quantification was pervasive in sociology and so was the arrogance and indifference to reality that accompanied it. And there was something else in common: both the Johnson administration and the sociological quantifiers in sociology in this particular generation hated dissent. A necessary and important part of the agenda, in both cases, was to shut their critics up and squeeze them out of positions of influence.

Parsonian and Mertonian sociological theory had the same kind of agenda — progress for them meant little more than accumulating more power and getting rid of their critics. Robert Merton was allied with Paul Lazarsfeld, who was among the most brutal and aggressively nasty proponents of quantification in the history of sociology. Merton's talk about "theories of the middle range" was an attempt to give a "theoretical" interpretation and justification of Lazarsfeldian "sociology," a sociology that had no theoretical content at all in the sense of the classical questions of social theory. The term "middle range" was fake, as Lazarsfeld himself pointed out, since neither of them believed there were theories of the "upper" range worth talking about. Merton poured scorn on people who regarded the classics of social theory as living texts to be learned from and insisted that a science that hesitates to forget its founders was lost. Parsons, with his talk of systems and his abstracted diagrams of the social process, had a strategy that can best be described as operations research without the numbers — abstractions made up of boxes with names like "cultural system" and arrows with fictional quantities of fictional resources moving between them. Parsons had his own theoretical reasons for hostility to dissent — the idea that societies had a central value system — which in itself delegitimated and marginalized critics as the enemy, to be psychoanalyzed or denounced as retrograde. In a bit of Parsonian logic that is both absurd and sinister, he reflexively applied this idea of a central value system to his own sociology, which he took to be itself the embodiment of the central values of modernity.

Vanity is the besetting sin of academics but also of bureaucrats and power holders. The Viet Nam advisers — McNamara, Bundy, Walter Rostow, and the rest — believed that they were the best and the brightest and that their critics were simply inferior. They surrounded themselves with ambitious sycophants who had the same background, did their bidding, shared these attitudes, and were similarly blind. They didn't grasp, if they had even cared to grasp, that their own power distorted the advice they were getting, corrupted the information flow, and blinded them. The same held in spades for the sociological quantifiers and the dominant "theorists." They had plenty of power—to place students, to promote careers, to get books supporting them to appear in print with prominent presses and "good" journals—and they thought that this validated their superiority. Merton devoted much of his career as a sociologist of science to an argument that academic power was justly distributed—because scientists at the top of the heap had more citations—and that his own sociology of science was a self-exemplifying success story. They didn't grasp, or care to grasp, that this reasoning was circular: their "success" was a product of their power. They were happy to congratulate themselves endlessly on their superiority. It was this mentality that led to the equation of the defense of quality with the defense of their own styles of sociology.

This may seem like an exaggeration. It is not. They were hostile, and the hostility was returned. I once asked one of my social psychology teachers, a psychologist who was to go on to a very distinguished career, if he and others looked up to the leading lights in their field at the high prestige universities. "Only long enough to give them the finger" was his response. And this was quite in tune with the general academic violence of the time. Sociology was the discipline in which the conflicts were the most extreme. The nearby sociology department at Washington University, where I spent the summer of 1969, had disintegrated. The leading figures were packing up as I arrived. The younger faculty regaled us with stories of the 1968 American Sociological Association (ASA) meetings, with the dramatic pronouncement of Martin Nicolaus and the Sociology Liberation Movement. Students and faculty were pushed out of departments, most notoriously at Ohio State, where Hans Zetterberg (whose archpositivist *Theory and Verification in Sociology* [1963] was widely read) got rid even of tenured faculty. We had some refugees from this event at Missouri. At Chicago, Marlene Dixon was ousted (and toured the country telling her story to women's groups), and Richard Flacks, who was denied tenure, was beaten nearly to death in his office by an unknown assailant.

By 1970 I was a graduate student in sociology. I had delayed my BA to keep my student deferment and received both that and an MA in 1971. I had worked though the graduate sociology curriculum as an undergraduate, and by 1970 I was primarily taking courses in philosophy. Missouri sociology had a long tradition of hostility to establishment sociology and a rich, theory-oriented graduate student culture. The university was also highly egalitarian and unstuffy. My interests were indulged. But I was well aware that we were outsiders and I was sensitive to the massive weight of standard sociology. I also had the draft to contend with.

The fact of the draft breathing down my neck made me question my own motives throughout the period. I was not well attuned to the moralism of the antiwar movement and was not an activist, though I went to the usual marches and free speech demonstrations within the university and the department. What troubled me most was what I only later came to understand as the tragic character of great power politics. Johnson and his advisers were perfectly willing to sacrifice the lives of innocent people — draftees and Vietnamese civilians — for an ideology. But this ideology, and any ideology, is inevitably more flimsy than the reality of the slaughter of the innocents. How should one strike a balance here? I was on the side of the innocents, whoever was slaughtering them and for whatever reason. But I also knew that sometimes innocents must suffer in the course of stopping the suffering of other innocents. I was a conscientious objector with a troubled conscience. The draft board promptly rejected my application and turned down my appeal. In the draft lottery, I received a very low number — fourteen out of 366 — which meant I was certain to be drafted. In early 1971, I had been given my physical and was waiting for the induction notice.

It never came. With the help of the very generous and decent local peace movement in Columbia, Missouri, and a lawyer who worked with them, I delayed it by appealing to the next level and then by asking that the appeal be heard in Missouri rather than Illinois. The system was in fact jammed with appeals of the same kind, and the courts had ruled that the perfunctory one-minute rejections of appeals at the meetings of the state appeals boards didn't constitute meaningful "review." In my case and others, the system simply gave up. The appeals were never acted on. The people making the appeals were simply put into a new category and left alone, though the solution was Kafkaesque. Eventually we received a draft card that said 1-H. We were never told what the category meant or that we were free of the process.

Another psychic weight was the job market. When I began graduate school in 1970, there was still a strong demand for sociologists, and even getting a job in "theory," meaning in a department big enough to support a theory person, was not out of the question, especially if one was willing, as I was, to go to an unprestigious department in the South. None of us knew that the job market and sociology enrollments were about to spectacularly collapse, though an article in the *American Sociologist* by Bob McGinnis and Louise Solomon in 1973 pre dicted, using standard labor market tools, that this was about to occur. The prediction was uncanny in its accuracy. When the extent of the damage became apparent, I was faced with the question of survival.

I was naively optimistic about my intellectual prospects. There was no lack of topics to take up. The problem of what a "theory" was seemed to be the way into the big issues and, indeed, was the Achilles heel both of sociological positivism and theory. Explanation theory, which I knew from the philosophy of science, cut through these issues like a sharp knife. I could read the first eight pages of Arthur Stinchcombe's newly published *Constructing Social Theories* (1968) and see that it had nothing to do with theory and made no sense.[8] When some unfortunate published a formal theory (complete with bogus logical operators) in the *American Sociological Review* (ASR), I jumped on it with a reply (1971). It might have appeared that I was making spectacular headway. How many things written by nineteen-year-olds had appeared in the ASR? But I soon realized that all of this effort was caught in a weird dilemma. The supposed "positivism" of positivist sociology was a sham. A glance at the sources cited by people like Peter Blau, such as Richard Braithwaite's elegant *Scientific Explanation* (1953) was enough to show why. Blau hadn't read the sources he cited, much less understood them. But to explain what was wrong with their appropriations of these texts required a level of competence with the basic philosophy and logic that neither they nor the audience of American sociologists possessed, as I quickly discovered by corresponding with various "methodologists." I published a few papers in sociology journals on these topics anyway but to no avail. Clearly I couldn't hope to get into the top journals with this stuff, though at first I tried. If this was what I needed to do to survive, it wasn't going to work.

The job market now made the Missouri degree a huge liability. So I decided to put my tail between my legs and go to a department where I could fake it long enough to get a degree that would get me a job. In the end I wound up at the known devil of Chicago, with a plan to take a second degree in a program called Conceptual and Historical Foundations of Science. I had support, I was looking for an apartment, and was working out the details. They could not be worked out.

8. As it turned out, *Constructing Social Theories* was even more wrong than I imagined — every single correlation in the model Stinchcombe took as "good theory," namely, Blau and Duncan's *The American Occupational Structure* (1967), was spurious, and the eventual consensus among statisticians on this famous text is that it failed to explain anything.

I had already broached the idea of a theory dissertation with various people at Chicago and been told to forget it. Morris Janowitz, the chair, was irate at the very thought of my taking philosophy courses—though he also seemed to be irate about anything that indicated that I had a mind of my own.

The end of this episode came as I sat in the foyer of Janowitz's office, in a long line of students. I could hear through his open door the abuse he was dishing out to each of them. By the time I had my turn, I had had enough of Janowitz and Chicago. Nothing was worth this kind of demeaning treatment. I had caluculated the price of success. I was unable to pay it. The bile rose in me. Raymond Chandler's hero, and mine, Philip Marlowe, said that "I test very high on insubordination." So did I. I quit the program before I began and went back to Missouri and cut a deal with my committee, which gave me the wise advice that I needed to be able to claim to teach complex organizations, and I accepted that even with this I was likely never to get a job.

Why didn't I just give up? I considered it a point of honor to finish the degree, and in my early twenties there were few other options. One of my philosophy professors had remarked that one learned more in the first year of teaching than in the whole of graduate school. So I resolved to see it through, try the market at least in the South (which I could do as a methodologist, which was still an employable category), and if nothing turned up, I would go to law school. A theory job was now out of the question. As I soon learned, in the departments I might have gone to, the teaching of theory was typically monopolized by a senior faculty member who had never published a line on theory but who considered it a "prestige" role. I did finish, though it took until 1975. Much of the intervening time was spent quite pleasantly in New Orleans contemplating the unpleasant question of whether I had a future.

During the period I was working on my dissertation, the situation of sociology got worse and worse, and the struggles within sociology grew even more brutal. The assistant editor of the *ASR* announced that the role of *ASR* editing was not to act as "paradigm enforcers" even as the journal was filled with papers by the Wisconsin school on status attainment. Peter Rossi tried to shut down the *American Sociologist*, which had been one of the few outlets for critics of establishment sociology and was popular and widely read, unlike the *ASR* itself. Eventually it was pushed out of the ASA. This was an exceptionally cynical act of bullying, aimed at suppressing honest differences that should have been argued out in full view of the profession. For me, it was the emblematic act of the era; it simultaneously affirmed the power of the oligarchy, cut their opponents out of a platform, and cloaked all of this in self-congratulatory concern for quality. Rossi himself was a specialist in getting money out the federal government.

I knew very well by then that the sun of American sociology was not going to shine on me. Nevertheless, I found it difficult to abandon all hope of a scholarly life, of being a participant in the great discussion. I puzzled over the phenomenon of academic power, and the differences between what I was experiencing in my dealings with the profession and the idealized view of science as consisting of conjectures and refutations that I had imbibed from Karl Popper. Of course, I did not know whether I had any talent, and I would have been grateful if someone had told me "do something else with your life." But no one did. I realized that any hope for a job depended on luck and on a vita that included a few things in print in reputable journals. I accepted that whatever I was to make out of my life as an academic had to be a matter of setting my own goals and not a matter of climbing some sort of career ladder. Merton wrote about the Matthew effect, in which those who are given advantages, get much greater advantages. The Matthew effect was not going to work for me but against me.

The disorienting thing about being an outsider is that one is unable to separate the question of whether one is any good, of whether one is doing something worthwhile, whether one is being fairly treated, whether the system is stacked against you, whether the snobs with whose contempt one dealt on a constant basis were perhaps right, or whether history has taken a turn that makes what you are doing pointless—they all come mixed together. The stakes are high. Bet wrong and one has wasted a life. Like Weber's anxious predestinarians, one looks for signs. But the positive signs are all ambiguous. The negative ones were not. I sent a proposal for a session titled "Wittgenstein and Sociology" to the 1974 ASA program committee, run by the incoming president, Peter Blau (I had been tipped by a friend that this notoriously clubby bunch had a member that was willing to listen to proposals from people outside the major departments). I received an incredibly condescending reply to the effect that if there was anything to the topic I might try to submit a paper on it. Within a few years, of course, the literature of sociology—though naturally not American sociology—was full of Wittgenstein.

Friedrich Nietzsche uses a term, *Vergeltung*, which is rendered as "requital" in the standard translations but is better translated "payback." He says that the origin of justice is payback and exchange under the presupposition of a rough equality of power, by which he means that justice begins as a relation between people who can exact revenge from one another and thus both act generously and express gratitude toward one another without servility. Servility was not my style — not that it would have done me any good in my situation. But payback was not out of the question. And getting even was a nice motivator. I later took my revenge on Peter Blau by writing a paper on his "deductive" Theory of Differentiation (Turner 1977). Stewing over the institutional injustices of academic life itself produced something. I wrote, with Daryl Chubin, two papers on issues related to Mertonian elitism, which showed that what the data demonstrated was not the virtue of the elite but the wastefulness of the system (1976, 1979).

Continuing was not entirely irrational. There appeared to be some grounds for hope. The journal system seemed, miraculously, to be opening up. While I was in New Orleans, I received the initial ads for *Theory and Society*. It looked as though the millennium had arrived. The list of editorial advisers included almost everyone who counted in theory internationally and in the United States, except for the Parsonians. It promised in its brochure to be a place for discussing philosophy of social science issues as well as theory. It was a gathering of the best of social theory at the time, and the best was very good. It was a false dawn, but in fact things were opening up a bit. I also enjoyed what I was doing — a dissertation on the "rationality of other cultures" problem, which took me out of sociology and into anthropology.

I went onto the job market in 1975 — in Florida, where I had moved from New Orleans with my wife. The state university system was undergoing a budget crisis and job freeze, but there were opportunities. I was very fortunate to get a job at one of the branch campuses of one of the larger universities, in a two-person program. The teaching load was nine courses a year, and over time I taught virtually the whole sociology curriculum. But it was comfortable, and it brought me into contact with colleagues outside of sociology. Most important, no one cared what I published, or where, as long as I was doing something.

There were, of course, prices to be paid, beyond the heavy teaching loads. My marriage broke up. A forerunner of countless others' academic marriages, our marriage was already strained by long separations, and under the new stress of finding two satisfactory jobs in one place, her desire to finish her PhD, the problems of reconciling expectations, and my inability to get a job that allowed her to do what she wanted to do. This formed an endless braid of troubles that had to be cut, however painfully. I knew that this job was as good a job as I was going to get. If I needed a reminder of how lucky I was to have gotten that far, I got one during the first week of classes: one of the women faculty in the department on the main campus called to tell me not to take it personally but that the women's group was trying to get me fired because they believed that affirmative action guidelines hadn't been followed in my appointment.

I sent my dissertation out for review at various publishers—none would even read it. But as a member of the ASA, I could send it in to the Rose Monograph series and at least expect the courtesy of a reply. I got a review—indeed, a split review, with one of the reviews being so violently hostile that the editor, Robin Williams, was taken aback. In an act of genuine academic decency and generosity, he consulted with me and commissioned a third review. It was accepted and published as *Sociological Explanation as Translation* (1980). I was thrilled. But even a success such as this turns out to be profoundly ambiguous for someone at the bottom of the academic hierarchy. If I had been on a normal career path, I supposed, it would have been an achievement that got me something— partway to tenure in a reputable department, for example, or an audience that had to respond to it.[9] For an outsider, however, it was just another oddball achievement, meaningless, clawed from the largely unwilling grasp of those who held the power. And my experience of the arbitrariness of the processes of evaluation pointed to the conclusion that these "achievements" were useless even for keeping score for oneself.

When I knew I had a job, I thought about a long-term plan, of writing either a comprehensive study on the methodological ideas of classical social theory or a parallel study of the implicit ethical theory of the classics, or both. My idea was to trace the consensus sociology of the present to its roots. I was still under the illusion that the standard story was more or less right and that Durkheim and Weber were in some way the progenitors of standard sociology. I began this in earnest in the summer of 1976. Returning to the classics, especially after learning to read them in a close, more or less "Straussian" way, freed me from the limited vision of contemporary sociology. I had already worked on Marx and Weber and the problem of the origins of capitalism. I continued with Durkheim, the supposed source of "positivist" sociology. It was immediately obvious that he was no positivist and that he was very different from the "classic" functionalist that he had been homogenized into by the disciplinary tradition—indeed that he was not a functionalist at all. It was also obvious that he and Weber had seriousness

9. There was a serious use of the argument by Steven Lukes (1982, 283–90), and elsewhere internationally there was a response. If I had any doubts about where I was welcome, they were evaporating.

and depth beyond the understanding of careerist sociology. It was easy enough to ridicule papers on "what Weber meant," as was routinely done by *ASR* editors and even "theorists" in the ASA Theory Section. It was much more difficult to say anything equally meaningful without having understood what they meant. And one soon realized as well that there was a huge gulf between those who had made the effort to come to terms with the great thinkers and those who got their opinions second-hand from theory textbooks or wrote textbooks that represented them as possessing a catalog of "positions" or "perspectives" or, for that matter, "propositions."

I had come to critique the classics but came away something more like a convert. I discovered that the classics were the best critics of Parsons and Merton.[10] I also discovered that it was possible to publish on them — the specialist literature was effectively outside the control of the oligarchs of American sociology. I immersed myself in the literature on Weber, much of which was outside sociology. With a colleague, Regis Factor, who knew both Germany and political theory, I produced a series of papers and then a book manuscript on Weber's value theory and its reception — and distortion. In the course of this, we found Jacob-Peter Mayer, then nearly ninety, the discoverer of the early Marx manuscripts and the author of a classic text on Weber as a political thinker. We invited him to Florida. As I had no network of theorists to support me, I went about creating one, with people like John O'Neill, Stanford Lyman, and Edward Shils. And I was treated generously. Mayer, who had been the discoverer of Jean Baudrillard and had written the preface to *La société de consommation: Ses mythes, ses structures* (1970), did the same for the first translation of mine (1984). And each of the others did me good turns as well.

By the early 1980s, I had escaped American sociology in spirit, if not yet in institutional reality. I had a few more body blows to suffer. But I no longer had any concern that the people doing the battering might be right. I tried the Weber book manuscript out at Cambridge New York, where I was known because of my first book, and received a very favorable first review. The second review, however, was a personal attack on me and my coauthor as ideological fanatics. It killed the

---

10. In a later work, *Max Weber: The Lawyer as Social Thinker* (1994), Factor and I explained why. Weber was intentionally getting away from the teleological model of social action (represented for him by the legal theorist Rudolf von Ihering) Parsons had simply gotten the historical development backward: this is what Parsons thought Weber was groping *toward*.

book for that press. I went through the same process, with the same result, at the University of Massachusetts Press. In fact, the book was largely a dry record of the facts—useful scholarship, as one of the nonsociology reviews of the published book put it. Through the intervention of John O'Neill, it was read at Routledge and published (1984). In the United Kingdom, I was free of the burdens of the American publishing system, which weights the scales toward orthodoxy and allows for decisions based on cronyism and vendettas by soliciting too many opinions and taking the worst one seriously. When published, it was reviewed favorably by Anthony Giddens in the *Times Higher Education Supplement*. Other related texts on Weber were published in political theory at the same time. We were, all of a sudden, part of a moment of thought.

While I was working on the final draft of this book, during a brief stint at Virginia Tech in science studies, I sent a very bland but technically perfect paper on Weber to the *ASR*. It was, predictably, trashed, on the grounds that it was "just history." I wrote a scathing letter to Sheldon Stryker, then editor, explaining just how and why this was an absurd judgment that could only have been made by a semiliterate idiot. When I reread the letter I decided not to send it. As I held it in my hand ready to throw it out, the secretary who had typed it said "You write a good nasty letter." On aesthetic grounds alone, I put it in the mail. After some negotiations, which involved the charade of writing a new section and then having it deleted, it was accepted.

By this time, publishing in the *ASR* no longer mattered to me. No one read it that I cared about reaching, and I had no respect for the system, those who ran it, and those who benefited from it. I had been confirmed in my view of these journals by Edward Shils, from whom I had taken a National Endowment for the Humanities Summer Seminar a few months before, and whose lordly disdain for them was based on inside knowledge dating back to the 1930s, as well as decades of experience as an editor of his own journal. I now no longer cared about payback, either. I was simply happy to get off a ship of fools and embarrassed that I had ever taken people like Blau seriously. The people who had looked kindly on me—Shils, Mayer, O'Neill, and Lyman—also seemed to me to be admirable role models. They were tough as nails, knew things that ordinary academics did not, read books that careerist academics do not read, and persevered outside, or largely outside, the machine of disciplinary academia. Yet they kept their intellectual balance. The people I myself read and profited from reading were often in this category anyway. I had lost a discipline and gained a tradition.

There was, however, a last act as a sociologist.[11] In 1987, I was, by accident, given a chance to work through the puzzle of the peculiar awfulness of American sociology. I had never worked on an American topic before, except for a few pages at the end of *The Search for a Methodology of Social Science* (1986), the fulfillment of my project on the methodology of the classics, and in an unpublished paper on Giddings that followed up on it. Giddings was the real brains behind the American quantitative tradition; he was ridiculed or unmentioned in the standard texts. I was curious about what came after. Jon Turner had signed up to do a volume in Polish for a series on national sociologies that was the brainchild of Edmund Mokrcynski — a great man with whom I was honored to have an association. I was supposed to fill in the methodology sections of a draft that was already written. As I got into it, and into the role of foundation funding, the Sociological Research Association, and the personal relations and enmities that made up the history of methodology, the project turned to something else: an exploration of the bases of the bitter conflicts with which I had grown up (Turner and Turner 1990).

In the context of the larger history, the bullying, the resistance, the compulsion to stigmatize and denounce, and the historical amnesia of American sociology came to make more sense. The conflicts had been there from the start, with the founders eagerly engaged in pushing one another out of the boat. Sociology had developed as a complex institutional order without ever resolving the conflicts. The theme of getting your opponents excluded and defined as backward and of foundations putting a thumb on the scale by pushing first one than another model of science — all this was there very early on. The personal side was also compelling, full of unsavory characters whose nastiness and vanity spilled from the archives as well as of serious people who had been misrepresented and trashed, such as Charles Ellwood, but whose decency was palpable. Who was a villain and who was not depended in part on where you stood, but it was evident enough that there was no simple storyline of good and evil, as it had seemed in

11. In 1987, I was raised to the rank of graduate research professor, which eventually led to my being moved to the philosophy department on the main campus of the university. I have omitted any discussion of this later period, though the themes pursued there have roots in the 1960s as well. They include the whole complex of ideas that are represented in Parsons, notably his functionalism and his appeal to a mysterious notion of culture, which reappears in Clifford Geertz and Pierre Bourdieu, in different form, and the idea of normativity and collective agency, which share their troubles.

the 1960s. There were decent quantifiers, relentlessly careerist Leftists, and so on. But there were also many knaves, and much of the knavery arose in connection with the quest for academic power and the purposeful confusion of considerations of quality and considerations of content and through the willingness to pervert the institutions of the discipline through this confusion, typically in the guise of saving them.

The New Left and the student movement of the 1960s in the United States had been an unstable mixture of classical liberal ideals — the ideas of free speech and participation in democratic processes — and a humanistic socialism concerned with alienation. For me, the free speech elements were the connecting link between sociology and the larger struggles of the day. But for many others, the movement was all about the thrills of solidarity. And these were genuine — to participate in a huge march to end the war along with thousands of others, to shout down the defenders of the status quo, to be morally right, and to have an impact on "the real world" was a tremendous experience. It is no surprise that there were people who wanted to reenact these experiences in different forms when the political moment had passed. But in the end, there was a conflict between the solidaristic shouting down of opponents and the idea of free speech and open discussion.

Sociology deals with ideological materials and is, in part, made up of them. But as a discipline, it ought to be a site of controlled contention — controlled by the facts, by a common tradition, and by considerations of what makes sense. The bad habit of closing off discussion, which predated 1968, and the habit, which the 1960s legitimated, of denouncing opponents in ideological terms is in conflict with this "ought." The inability of sociology to deal with race, the most complex and intractable, moralized, ideologically loaded, and tragic of all issues in American society, is the dead canary in the mine: the historical greatness of American sociology came at those moments when it did create a zone in which discussion was possible, even when these successes were partial and limited. I was loyal to the ideal of free discussion and never happy with the flight to solidarity and comforting moralisms. I had always tried to create possibilities for discussion free of the professional hierarchy. As a graduate student, I had cofounded the *Review of Social Theory*. One afternoon, sitting in my graduate student office, David Maines and I had gone through the exercise of naming names of people who might support an alternative to the ASA. Perhaps it was the kernel of the Society for Symbolic Interaction, which he had a major role in creating a few years later. I used every chance I could as an editor, for example, as chair of a university press editorial board, to open up discussion. From this position I was able to rescue Bob Eden's terrific book on Nietzsche and Weber. I edited books that gave opportunities to discuss things that weren't going to be discussed in the journals, organized conferences, and even started a new social theory organization. These were very small victories. This struggle continues.

References

Birmingham, Stephen. 1977. *Certain People: America's Black Elite.* Boston: Little Brown.

Blau, Peter M., and Otis Dudley Duncan. 1967. *The American Occupational Structure.* New York: Wiley.

Braithwaite, Richard. 1953. *Scientific Explanation: A Study of the Function of Theory, Probability and Law in Science.* Cambridge: Cambridge University Press.

Burnham, James. 1943. *The Machiavellians.* New York: John Day Co.

Dubin, Robert. 1969. *Theory Building.* New York: Free Press.

Fall, Bernard. 1966. *Hell in a Very Small Place: The Siege of Dien Bien Phu.* Philadelphia: Lippincott.

Freud, Sigmund. 1939. *Moses and Monotheism.* New York: A. A. Knopf.

———. 1953. *The Future of an Illusion,* trans. W.D. Robeson-Scott. New York: Liveright. (1st edn., 1928.)

Frazier, E. Franklin. 1956. *Black Bourgeoisie.* Glencoe, IL: Free Press.

Fromm, Erich. 1941. *Escape from Freedom.* New York: Holt, Rinehart, & Winston.

———. 1955. *The Sane Society.* New York: Rinehart.

Gosse, Edmund. 1934. *Father and Son.* New York: Oxford University Press.

Lévi-Strauss, Claude. 1966. *The Savage Mind.* Chicago: University of Chicago Press.

Lindner, Robert. 1956. *Must You Conform?* New York: Rinehart.

Lukes, Steven. 1982. "Relativism in Its Place." Pp. 260–305 in *Rationality and Relativism,* edited by Martin Hollis and Steven Lukes. Cambridge, MA: MIT Press.

Malcolm X. 1966. *Malcolm X Speaks.* New York: Grove Press.

Mayer, J. P. 1970. Preface to Jean Baudrillard, *La société de consommation: Ses mythes, ses structures.* Paris: Gallimard.

———. 1984. Nota previa to Stephen Turner, *La Explicacion sociologica como traduccion.* Translated by Mario Usabiaga. Mexico City: Fondo de Cultura Economica, 9.

McGinnis, Robert, and Louise Solomon. 1973. "Employment Prospects for Ph.D. Sociologists during the Seventies." *American Sociologist* 8:57–63.

Mills, C. Wright. 1959. *The Sociological Imagination.* New York: Oxford University Press.

Niebuhr, Reinhold. 1960. "The Christian in Politics." Pp. 193–209 in *Reinhold Niebuhr on Politics,* edited by Harry A. Davis and Robert C. Good. New York: Scribners.

Overstreet, Harry. 1949. *The Mature Mind.* New York: W. W. Norton.

Packard, Vance. 1958. *The Hidden Persuaders.* New York: Pocket Books.

Rosen, Louis. 1998. *The South Side: The Racial Transformation of an American Neighborhood.* Chicago: Ivan R. Dee.

Stinchcombe, Arthur. 1968. *Constructing Social Theories.* New York: Harcourt, Brace & World.

Turner, Stephen. 1971. "The Logical Adequacy of 'The Logical Adequacy of Homans' Social Theory.'" *American Sociological Review* 36:709–11.

———. 1977. "Blau's Theory of Differentiation: Is It Explanatory?" *Sociological Quarterly* 18:17–32.

———. 1980. *Sociological Explanation as Translation.* Rose Monograph Series of the American Sociological Association. Cambridge, MA: Cambridge University Press.

———. 1986. *The Search for a Methodology of Social Science: Durkheim, Weber, and the Nineteenth Century Problem of Cause, Probability, and Action.* Boston Studies in the Philosophy of Science, 92. Dordrecht: Reidel.

Turner, Stephen, and Daryl Chubin. 1976. "Another Appraisal of Ortega, the Coles, and Science Policy: The Ecclesiastes Hypothesis." *Social Science Information* 15:657–62.

———. 1979. "Chance and Eminence in Science: Ecclesiastes II." *Social Science Information* 18:437–49.

Turner, Stephen, and Regis Factor. 1984. *Max Weber and the Dispute over Reason and Value: A Study in Philosophy, Ethics, and Politics.* London: Routledge & Kegan Paul.

———. 1994. *Max Weber: The Lawyer as Social Thinker.* London: Routledge.

Turner, Stephen, and Jonathan Turner. 1990. *The Impossible Science: An Institutional Analysis of American Sociology,* Beverly Hills and London: Sage.

Weber, Max. [1919] 1946. "Politics as a Vocation." In *From Max Weber: Essays in Sociology,* edited and translated by H. H. Gerth and C. W. Mills. New York: Oxford University Press.

Weber, Max. 1958. *The Protestant Ethic and the Spirit of Capitalism.* Translated by Talcott Parsons. New York: Scribner's.

Wilson, William J. 1966. *When Work Disappears: The World of the New Urban Poor.* New York: Knopf.

Zetterberg, Hans. 1963. *On Theory and Verification in Sociology.* Rev. ed. Totowa, NJ: Bedminster Press.

Ontological Disobedience — Definitely! {Maybe}

Steve Woolgar is a sociologist who holds the chair of marketing at the Oxford University. He was formerly professor of sociology, head of the Department of Human Sciences and director of Centre for Research into Culture and Technology at Brunel University. He took his BA (first class honours), MA, and PhD from Emmanuel College, Cambridge University. He has since held visiting appointments at McGill University (sociology), MIT (Program in Science Technology and Society), École Nationale Superieure des Mines, Paris (Centre de Sociologie de l'Innovation), and University of California, San Diego (sociology). He is the winner of a Fulbright Scholarship, a Fulbright Senior Scholarship, and an Economic and Social Research Council (ESRC) Senior Research Fellowship. From 1997 to 2002 he was director of the ESRC Programme: Virtual Society?—the social science of electronic technologies comprising twenty-two research projects at twenty-five universities throughout the United Kingdom. He has published widely in social studies of science and technology, social problems, and social theory and has been translated into Dutch, French, Greek, Japanese, Portuguese, Spanish, and Turkish. His latest

This chapter is dedicated to the memory of Sheila McKechnie (1948–2004), a self-professed, "fully paid up member of the awkward squad," who purveyed an admirably influential and fruitful form of disobedience.

For their comments and suggestions, I thank Catelijne Coopmans, Paul Drew, John Holmwood, Janet Low, Daniel Neyland, Alan Sica, and Steve Turner. And also my therapist.

The quote from Pirandello ([1913] 1962), 21.

book is Virtual Society? Technology, Cyberbole, Reality. *His current projects include research into the governance and accountability relations of mundane technical solutions to social problems; whether science and technology studies really means business; and an inquiry into the nature and dynamics of provocation. He has served on various U.K. and European government advisory bodies and research councils. He is a member of Council of Which? The Consumer's Association, and chair of Auditory Verbal UK, the charity that enables speech and language in hearing-impaired children.*

> LAUDISI: All I'm trying to say is that your curiosity . . . is insufferable. If for no other reason than it's quite pointless.
>
> SIRELLI: Pointless?
>
> LAUDISI: Pointless! . . .
>
> MRS. CINI: Pointless? Our trying to find out?
>
> LAUDISI: Forgive my asking . . . find out *what?* What can we really know about other people? Who are they? What sort of people they are? What they do? Why they do it?
>
> Pirandello [1913] 1962

Introduction: How to Respond to This Exercise?

The construction of this little piece has been a struggle, not least because the exercise of writing autobiographically poses several temptations. First, I have to overcome the intuition that an exploration of my personal background and experiences is a conceit. Who on earth could be remotely interested in my personal biography? I myself find it pretty boring. Second, my training (qua sociologist) tells me to be suspicious of narratives that overly individualize personal experiences. The temptation is to fashion, instead, a narrative that stands as "an account of anyone." The narrative options here include generalized historical and sociological forms—please understand everything related here as typical of "the period" or of "the generation." Sometimes the tension between the personal and the general is addressed through the classic compromise of the lucky witness—I just happened to be in the right place at the right time—as classically found in the false modesty of Nobel Prize acceptance speeches and Academy Award ceremonies. Third, we need to avoid the temptation of retrospective reconstruction, the writing of Whiggish histories that repopulate the past with just those events that must have happened in order to lead to the present.

Characteristic of all these temptations is the concept of "influence." The editors invite us to identify, reflect on, and discuss "influences" on our position, approach, or perspective. So the biggest temptation of all, a sort of metatemptation if you will, is to present a story of the past that embodies this orthodox view of the relation between influence and action. An ethnographically skeptical treatment of "influence" starts from the view that there is no clear connection between influences and outcomes. Yet trying to resist this temptation is especially difficult because it requires going against ingrained conventions of narrative construction. These conventions not only enact and support the idea of influence, they also reaffirm the basic premises of causal relationships and explanations (e.g., that influences gave rise to a view, perspective, or action).

We could try to reject the tyranny of influences either by adopting a form of "postmodernist" exposition, a kind of radically alternative narrative form,[1] or, in contrast, by espousing a purportedly more "rigorous scientific" procedure for identifying the actual causal connections. Both responses are inadequate because they in effect "jump out of" the problem frame. The preferred alternative is to stay engaged with the problem while remaining skeptical. In a sense this merely follows a familiar anthropological mode of managing being an insider and an outsider at the same time. One is simultaneously a member of and a stranger to one's (own) argument, so that one produces (what looks like) a "conventional" text that at the same time develops and advances its own critique. The aim here is to see if we can produce an unstable argument that needs to be taken seriously, an argument that also constitutes its own ethnography, a text that is simultaneously at rest with and critical of itself.[2]

So let us be clear that this whole project is nuts.[3] The editors invite contributions to a volume that documents the influences on the early careers of social scientists. Are they really asking us to present an account of knowledge activities, ca-

1. No, it's okay this is not one of those weird postmodern pieces. I fully subscribe to the argument that we have never been modern (Latour 1991), let alone postmodern.

2. Sorry about this last cliché. "Sounds very much like a ton of lit crit stuff I've read over the last 20 years" (Sica, e-mail message to author, 2004). But I do think the aspiration is correct. It's just that during all those years nobody bothered to try to work out what it means.

3. "Nuts"? I here, after all these years, such an exalted standard of erudition.

reer moves, intellectual direction in terms of the influences that gave rise to them? They clearly fail to understand that a key article of disobedience, at least to this member of "the generation," is the rejection of just this kind of proposition. Come on, give me a break. Surely, one of the key achievements of the disobedient generation was the disavowal of precisely this kind of conventional style of argument.[4] This means, then, that our response should take the path of itemizing the long list of problems with the editors' expectations. This list would constitute a pretty much watertight case for not going along with the editors' request.

And yet. . . .

This whole project is delightful. The whole point of disobedience is noncompliance. The editors invite us, representatives of a "generation," to reflect on our own noncompliance while still compliantly operating within the editors' framework. To be truly disobedient, and so deserving inclusion in this volume, one would have to refuse to be included. In a nice inversion of the old Groucho Marx joke, one could only really qualify as a fully paid-up member of the disobedient generation by refusing to become a member. So the very nature of the project admits and encourages explorations of a series of complex contradictions and reflexive loops. Of course, some objectivist philosophers still depict these issues in terms of inconsistencies or as aporias. They are viewed as logical traps to be avoided lest they threaten the entire basis of reasonable (?) argument. By contrast, for the rest of us, these same issues offer a great opportunity to lift ourselves from the humdrum hagiographies of linear retrospective flat text autobiography.

Two Kinds of Disobedience

Did the disobedience of our generation lead merely to the displacement of the status quo by an alternative but stable project? Or did it open the way to more lasting critique? The contrast is simple but important. Crudely expressed, it is a contrast between disobedience designed to bring about change, and in particular a move to an alternative stable state—which we can call instrumental disobedience—and disobedience that takes the form of an enduring restlessness, discomfort, dissatisfaction, and skepticism—which we shall call dynamic or ontological disobedience. The first kind is an instrumental means for articulating

4. "Surely"? One of my school teachers impressed me with the observation that a speaker's use of "surely" is a (sure) sign that the speaker is about to lose the argument.

and achieving an alternative position; the second is more a kind of credo, an attitude and perspective for sustaining a form of life.

The first sense of disobedience is directed against an existing orthodoxy. But it is limited in the sense that it often seems destined merely to usher in another, alternative orthodoxy. As is widely documented in the analysis of political change, from George Orwell to Nelson Mandela, yesterday's protesters become members of today's establishment. The radical terrorists who succeed commonly go on to assume positions of orthodox political power. In Tony Benn's apt phrase even the most heinous enemies of the state frequently end up "taking tea with the Queen" (Benn 1995). In respect to the political protests of "our generation" such transformations give rise to ironic renditions of the "fate" of the radical student revolutionaries of the 1960s. Under newspaper and journal headlines such as "Where Are They Now?" we learn that a prominent student radical figure on the barricades in 1968 Paris—"Danny the Red"—is now selling life insurance. Ironic treatments of radical theoretical and intellectual change in the social sciences are less common. A notable exception is Mel Pollner's (1991) well-known account of the institutionalization of ethnomethodology. The radical reflexivity of early ethnomethodology, writes Pollner, has now "settled down and moved out to the suburbs." Did the apparently radical disobedience of 1967 ethnomethodology—the bête noire of much traditional sociology at the time—merely presage the routinized, formulaic, normal science practice of conversational analysis? Or, to take another example, has the angry relativism of early sociology of scientific knowledge—which throughout the 1970s and 1980s sent legions of objectivist philosophers of science spinning in their graves—now given rise to a tamed formula for representing the social dynamics of science entrepreneurship and science policy? Has the provocative disobedience of subsequent calls to flatten the ontological landscape, to advance a symmetry between the attributes of humans and nonhumans as a heuristic starting point, now merely led to the mechanical application of actor network "theory"?[5]

---

5. These questions raise further questions about the nature of instrumental disobedience. If this kind of disobedience inevitably gives rise to the appropriation and institutionalisation of radical ideas, in what sense was it ever truly radical? No sociologist sensitive to the problems of essentialism and its attribution would want to claim that ideas are intrinsically (essentially) radical. This alerts us, instead, to enquire about the nature of the social dynamics and the sets of social relations that sustain perceptions of disobedience and how these relations change so that disobedience becomes attenuated. For-

By contrast, dynamic or ontological disobedience envisages a form of continual revolution. The central question here is what sustains persistent disobedience. If the target is less specific than in instrumental disobedience, the related question is why is persistent revolution necessary or desirable? The disobedience envisaged here is intended to be constantly unsettling, challenging, destabilizing but with no specific end in mind. It provides a reservoir of continual questioning but for what purpose? Where does it end? And if it is indeed "without purpose," does not continual disobedience imply a kind of petulance, a form of disobedience for its own sake?

For ontological disobedience, merely to ask these questions is already to embrace unwarranted compromise. For ontological disobedience there is no end. Rather, there is a constant injunction to be disturbing and challenge. This also begins to account for an important difference between the instrumentality of many forms of political radicalism and the open-endedness of dynamic disobedience. Ontological disobedience is far more radical than mere political disobedience. It is especially important to note that the former also challenges the presumption of the latter that political action necessitates objective commitment (see, e.g., Herrnstein Smith 1997).

This simple contrast enables us to discern some important constraints endemic to our task. For the very phrase "disobedient generation" connotes a form of instrumental rather than ontological disobedience. It does so because it ties the nature of the disobedience to a social category (a younger generation), which is directed against its contrastive pair part (the older generation). This implies a lot about the kind of disobedience. It is the voice of the child raised against the dominant parental authority, a parental authority that can be played out also in the guise of the state, government, or scientific authority. But there is more than a suspicion of temporary, limited disobedience about it. Children, after all, are just like that. It's just a generational thing. In the end the disobedient generation will grow up.[6]

---

tunately, there is insufficient space here fully to examine the processes of retrospective construction of "Steve Woolgar" as a disobedient theorist.

6. The same grown-ups sometimes evince disappointment that their own offspring are insufficiently disobedient. Harking back to his own disobedient teenage treatment of texts with which he disagreed, my famous French friend is concerned that his teenage son "is yet to burn his first novel."

Some Autobiographical Origins of Ontological Disobedience

So in autobiographical terms, where does this leaning toward dynamic disobedience come from? I went on some of the marches in central London in 1967 and 1968. I don't much recall feeling especially politicized or that some political motive was my reason for going. But I do recall being impressed by the volume and raucousness of the crowd, by the power and energy of the protest. Especially impressive was the look on the faces of the police and the passersby. They seemed to be looking at us in awe of disobedience itself, not because they feared the perspective of specifically left-wing politics or whatever. I remember thinking that maybe "anarchy" was an interesting idea and struggled with one or two worthy but seemingly opaque tracts on the topic.

But this was also the time of satire. A school trip was organized to a theater in London's West End where I watched a production of "Behind the Fridge," itself a parodic successor to "Beyond the Fringe," the shows that brought Peter Cook, Dudley Moore, Alan Bennett, and Jonathon Miller to prominence, the precursor to traditions of irreverent British humor including *That Was the Week That Was*, David Frost, and *Monty Python*. Again, it seemed to me, the vitality of the protest, the extent of the trouble and unnerved reaction that it provoked, was much more impressive than any specific, let alone coherent, political standpoint that prompted the protest in the first place. At school, a brave friend started an "underground" magazine titled *Yellow Socks*. Brave because these very garments of clothing had recently sent our headmaster into paroxysms of rage when one of the boys was discovered wearing them. A clearly deliberate violation of the rules of school uniform (a uniform "royal" blue from head to toe). The whole school was brought to a special assembly to have the matter expurgated. What seemed both delightful and absurd was the vehemence of "their" reaction to this episode. In and through the reaction to it, the behavior became a gesture of defiance. One could dress up this episode, so to speak, as a(nother) manifestation of the more general eruption of a whole generation of youth in the face of stifling postwar orthodoxy. But it didn't seem that way at the time.

Of course, this was also the time of significant new musical trends. Many, such as Joan Baez and Bob Dylan, were associated with protest and antiwar movements. Although these were clearly worthy sentiments, to me they seemed rather dull compared to the shock value of the Pretty Things, the Rolling Stones, and the Velvet Underground. Again, although it is possible in retrospect to enroll these latter forms of expression into an account of cultural upheaval aimed at prevailing political orthodoxy, the notably striking effects at the time were the outrage and consternation generated by these new musical forms. They seemed to me, to the extent that I could then articulate the feeling, to promise an engine of continual disruption and challenge, more than an instrument for targeted political change.

So the emerging sense of disobedience here is one of being awkward or difficult in the face of orthodoxy — dynamic or ontological disobedience. These latter terms seem to capture my experiences of disruption and challenge much better than the idea of "rebellion" — instrumental disobedience — with its rather earnest, steely Leninist overtones and associated suggestions of political (re)organization.

If I was looking for a forum for articulating my sense of the intrigue and challenges of awkwardness and disobedience, the move from a minor public school to Cambridge did not at first seem promising. The Cambridge degree course in engineering afforded few possibilities for disobedience. On the whole, my fellow engineering undergraduates seemed gray (as I no doubt also seemed to them) — we attended lots of lectures, experiments, practicals, and demonstrations — while our contemporaries seemed to have lots of time to engage in more exciting diversions. We seemed overconcerned with the dull aspects of mechanical science, and our rooms bore few of the flamboyant, colorful posters and decorations of fellow students in the arts and humanities. When one of the lecturers in the introductory thermodynamics course made a joke about the operation of the internal combustion engine — "everyone knows that to start a revolution you need a crank" — he seemed to embody a kind of engineering mindset that casts aspersions on political figures. I was intrigued to learn that engineering students at one university on the other side of the world (Simon Fraser University, I think it was) wore bright red jackets with "engineering" emblazoned across the back and operated as a kind of vigilante force for breaking up student demonstrations. Not surprising that few Cambridge engineers turned out for the demonstration against the junta at the Garden House Greek Restaurant; very surprising to me that some minor damage to property was subsequently transformed through media descriptions into the "the Garden House riots."

The lack of disobedience seemed enshrined in the degree-course organization. Interminable practicals required routine but uncommitted engagement. They needed to get done, not to be thought about. It was shocking to discover that many investigations were simply copied from reports submitted by previous years' students. There seemed little intellectual challenge. One was not encouraged to wonder and reflect, just to get through — and to do so by means of ferocious organization. Engineering seemed the scientific/technical equivalent of what I imagined to be training in the law. Stamina and organization, rather than curiosity and challenge, were the necessary virtues.

But a great virtue of Oxbridge was (and is) its interdisciplinarity, founded on the enduring conceit of the Renaissance Man, that if you are clever and knowledgeable about any one subject, you are potentially clever and knowledgeable about many others. This view is institutionalized through the college system that encourages undergraduates to mix lives and social activities irrespective of their degree course. In this context, one Cambridge friend, John Holmwood, provided me with an introduction to social science or, at least, to one image of it. Social science was clearly about argument. John argued with gusto, great seriousness, determination, intensity, and enormous conviction. Things in the world beyond engineering were clearly not black and white but, strikingly, they needed to be argued that way. It was enormously impressive to experience John in full flow: this was bravado intellectual performance. For someone unenculturated into this (social science) mode of argument it was also intriguing to notice the catastrophic effect of interjecting the occasional flat denial. These were moments when I am sure I just came across as being difficult.

John subsequently spent a year as a teaching assistant at the University of California, Los Angeles, Department of Sociology. Before he went, he presented me with a copy of *Studies in Ethnomethodology* (Garfinkel 1967). On his return a year later, he gave me some incomprehensible notes he had taken from a Garfinkel lecture (circa 1972).[7] The book and the notes joined my embryonic, eclectic collection of obscure sources that I felt I should one day try and make some sense of. I put considerable energy into investigating alternatives to a third year of undergraduate engineering, even arranging to transfer to a medical sciences degree course, before finally signing up for the "management option" of the Engineering Tripos. Academic management at Cambridge at that time comprised sociology of organizations and industrial relations, mathematically based operations research, and statistics. I suddenly discovered I enjoyed reading the sociology books and writing essays, to the extent that I was invited to stay on to do a PhD.

After a year, my Cambridge PhD supervisor Mike Mulkay moved to take a po-

---

7. It took some time to realize that these were actually: "Notes on an Incomprehensible Garfinkel Lecture." As a comparatively junior academic, I was surprised when Garfinkel turned up in Oxford some ten years later and gave exactly the same lecture. A version of it appears in the discussion of "hearably summoning phones" (Garfinkel 2002).

sition at York, "a real university," and suggested I follow him. I joined a "real" department of sociology but headed by a strange bloke called Laurie Taylor, who always seemed to be away in London appearing on the radio and television. Laurie had made his reputation as a leading light in the new wave of sociology of deviance. It was curious to observe some of the more politically radical graduate students at York accusing Laurie of backsliding on issues such as whether or not International Marxist Group should join forces with student movements in open rebellion on the streets. Another newcomer to the department was Paul Drew. Paul taught graduate classes in ethnomethodology and purveyed an especially impressive, well-honed version of skepticism directed at just about every known form of traditional sociological theorizing. This was high church ethnomethodology and conversational analysis at its ascetic best. It involved the articulation of difficult and devastating questions that could be addressed to any conceivable sociological claim. My neophyte attempts at flat denial in the face of sweeping sociological argument now admitted some minor refinement. I learned to ask, "Exactly what do you mean by. . . ?" I also learned that "the social," insofar as it could be said to exist anywhere, was achieved and accomplished as part of the enormous richness and complexity of everyday, ordinary, commonsensical, mundane, practical activities. Paul and I shared a house for a year, during which I struggled over (what I later recognized as) the enormous and profound awkwardness of our everyday, ordinary, commonsensical, and so on exchanges:

> (*Paul is vacuum cleaning the stairs.*)
> ME: What are you doing Paul?
> PAUL (*gives me a fixed stare, five seconds silence, clutching vacuum cleaner*).

Or,

> (*Phone rings*)
> PAUL: (*picking up the phone*). Yes.

There is no question that this, the lived experience of the actual whatness of the everyday, ordinary (etc.) enormously aided my subsequent appreciation of Garfinkel.[8] In particular, it became clear that the famous "breaching experiments" are actually paradigmatic exercises in disobedience. They are awkwardness-

---

8. The technical term for "whatness" is "quiddity."

generating practices that show up our profound reliance on order and structure. The awkwardness arises because they profoundly challenge what we take for granted. And the program that they suggest is in principle unlimited in its potential application to all areas of activity. Arguably, the ontological disobedience at the heart of these and other features of early ethnomethodology has since been lost in the move to institutionalize a formulaic, "scientific" perspective on practical actions. Thus a resulting institutionalized response to what was called traditional sociology is the "science" of conversational analysis. The profound skepticism to be found in early Garfinkel has since been rewritten as a form of merely instrumental disobedience.[9]

My path through ethnomethodology reached its apogee a few years later when I joined the unsung elite who had been "ripped off by Harold." When the great man visited Oxford on sabbatical, he persuaded me that the glittering prizes awaited just those sociologists who could bring to bear a unique perspective on the work of science. My thesis work on the discovery of (radio) pulsars had involved my acquiring, from the American Institute of Physics, an audiotape of the first optical pulsar discovery. The discoverers had unwittingly left the audio channel of their recording equipment running as they tried to make sense of the observations unfolding before them. Through an analysis of the actual whatness of the night's work, Garfinkel explained to me, and in virtue of the unique adequacy of our methods, we would have access to the very kernel of what is special about scientific discovery. He should "get me to California" to work with him and his team on this. I handed over the tape. The next time I heard of it/from him was when he presented a paper on its analysis at a Toronto conference in 1980 (Garfinkel, Lynch, and Livingston 1981).

I had previously met Bruno Latour at the 1976 conference "The Use of Quantitative Methods in the History of Science" in Berkeley. Who knows what either of us was doing at that meeting? I was invited on the strength of my first ever publication, a sustained whine about the theoretical paucity of some contemporary quantitative analyses of science (Gilbert and Woolgar 1974), to speak about the emerging field of social studies of science in the United Kingdom. In the context of the feeling that U.S., predominantly Mertonian-inspired sociology of science,

---

9. While this reading of the radical origins of ethnomethodology is contentious, it is underpinned by the memory of various aphorisms offered to me by Garfinkel along the lines that "everything is programmatics" or that "conversational analysis is the jewel in the crown of ethnomethodology but we don't believe a word of it."

had yet to take seriously the emerging British traditions in the sociology of scientific knowledge, I had entitled my conference paper, with what I imagined to be telling irony, "News from Nowhere." Bruno was there because he was just starting work at the Salk Institute on a project that set out to research the careers of great scientists. I was probably the first person from civilization — by which I mean the world of social studies of science — to visit him there among his tribe. In giving me an initial tour of the laboratory he introduces me to the equipment (not the people) that populates the spaces in and around the laboratory. He gently picks up a pipette and explains to me: "This, they believe, is something that measures what they call a 'volume' of liquid." Such delightful disrespect for the given, such wonderful ethnographic distance, such promise of ontological disobedience!

I had only barely heard of Mary Douglas's (1978) famous distinction. Yet the danger associated with thinking along lines similar to Garfinkel and Latour seemed much more attractive than the aspirations to purity associated with attempts to establish safe explanatory formulas as offered, for example, by the strong program in the sociology of scientific knowledge or SSK. The great disappointment of the latter, it turned out, was that its disobedience led merely to replacing one relatively stable system of explanation with another. Meanwhile, at York, the emerging dynasty of Mike Mulkay's postgraduate students began a series of workshops exploring the dangers of discourse and reflexivity.

On Sustaining Disobedience (and Concealment)

> SIRELLI: You'll forgive my asking, but what do you hope to achieve with all this rigmarole? [10]

This is all very well. My account has thus far offered a few characterizations of "the time," which are loosely tied to my emerging analytic proclivities. I've tried to organize these observations around a distinction between instrumental and ontological disobedience. Are you kidding? Only two kinds of disobedience? Are they really so distinct? Can we so easily categorize some forms of political protest as merely instrumental, and others as dynamic? Can we not argue that the disobedience of musicians is often instrumentalized as part of their marketing? [11]

10. Pirandello [1913] 1962, 24.
11. Come to think of it, just about every Rolling Stones record I've heard includes an instrumental break.

For example, the brothers Gallagher achieved fame to some extent for being disobedient.[12] Artists like Eminem thrive on their reputation for disobedience. But does this kind of notoriety necessitate ontological disobedience? Whether forms of disobedient action and behavior are ontological or instrumental presumably has a lot to do with how these behaviors are appropriated and reformulated. And, in any case, is the nonenduring, finite quality of instrumental disobedience always such a bad thing? What about the clear benefits of temporary disobedience, for example, in the emerging argumentative genre of the "rant" (Osborne 2003)? By contrast, is not enduring disobedience sometimes rather negative; one thinks for example of the embarrassing specter of the Rolling Stones still carrying on after all these years?[13] And is not a key feature of disobedience that responses will vary between audiences and over time? Disobedience for whom, how, and when?

Surely?

So the central question is still left hanging: what origins might eventually lead an aspiring engineer to become a quasi-Garfinkelian archreflexive tropist ontologically disobedient chair of marketing?[14]

To dig a bit deeper we need to follow a different tack: I must now reveal that the biggest influence on my early thinking was undoubtedly the playwright Luigi Pirandello. But to be entirely consistent with the earlier point about the problematic nature of influences, I should make it clear that Luigi didn't realize this at the time. More to the point, nor did I. Indeed, it was only many years later that I realized this influence, when I first met him through a popular revival of his play *Absolutely {Perhaps}* in London's West End.[15]

A popular conception of social action derives from Goffman's (1990) dramaturgical vision of social players on the stage. But Pirandello proposes some very contrasting views. For Pirandello, the settled, fathomable outcome of narrative and plot is anathema. *Absolutely {Perhaps}* is built around two characters, each

12. Thanks to Catelijne Coopmans for reminding me that Oasis released a 1994 album entitled *Definitely maybe*.
13. I owe this example to Daniel Neyland.
14. A yet more central question, of course, if we take seriously anything about ontological disobedience, is how can we begin to address this former question without taking into account the kind of answer with which the person in question would feel comfortable?
15. Written in 1913, *Così e {se vi pare!}* has been variously translated as *And That's the Truth* in 1925; as *Right You Are (If You Think So)* in 1962; as *Absolutely! {Perhaps}* in 2003; and as *Definitely! {Maybe}* in 2004.

of whom says the other is mad. The play revolves around the morally charged efforts of the other characters to settle who is right. The playwright "intrigues us into chasing as excitedly as the neighbors after the solution to the mystery; and he leaves us, as he leaves them, with the mystery returned to [us]" (Browne 1962, 8).

MRS. PONZA: ... I am just whoever you think I am![16]

Pirandello is precisely concerned with the absence of a solution to puzzles about the relation between the act and its underlying reality, between imagination and reality. But this is much more than mere games playing. "Mine is a serious theatre. It requires the total participation of that moral entity — man. It is not comfortable theatre. It is a difficult theatre, even a dangerous one" (Pirandello 1935). By "the total participation of that moral entity — man," I think Pirandello means to articulate and explore situations where there is no escape, no boundaries that can keep the phenomenon being discussed safe, divided off, stable, contained. Indeed, toward the end of the play, several presumed boundaries are shown not to be what they appear. The distinction between actors and audience dissolves when several "members of the audience" start to join in the discussion with those on stage. The distinction between actors and playwright breaks down when it eventually becomes apparent that the central character of the Professor (ahh!) is actually (playing) the playwright. Right at the end, the principles huddle together to form an impenetrable circle around which we now see has flowed the whole course of accusation and counteraccusation of madness, consternation, and irresolution. "I think that life is a very sad piece of buffoonery because we need to deceive ourselves constantly by creating a reality (one for each and never the same for all) which from time to time is discovered to be in vain and illusory" (Pirandello 1935). In Pirandello, then, the instability and unresolvability of the reality/illusion couple is paramount.[17] So Pirandello injects a fluidity and uncertainty into the idea of social action that far surpasses Goffman. A sign of our postmodern times? Well, no, since Pirandello wrote *Absolutely {Perhaps}* in 1913! So was he "ahead of his time"? A postmodernist stuck

16. Pirandello [1913] 1962, 87. Surprisingly, it turns out that Pirandello was also a major influence on Eminem: "I am whatever you say I am" (Eminem, *The Marshall Mathers LP*, Aftermath Ent./Interscope Records, 2000).

17. This is, of course, perfect for a chair of marketing, to whom issues of the relation between reality and illusion are paramount (cf. Woolgar and Simakova 2003).

in the 1900s? Perhaps there is something in this since he is now hailed as a fore-runner of existentialism, the theater of the absurd, and Eugene Ionesco, and direct lines are drawn from him through surrealist comedy to Monty Python.

The importance, then, of Goffman-type models of social action is not (just) that they provide another convenient way for analysts to divide up the world but that, in suggesting that the world is other than it seems, they signal a moment of uncertainty and instability, of suggesting that what seems to be the case is not the case. On the whole, we respond to these moments of uncertainty by trying to get through them as quickly as possible, to get to the other side, to return to a normal order. Indeed, the extent of our dependence on order and normality is indexed by the extent of consternation (alarm, upset, or humor) associated with disruptive moments. But the point of the Pirandellan, as opposed to the Goffman, reading is that we glimpse the possibility of constant consternation and hence appreciate the continual work needed to maintain and renew social order.

Consideration of Pirandello underscores the difference between relatively static (or stipulative) and relatively dynamic (or technographic) models of social action. This difference maps well on to our earlier distinction between instrumental and ontological disobedience. The former stresses stability and certainty, whereas the latter encourages us to emphasize the uncertainties associated with interpretation.

Conclusion

We can conclude that the forms of disobedience that differentially inform our perspectives as social analysts definitely have profound consequences for the nature and kinds of inquiry that we perform. Whereas instrumental disobedience is aimed primarily at the safe displacement of one orthodoxy with another, ontological disobedience (maybe) encourages a much more theoretically dangerous attitude.

If our own (social scientific) theater is one-dimensional, static, predictable, safe, we will doubtless continue to pull in the crowds. Audiences may be attracted, perhaps by the promise of becoming better informed about the nature of the (social) world. But if we also want to make them think, to disturb existing preconceptions and assumptions, our theater will have to espouse a form of disobedience that is much more dynamic, unpredictable, unstable, provocative, and, above all, dangerous. "The audience was outraged at the play's conclusion. They were shocked by it. There had never been an ending like that in the history of drama. It broke all the rules. At the curtain call when the author appeared some of the audience cheered. But some of them yelled obscenities. One irate customer tore his theater seat from its moorings and hurled it onto the stage. It narrowly missed Pirandello's head" (Zeffirelli 2003). Clearly, some members of the audience concluded that the playwright had willfully concealed the very information they were expecting from him.

References

Benn, Tony. 1995. *The Benn Diaries.* London: Arrow Books.

Browne, E. Martin. 1962. Introduction to Luigi Pirandello, *"Right You Are! (If You Think So)," "All for the Best" and "Henry IV."* Edited by E. Martin Browne. London: Penguin Plays.

Douglas, Mary. 1978. *Purity and Danger: An Analysis of the Concepts of Pollution and Taboo.* London: Routledge.

Garfinkel, Harold. 1967. *Studies in Ethnomethodology.* Englewood Cliffs, NJ: Prentice Hall.

———. 2002. *Ethnomethodology's Program: Working out Durkheim's Aphorism.* Oxford: Rowman & Littlefield.

Garfinkel, Harold, Michael Lynch, and Eric Livingston. 1981. "The Work of a Discovering Science Construed with Materials from the Optically Discovered Pulsar." *Philosophy of the Social Sciences* 11:131–58.

Gilbert, G. Nigel, and Steve Woolgar. 1974. "The Quantitative Study of Science: An Examination of the Literature." *Science Studies* 4:279–94.

Goffman, I. 1990. *The Presentation of Self in Everyday Life.* Harmondsworth: Penguin Books.

Herrnstein Smith, Barbara. 1997. "The Unquiet Judge: Activism without Objectivism in Law and Politics." Chap. 1 in *Beliefs and Resistance: Dynamics of Contemporary Intellectual Controversy.* Cambridge, MA: Harvard University Press.

Latour, Bruno. 1991. *We Have Never Been Modern.* Translated by Catherine Porter. London: Harvester Wheatsheaf.

Osborne, Thomas. 2003. "Against Creativity: A Philistine Rant." *Economy and Society* 32 (4): 507–25.

Pirandello, Luigi. 1935. Interview by Franco Zeffirelli. Cited in Franco Zeffirelli, "The Division between Reality and Imagination: Martin Sherman Talks to Franco Zeffirelli about Pirandello," in *Programme Notes for "Absolutely! {perhaps}."* London: Wyndhams Theatre, 2003.

———. [1913] 1962. *"Right You Are! (If You Think So)," "All for the Best" and "Henry IV."* Edited by E. Martin Browne. London: Penguin Plays.

Pollner, Mel. 1991. "Left of Ethnomethodology: The Rise and Decline of Radical Reflexivity." *American Sociological Review* 56 (3): 370–80.

Woolgar, Steve, and Elena Simakova. 2003. "Marketing Marketing." Paper presented to Skebo Workshop on Marketing Practices, Sweden, June 15.

Zeffirelli, Franco. 2003. "The Division between Reality and Imagination: Martin Sherman Talks to Franco Zeffirelli about Pirandello." In *Programme Notes for "Absolutely! {perhaps}."* London: Wyndhams Theatre.

Falling into Marxism; Choosing to Stay

Erik Olin Wright received his PhD from the University of California, Berkeley, and has taught at the University of Wisconsin since then. His academic work has been centrally concerned with reconstructing the Marxist tradition of social theory and research in ways that attempt to make it more relevant to contemporary concerns and more cogent as a scientific framework of analysis. His empirical research has focused especially on the changing character of class relations in developed capitalist societies. Since 1992 he has directed the Real Utopias Project, which explores a range of proposals for new institutional designs that embody emancipatory ideals and yet are attentive to issues of pragmatic feasibility. His principle publications include The Politics of Punishment: A Critical Analysis of Prisons in America; Class, Crisis and the State; Classes; *Reconstructing Marxism (with Elliott Sober and Andrew Levine);* Interrogating Inequality; Class *Counts: Comparative Studies in Class Analysis; and* Deepening Democracy: Innovations in Empowered Participatory Governance *(with Archon Fung). He is married to Marcia Kahn Wright, a clinical psychologist working in community mental health, and has two grown daughters, Jennifer and Rebecca.*

I have been in school continuously for more than fifty years: since I entered kindergarten in 1952, there has never been a September when I wasn't beginning a school year. I have never held a nine-to-five job with fixed hours and a boss telling me what to do. In high school, my summers were always spent in various kinds of interesting and engaging activities — traveling home from Australia where my family spent a year (my parents were Fulbright professors at the University of Western Australia); music camp (I played viola); assisting in a lab. And in college, it was much the same: volunteering as a photographer on an archaeological dig in Hawaii; teaching in a high school enrichment program for minority kids; traveling in Europe. The closest thing to an ordinary paying job I ever had was occasionally selling hot dogs at football games in my freshman year in college. What is more, the ivory towers that I have inhabited since the mid-1960s have been located in beautiful physical settings, filled with congenial and interesting colleagues and students, and animated by exciting ideas. This, then, is the first fundamental fact of my life as an academic: I have been extraordinarily lucky and have always lived what can only be considered a life of extreme privilege. Nearly all of the time I am doing what I want to do; what I do gives me a sense of fulfillment and purpose; and I am paid well for doing it.

Here is the second fundamental fact of my academic life: since the early 1970s, my intellectual life has been firmly anchored in the Marxist tradition. The core of my teaching as a professor has centered on communicating the central ideas and debates of contemporary Marxism and allied traditions of emancipatory social theory. The courses I have taught have had names like Class, State and Ideology: An Introduction to Marxist Sociology; Envisioning Real Utopias; Marxist Theories of the State; Alternative Foundations of Class Analysis. My energies in institution building have all involved creating and expanding arenas within which radical system-challenging ideas could flourish: creating a graduate program in class analysis and historical change in the Sociology Department at the University of Wisconsin–Madison; establishing the A. E. Havens Center, a research institute for critical scholarship at Wisconsin; organizing an annual conference for activists and academics, now called RadFest, which has been held every year since 1983. And my scholarship has been primarily devoted to reconstructing Marxism as a theoretical framework and research tradition. While the substantive preoccupations of this scholarship have shifted over the past thirty years, its central mission has not.

As in any biography, this pair of facts is the result of a trajectory of circumstances and choices: circumstances that formed me and shaped the range of choices I encountered, and choices that in turn shaped my future circumstances. Some of these choices were made easily, with relatively little weighing of alternatives, sometimes even without much awareness that a choice was actually being made; others were the result of protracted reflection and conscious decision making, sometimes with the explicit understanding that the choice being made would constrain possible choices in the future. Six such junctures of circumstance and choice seem especially important to me in shaping the contours of my academic career. The first was posed incrementally in the early 1970s: the choice to identify my work primarily as contributing to Marxism rather than simply using Marxism. The second concerns the choice, made just before graduate school at the University of California, Berkeley, to be a sociologist, rather than some other *ist*. The third was the choice to become what some people describe as multivariate Marxist: to be a Marxist sociologist who engages in grandiose, perhaps overblown, quantitative research. The fourth choice was the choice of which academic department to be in. This choice was acutely posed to me in 1987 when I spent a year as a visiting professor at the University of California, Berkeley. I had been offered a position there, and I had to decide whether I wanted to return to Wisconsin. Returning to Madison was unquestionably a choice that shaped subsequent contexts of choice. The fifth choice has been posed and reposed to me with increasing intensity since the late 1980s: the choice to stay a Marxist in this world of post-Marxisms when many of my intellectual comrades have decided for various good, and sometimes perhaps not so good, reasons to recast their intellectual agenda as being perhaps friendly to, but outside of, the Marxist tradition. Finally, the sixth important choice was to shift my central academic work from the study of class structure to the problem of envisioning real utopias.

To set the stage for this reflection on choice and constraint, I need to give a brief account of the circumstances of my life that brought me into the arena of these choices.

Growing Up

I was born in Berkeley, California, in 1947 while my father, who had received a PhD in psychology before World War II, was in medical school on the GI Bill. When he finished his medical training in 1951, we moved to Lawrence, Kansas, where he became the head of the program in clinical psychology at Kansas University (KU) and a professor of psychiatry in the KU Medical School. Because of antinepotism rules at the time, my mother, who also had a PhD in psychology, was not allowed to be employed at the university, so throughout the 1950s she did research on various research grants. In 1961, when the state law on such things changed, she became a professor of rehabilitation psychology.

Life in my family was intensely intellectual. Dinner table conversation would often revolve around intellectual matters, and my parents were always deeply enthusiastic and involved in their children's school projects and intellectual pursuits. My mother would carefully go over term papers with each of us, giving us both editorial advice and substantive suggestions. We were members of the Lawrence Unitarian Fellowship, which was made up of, to a substantial extent, university families. Sunday morning services were basically interdisciplinary seminars on matters of philosophical and social concern; Sunday school was an extended curriculum on world religions. I knew by about age ten that I wanted to be a professor. Both of my parents were academics. Both of my siblings became academics. Both of their spouses are academics. (Only my wife, a clinical psychologist, is not an academic, although her father was a professor.) The only social mobility in my family was interdepartmental. It just felt natural to go into the family business.

Lawrence was a delightful, easy place to grow up. Although Kansas was a politically conservative state, Lawrence was a vibrant, liberal community. My earliest form of political activism centered on religion: I was an active member of a Unitarian youth group called Liberal Religious Youth, and in high school I went out of my way to argue with Bible Belt Christians about their belief in God. The early 1960s also witnessed my earliest engagement with social activism. The civil rights movement came to Lawrence first in the form of an organized boycott of a local segregated swimming pool in the 1950s and then in the form of civil rights rallies in the 1960s. In 1963 I went to the Civil Rights March on Washington and heard Martin Luther King Jr.'s "I have a dream" speech. My earliest sense of politics was that at its core it was about moral questions of social justice, not problems of economic power and interests.

My family, also, was liberal, supporting the civil rights movement and other liberal causes; but while the family culture encouraged an intellectual interest in social and moral concerns, it was not intensely political. We would often talk about values, and the Unitarian Fellowship we attended also stressed humanistic, socially concerned values, but these were mostly framed as matters of individual responsibility and morality not as the grounding of a coherent political challenge to social injustice. My only real exposure to a more radical political perspective came through my maternal grandparents, Russian Jewish immigrants who had come to the United States before World War I and lived near us in Lawrence, and my mother's sister's family in New York. Although I was not aware of this at the time, my grandparents and the New York relatives were Communists. This was never openly talked about, but from time to time I would hear glowing things said about the Soviet Union, socialism would be held out as an ideal, and

America and capitalism would be criticized in emotionally laden ways. My cousins in New York were especially vocal about this, and in the mid-1960s when I became more engaged in political matters, intense political discussions with my New York relatives contributed significantly to anchoring my radical sensibilities.

My interest in social sciences began in earnest in high school. In Lawrence it was easy for academically oriented kids to take courses at the University of Kansas, and in my senior year I took a political science course on American politics. For my term project I decided to do a survey of children's attitudes toward the American presidency and got permission to administer a questionnaire to several hundred students from grades 1–12 in the public schools. I then organized a party with my friends to code the data and produce graphs of how various attitudes changed by age. The most striking finding was that, in response to the question, "Would you like to be President of the United States when you grow up?" there were more girls who said yes than boys through third grade, after which the rate for girls declined dramatically.

By the time I graduated from high school in 1964, I had enough university credits and advanced placement credits to enter KU as a second-semester sophomore, and that is what I had planned to do. Nearly all of my friends were going to KU. It just seemed like the thing to do. A friend of my parents, Karl Heider, gave me, as a Christmas present in my senior year in high school, an application form to Harvard. He was a graduate student at Harvard in anthropology at the time. I filled it out and sent it in. Harvard was the only place to which I applied, not out of inflated self-confidence but because it was the only application I got as a Christmas present. When I eventually was accepted (initially I was on the waiting list), the choice was thus between KU and Harvard. I suppose this was a "choice" since I could have decided to stay at KU. However, it just seemed so obvious; there was no angst, no weighing of alternatives, no thinking about the pros and cons. Thus, going to Harvard in a way just happened.

Like many students who began university in the mid-1960s, my political ideas were rapidly radicalized as the Viet Nam War escalated and began to impinge on our lives. I was not a student leader in activist politics, but I did actively participate in demonstrations, rallies, fasts for peace, and endless political debate. At Harvard I majored in social studies, an intense interdisciplinary social science major centering on the classics of social theory, and in that program I was first exposed to the more abstract theoretical issues that bore on the political concerns of the day: the dynamics of capitalism, the nature of power and domination, the importance of elites in shaping American foreign policy, and the problem of class and social change. I found all of this intellectually exciting, and wrote numerous term papers on these kinds of macrosociological issues, but these themes did not constitute for me an overriding intellectual preoccupation as an undergraduate. I wrote my senior thesis not on problems of political economy, classes, and the state but on a social psychological theme: the causes and effects of student leaves of absence from universities. I conducted a survey on this problem and analyzed the data using punchcards in order to understand the conditions under which leaves of absence would have a positive or negative impact on the students involved. The thesis was well received, but one would be hard put to find any hint of radical sensibilities in it.

As graduation approached in 1968 I faced a problem confronted by most healthy American males of the time: how to cope with the prospect of being drafted. It was impossible to get a conscientious objector deferment from my draft board in Kansas since I could not prove that I was a long-standing member of a pacifist religious group. I knew people who become expatriates, and others who were prepared to go to jail rather than be drafted. I was unwilling to make either of these sacrifices. Instead, I decided to enroll in a Unitarian seminary — the Starr King School for the Ministry in Berkeley — and thus get a ministerial deferment. I enrolled in the seminary not out of a deep and abiding commitment to the ministry as a possible vocation — that never occurred to me as something I would actually do — but because it was the only way I could think of at the time to keep out of the army in the context of the Viet Nam War. The enrollments at seminaries, especially in Unitarian seminaries, increased dramatically in the late sixties. When I received a scholarship to study history at Balliol College, Oxford, I therefore organized a way to be formally enrolled in the seminary while taking courses at Oxford. I made a point of specializing in the English Puritan Revolution under the tutorship of Christopher Hill so that if the draft board ever questioned this arrangement I could show that I was studying something connected to religion.

After two extraordinary years of wallowing in intellectual pleasures at Oxford, I returned in the fall of 1970 to the United States and entered the Unitarian Seminary in Berkeley. This is when the decisive choices through which my academic identity would be forged began.

Becoming a Marxist: Accountability and Eclecticism

When I entered the seminary I was already quite radicalized intellectually and politically. The general terms of political debate in England were more permeated with Marxian-inspired ideas than was generally the case in the United States. At Oxford, under the stimulating guidance of Steven Lukes, I had read much more thoroughly a range of Marxist work than I had earlier and wrote a series of papers on various Marxist themes, including my first paper on the problem of class. Still, in 1970 I would not have said that the central focus of my scholarly work was the reconstruction of Marxist approaches to understanding social and political questions. That changed in the course of the next few years.

At the seminary I had two crucial formative experiences. First, I initiated and then led a seminar at the Berkeley Graduate Theological Union called Utopia and Revolution. Fifteen or so students from various seminaries participated in the seminar in which we read and energetically debated socialist, Marxist, anarchist, and various strands of utopian literature. This was the first extended academic context in which I was involved where the primary motivation was not simply the scholarly task of clarifying ideas and weighing the intellectual merits of arguments but, rather, sorting out our political vision and thinking about how to connect our concrete activities to a broad agenda of social change. The seminar was an exhilarating experience. Thirty years later I still teach a graduate seminar in the same spirit—Envisioning Real Utopias.

The second critical experience was a year-long internship as a student chaplain at San Quentin Prison. Every week I would drive from Berkeley to the prison north of San Francisco and spend the day in the Protestant chaplain's office talking to prisoners. This was the height of the militant period of the Black Panthers, and many black prisoners in San Quentin were highly politicized. When prisoners would come to me and ask me to pray with them, I would send them to the real chaplain saying that he was better at that. Very quickly it became known among prisoners that I was a sympathetic ear for political discussions, both about the conditions in the prison and about broader issues in American society. Through the prisoners I met, I became involved in an activist organization called the Prison Law Project, which linked radical, mainly black, prisoners with left-wing lawyers and was devoted to challenging prison conditions through litigation and other forms of activism. In the context of my work with the Prison Law Project and my role in the prison, I decided with my friends in the project to write a book about San Quentin, which eventually became published as the *Politics of Punishment* in 1973, about half of which was written by myself, and the rest by prisoners and others connected with the Prison Law Project.

The Politics of Punishment was by far the most ambitious piece of writing I had ever attempted. I remember when the book was finally done saying that my respect for even very bad books had increased since I now knew how much work they entailed. Writing the book was also the first context in which I had to navigate the analytical imperatives of serious scholarly exposition with the political imperatives of popular accessibility and political relevance. I discovered that I could do academic work that was not just fun intellectually but that had moral and political aspirations as well.

In January 1971, the rules of military conscription changed and a lottery replaced the previous system. When the first lottery was conducted, I received a good number—somewhere above 250 as I recall—and since the expectation was that no one with a number above the low 100s would be drafted in 1971, I gave up my seminary student deferment and decided to enter graduate school in sociology.

Although I was formally enrolled as a graduate student in the Berkeley Sociology Department, the real core of my intellectual formation occurred in what might be called the Bay Area Student Run University of Radical Intellectual Thought. Almost from the start, I was heavily involved in a series of organizations and activities that brought radical students together across departments within the University of California and across universities within driving distance:

- I regularly attended a Bay Area–wide political economy seminar loosely linked to the Union for Radical Political Economics that usually met at Stanford in which problems in Marxist political economy were discussed. Over the years, I presented a number of papers in that seminar, including the earliest version of my work on rethinking the concept of class. At one seminar I laid out the problem of the "middle class" in which I described the class location of managers as ambiguous because of the way they combined relational attributes both of workers (they did not own the means of production) and of capitalists (they dominated other employees). Brigit O'Laughlin, an anthropologist at Stanford, suggested that these kinds of locations might better be thought of as contradictory rather than merely ambiguous, and thus the term for my contribution to the analysis of the middle class was born: contradictory locations within class relations.
- I was part of the founding editorial collective of *Kapitalistate*, a journal devoted to debates over Marxist theories of the state organized by the Marxist economist James O'Connor, then at San Jose State University. The collective involved students and unattached intellectuals from all over the San Francisco Bay Area and, through reading and commenting on papers, it linked us to students in Eu-

rope (especially Germany) and other places in the United States (especially Wisconsin). Through my involvement in the journal collective, I read a paper on state theory written by Roger Friedland and Gosta-Esping Anderson, at the time sociology graduate students at the University of Wisconsin, sent them detailed comments, and ended up coauthoring with them the final published version of the paper. Through them I became linked to students at Wisconsin and began to think of the Wisconsin Sociology Department as an exciting place.

• I was heavily involved in founding an organization of socialist-oriented academics called the Union of Marxist Social Scientists, which was organized to increase dialogue among activists and left-oriented academics. Its main activity was an annual conference held each spring at a summer camp called Camp Gold Hollow in the Sierra foothills, which was attended by several hundred people from up and down the West Coast. By the mid-1970s this conference became a politically charged venue in which students, a scattering of faculty, grassroots activists, and militants from various sectarian Marxist-Leninist quasi-parties gathered to debate theoretical and political matters. At the last camp I attended, in the spring of 1976, my work on social class was denounced in a large meeting by members of the League for Proletarian Socialism (a self-styled Maoist group) for reflecting "petty bourgeois socialism." That annual conference is the direct ancestor of RadFest.

• In order to enable students to get formal academic credit for the kinds of study groups in which we were involved, I convinced a number of faculty members in the Berkeley Sociology Department to act as passive sponsors of a series of student-organized on-going graduate seminars exploring debates in radical theory. One of these — Current Controversies in Marxist Social Science — met continuously for four or five semesters and formed the basis for several courses I subsequently taught when I became a professor.

Through these activities I discovered that there existed an on-going, energetic intellectual tradition in which one could be a radical critic and engage in careful, rigorous, intellectually sophisticated academic work. The attraction was as much intellectual as political. The debates were exciting and demanding. When we read Louis Althusser, Nicos Poulantzas, Elmar Altvatar, Perry Anderson, Claus Offe, Antonio Gramsci, Jürgen Habermas, James O'Connor, Barry Hindiss and Paul Hurst, Goran Therborn, and the other writers in the Marxist renaissance we felt we were at the cutting edge of ideas, really learning something important and gaining depth. These texts were usually hard, and it took work to sort them out, but this also was part of the attraction: we were not doing something easy. There were many people joined together in the effort, and the dialogue created a sense of common purpose and community.

Some people in these circles were deeply involved in self-styled Marxist, Marxist-Leninist, Maoist, or Trotskyist parties, but most were not. Generally, most people in my intellectual circle saw party activists as disruptive, as infusing self-righteous dogmatic styles of argument into theoretical debates. Many of us were or had been activists in specific movements — the antiwar movement, the student movement, the prison rights movement — but above all, this intellectual community was academic: mostly graduate students and a few faculty engaged in the project of forging a new Marxist social science in the university.

That the intellectual anchor of debates in this community was Marxist, there can be no doubt. Still, not everyone who participated in these activities called themselves Marxist. Among radical intellectuals of the early 1970s many people saw their work as drawing from the Marxist tradition or being inspired in various ways by that tradition without defining their central goal as contributing to the reconstruction of Marxism. One can use Marxism without being a Marxist.

Most of what I have published, if you strip away the rhetorical parts that proclaim how the work tries to contribute to Marxism, could almost as well have been written in the softer spirit of having a Marxist inspiration. I could have framed my arguments by saying something like "the Marxist tradition is a rich and interesting source of ideas. We can learn a lot from it. Let's see where we can go by taking these traditional notions of class and massaging them, changing them, combining them with Weberian and other elements in various ways." I could have cast my class analysis this way without invoking any commitment to Marxism per se as a tradition worth reconstructing.

Many sociologists in the late 1960s and early 1970s, radical intellectuals of my generation, made that kind of choice. Consider Theda Skocpol's early work, especially *States and Social Revolutions*. This book could have been written as a Marxist work with no real change in any substantive thesis. It could have been written as a book that was amending and reconstructing certain weaknesses in the Marxist tradition, particularly its inattention to the problem of state capacity and state breakdown, in order to rebuild and strengthen that tradition. Instead she chose, for reasons that she would have to explain in her own set of intellectual and personal coordinates, to treat the book as a dialogue with the Marxist tradition but firmly, rhetorically, outside it. I made the opposite choice. The question is, why did I do this, what was my thinking behind it?

Let me give you a vignette that I think helps to reveal what's at issue here. In 1986 I gave a talk in Warsaw called "Rethinking Once Again, Alas, the Marxist Concept of Class." In the talk, I discussed such things as contradictory class locations, exploitation in Soviet-type postcapitalistic society, the role of control over different kinds of assets for constructing new kinds of exploitation, and so on. Afterward, the first question was the following: "Professor Wright, I find your ideas very interesting and very compelling. I think there is a lot to be discussed about them, but why do you call this *Marxist*? Why deflect attention from what you are really talking about by saying that this has anything to do with Marxism?" What is at issue here is a dramatic difference in the contexts for pursuing radical intellectual work. In the Polish context of 1986, to declare that this was a reconstruction of Marxism meant something utterly different from what the same words mean when they are declared in the context of American sociology. In Poland, to reconstruct Marxism in the 1980s was to salvage an ideology of state repression. In the United States, to embed one's work in a rhetoric of reconstructing Marxism means, in contrast, to declare one's solidarity with struggles against capitalism, class inequality and oppression.

Thus, I think the first motivation behind the declaration of my work as contributing to Marxism centers on a point in the sociology of knowledge. What does it mean to define one's work as integral to an oppositional current within an established set of institutions? This is very close to what sociologists talk about when they talk about "reference groups." What really was at stake to me was the nature of the constituency or audience to whom I wanted to feel accountable. Whose criticisms did I want to worry about, and whose did I want to simply be able to dismiss?

These psychological issues are an important part of what is at stake in making the choice to see my work as embedded in the Marxist tradition, as contributing to the reconstruction of that tradition rather than simply drawing on it. Defining my work this way establishes to whom I am accountable, whose opinions are going to matter. The issue of reference group, however, is not just psychological, since reference groups are also social networks that dispose of real resources and impose real pressures of various kinds. Choosing a reference group, then, has the effect of creating a set of constraints that one faces in the future.

In the decision to describe my work as contributing to Marxism, then, there is a kind of Ulysses and the Siren story at work (to use a metaphor elaborated by Jon Elster). It is an attempt, however imperfect, at blocking certain pressures of co-optation that one experiences once one enters a profession. It is an attempt to make life more difficult for oneself. The same holds true for feminist sociologists today. Some feminists say that their work is contributing to feminism as such. Rather that just contributing to sociology inspired by feminism, they see their work as contributing to building feminist theory. Such declarations make life more difficult, since you could say most of the same things without framing your agenda in this more provocative manner. Making one's life more difficult in this way, however, is not a sign of masochism; it is a strategy that makes it harder to slide inadvertently into a theoretical and intellectual practice that is overwhelmed by its professional acceptability. The pressures for mild, nonconfrontational, acceptable scholarship are enormous, and situating one's work firmly in a radical oppositional current is one way of partially neutralizing those pressures.

There is another side to the choice to contribute to building Marxism as an intellectual tradition rather than simply using it that entered my own decisions and that has become increasingly important in my subsequent on-going decision to stay in Marxism rather than to become, as is more fashionable these days, post-Marxist. This second aspect of the choice raises issues in philosophy of science rather than sociology of knowledge. What is the best way to contribute to the enhancement of our knowledge of social life? Is the most productive strategy to work within what one considers the best available paradigm, or is it better to take a more eclectic approach, avoiding any strong commitment to a single perspective but instead picking and choosing from different traditions as is appropriate for different particular questions one might ask? In a somewhat overstylized way we can contrast two stances toward these issues: a stance that places great value on ambitious programs for theoretical coherence and integration in the form of a sustained paradigm and a stance, sometimes referred to as a more empiricist approach, that argues that what we want to do is deeply and intensively describe the world while eclectically drawing from different sorts of ideas as we see fit for different problems.

My view on this contrast of intellectual practices is not the conventional one for someone who is committed to a paradigmatic view of knowledge in his own work. Most people who are committed to some kind of effort at building strong paradigms are antieclectic: eclecticism is viewed as the enemy of paradigm building. I believe, to the contrary, that there is a constructive symbiotic relationship between paradigm-mongers and carefree eclectics. The optimal intellectual terrain for radical theory — or for any sociological knowledge, for that matter — is a mixture of people who are committed eclectics and people who are committed paradigmists. If I could snap my fingers and make every radical intellectual a committed Marxist, I wouldn't do it. I think it would be bad for Marxism and certainly bad for the Left. If I could snap my fingers and make everybody a committed eclectic, if that's not an oxymoron, I would also not do it. Eclecticism is in a certain sense parasitic on committed paradigms. To be an effective eclectic, there must be other scholars around who are worrying obsessively about how to rebuild paradigms and maintain the maximum coherence possible within them. But if that's what everyone did, it would be a constraint on the possibility of effectively reconstructing paradigms because the puzzles and worries and anomalies that a reconstructive project faces often come from the insights generated by the eclectics.

The environment of intellectual work that I see as optimal, and that I try to achieve to the extent possible in the intellectual settings within which I work, thus values an intellectual pluralism in which no one is holier-than-thou about metatheoretical principles. Dialogue between the doubts of the eclectics and the commitments of the paradigmists strengthen both. These issues hold for contemporary feminism as well as Marxism. In the feminist tradition radical feminism is crucial for healthy feminism, even though I think radical feminism is not the most plausible version of feminism. Still, it would be a shame for the feminist tradition if radical feminists were somehow persuaded to abandon the most radical and extreme forms of feminism. Similarly for the socialist tradition of intellectual work, it is important to have a body of scholarship and intellectual work that remains committed to rebuilding rather than simply drawing from the Marxist tradition.

Becoming a Sociologist: Fuzzy Disciplines and Intellectual Pluralism

The second choice in the early 1970s that helped forge my academic identity was the fateful decision to become a sociologist. When I entered sociology, I saw it more as a platform on which to do my work than as a discipline to which I felt any commitment as such (although I have to admit that over time my sense of loyalty to the field has grown considerably). As an undergraduate I majored in an interdisciplinary social science program (social studies), after which I studied history for two years at Oxford. I currently participate actively in an academic network sponsored by the MacArthur Foundation in which most participants are economists, and since 1975 I have been on the editorial board of the journal *Pol-*

itics and Society, which has stronger roots in political science than in sociology. I see myself as a social scientist and social theorist rather than a capital S Sociologist. Why, then, did I choose sociology as an academic home?

Of all the social sciences, sociology seemed to me to be the least disciplinary; it had the fuzziest boundaries. But even more significantly, sociology has valued its own marginal traditions in a way that other social sciences don't. Even anti-Marxist sociologists recognize the importance of Marx as one of the intellectual founders of what has become sociology. All graduate courses in theory contain at least some reading of Marx. There are economics departments in which the name Marx would never be mentioned. The only social science discipline that might have served as well as sociology was political science, and I suppose if I had been at some other university I might have become a political scientist. But at Berkeley I felt that sociology was a more congenial place in which to be a radical, and in general I now think political science tends to be somewhat less hospitable to radicalism because of the tight relationship between political science and the state. Political science is a breeding place for government advisers and policy analysts, and that aspect of political science as a discipline would be a constraint that I did not want to choose. So, I chose sociology.

Becoming a Multivariate Marxist: Legitimating Marxism and Careerism

Very quickly in graduate school, even in a place like Berkeley, it becomes clear where the intellectual core of sociology as a discipline lies. Having decided to be a sociologist and having as a mission the reconstruction of Marxism as social science, I saw a crucial task of my work as trying to increase the credibility of Marxism within the academy, and I felt that quantitative research was a good way to accomplish this. As I wrote in 1987, reflecting on my early theoretical ambitions: "I originally had visions of glorious paradigm battles, with lances drawn and the valiant Marxist knight unseating the bourgeois rival in a dramatic quantitative joust. What is more, the fantasy saw the vanquished admitting defeat and changing horses as a result"

My decision to launch a series of projects involving large-scale data gathering and sophisticated statistical analysis was not driven by any epistemological conviction that these techniques generated deeper insights or more reliable knowledge. Indeed, on that score I have generally found that I learn more from good qualitative and historical research than from quantitative research. But I felt that, at that point in the history of Marxism in sociology (the mid-1970s), establishing the credibility of Marxism using a quantitative methodology had the greatest chance of making a difference in the intellectual space Marxists could occupy within the academy. I also just like playing with numbers and was pretty good at it.

This decision to pursue quantitative research was also bound up with particular personal relations in graduate school. My closest friend at Berkeley was an Italian student, Luca Perrone. Luca was a sophisticated European intellectual, at ease with the various theoretical currents of left-wing thought, but also enthusiastic about quantitative research. He was the perfect kindred spirit with whom to forge a quantitatively oriented Marxist research program. My first publication engaged with Marxism was written with Luca, a long theoretical essay published in Italian in 1973 comparing the conception of the state and politics in the work of Talcott Parsons and Nicos Poulantzas, and subsequently, my first quantitative publications in class analysis, including my first *American Sociological Review* (ASR) article in 1977, were also written jointly with him. As we approached the end of our time together in Berkeley we wanted to concoct a long-term project that would enable us to continue working together—a project that would bring me regularly to Europe and Luca to the United States. A large well-funded cross-national quantitative study on social class seemed a good way to do this. Tragically, Luca died in a skindiving accident in 1981 and, thus, did not live to see the results of our early collaboration.

To be honest, there was also, from the start, a darker side to the appeal of quantitative research. All academic disciplines, as institutions, contain a system of rewards and sanctions that channels work in particular directions, and there were clearly more resources to be had through quantitative research. I was very ambitious as a young scholar—ambitious in my search for what I considered to be the "truth," but also ambitious for status, recognition, influence, world travel. Embarking on a line of research anchored in conventional survey research thus offered tangible rewards.

I cannot reconstruct exactly what the balance of these motives were in the mid-1970s when I did my dissertation research, a quantitative study of class structure and income determination, or in the late 1970s when I began my twenty-year comparative project on class structure and class consciousness. But whatever the balance between grantsmanship and intellectual purpose, the choice to direct my research in this way was enormously consequential, and not always in ways to my liking. It resulted in a narrowing of askable questions and a divergence between much of my best theoretical work and my empirical research. Originally, the idea in 1978 when I began the comparative class-analysis project was to do a survey of class structure and class consciousness in the United States, Italy, and Sweden. This was meant to be a brush-cleaning operation: settling and clarifying a range of empirical issues before returning to the problems I cared about the most—the state, politics, social change. But quickly the project expanded as scholars in various other countries asked to join the research, leading eventually to surveys more or less replicated in more than a dozen countries. This enlarged scale of the enterprise created a set of expectations and commitments that could not be easily (or responsibly) abandoned, and yet the work did not always yield intellectual insights in proportion to the time and resources the project absorbed.

Choosing a Department: Professional versus Intellectual Sociology

I initially went to the University of Wisconsin without a great deal of thought and deliberation. Through my involvement in *Kapitalistate*, I had made friends with a number of graduate students there, and through them various faculty in the department became aware of my work even before I was on the job market. In 1975, I was asked by the department to apply for an assistant professorship and was quickly offered a job even before I went for an interview, so I never really went on a national job search to explore all options. In 1987, however, I was offered a job at the University of California in Berkeley and spent a year there "trying it out." By the spring of 1988, I was clearly faced with a genuine, unmistakable choice, a choice laden with "road not taken" potentials.

Here is how, at the time, I characterized the big difference between these two departments in the late 1980s. If you think of the famous people in the Berkeley department what comes to mind are titles of books: *TVA and the Grass Roots, Alienation and Freedom, Habits of the Heart, Mothering.* When you think of the famous people in the Wisconsin department what comes to mind is the journals in which they publish, the topics that they pursue, the datasets they have developed: the *ASR* and *American Journal of Sociology*, mobility and status attainment, the Wisconsin Longitudinal Study, log-linear analysis. Wisconsin was an article-writing department and Berkeley a book-writing department.

This contrast between the two departments is also reflected in the nature of their graduate programs: at Wisconsin a significant number of graduate students write dissertations that are spin-offs in one way or another from large, on-going research projects. The model of education is that of an apprenticeship, and while students are expected to do original and innovative work, many do so within the context of some professor's research shop. At Berkeley, it is quite rare for students to play this apprenticeship role. Students are expected to be autonomous intellectuals; dissertations are supposed to be first drafts of books; it is rare that dissertations are in any direct way derivative from the data and projects of their advisers.

In agonizing about the choice of where to be, I stylized the contrast between these two settings by saying that Berkeley was one of the leading intellectual departments in which I would be on the discipline-oriented wing, whereas Wisconsin was one of the leading discipline-oriented departments in which I would be on the intellectual wing. Which of these settings, I thought, do I want to be in? Which would provide the most creative context for my future work? The irony was that although I actually found the intellectual climate of Berkeley more comfortable in many ways than that of Wisconsin, I felt that I would be more challenged and pushed in more interesting ways if I was more an intellectual maverick in a disciplinary department than a disciplinary maverick in an intellectualized one. I felt that at that point in history and at that point in my life, perhaps, the creative tension would be more constructive in Madison. At Berkeley I would be constantly contending with postmodernist currents that argued for the centrality of culture for everything and the impossibility of explaining anything. In Madison I would be arguing for the importance of an open and dialectical perspective on the relationship between social change and social action and the need for unconventional voices in sociology. So, I returned to Wisconsin, although I have retained close ties to Berkeley and frequently return to give talks.

In the years since that choice, the two departments have converged somewhat. I recently did a ministudy of dissertations done at Wisconsin and Berkeley since the 1960s in order to better characterize the two departments. Berkeley has been fairly consistent over the entire period: 75–90 percent of dissertations in each decade used qualitative methods. At Wisconsin there has been a sharp change: from the 1960s through the 1980s, roughly 70–80 percent of dissertations were quantitative. In the 1990s this dropped to just over 50 percent. This methodological shift in dissertation research reflects a change in the composition of faculty and, more broadly, in the intellectual culture of the Wisconsin department.

Staying a Marxist

When I became politically radicalized and first began my intellectual work in the late 1960s, Marxism really was the only game in town: if you were a serious intellectual and really wanted to develop theoretical groundings for radical critique of the status quo, in some way or another you had to find a home in or make peace with the Marxist tradition, whether or not you then used the label as a self-designation. Marxist theorizing was at the cutting edge of sophisticated intellectual debate, and, while Marxism never became part of the academic mainstream, there was a certain intellectual cachet in calling oneself a Marxist within the academy. In sociology, Marxism was treated as a real rival to more mainstream traditions, so even though most sociologists disagreed with me, I felt that my ideas were taken seriously.

Beginning in the mid-1980s and accelerating in the 1990s, Marxism became increasingly marginal to academic life and intellectual debate. It is not that Marxist ideas have disappeared — many in fact have become absorbed into the mainstream — but rather that Marxism as an intellectual terrain is no longer the site of wide-ranging, energetic, innovative theoretical work. Particularly since the "fall of Communism," to many people Marxism now seems an archaic discourse, and discussions of exploitation, class struggle, revolution, and socialism seem faintly ridiculous rather than hard-edged, nuanced challenges to the status quo. Many radical intellectuals who, in the early 1980s, firmly identified their own work with Marxism now no longer do so. They have not necessarily become self-described ex-Marxists and certainly not rabid anti-Marxists — as happened in the 1950s when the exit from Marxism was deeply bound up with anti-Communism — but they do longer see the reconstruction of Marxism as a pressing, or even relevant, task.

I have remained stubbornly working inside of Marxism and continue to work for the reconstruction rather than abandonment of this intellectual tradition. I do so, above all, because I continue to believe that many of the core ideas of this tradition are indispensable for any project of emancipatory social change. Specifically, the diagnosis of capitalism as a system of oppression built around class and exploitation, and the normative vision of a radically egalitarian democratic alternative to capitalism, are fundamental insights integral to Marxism. While I no longer see Marxism as a comprehensive theoretical paradigm capable of constituting a general theory of history and society, I still believe that the Marxist tradition contains a coherent framework of ideas that can provide a solid grounding for a socially engaged research program.

I have not, however, pursued this goal simply as an individual project of my own. To sustain these commitments and the hope to accomplish these goals requires embedding oneself in a particular set of social networks, a particular circle of people whose work one reads, with whom one discusses issues, and whose judgments matter. A reference group is not just an impersonal audience defined by some social category; it is also a circle of people with names and addresses who constitute the active, ongoing basis for the intellectual interactions and support that spur one's own intellectual development.

In my case, there are two such concrete reference groups that have anchored my work since the 1970s. The first is a group of scholars that was at the core of an intellectual current known as analytical Marxism in the 1980s. The group has a less high-blown name that it gave to itself: the NBSMG — the No-Bullshit Marxism Group. The NBSMG is a group of a dozen or so philosophers, economists, sociologists, political scientists, and historians from five countries that has met every September in London, Oxford, or New York for a three-day conference from 1979 to 2000 (and, since then, once every two years). Many of the names associated with the NBSMG over the past two decades are relatively familiar — Pranhab Bardhan, Sam Bowles, Robert Brenner, G. A. Cohen, Josh Cohen, Jon Elster, Adam Przeworski, John Roemer, Hillel Steiner, Robert van der Veen, and Philippe van Parijs.

The term "analytical" in analytical Marxism reflects its central intellectual style: bringing the concern with conceptual precision, clarity, and rigor that is characteristic of analytical philosophy to bear on Marxian themes. Substantively, the central mission of the group was initially to explore systematically the theoretical and normative foundations of a series of pivotal Marxian ideas: exploitation, class, the theory of history, economic crisis. Subsequently, the preoccupations became less narrowly focused on Marxist concepts and more broadly directed toward the normative concerns with equality and social justice.

The group was initially formed around discussions of G. A. Cohen's extraordinary book *Karl Marx's Theory of History: A Defense* (Princeton, NJ: Princeton University Press, 1978). I read this book in the summer of 1979 (while in the process of adopting a baby in Costa Rica) and was completely blown away by it. This book is by far the most rigorous and profound book on Marx's work that I have ever read, and certainly the book that has most influenced the way I think about Marxism. I wrote a long review essay of the book with Andrew Levine that was published in *New Left Review* in 1980. Cohen read it, and invited me to attend the 1981 NBSMG meeting. I was invited back in 1982 and have been a member of the group since then.

For the first fifteen years or so, the group met in the same room every year and ate at the same restaurants. Mostly, we only saw each other during this three-day period. For me it was like a little chunk of the year snipped out, reserved for this special world. I had the rest of the year, then the three-day no bullshit meeting in London.

Most years, of the ten or eleven people who attended a meeting about half presented papers. These got distributed five or six weeks in advance and were generally read quite carefully by participants. At the meeting itself, someone other than the author would introduce and comment on a given paper. Roughly an hour and a half or so would be spent demolishing/discussing the paper in a no-holds-barred manner. The intellectual style was intense and analytically exhausting. To an outsider, many of the discussions might seem destructive, but I think that impression would be mistaken. The interactions involved a particular form of intellectual aggressiveness that is not inherently invalidating; the very act of taking each other's work so seriously is itself an affirmation of respect and support. An outsider wouldn't really see this. Many people looking at this behavior would think this was a gladiatorial combat in which death was the only possible outcome. But from the inside it can be an enormously exciting setting for coming to terms with the subtle problems and gaps in one's ideas and gaining insights about the inner workings of other people's work.

The group is, as one might predict, all men. We have had discussions in the group from time to time about gender issues, both as a topic — I presented a paper on Marxism and feminism at one meeting — and as an issue in the group's composition. For better or worse, nobody in the group knew well any women scholars who both shared an interest in the substantive topics about which we were concerned and engaged those topics in the intellectual style that marked the group. It was probably also the case, I suppose, that many members of the group felt that the kind of intensity of the group would be harder to sustain if it was gender mixed. In any event, no women have been recruited as members of the "club," although several have been invited to attend at various times. In these terms the NBSMG raises important, and troubling, issues in the sociology of gender. Networks of this sort are crucial sites where productive intellectual development occurs, where ideas are forged and refined. While the NBSMG does not control any financial resources — it gives no grants and everyone always pays for his own travel and expenses — nevertheless as a vigorous interpersonal network of intellectual exchange, it is influential and valuable. Undoubtedly the gender composition of the network both reflects the historically marginalized role of women intellectuals in the Marxist tradition and contributed in some way to sustaining such gender inequality.

From the early 1980s to the late 1990s, the NBSMG was the organized reference group that mattered most to me. When I wrote papers in that period, the ghosts who sat in the back of my room and periodically jumped up to tell me that what I had written was ridiculous, and made me worry about whether I got it right, were mainly from this group (and some kindred spirits to this group). The group has unquestionably given my work a particular direction and cast because I have to worry, by virtue of this reference group, about certain issues while others seem less pressing.

Gradually, in the course of the 1990s, the intellectual agendas and theoretical commitments of many of the members of the group changed. Two participants—Jon Elster and Adam Przeworski—decided to leave the group, feeling that in the context of busy schedules it no longer served their needs in a useful way. A number of others felt that while the normative issues at the core of group, especially a radical egalitarian stance toward issues of social justice, remained central to their work, the specific preoccupation with Marxism as a source of ideas and debates for advancing that normative agenda was no longer so important. By the year 2000, several people in the group expressed the sentiment that perhaps it was time to end the annual gathering, but we voted to continue, as much because of the value we all placed on the fellowship and durability of the group as on its intellectual pay-offs. The 2001 meeting was scheduled for New York in mid-September but had to be cancelled because of the 9/11 attacks. When we met the following year, September 2002, we decided to move to an every-other-year cycle. At the moment, it is uncertain whether this is simply a gentle way of incrementally ending the group or whether it will continue in a less energetic way. In any event, the drift in its intellectual priorities and the decline in its intensity have reduced its role as an anchor for my academic work.

My second reference "group" has, if anything, increased in salience over time. It consists of a single person, Michael Burawoy, a professor of sociology at Berkeley. Michael and I have read nearly every page that either of us has written in the past twenty-five years or so. He is constantly reminding me not to lose sight of the ultimate point of it all by becoming preoccupied with analytical rigor at the expense of political relevance; I am constantly telling him to be more precise in his formulations, to be clearer about the underlying logic of the conceptual distinctions he makes. Our intellectual styles are quite at odds with one another in many ways. He does ethnographic research of an extraordinary fine-grained character; my research has been quantitative, typically obliterating much of the nuance and texture of the subjects I study. He is generally skeptical of claims about "objective" truth; I have generally defended rather conventional philosophical views of the scientific aspirations of Marxism and sociology. We have discussed these issues and their bearing on our respective work while walking my dog in the woods, biking the hills of Marin County, and looking for open restaurants in Moscow. In the late 1980s, this dialogue took the form of a series of published exchanges between the two of us in the 1987 and 1989 issues of the *Berkeley Journal of Sociology*. (The first of these exchanges is reprinted in my 1990 book, *The Debate on Classes*; the second appears as chap. 9 in *Interrogating Inequality*). Subsequently, we coauthored a number of papers, most recently "Sociological Marxism" in the *Handbook of Sociological Theory*. As of 2003, we began the process of trying to write a book together based on this paper. The idea is to reflect on the past twenty-five years or so of empirical research and theoretical development within Marxist-inspired social science and identify what we feel to be its enduring, robust core. Our hope is to elaborate a distinctive sociological Marxism around this core. The particular way in which personal loyalty and closeness is combined with intellectual difference in our relationship has been for me a vital source of intellectual challenge and encouragement. It is also, surely, at least part of the personal dimension of "staying" Marxist.

Envisioning Real Utopias

In my work with Burawoy, we have identified the robust core of the Marxist tradition as consisting of two theoretical clusters: first, a diagnosis of capitalism, both of the ways it imposes harms on people and of its logic of development and reproduction; and second, an account of the possibilities of a radically democratic, egalitarian alternative to capitalism. Class analysis pervades both of these: the analysis of class and exploitation is central to understanding how capitalism works, and the transformation of class relations is central to understanding a future beyond capitalism.

For two decades, from the mid-1970s until the mid-1990s, most of my scholarly work was dominated by the first of these theoretical clusters, above all, by the problem of strengthening the Marxist concept of class as a tool for studying capitalist societies. Except for occasional essays, I had given relatively little attention to the problem of emancipatory alternatives to capitalism. It now seems urgent to grapple with this issue. With the end of the cold war and the rise of capitalist triumphalism, this second theoretical cluster of the Marxist tradition has lost much of its credibility even among critics of capitalist society. For all of their oppressive flaws, the existence of the statist economies of the USSR and elsewhere were a practical demonstration that alternatives to capitalism were possible. Marxist critics of those societies could then make a plausible argument that what these societies needed to become socialist was a radical democratic transformation. By the early 1990s those arguments no longer seemed credible to most people.

In this historical context, as my work in the Comparative Class Analysis Project was winding down in the middle-1990s and I faced the question of what research to pursue next, I decided to embark on what has since become the Real Utopias Project. The project directly grew out of my interactions with my closest colleague at Wisconsin, Joel Rogers. Joel is deeply engaged in both the theoretical and practical problems of progressive policy reform, ranging from issues of reinvigorating democratic institutions (he was the central founder of the New Party in the 1980s) to the problem of creating new labor market institutions that advance both economic equality and productive efficiency. He coined the expression "high road capitalism" to describe this endeavor and characterizes the strategy of reform as "paving the high road and closing off the low road." I wanted a project that would be relevant to this kind of pragmatic concern with change within the limits of existing possibilities while also advancing the traditional Marxist concern with understanding alternatives outside of those limits. I initially called this endeavor "society by design" but felt a bit squeamish about the elitest social engineering tone of the expression. On a Sunday morning dog walk together (which we have done nearly every Sunday when both of us are in town since the late 1980s), Joel suggested that I call this enterprise "designing realistic utopias." Soon this became the Real Utopias Project. As in many intellectual enterprises, getting the brand name right helped a lot in giving the project greater coherence and focus.

The idea of the project is to investigate systematic proposals that attempt both to embody emancipatory values and to take seriously the problem of institutional feasibility. The project is organized around a series of international conferences at which specific proposals are elaborated and debated. Each conference has resulted in the publication of a book containing the proposal and a range of the commentaries. The first of these books, published in 1995, revolved around work by Joel Rogers and Joshua Cohen on the problem of associative democracy. Subsequent books have dealt with market socialism (John Roemer, 1996), asset redistribution within capitalist markets (Sam Bowles and Herbert Gintis, 1999), empowered participatory governance (Archon Fung and Erik Olin Wright, 2003), and universal basic income and stakeholder grants (Bruce Ackerman, Ann Alstott, and Philippe van Parijs, 2004).

• • •

My academic career embodies a series of deep, probably unresolvable tensions: tensions between radical egalitarian values and elite academic professionalism; between the commitment to Marxism as a vibrant intellectual and political tradition and the fear of being trapped in indefensible, outmoded assumptions; between being relevant to real struggles and devoting my energies to refinements of abstract concepts. These tensions are impossible to escape, at least for me, but I hope in the end that they have been creative tensions that have pushed my ideas forward and kept me from sliding into comfortable complacency.

Bibliography

Books in the Real Utopias Project

Volume 1. 1995. *Associations and Democracy*, compiled by Joshua Cohen and Joel Rogers, with contributions by Paul Q. Hirst, Ellen Immergut, Ira Katznelson, Heinz Klug, Andrew Levine, Jane Mansbridge, Claus Offe, Philippe Schmitter, Wolfgang Streeck, Andrew Szasz and Iris Young. Edited and introduced by Erik Olin Wright. London: Verso.

Volume 2. 1996. *Equal Shares: Making Market Socialism Work*, compiled by John Roemer, with contributions by Richard J. Arneson, Fred Block, Harry Brighouse, Michael Burawoy, Joshua Cohen, Nancy Folbre, Andrew Levine, Mieke Meurs, Louis Putterman, Joel Rogers, Debra Satz, Julius Sensat, William H. Simon, Frank Thompson, Thomas E. Weisskopf, Erik Olin Wright. Edited and introduced by Erik Olin Wright. London: Verso.

Volume 3. 1999. *Recasting Egalitarianism: New Rules for Equity and Accountability in Markets, Communities and States*, compiled by Samuel Bowles and Herbt Gintis, with contributions by Daniel M. Hausman, Erik Olin Wright, Elaine McCrate, Elinor Ostrom, Andrew Levine, Harry Brighouse, David M. Gordon, Paula England, John E. Roemer, Karl Ove Moene, Michael Wallerstein, Peter Skott, Steven N. Durlauf, Ugo Pagano, Michael R. Carter, Karla Hoff. Edited and introduced by Erik Olin Wright. London: Verso.

Volume 4. 2003. *Deepening Democracy: Innovations in Empowered Participatory Governance*, compiled by Archon Fung and Erik Olin Wright, with contributions by Rebecca Neaera Abers, Gianpaolo Baiocchi, Joshua Cohen, Patrick Heller, Bradley C. Karkkainen, Rebecca S. Krantz, Jane Mansbridge, Joel Rogers, Craig W. Thomas, T. M. Thomas Isaac. London: Verso.

Volume 5. 2005. *Redesigning Distribution: Basic Income and Stakeholder Grants as Cornerstones of a More Egalitarian Capitalism*, compiled by Bruce Ackerman, Ann Alstott, and Philippe van Parijs, with contributions by Barbara Bergmann, Irv Garfinkle, Chien-Chung Huang, Wendy Naidich, Julian LeGrand, Carole Pateman, Guy Standing, Stuart White, Erik Olin Wright. London: Verso, in press.

Other books referred to in the essay

Cohen, G. A. 1978. *Karl Marx's Theory Of History: A Defense*. Princeton, NJ: Princeton University Press.

Wright, Erik Olin. 1973. *The Politics of Punishment: A Critical Analysis of Prisons in America*. New York: Harper and Row; New York: Harper Colophon Books.

———. 1978. *Class, Crisis and the State*. London: New Left Books. Translations in Spanish, Portuguese, Japanese, Korean.

———. 1985a. *Class Structure and Income Determination*. New York: Academic Press.

———. 1985b. *Classes*. London: Verso.

———. 1990. *The Debate on Classes*. London: Verso.

———. 1994. *Interrogating Inequality*. London: Verso.

———. 1997. *Class Counts: Comparative Studies in Class Analysis*. Cambridge: Cambridge University Press. Student edition published 2000.

Wright, Erik Olin, Elliott Sober, and Andrew Levine. 1992. *Reconstructing Marxism: Essays on Explanation and the Theory of History*. London: Verso. Portuguese translation, 1993.

Jeffrey C. Alexander

Craig Calhoun

Patricia Hill Collins

Karin Knorr Cetina

Michel Maffesoli

Photo by Alan Rusbridger

Saskia Sassen

Laurent Thévenot

Bryan Turner

Stephen Turner

Steve Woolgar

Erik Olin Wright

Index

Douglas, Mary, 320

draft, the, 21, 29–32, 34, 36, 79, 293, 296–97, 330–31; board, 5, 29–30, 80–81; and class, 99–100; conscientious objector, 30–33, 78–81, 297, 330; deferment, 2, 12, 30, 80, 332; ending of, 134; lottery, 30–32, 85, 297, 332. *See also* peace movement; Viet Nam

Drew, Paul, 318

Dreyfus, Herbert, 188

Duarte, José Napoleon, 247, 248

Dubin, Robert, *Theory Building*, 294

DuBois, William E. B., 102; *African Slave Trade*, 110; *The Philadelphia Negro*, 110

Durkheim, Émile, 38, 46, 47, 200, 260, 280; anomie, 202; *Division of Labor in Society*, 171; *The Elementary Forms of Religious Life*, 199; and Marx, 61; Parsons and, 212; and positivist sociology, 302; ritual effervescence, 277

Dylan, Bob, 4, 73, 314

Ear Inn, The, 241, 250

Earth Day, 73, 84

eclecticism, 336–7

economics, 2, 10, 42, 104, 181–82, 206, 258; and history of, 7, 230; political, 9, 134, 207, 231

Economy and Class Structure (Sohn-Rethel), 274

Eden, Bob, 307

Edgley, Roy, 215

Edmunds, June, *Generations, Culture and Society*, 277

effervescence, 199, 201, 202, 203, 256, 276–77; intellectual, 136. *See also* Mai 1968

Eisenstadt, Shmuel, 171

Electronic Frontier, 250

Elementary Forms of Religious Life (Durkheim), 199

Elias, Norbert, 213; *The Germans*, 211

elites, 286, 301, 329

Ellwood, Charles, 305

El Salvador, 237–39, 246–49

Elster, Jon, 335, 345

emancipatory social theory, 326, 346

Emerson, Richard, 119, 121–22

Engels, Friedrich, 61, 89, 215; *The Condition of the Working Class in England*, 90

environment, 74, 217

Epstein, Barbara, 246

Escape from Freedom (Fromme), 290

Essential Left, The, 206

ethnicity, 23–4, 77, 219, 226. *See also* intersecting social hierarchies

ethnography, 35, 69, 82, 188, 345

Ethnography Unbound (Burawoy), 69

ethnomethodology, 171, 313, 318, 319

Etzioni, Amitai, 174; *The Active Society*, 173; *The Moral Dimension*, 171

Evans-Pritchard, Edward, 87

events of '68, x, 2–4, 10–12, 282; American Sociological Association meetings, 296; Columbia University, 3, 8, 14; Czechoslovakia, 4, 8, 12, 14, 133, 161–62, 206; and sociology, 273, 282; Sociology Liberation Movement, 275; student revolts, 275, 277–81. *See also* Mai 1968; May 1968; 1968; Prague spring

everyday life, 112, 144, 164, 197, 198, 200, 276, 282; race and, 101; sociology of, 152; subversive character of, 199; whatness of, 318, 319

Fabianism, 47, 51

Fabian Society, 88

Factor, Regis, 303; *Max Weber and the Dispute over Reason and Value*, 304

Faculté de Sciences Humaines, 233

Faculty for Human Rights, 246

Fall, Bernard, *Hell in a Very Small Place*, 293

Fanon, Franz, 14, 61, 102; *The Wretched of the Earth*, 55

Fantasia, Rick, *Cultures of Solidarity*, 60

Fassbinder, Ranier, 146

Father and Son (Gosse), 288n4

Fay School, 22, 24

Fellini, Frederico, 146

feminism, 15, 36, 112, 125, 144, 217, 336–37, 344; early, 8, 118; neo, 152; socialist, 214. *See also* gender; intersecting social hierarchies; transgender theory

Feminist Mystique (Friedan), 118

Feyerabend, Paul, 183

Fighting Words (Collins), 98n3, 103n8, 105n9

Fish, Hamilton, 238–39

Fitzgerald, Frances, *Fire in the Lake*, 238

Flacks, Dick, 52n2

Fo, Dario, 146

Forché, Carolyn, 238

Ford Foundation, 228

Fortes, Meyer, 87, 88

Foucault, Michel, 38, 58, 62, 168, 213, 231, 262, 281; and Gramsci, 61

Frank, Gundar, 55

Frankfurt School, 144, 163, 168, 290. *See also* critical theory

Frazier, E. Franklin, *Black Bourgeoisie*, 291

Freedom Summer. *See* civil rights movement

free speech movement, 13, 50, 118, 119, 297, 306

Free University of Berlin, 156, 163–65, 172

Fremont Project, 46

French Bureau of Statistics, 258

French Communist Party, 15, 201

Freud, Sigmund, 27, 85, 102, 145, 176; *Future of an Illusion*, 290; *Moses and Monotheism*, 290

Friedan, Betty, *Feminist Mystique*, 118

Fromme, Erich: *Escape from Freedom*, 290; *The Sane Society*, 290

Fuchs, Laurence, 104, 106

functionalism, 102, 148, 149, 172, 302, 305

Future of an Illusion, The (Freud), 290

Gadamer, Hans-Georg, 186

Garden House riots, 316

Garfinkel, Harold, 152, 179, 319, 321; *Studies in Ethnomethodology*, 317

Geertz, Clifford, 136, 305n11

Gehlen, Arnold, 163–64, 281

Gellner, Ernest, 129, 136, 138; *Mind*, 135; *Words and Things*, 135

gender, 74, 82, 110, 125, 210, 216, 219, 265, 281, 344. *See also* feminism; intersecting social hierarchies; transgender theory

generational experience, 2, 12, 40, 185, 277, 312–14, 281. *See also* 1968; Sixties

Generational Generations Culture and Society (Edmunds and Turner), 277

Genesis of Values, The (Joas), 172–74

Germans, The (Elias), 211

Gervasi, Sean, 207

Geymonat, Ludvico, 145

ghetto, 291, 292, 293

Giddens, Anthony, 168, 170, 213, 215, 219, 304; *Capitalism and Modern Social Theory*, 212

Giddings, Franklin, 305

globalization, 69, 70, 78, 97, 207, 219, 283

Gluckman, Max, 54, 79, 87–91

Goffman, Erving, 69, 85, 130, 152, 263, 321, 323

Goldmann, Lucien, 209, 275

Goldschmidt, Dietrich, 169

Gompers, Samuel, 43–44

Goodman, Paul, 40

Goody, Jack, 87

Gorz, André, 42

Gosse, Edmund, *Father and Son*, 288n4

Gouldner, Alvin, 88

Gramsci, Antonio, 42, 46, 58, 61, 200, 333; "Gruppo Gramsci," 143; *Prison Notebooks*, 57

Group of Political and Moral Sociology (GSPM), 261

Growtowski, Jerzy, 147

Guatemala, 237–38, 246, 249

Guattari, Felix, 231

Guevara, Ché, 14

Gumperz, John, 188

Habermas, Jürgen, 38, 62, 157, 162, 163, 166, 183, 186, 333; *Knowledge and Human Interests*, 214; "Labor and Interaction," 165; *On Logic of the Social Sciences*, 214; *Theory of Communicative Action*, 168, 170

Hannan, Michael, 117

"Hanoi Hilton," 78

Haraszti, Miklos, 65; *A Worker in a Worker's State*, 63

Harré, Rom, 183, 208, 215

Harrington, Michael, *The Other America*, 11

Harris, David, 117–18

Hartwell, Max, 92

Harvard, 25, 26–29, 32, 44, 95, 109, 111, 235, 329; Center for European Studies, 138, 263; Center for International Affairs (CFIA), 234; and critical liberalism, 43, 110; Population Center, 27–28, 34, 35

Harvard *Crimson*, 40

Sohn-Rethel, Alfred, 273; *Economy and Class Structure*, 274; *Manual and Mental Labour*, 274
Solidarity, 63–65
solidarity, 204, 253, 256, 257, 270, 264, 306; emotional, 203; movement (Latin American), 236–38, 247; political, 12–13
Sontag, Susan, 239, 250
Sorbonne, 200
Sorokin, Pitirim, 93
sound poetry, 241
South Africa, 51, 54, 56, 88, 91; African National Congress, 68; civil rights, 101; color bar, 53; Communist Party, 52, 68. *See also* apartheid
South Side, The: The Racial Transformation of an American Neighborhood (Rosen), 287
Soviet communism. *See* Marxism
Soviet Union, 66–67
Spindler, Louise, 125
SSK (sociology of scientific knowledge). *See* sociology
Stalin, Joseph, 44
standpoint epistemology, 98, 112. *See also* Collins, Patricia Hill
Stanford University, 116–17, 119, 121, 123; female / minority faculty, 124n2, 125; Union for Radical Political Economics, 332
State in Capitalist Society (Miliband), 57
States and Social Revolutions (Skocpol), 334
statistics, 258, 317; politics of, 259; Vietnam War and, 294–96. *See also* quantitative methods; representation
status attainment, 299, 240
Steel, Ronald, 239
Stephan, Alfred, 239
Stinchcombe, Arthur, *Constructing Social Theories*, 298
strangeness, 253, 266
Strawberry Statement, The (Kunen), 13
structuralism (French), 54, 57, 275
structural polytheism, 202, 203
Structure of Social Action, The (Parsons), 46, 211–12
student movements, 276–82, 306; France, 4, 13–14, 206, 275, 277, 278; Germany, 160–63, 206; Italy, 142, 143, 147, 154; U.K., 79, 275–76, 278, 313, 318; U.S., 3, 8, 12–14, 27, 29, 50, 73, 81, 95, 107, 118,

134, 334; Vienna, 179, 180–84. *See also* free speech movement; Sixties
Students for a Democratic Society. *See* SDS
Studies in Ethnomethodology (Garfinkel), 317
Styron, Rose, 239
"Summer of Love," 7–8
Sunseri, Mary, 125
Susser, Ida, 56
Szelenyi, Ivan, 62, 64

Tarde, Gabriel, 14, 202
Tax, Sol, 86
Taylor, Charles, 169, 174
Taylor, Laurie, 318
Taylor, Maxwell, 293
teach-in. *See* Viet Nam
Teachings of Don Juan (Casteneda), 229
"Technique of Marx and Heidegger, The" (Maffesoli), 197
Theoretical Logic in Sociology (Alexander), 43
theory. *See* social theory
Theory and Society, 301
Theory and Verification in Sociology (Zetterberg), 296
Theory Building (Dubin), 294
Theory of Communicative Action (Habermas), 168
Theory of Justice (Rawls), 172
things, 261–63
Thompson, E. P., 54; *The Making of the English Working Class*, 90–91, 279; *Warwick University Limited*, 218
Time magazine, 3, 8. *See also* May 1968
Times Higher Education Supplement, 304
Timm, Edward, 177
Tiryakian, Edward, 174
Tocqueville, Alex de, 263
Torrance, John, 212
Touraine, Alain, 171, 172, 253, 262
transgender theory, xii, 112
Trevor, William, *Old Boys*, 130n1
Tuana, Nancy, 117
Turner, Bryan: *The Dominant Ideology Thesis*, 276; *Generational Generations Culture and Society*, 277
Turner, Jonathan, 305